100 BULLETS: THE HARD WAY

100 BULLETS: THE HARD WAY

Brian Azzarello Writer

Eduardo Risso Artist

Patricia Mulvihill Colorist

Clem Robins Letterer

Dave Johnson   Original Series Covers

100 BULLETS **created by**
Brian Azzarello **and** Eduardo Risso

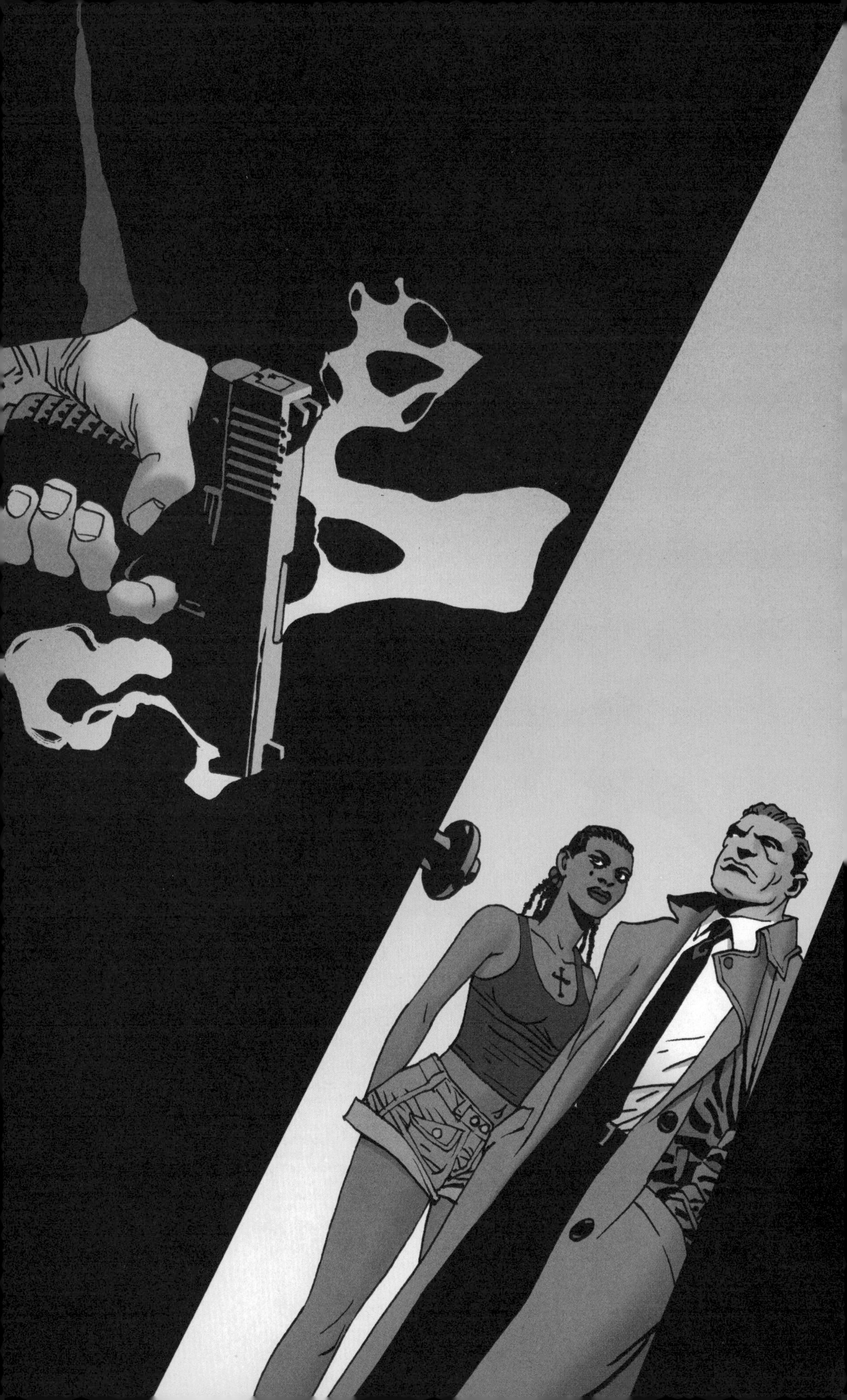

100 BULLETS: THE HARD WAY.
Published by DC Comics. Cover, introduction and
compilation copyright © 2005 DC Comics. All Rights Reserved.
Originally published in single magazine form as 100 BULLETS
50-58. Copyright © 2004, 2005 Brian Azzarello, Eduardo Risso
and DC Comics. All Rights Reserved. All characters, their
distinctive likenesses and related elements featured in this
publication are trademarks of DC Comics. The stories,
characters and incidents featured in this publication are
entirely fictional. DC Comics does not read or accept
unsolicited submissions of ideas, stories or artwork.
DC Comics, 1700 Broadway, New York, NY 10019.
A Warner Bros. Entertainment Company.
Printed in Canada. First Printing.
ISBN: 1-4012-0490-2.
Cover illustration by Dave Johnson.
Publication design by John J. Hill.
Special thanks to Eduardo A. Santillan Marcus
for his translating assistance.

INTRODUCTION BY JASON STARR

The best fiction — and art in general — stretches the constraints of its genre to such a degree that contemporary critics are unsure of how to characterize it. From the paintings of Vincent van Gogh to the writings of F. Scott Fitzgerald and Jim Thompson, history has been littered with the work of great artists that was disregarded or misunderstood at the time of its creation, only to be recognized later as truly groundbreaking.

In some ways, it's easy to dismiss 100 BULLETS as merely a series of comic books. It has all of the sensational artwork, hip dialogue and pure escapism that we expect from a great comic. But just because a work of fiction is entertaining, and reading it doesn't feel like homework, doesn't mean it can't be literary — and, while 100 BULLETS functions on one level as pure fun, it also happens to be some of the greatest neo-*noir* of our time.

It's unfortunate that *noir* has become such a murky word. Many books, films, and even albums are sloppily advertised today as *noir*. The entertainment industry, when at a loss for how to describe its products, uses *noir* as a synonym for "dark" or "dangerous" or "scary." In recent years, a broad range of fiction from mysteries to chick lit has been promoted as *noir*, and the Irish crime writer Ken Bruen has described this sort of proliferation as "*noir* light." This is no knock against the authors of these works, who often have no control over how their products are marketed, but there's no arguing that the clutter of *noir*-advertised material makes it harder for the public to recognize the real thing.

The term "*noir*," in respect to fiction, is derived from the term *film noir*, coined by French film critics to describe a certain style of American movies from the 1940s and '50s. Further exploring this newly defined genre, the French began to look at the works of such writers as Dashiell Hammett, Raymond Chandler,

James M. Cain and David Goodis — whose novels provided the foundations for many *films noirs* — and classifying them under the new category of *roman noir*. In France today, *noir* is still used to characterize a broad range of dark literature. In the United States, however, *noir* took on a much narrower definition during the late 1980s when Barry Gifford's Black Lizard Press began publishing writers such as Cain, Goodis and, most notably, Jim Thompson. The *noir* novels in most of Gifford's line had protagonists that weren't cops or detectives — at least not good ones. The plots focused on non-professional criminals, average Joes and/or losers who'd suffered bad breaks and were forever doomed and screwed.

Another term which gets misused as often as *noir* is "neo-*noir*." It seems like any book that is set in the present day and has any darkness in it at all is called neo-*noir*. But true neo-*noir* pays homage to the style and themes of previous *noir* works, occasionally taking on an in-the-know, tongue-in-cheek quality, while stretching the limits of the genre. Neo-*noir* is often lumped with other *noir* or crime fiction because, by definition, it doesn't fit neatly into the category. It's beyond the genre — something we haven't seen before. One of the first neo-*noir* writers was Charles Willeford. In his 1960 classic *The Woman Chaser*, Willeford took the familiar theme of a little man's quest for the American dream and spun it into a scalding sendup of the film industry.

100 BULLETS is true neo-*noir* in the Willeford tradition. The series is based on a simple revenge concept — a "little guy" is approached by the mysterious agent Graves and offered a once-in-a-lifetime chance to right all wrongs with a gun containing untraceable bullets. The person has a choice — to control his own fate or to let fate control him — and the decision he makes is inevitably the wrong one. It's a

...ascinating premise in itself, but Brian Azzarello and Eduardo Risso use this payback device as a springboard to explore a broad range of issues and ideas which extend far beyond the usual constraints of the genre. The series has dealt with everything from drug warfare to a Hall of Fame baseball player, from Kennedy assassination theories to a warped history of the United States — not the usual themes that come up in most comics.

Like all neo-*noir*ists, Azzarello and Risso are very aware of past masters. For example, Wylie Times, the hapless gas station attendant at the center of this volume, is a tribute to Frank Chambers in Cain's *The Postman Always Rings Twice*. Milo Garret, the P.I. with the bandaged face in THE COUNTERFIFTH DETECTIVE, is an homage to Chandler and Hammett and to Vince Parry, the protagonist of Goodis's *Dark Passage*. There are many other references to Goodis's novels throughout the series, and to the work of such writers as Thompson and Willeford. Similar to how neo-*noir* filmmakers Quentin Tarantino and Robert Rodriguez occasionally take on the styles of classic *film noir*, '70s blacksploitation films and classic kung fu cinema, Azzarello's dialogue often contains "shout-outs" to past classics, and Risso's artwork revels in the shadowed images and dark urban settings often associated with *noir*. But while there are many homages to the past in 100 BULLETS, the series never approaches the level of parody — an important distinction. In the same way that hip-hop artists "sample" the works of past rappers, Azzarello and Risso take aspects of previous *noir* and mix them together with up-to-the-second lingo and modern imagery to create something entirely their own.

In this latest volume of their singular creation, an already white-hot series gets even hotter. Azzarello's dialogue has never been sharper or funnier than it is here, and his ungodly synergy with Risso continues to amaze. The main storyline approaches a climax as two of the comic's best characters — Wylie and Dizzy — get plenty of page time: Wylie is put in the very *noir* predicament of trying to determine who is responsible for his actions — himself for using the gun, or Graves for giving it to him — and we learn more about Dizzy's mysterious relationship with Shepherd. The back-and-forth between Wylie and Dizzy, two truly lost souls, is hilarious and heartbreaking, and Risso creates a bleak, despairing New Orleans landscape with no Mardi Gras in sight. This volume also gives us one of the series' most moving characters in Gabe, a trumpet player who is living in a hell of ugliness, with music as his lone salvation.

100 BULLETS has a resonance that few comics — or novels, for that matter — can match. Its desperate, fateful characters linger with us for days and haunt us at night. This is, without a doubt, the crack cocaine of crime fiction — exhilarating, dangerous, and painfully addictive. It also may be an early glimpse into the future of *noir*.

— **Jason Starr**

JASON STARR is the author of six crime novels which have been published in nine languages. His novel **Tough Luck** *won the 2004 Barry Award for Best Paperback Original and was nominated for the 2004 Anthony Award for Best Paperback Original. His latest novel,* **Twisted City***, is available from Vintage Crime/Black Lizard.*

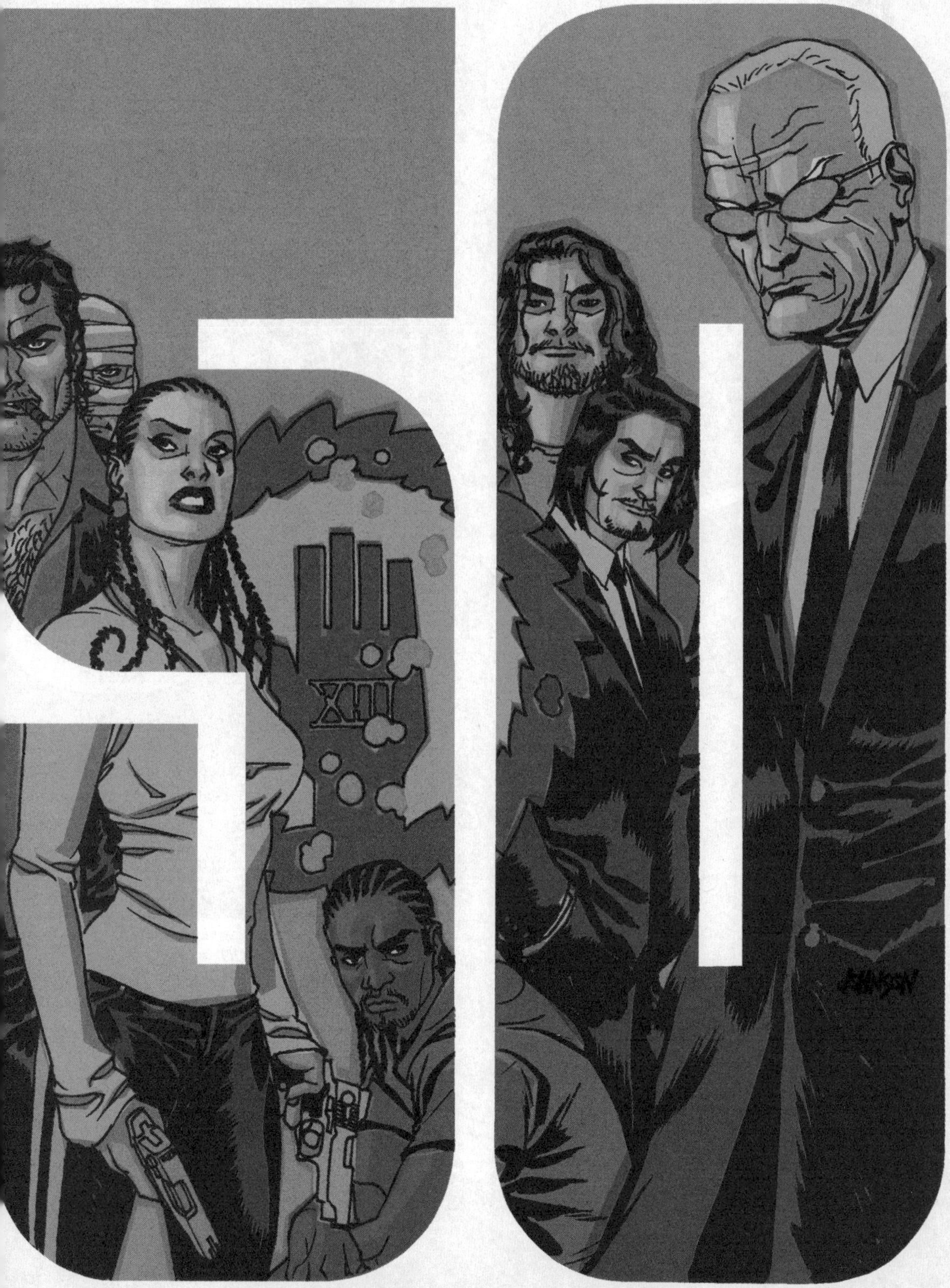
50
XIII

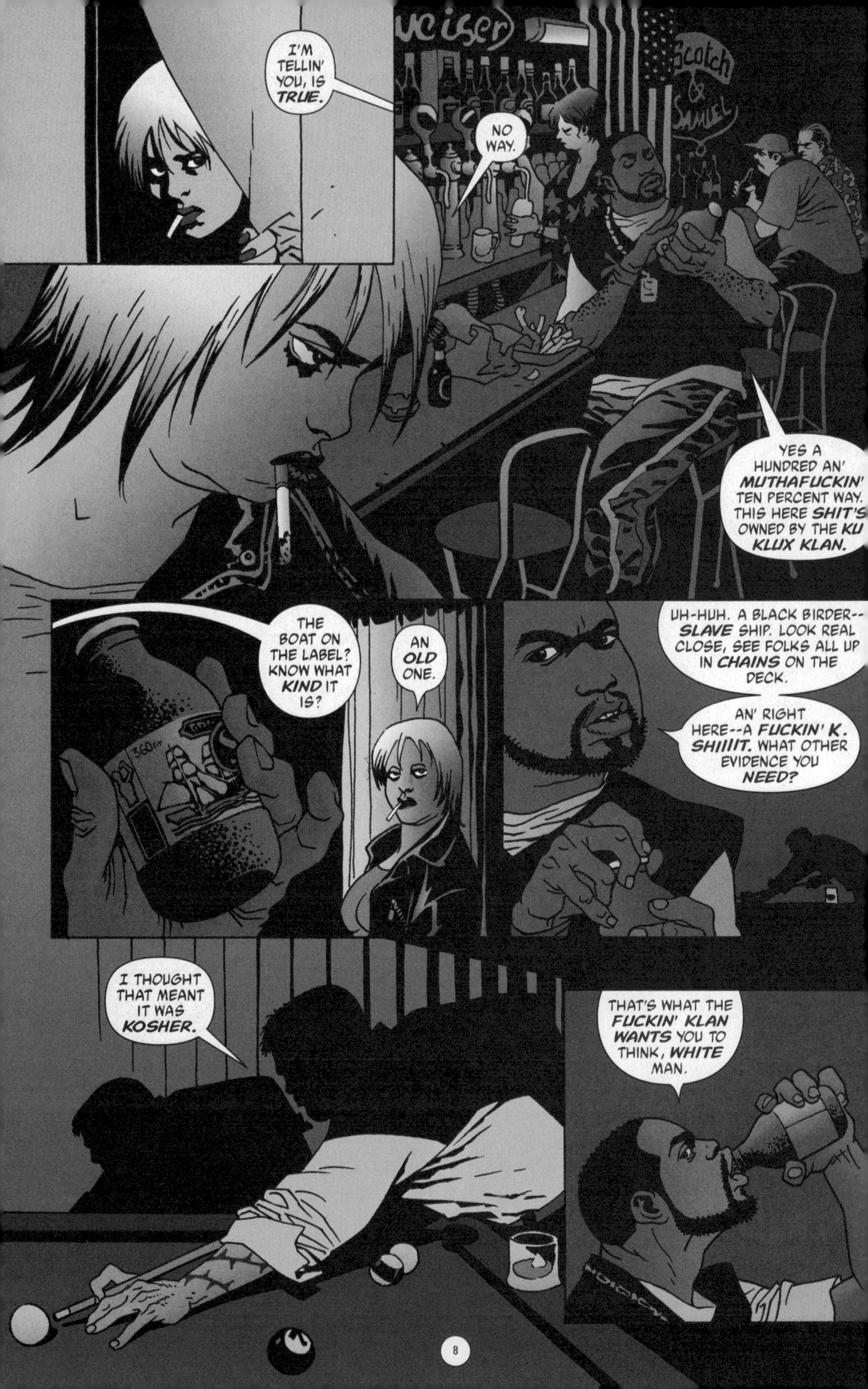
I'M TELLIN' YOU, IS TRUE.
Scotch & Samuel
NO WAY.
YES A HUNDRED AN' MUTHAFUCKIN' TEN PERCENT WAY. THIS HERE SHIT'S OWNED BY THE KU KLUX KLAN.
THE BOAT ON THE LABEL? KNOW WHAT KIND IT IS?
AN OLD ONE.
UH-HUH. A BLACK BIRDER-- SLAVE SHIP. LOOK REAL CLOSE, SEE FOLKS ALL UP IN CHAINS ON THE DECK.
AN' RIGHT HERE--A FUCKIN' K. SHIIIIT. WHAT OTHER EVIDENCE YOU NEED?
I THOUGHT THAT MEANT IT WAS KOSHER.
THAT'S WHAT THE FUCKIN' KLAN WANTS YOU TO THINK, WHITE MAN.

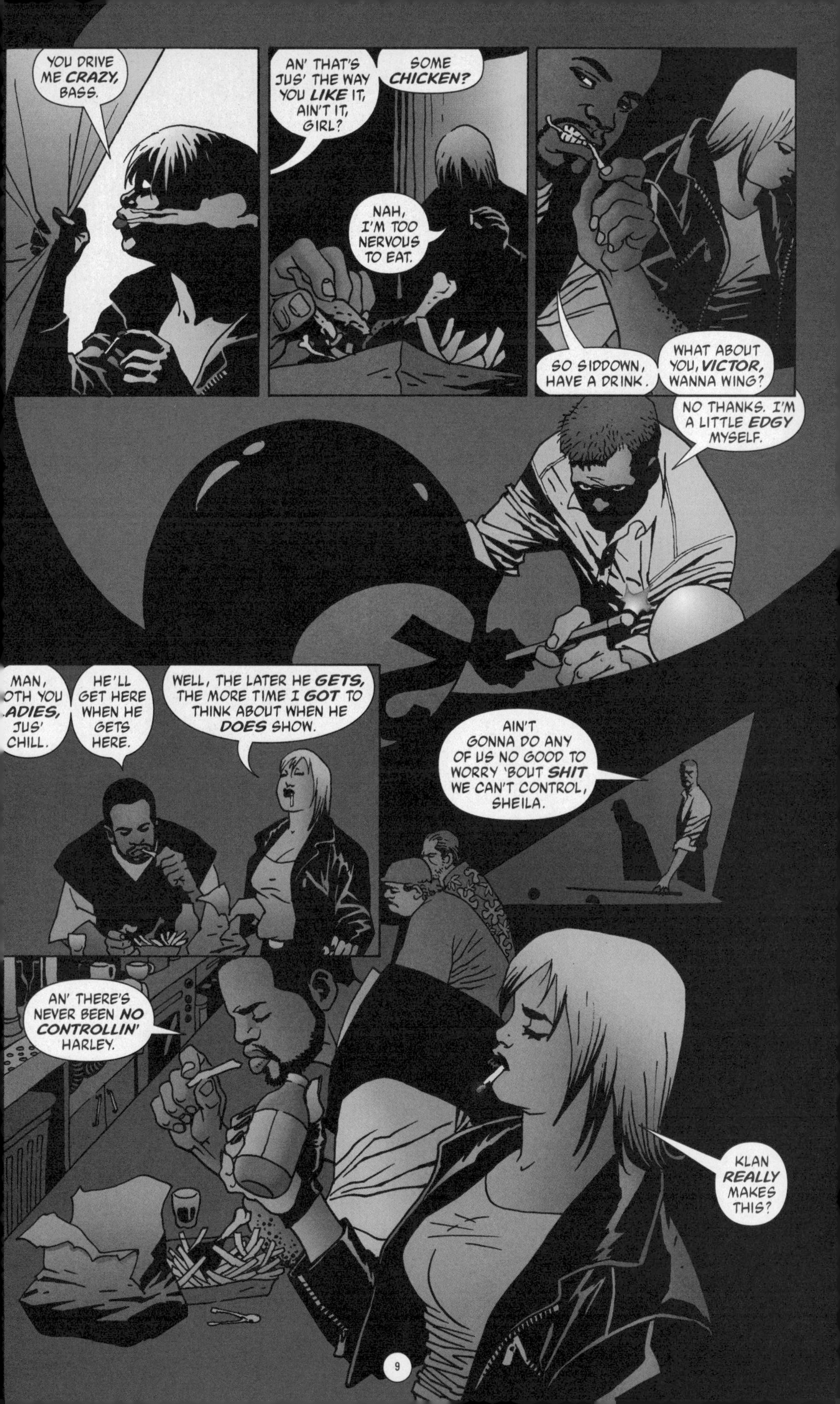

YOU DRIVE ME CRAZY, BASS.
AN' THAT'S JUS' THE WAY YOU LIKE IT, AIN'T IT, GIRL?
SOME CHICKEN?
NAH, I'M TOO NERVOUS TO EAT.
SO SIDDOWN, HAVE A DRINK.
WHAT ABOUT YOU, VICTOR, WANNA WING?
NO THANKS. I'M A LITTLE EDGY MYSELF.
MAN, OTH YOU ADIES, JUS' CHILL.
HE'LL GET HERE WHEN HE GETS HERE.
WELL, THE LATER HE GETS, THE MORE TIME I GOT TO THINK ABOUT WHEN HE DOES SHOW.
AIN'T GONNA DO ANY OF US NO GOOD TO WORRY 'BOUT SHIT WE CAN'T CONTROL, SHEILA.
AN' THERE'S NEVER BEEN NO CONTROLLIN' HARLEY.
KLAN REALLY MAKES THIS?

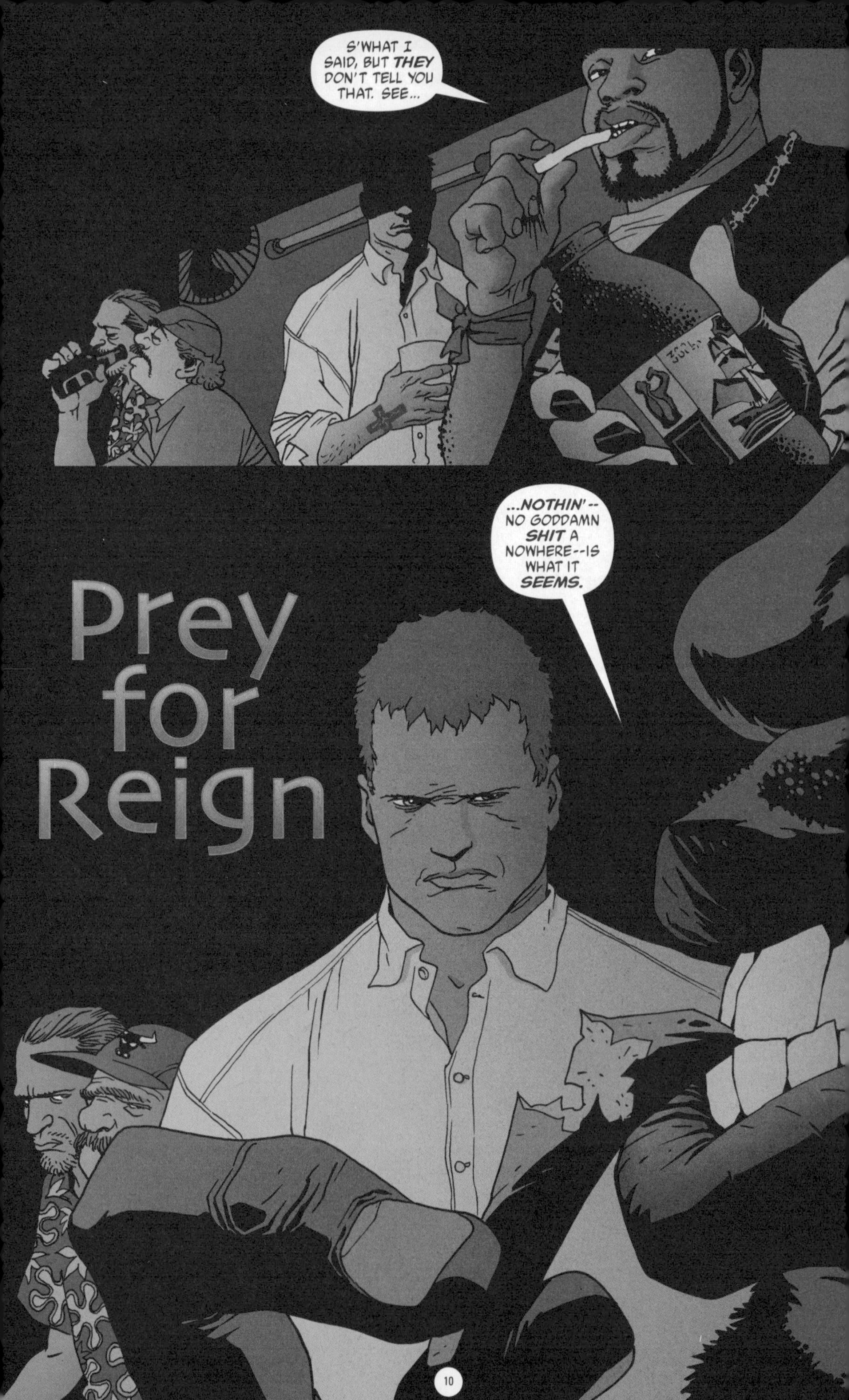
S'WHAT I SAID, BUT THEY DON'T TELL YOU THAT. SEE...
...NOTHIN' -- NO GODDAMN SHIT A NOWHERE--IS WHAT IT SEEMS.
Prey for Reign

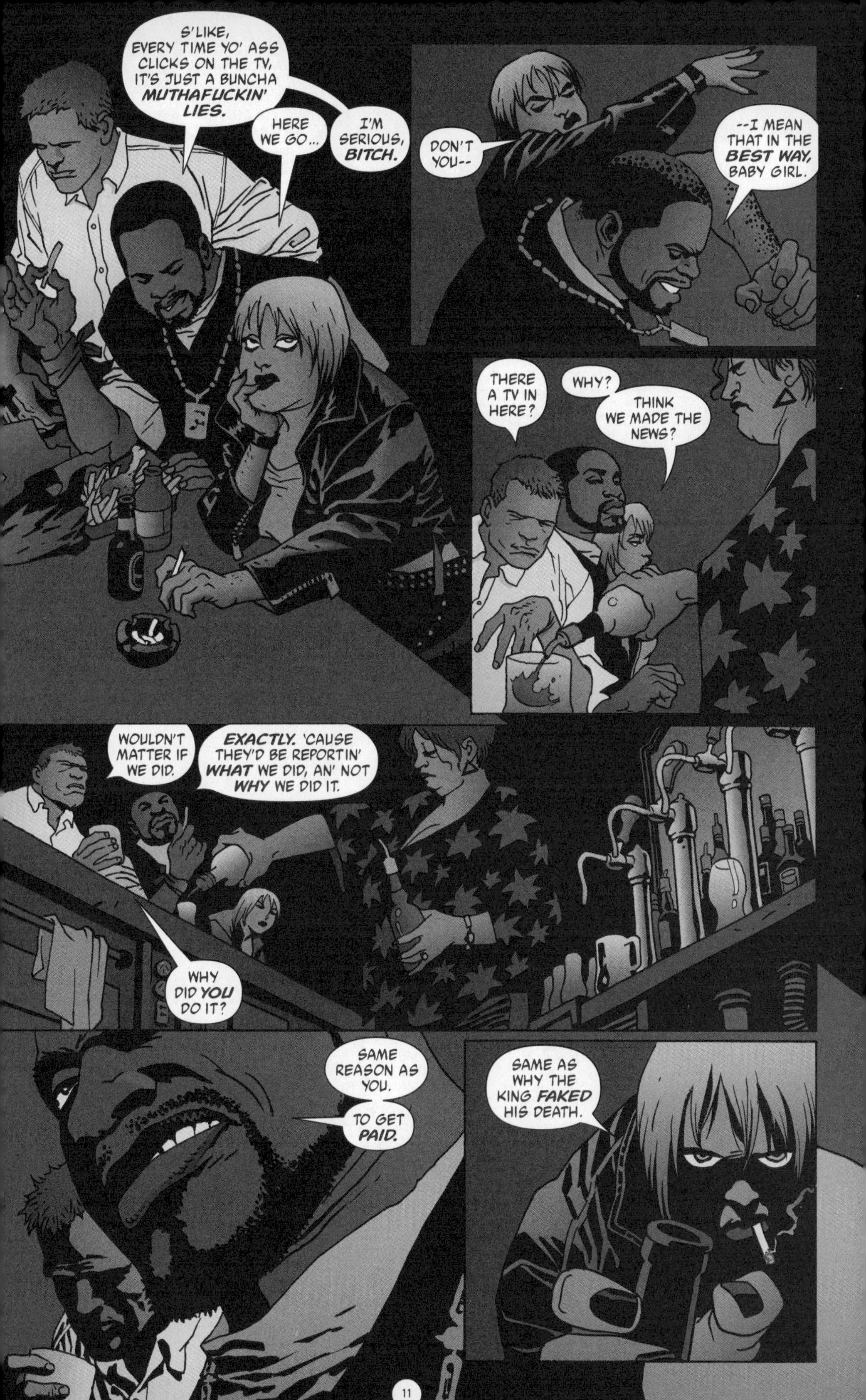
S'LIKE, EVERY TIME YO' ASS CLICKS ON THE TV, IT'S JUST A BUNCHA MUTHAFUCKIN' LIES.
HERE WE GO...
I'M SERIOUS, BITCH.
DON'T YOU--
--I MEAN THAT IN THE BEST WAY, BABY GIRL.
THERE A TV IN HERE?
WHY?
THINK WE MADE THE NEWS?
WOULDN'T MATTER IF WE DID.
EXACTLY. 'CAUSE THEY'D BE REPORTIN' WHAT WE DID, AN' NOT WHY WE DID IT.
WHY DID YOU DO IT?
SAME REASON AS YOU.
TO GET PAID.
SAME AS WHY THE KING FAKED HIS DEATH.

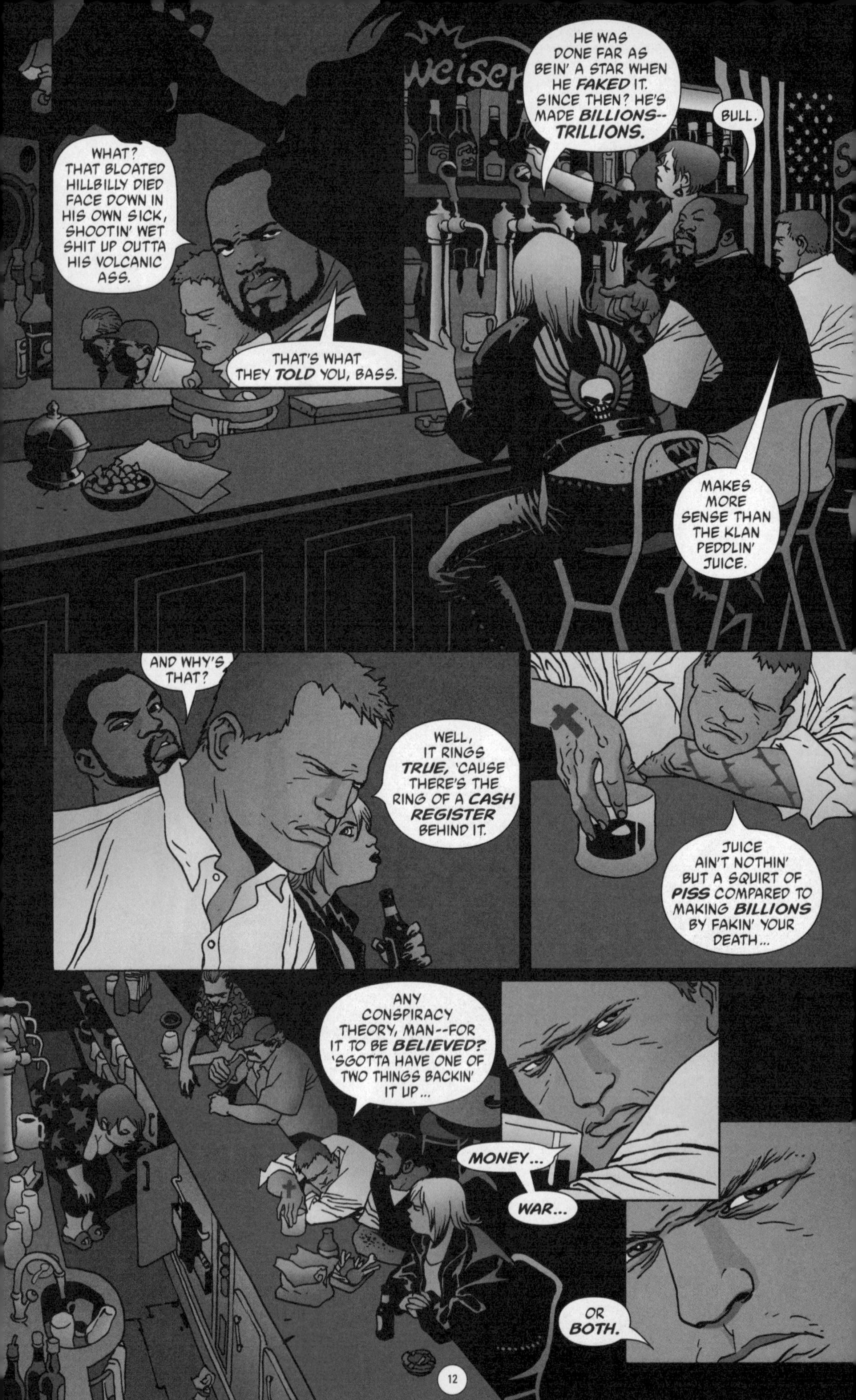
WHAT? THAT BLOATED HILLBILLY DIED FACE DOWN IN HIS OWN SICK, SHOOTIN' WET SHIT UP OUTTA HIS VOLCANIC ASS.
THAT'S WHAT THEY TOLD YOU, BASS.
HE WAS DONE FAR AS BEIN' A STAR WHEN HE FAKED IT. SINCE THEN? HE'S MADE BILLIONS-- TRILLIONS.
BULL.
MAKES MORE SENSE THAN THE KLAN PEDDLIN' JUICE.
AND WHY'S THAT?
WELL, IT RINGS TRUE, 'CAUSE THERE'S THE RING OF A CASH REGISTER BEHIND IT.
JUICE AIN'T NOTHIN' BUT A SQUIRT OF PISS COMPARED TO MAKING BILLIONS BY FAKIN' YOUR DEATH...
ANY CONSPIRACY THEORY, MAN--FOR IT TO BE BELIEVED? 'SGOTTA HAVE ONE OF TWO THINGS BACKIN' IT UP...
MONEY...
WAR...
OR BOTH.

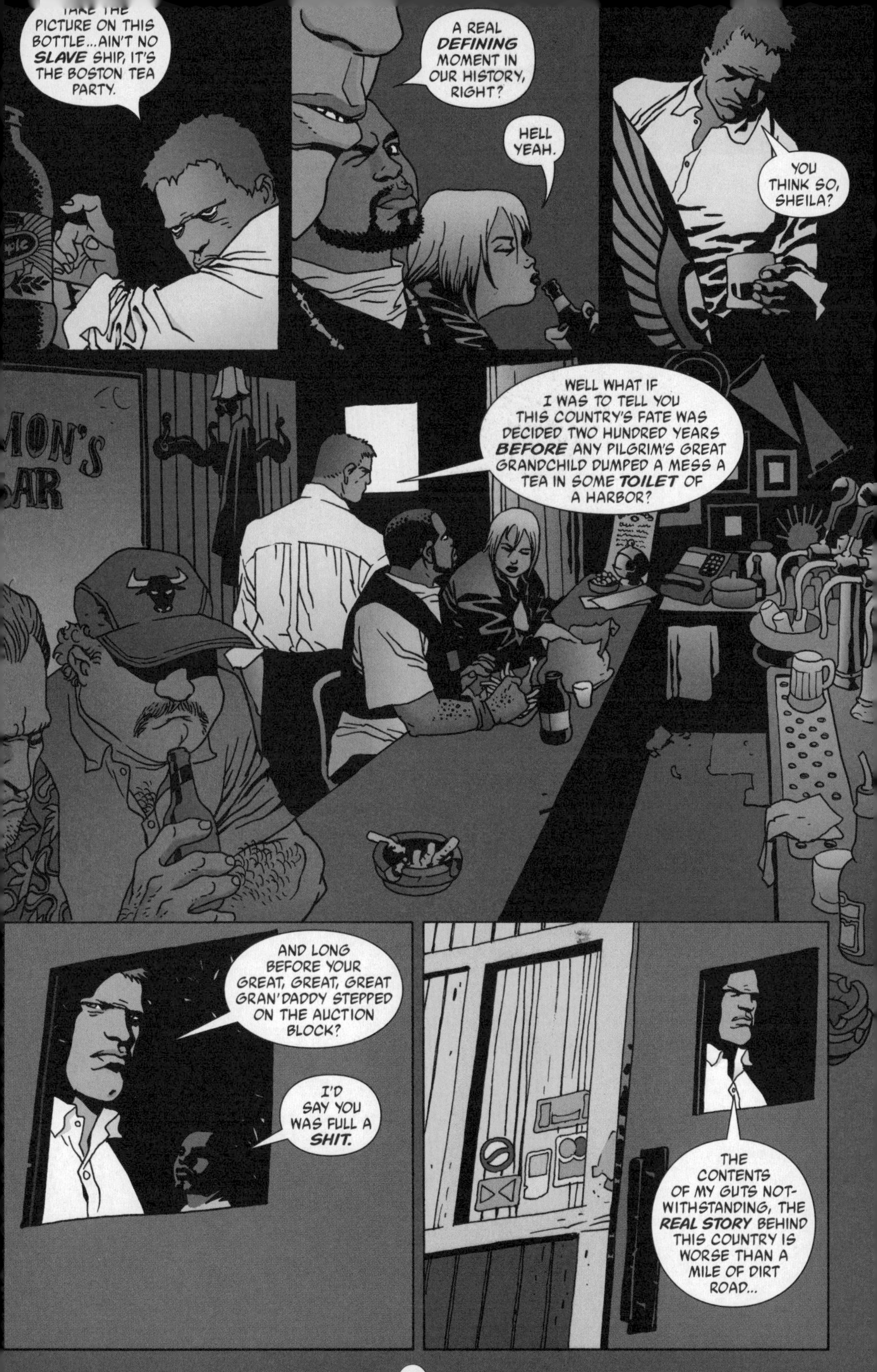
TAKE THE PICTURE ON THIS BOTTLE...AIN'T NO **SLAVE** SHIP, IT'S THE BOSTON TEA PARTY.
A REAL **DEFINING** MOMENT IN OUR HISTORY, RIGHT?
HELL YEAH.
YOU THINK SO, SHEILA?
WELL WHAT IF I WAS TO TELL YOU THIS COUNTRY'S FATE WAS DECIDED TWO HUNDRED YEARS **BEFORE** ANY PILGRIM'S GREAT GRANDCHILD DUMPED A MESS A TEA IN SOME **TOILET** OF A HARBOR?
AND LONG BEFORE YOUR GREAT, GREAT, GREAT GRAN'DADDY STEPPED ON THE AUCTION BLOCK?
I'D SAY YOU WAS FULL A **SHIT.**
THE CONTENTS OF MY GUTS NOT-WITHSTANDING, THE **REAL STORY** BEHIND THIS COUNTRY IS WORSE THAN A MILE OF DIRT ROAD...

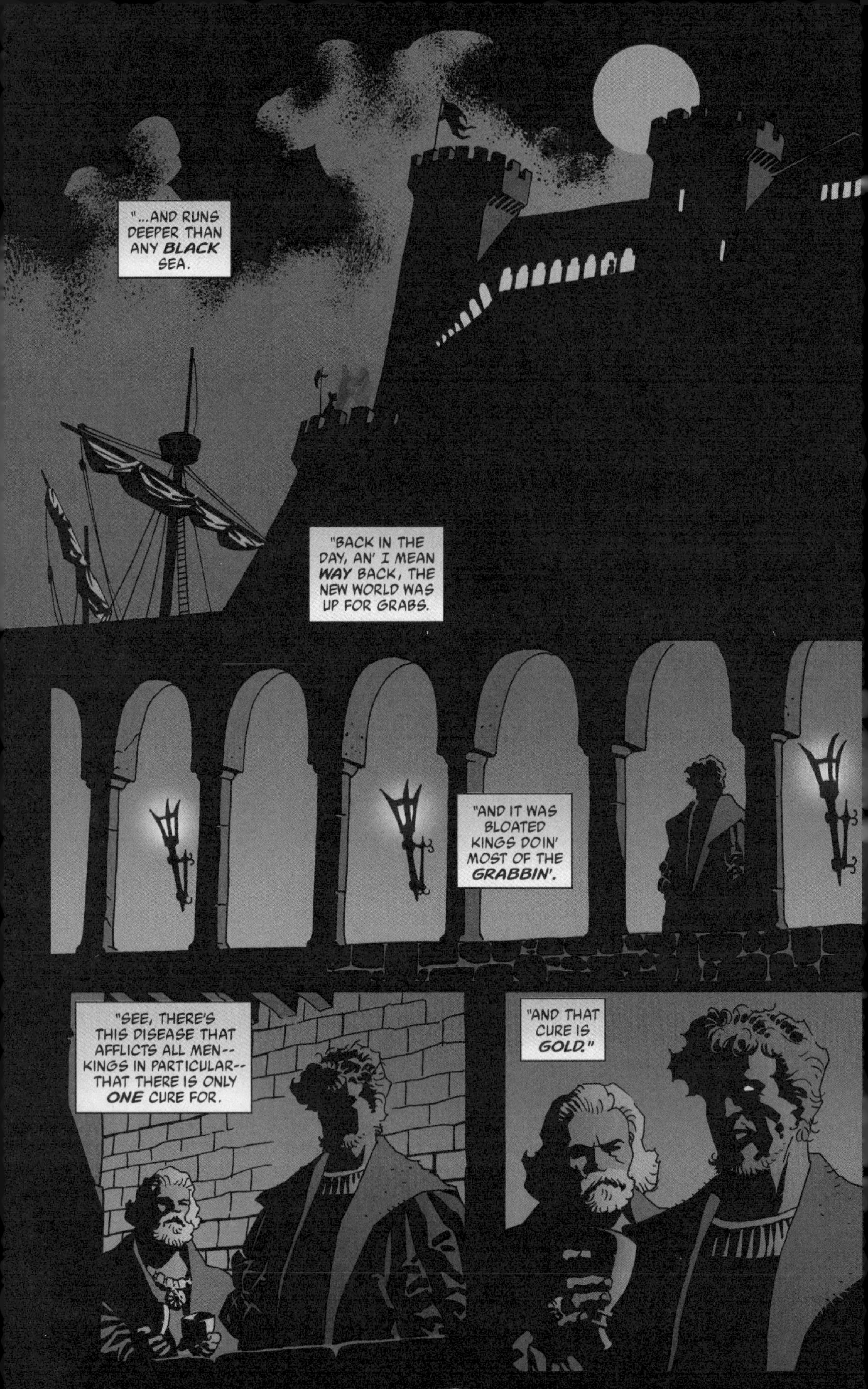
"...AND RUNS DEEPER THAN ANY BLACK SEA.
"BACK IN THE DAY, AN' I MEAN WAY BACK, THE NEW WORLD WAS UP FOR GRABS.
"AND IT WAS BLOATED KINGS DOIN' MOST OF THE GRABBIN'.
"SEE, THERE'S THIS DISEASE THAT AFFLICTS ALL MEN--KINGS IN PARTICULAR--THAT THERE IS ONLY ONE CURE FOR.
"AND THAT CURE IS GOLD."

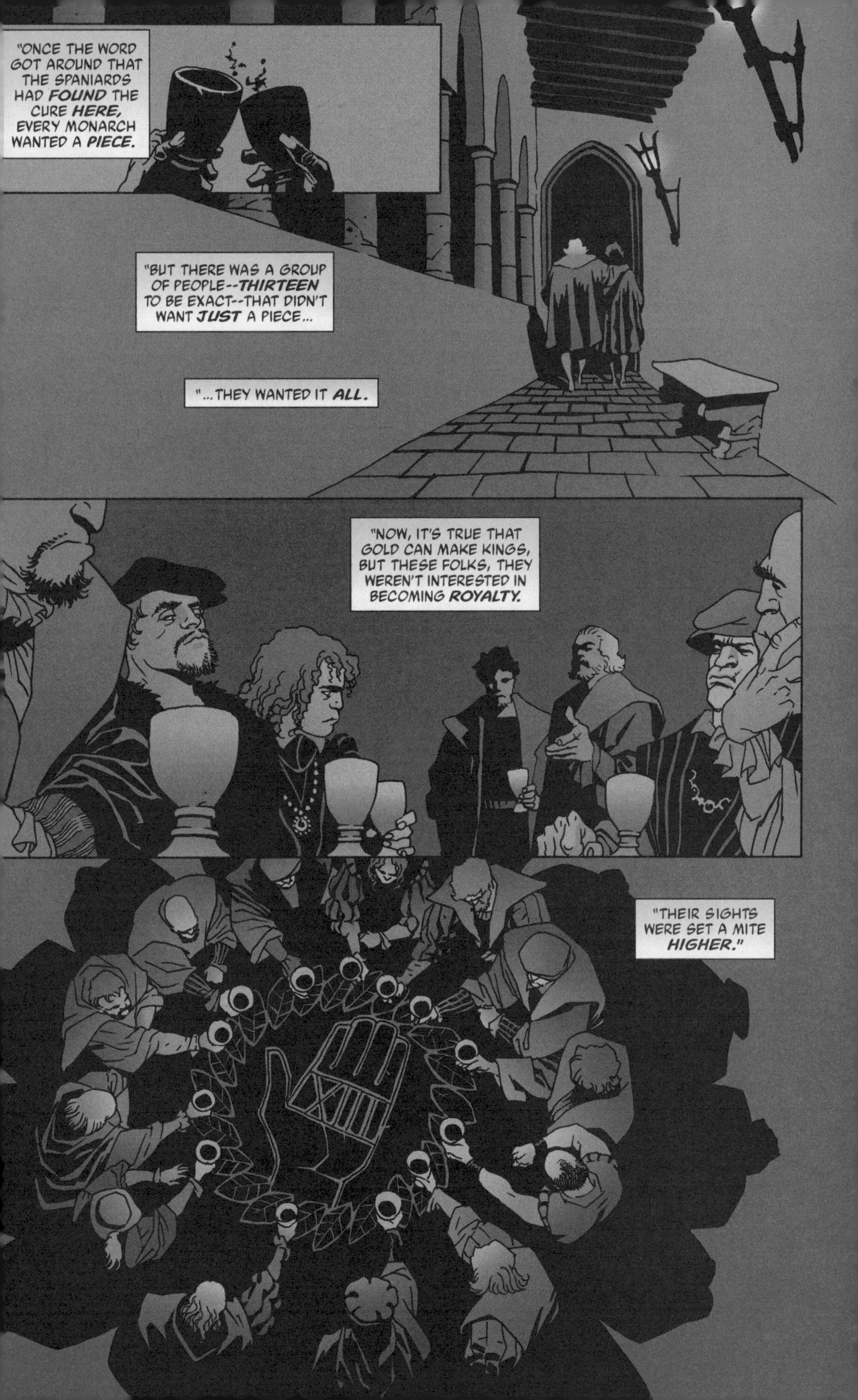
"ONCE THE WORD GOT AROUND THAT THE SPANIARDS HAD FOUND THE CURE HERE, EVERY MONARCH WANTED A PIECE.
"BUT THERE WAS A GROUP OF PEOPLE--THIRTEEN TO BE EXACT--THAT DIDN'T WANT JUST A PIECE...
"...THEY WANTED IT ALL.
"NOW, IT'S TRUE THAT GOLD CAN MAKE KINGS, BUT THESE FOLKS, THEY WEREN'T INTERESTED IN BECOMING ROYALTY.
"THEIR SIGHTS WERE SET A MITE HIGHER."

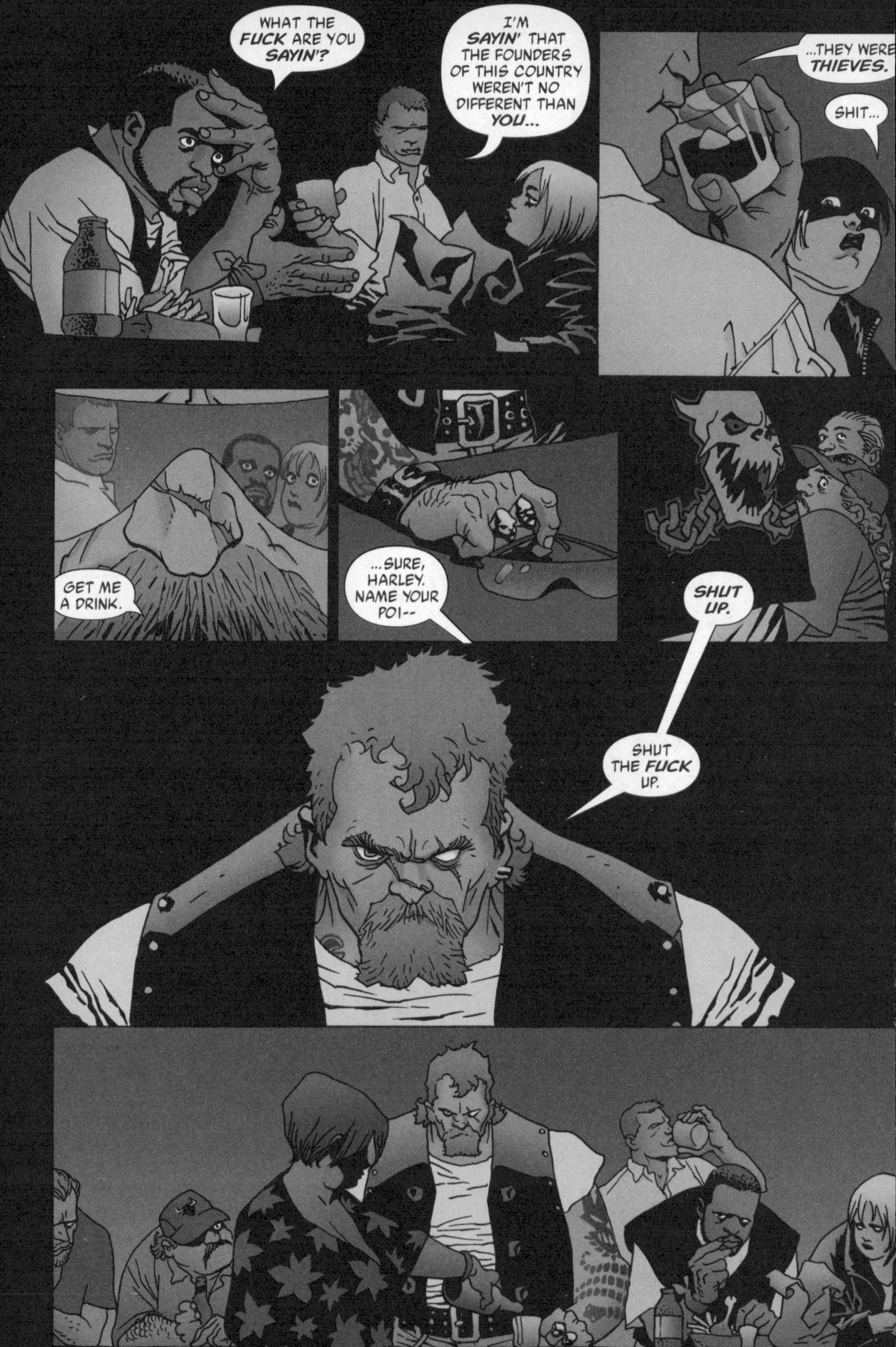
WHAT THE FUCK ARE YOU SAYIN'?
I'M SAYIN' THAT THE FOUNDERS OF THIS COUNTRY WEREN'T NO DIFFERENT THAN YOU...
...THEY WERE THIEVES.
SHIT...
GET ME A DRINK.
...SURE, HARLEY. NAME YOUR POI--
SHUT UP.
SHUT THE FUCK UP.

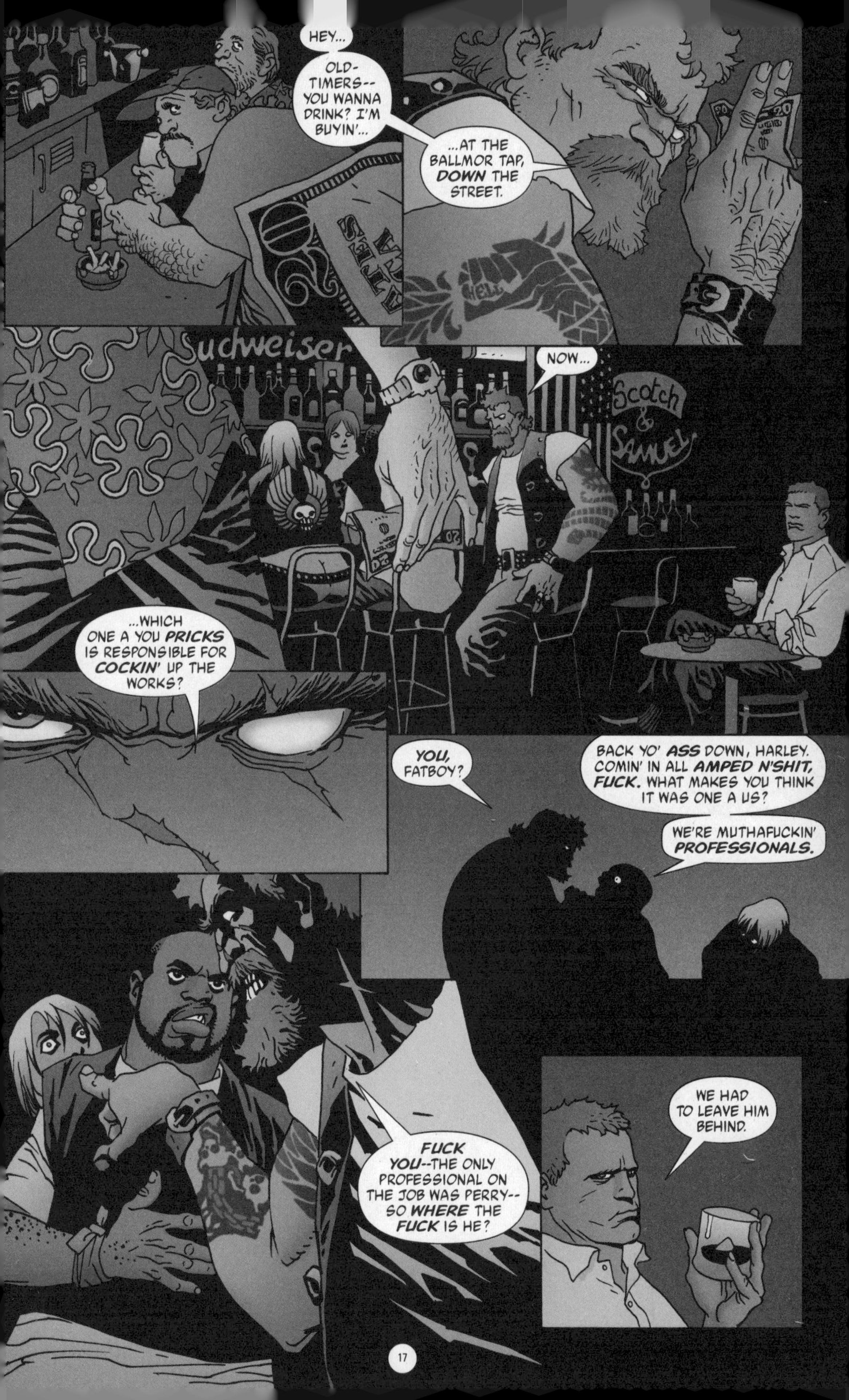
HEY...
OLD-TIMERS--YOU WANNA DRINK? I'M BUYIN'...
...AT THE BALLMOR TAP, DOWN THE STREET.
Budweiser
NOW...
Scotch & Samuel
...WHICH ONE A YOU PRICKS IS RESPONSIBLE FOR COCKIN' UP THE WORKS?
YOU, FATBOY?
BACK YO' ASS DOWN, HARLEY. COMIN' IN ALL AMPED N'SHIT, FUCK. WHAT MAKES YOU THINK IT WAS ONE A US?
WE'RE MUTHAFUCKIN' PROFESSIONALS.
FUCK YOU--THE ONLY PROFESSIONAL ON THE JOB WAS PERRY--SO WHERE THE FUCK IS HE?
WE HAD TO LEAVE HIM BEHIND.

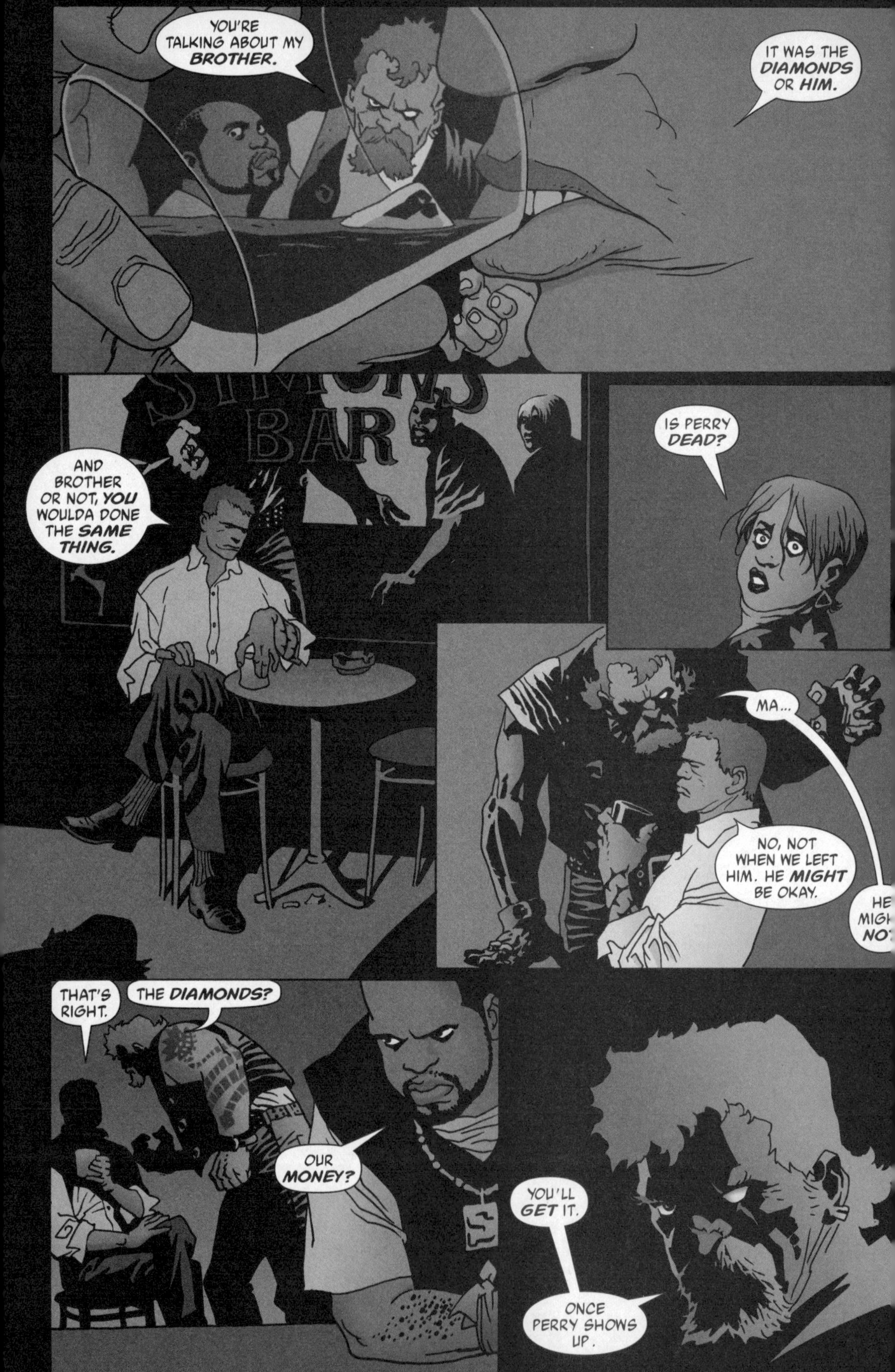

YOU'RE TALKING ABOUT MY BROTHER.
IT WAS THE DIAMONDS OR HIM.
BAR
AND BROTHER OR NOT, YOU WOULDA DONE THE SAME THING.
IS PERRY DEAD?
MA...
NO, NOT WHEN WE LEFT HIM. HE MIGHT BE OKAY.
THAT'S RIGHT.
THE DIAMONDS?
OUR MONEY?
YOU'LL GET IT.
ONCE PERRY SHOWS UP.

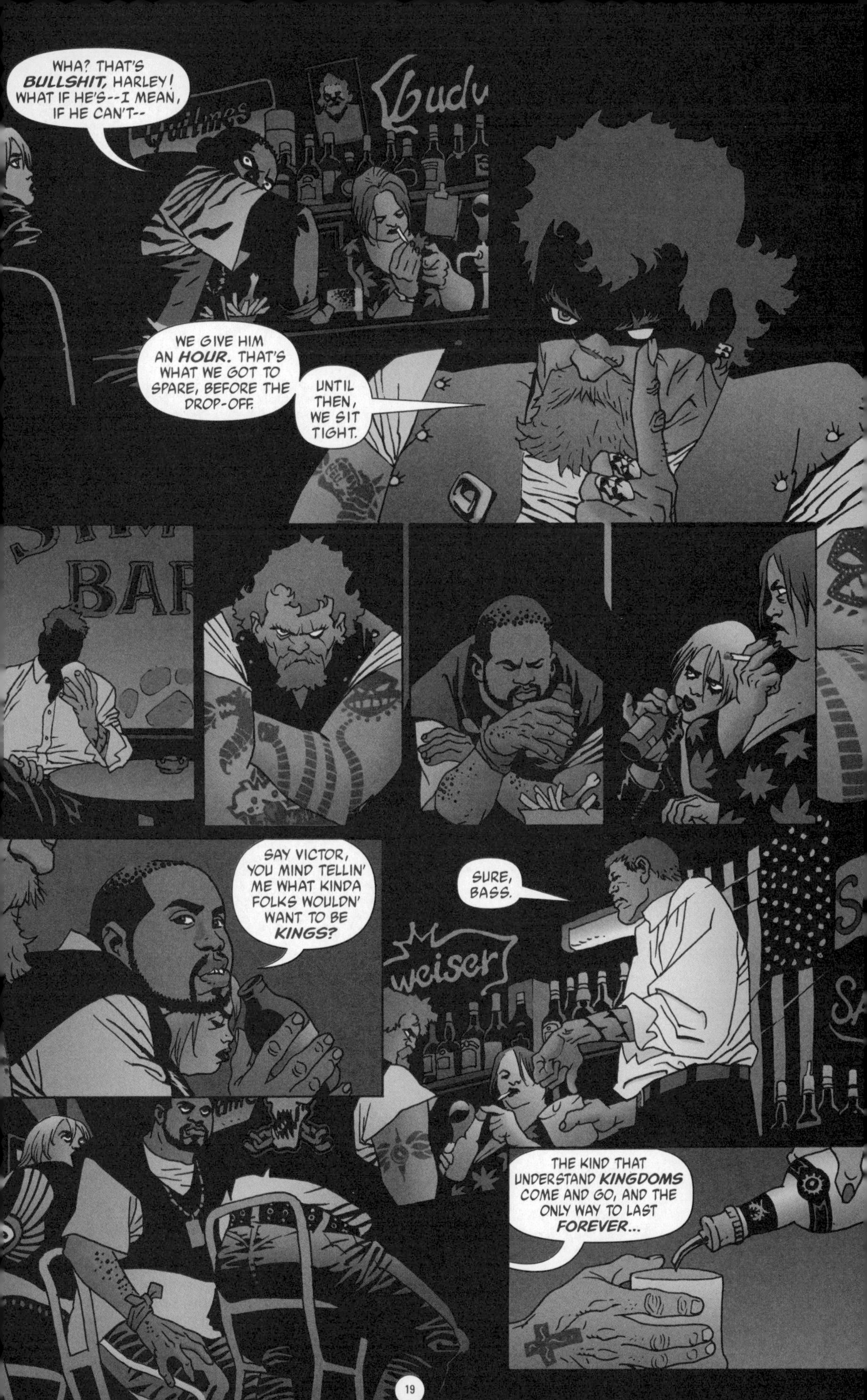

WHA? THAT'S **BULLSHIT,** HARLEY! WHAT IF HE'S--I MEAN, IF HE CAN'T--
WE GIVE HIM AN **HOUR.** THAT'S WHAT WE GOT TO SPARE, BEFORE THE DROP-OFF.
UNTIL THEN, WE SIT TIGHT.
SAY VICTOR, YOU MIND TELLIN' ME WHAT KINDA FOLKS WOULDN' WANT TO BE **KINGS?**
SURE, BASS.
THE KIND THAT UNDERSTAND **KINGDOMS** COME AND GO, AND THE ONLY WAY TO LAST **FOREVER...**

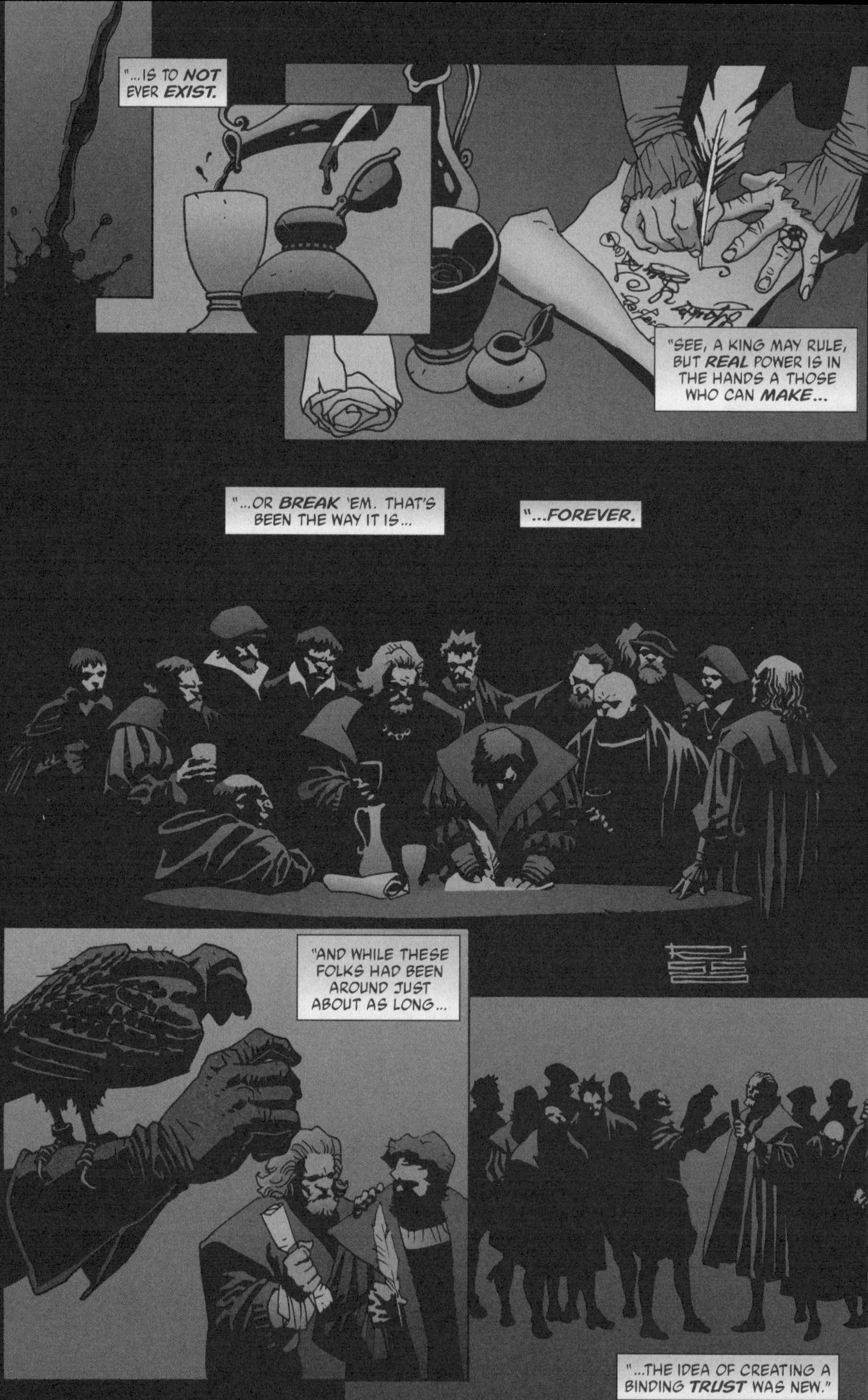
"...IS TO NOT EVER EXIST.
"SEE, A KING MAY RULE, BUT REAL POWER IS IN THE HANDS A THOSE WHO CAN MAKE...
"...OR BREAK 'EM. THAT'S BEEN THE WAY IT IS...
"...FOREVER.
"AND WHILE THESE FOLKS HAD BEEN AROUND JUST ABOUT AS LONG...
"...THE IDEA OF CREATING A BINDING TRUST WAS NEW."

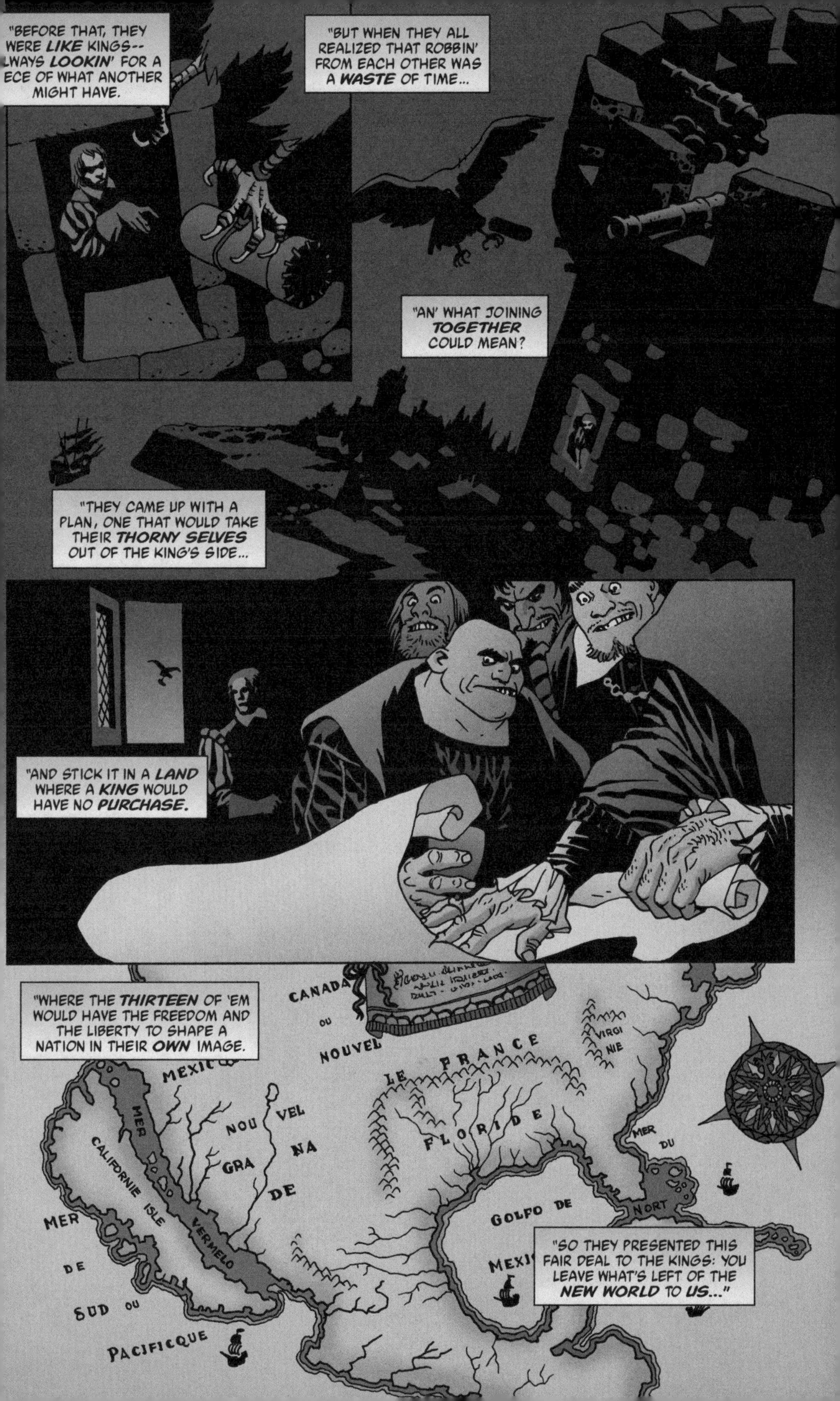
"BEFORE THAT, THEY WERE LIKE KINGS-- LWAYS LOOKIN' FOR A ECE OF WHAT ANOTHER MIGHT HAVE.
"BUT WHEN THEY ALL REALIZED THAT ROBBIN' FROM EACH OTHER WAS A WASTE OF TIME...
"AN' WHAT JOINING TOGETHER COULD MEAN?
"THEY CAME UP WITH A PLAN, ONE THAT WOULD TAKE THEIR THORNY SELVES OUT OF THE KING'S SIDE...
"AND STICK IT IN A LAND WHERE A KING WOULD HAVE NO PURCHASE.
"WHERE THE THIRTEEN OF 'EM WOULD HAVE THE FREEDOM AND THE LIBERTY TO SHAPE A NATION IN THEIR OWN IMAGE.
CANADA
OU
NOUVEL
LE FRANCE
VIRGI NIE
MEXIC
MER
CALIFORNIE ISLE
VERMELO
NOU VEL
GRA NA DE
FLORIDE
MER DU
NORT
GOLFO DE
MEXI
MER
DE
SUD OU
PACIFICQUE
"SO THEY PRESENTED THIS FAIR DEAL TO THE KINGS: YOU LEAVE WHAT'S LEFT OF THE NEW WORLD TO US..."

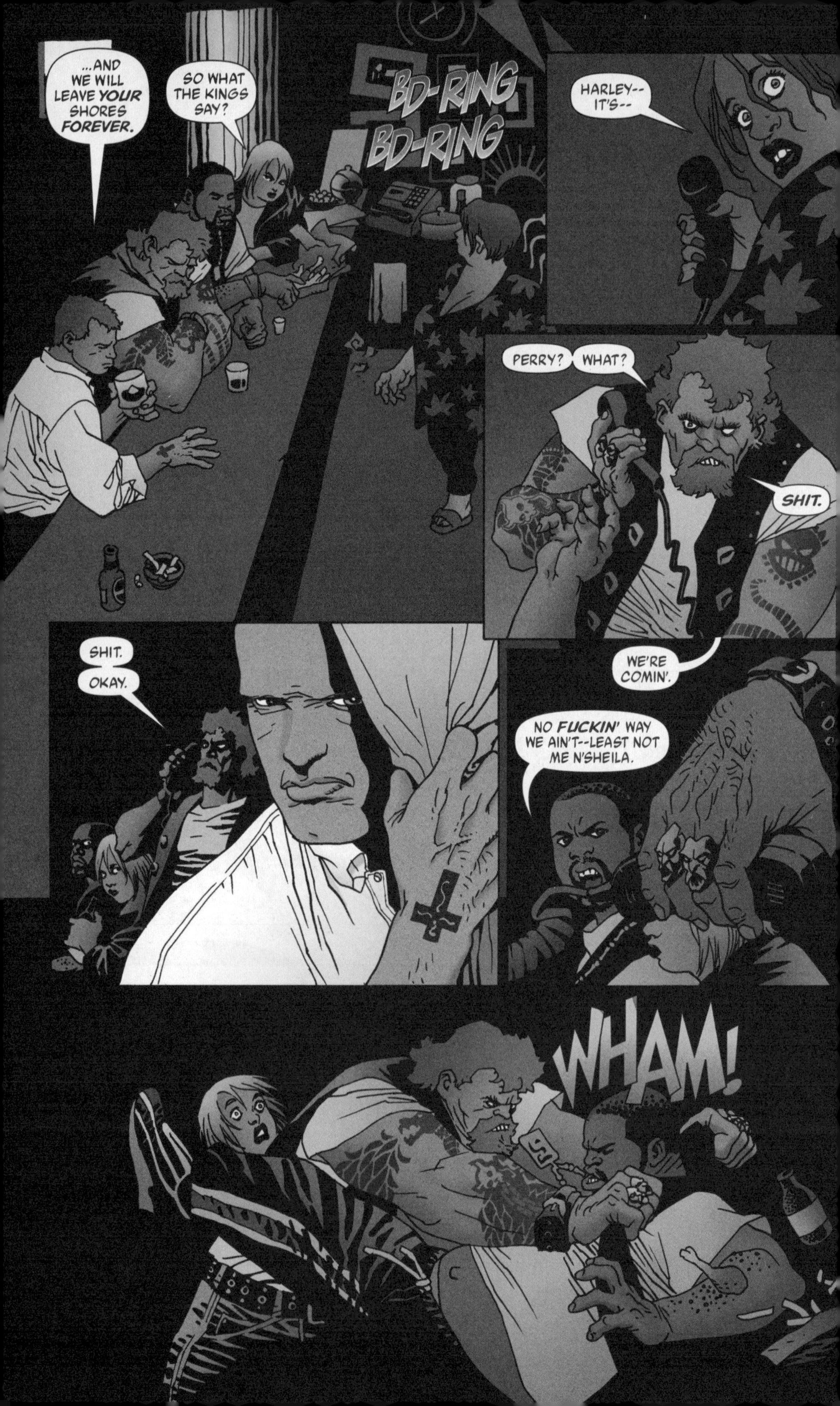
...AND WE WILL LEAVE YOUR SHORES FOREVER.
SO WHAT THE KINGS SAY?
BD-RING BD-RING
HARLEY-- IT'S--
PERRY?
WHAT?
SHIT.
SHIT.
OKAY.
WE'RE COMIN'.
NO FUCKIN' WAY WE AIN'T--LEAST NOT ME N'SHEILA.
WHAM!

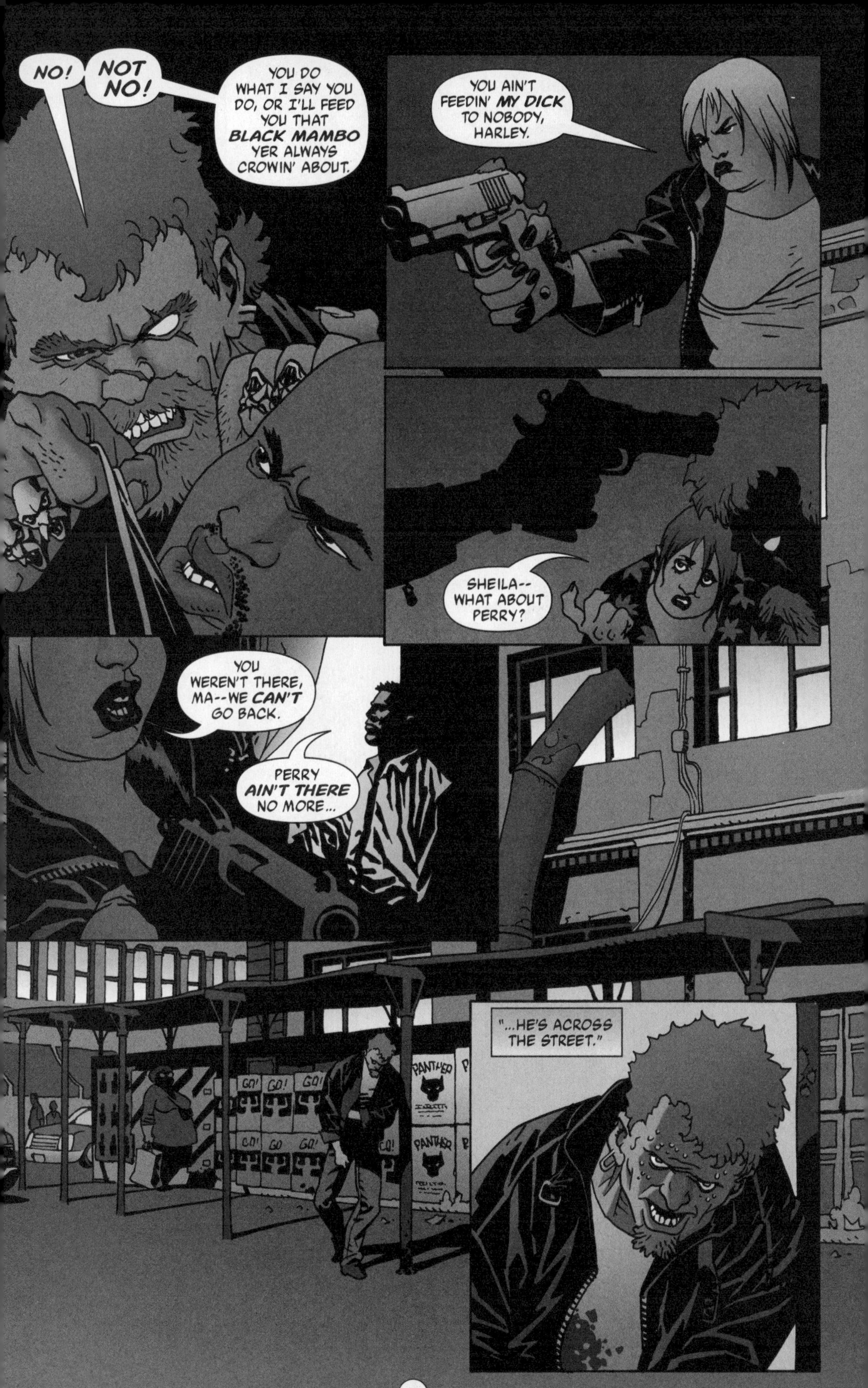
NO!
NOT NO!
YOU DO WHAT I SAY YOU DO, OR I'LL FEED YOU THAT BLACK MAMBO YER ALWAYS CROWIN' ABOUT.
YOU AIN'T FEEDIN' MY DICK TO NOBODY, HARLEY.
SHEILA-- WHAT ABOUT PERRY?
YOU WEREN'T THERE, MA--WE CAN'T GO BACK.
PERRY AIN'T THERE NO MORE...
"...HE'S ACROSS THE STREET."

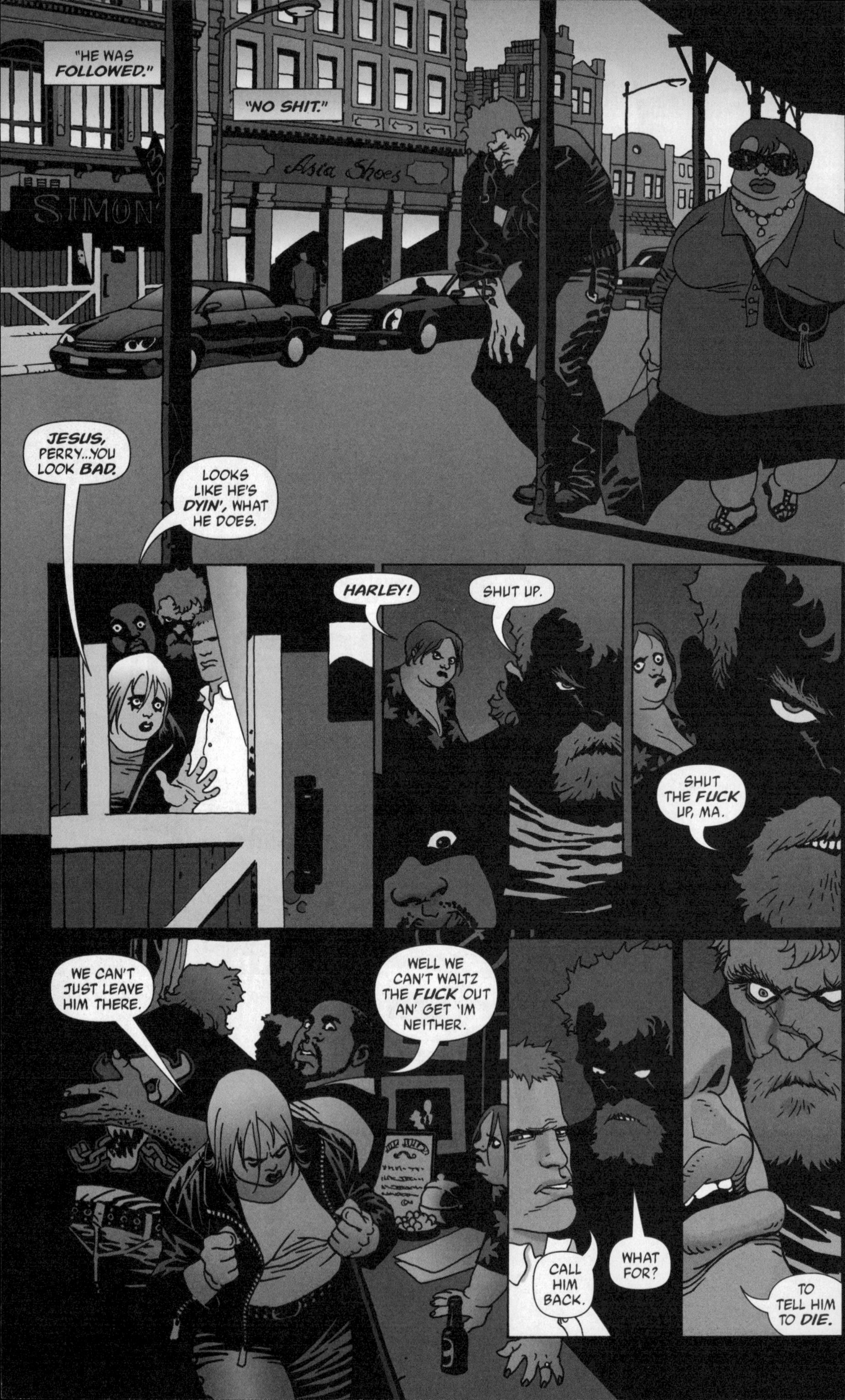
"HE WAS FOLLOWED."
"NO SHIT."
SIMON
Asia Shoes
JESUS, PERRY...YOU LOOK BAD.
LOOKS LIKE HE'S DYIN', WHAT HE DOES.
HARLEY!
SHUT UP.
SHUT THE FUCK UP, MA.
WE CAN'T JUST LEAVE HIM THERE.
WELL WE CAN'T WALTZ THE FUCK OUT AN' GET 'IM NEITHER.
CALL HIM BACK.
WHAT FOR?
TO TELL HIM TO DIE.

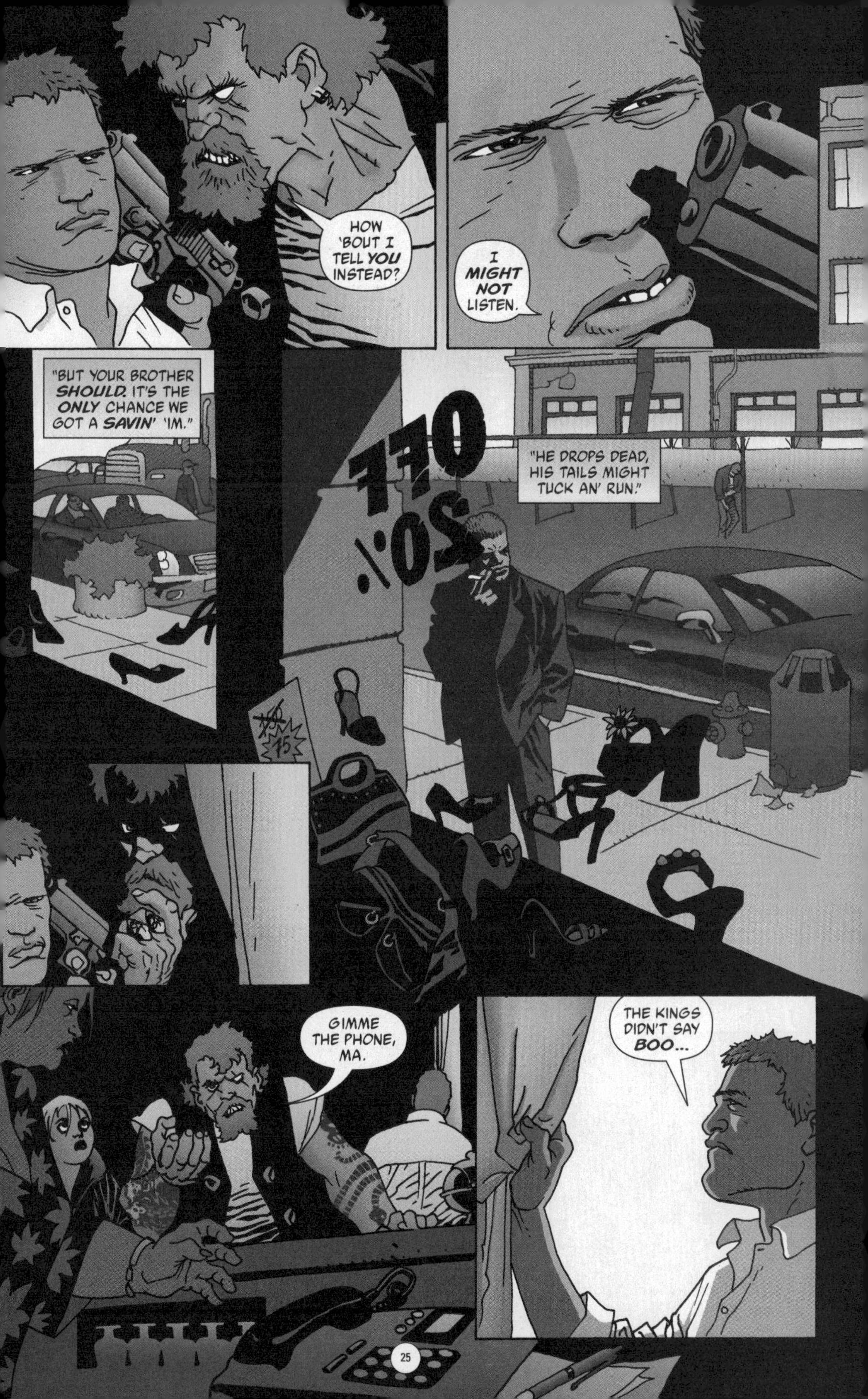
HOW 'BOUT I TELL *YOU* INSTEAD?
I *MIGHT NOT* LISTEN.
"BUT YOUR BROTHER *SHOULD.* IT'S THE *ONLY* CHANCE WE GOT A *SAVIN'* 'IM."
20% OFF
"HE DROPS DEAD, HIS TAILS MIGHT TUCK AN' RUN."
GIMME THE PHONE, MA.
THE KINGS DIDN'T SAY *BOO...*

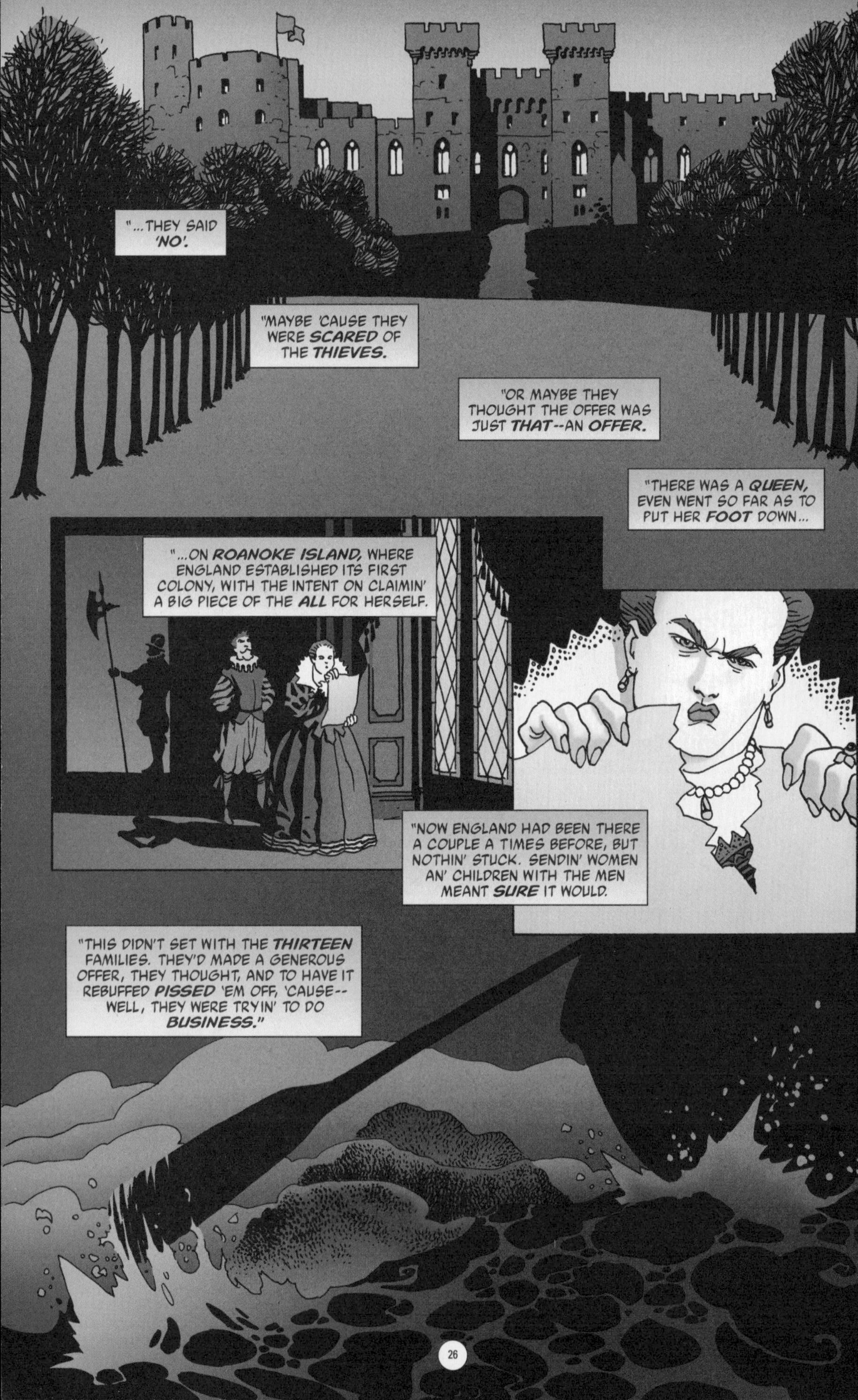
"...THEY SAID 'NO'.
"MAYBE 'CAUSE THEY WERE SCARED OF THE THIEVES.
"OR MAYBE THEY THOUGHT THE OFFER WAS JUST THAT--AN OFFER.
"THERE WAS A QUEEN, EVEN WENT SO FAR AS TO PUT HER FOOT DOWN...
"...ON ROANOKE ISLAND, WHERE ENGLAND ESTABLISHED ITS FIRST COLONY, WITH THE INTENT ON CLAIMIN' A BIG PIECE OF THE ALL FOR HERSELF.
"NOW ENGLAND HAD BEEN THERE A COUPLE A TIMES BEFORE, BUT NOTHIN' STUCK. SENDIN' WOMEN AN' CHILDREN WITH THE MEN MEANT SURE IT WOULD.
"THIS DIDN'T SET WITH THE THIRTEEN FAMILIES. THEY'D MADE A GENEROUS OFFER, THEY THOUGHT, AND TO HAVE IT REBUFFED PISSED 'EM OFF, 'CAUSE-- WELL, THEY WERE TRYIN' TO DO BUSINESS."

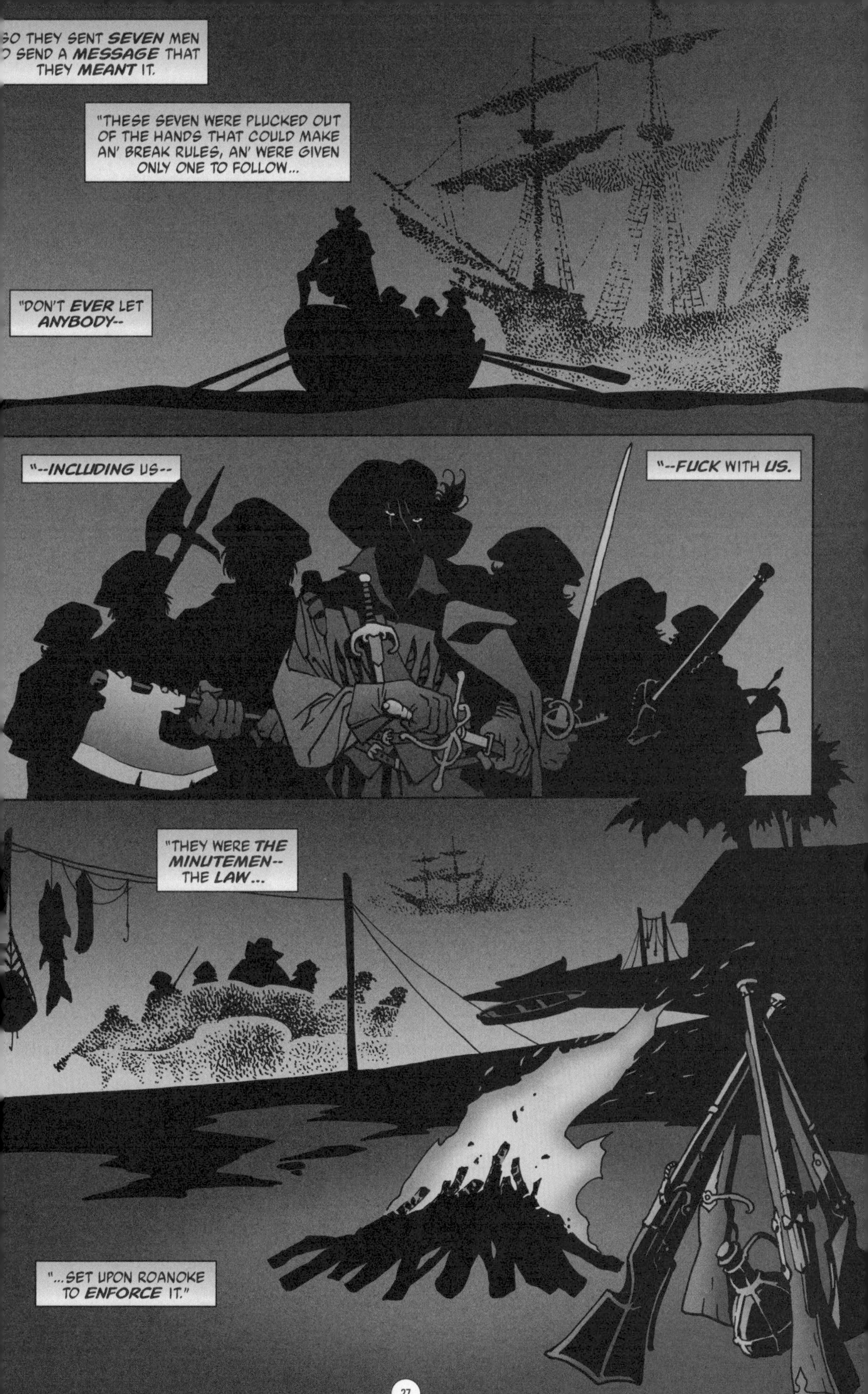
SO THEY SENT SEVEN MEN TO SEND A MESSAGE THAT THEY MEANT IT.
"THESE SEVEN WERE PLUCKED OUT OF THE HANDS THAT COULD MAKE AN' BREAK RULES, AN' WERE GIVEN ONLY ONE TO FOLLOW...
"DON'T EVER LET ANYBODY--
"--INCLUDING US--
"--FUCK WITH US.
"THEY WERE THE MINUTEMEN-- THE LAW...
"...SET UPON ROANOKE TO ENFORCE IT."

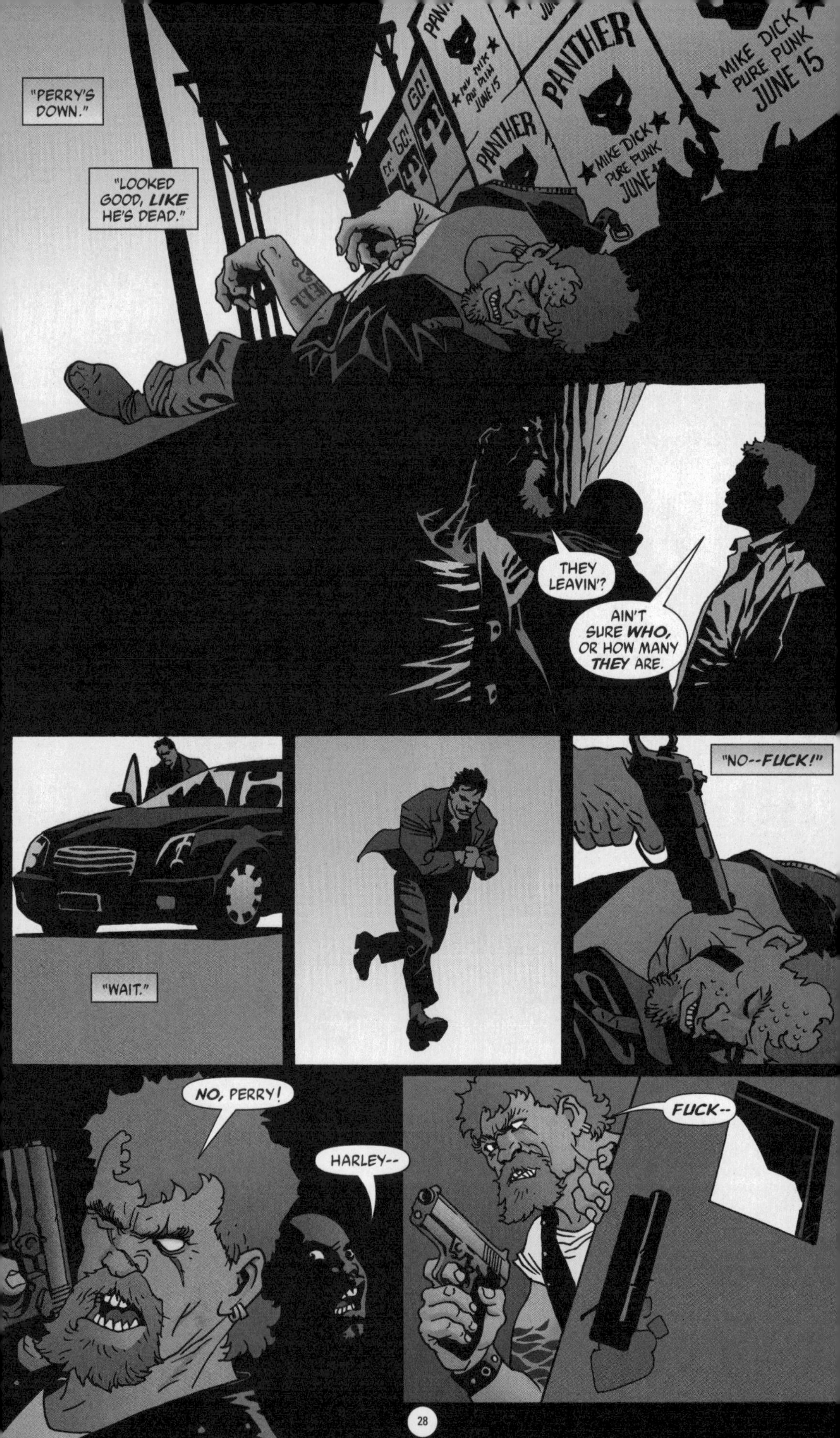
PANTHER
MIKE DICK
PURE PUNK
JUNE 15
"PERRY'S DOWN."
"LOOKED GOOD, LIKE HE'S DEAD."
THEY LEAVIN'?
AIN'T SURE WHO, OR HOW MANY THEY ARE.
"WAIT."
"NO--FUCK!"
NO, PERRY!
HARLEY--
FUCK--

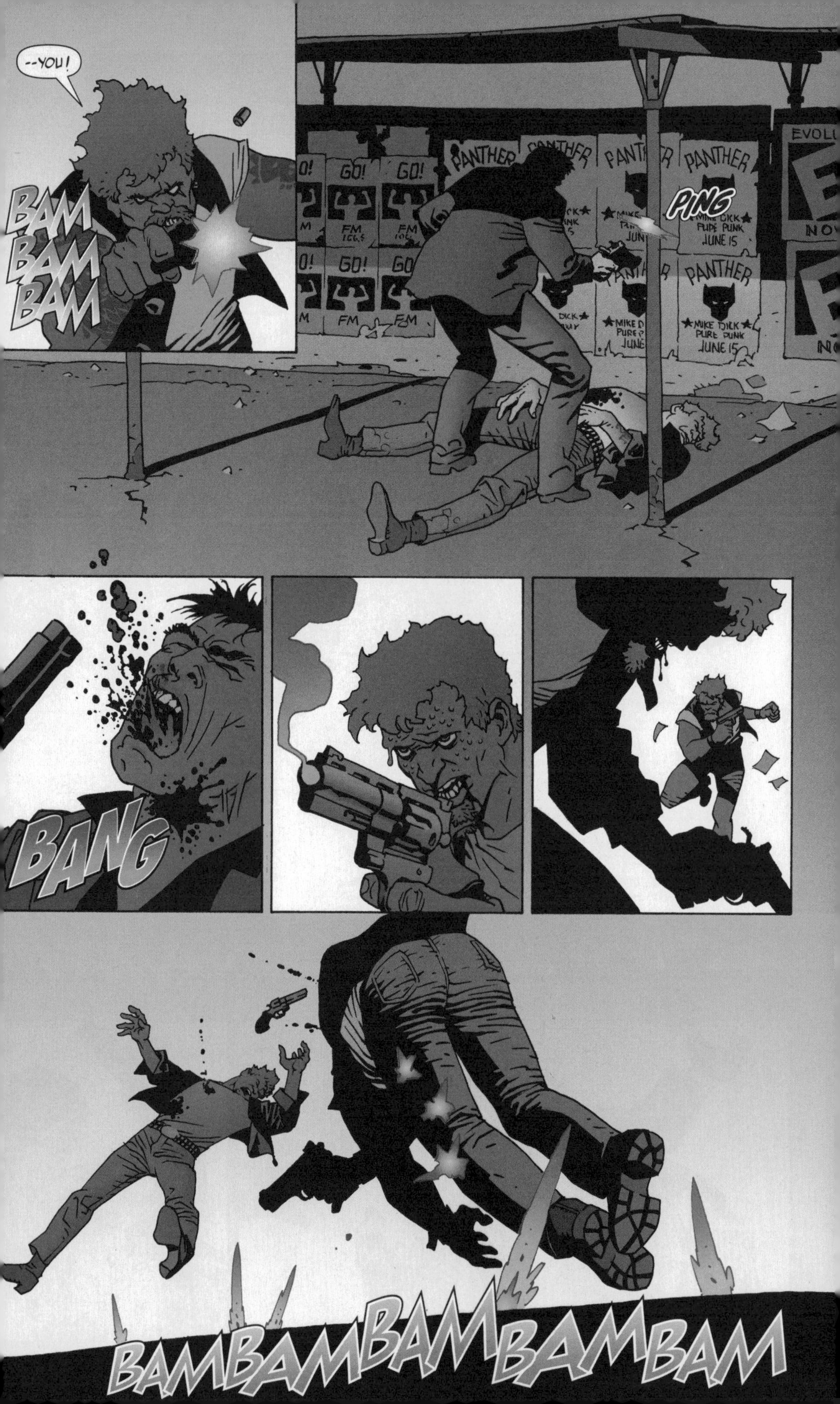

--YOU!
BAM BAM BAM
PING
BANG
BAMBAMBAMBAMBAM

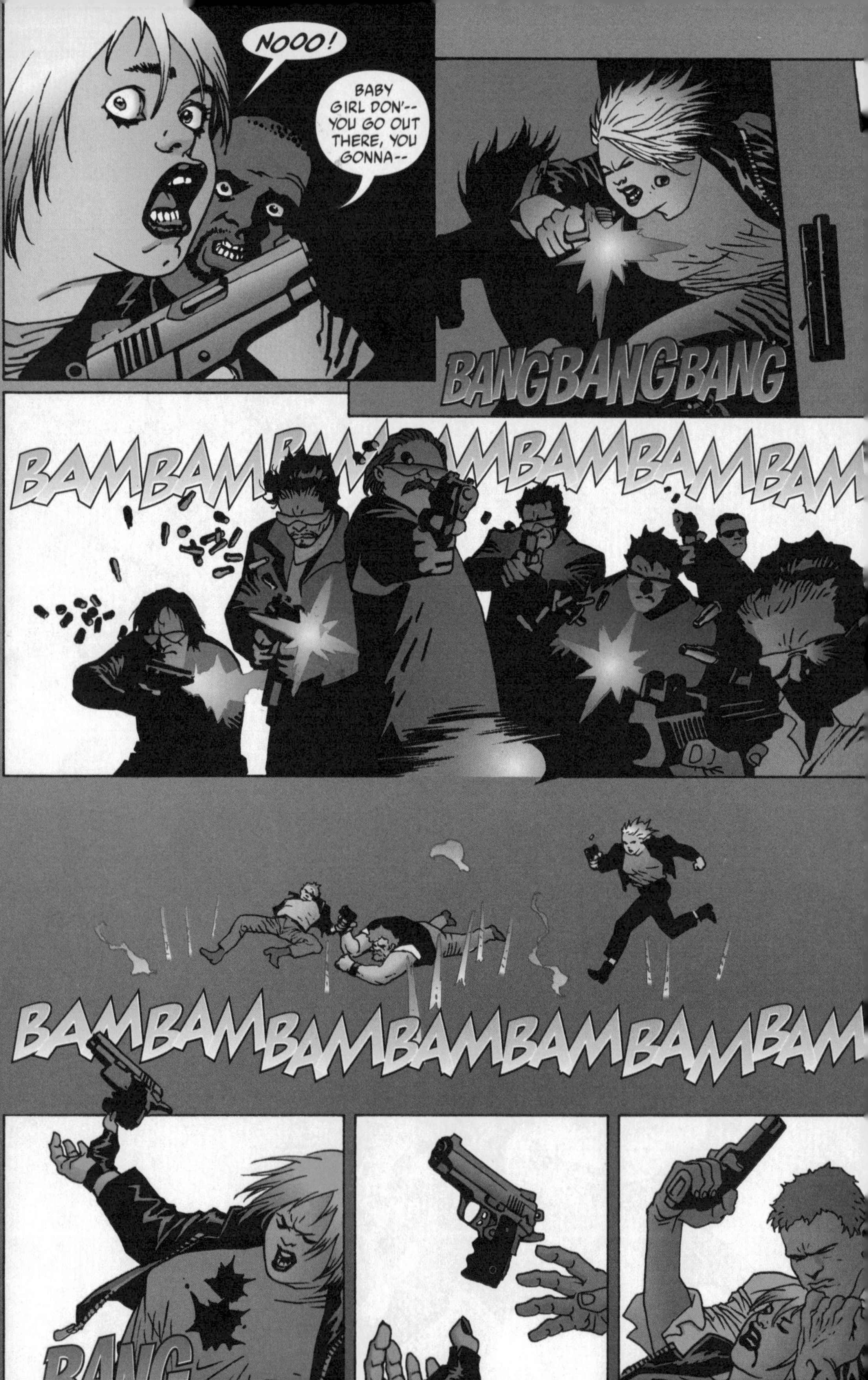

NOOO!
BABY GIRL DON'-- YOU GO OUT THERE, YOU GONNA--
BANGBANGBANG
BAMBAMBAMBAMBAMBAMBAM
BAMBAMBAMBAMBAMBAMBAM
BANG

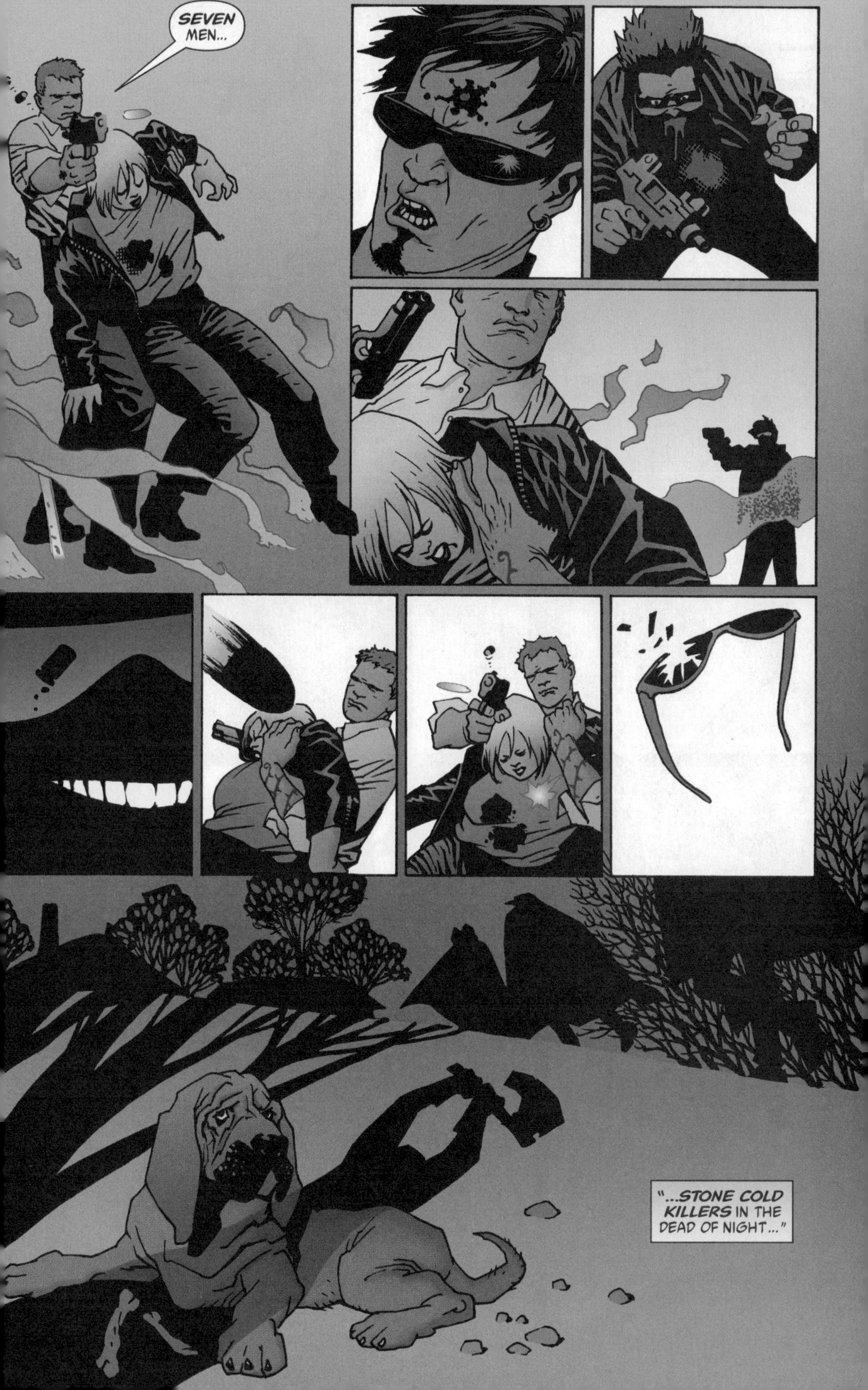
SEVEN MEN...
"...STONE COLD KILLERS IN THE DEAD OF NIGHT..."

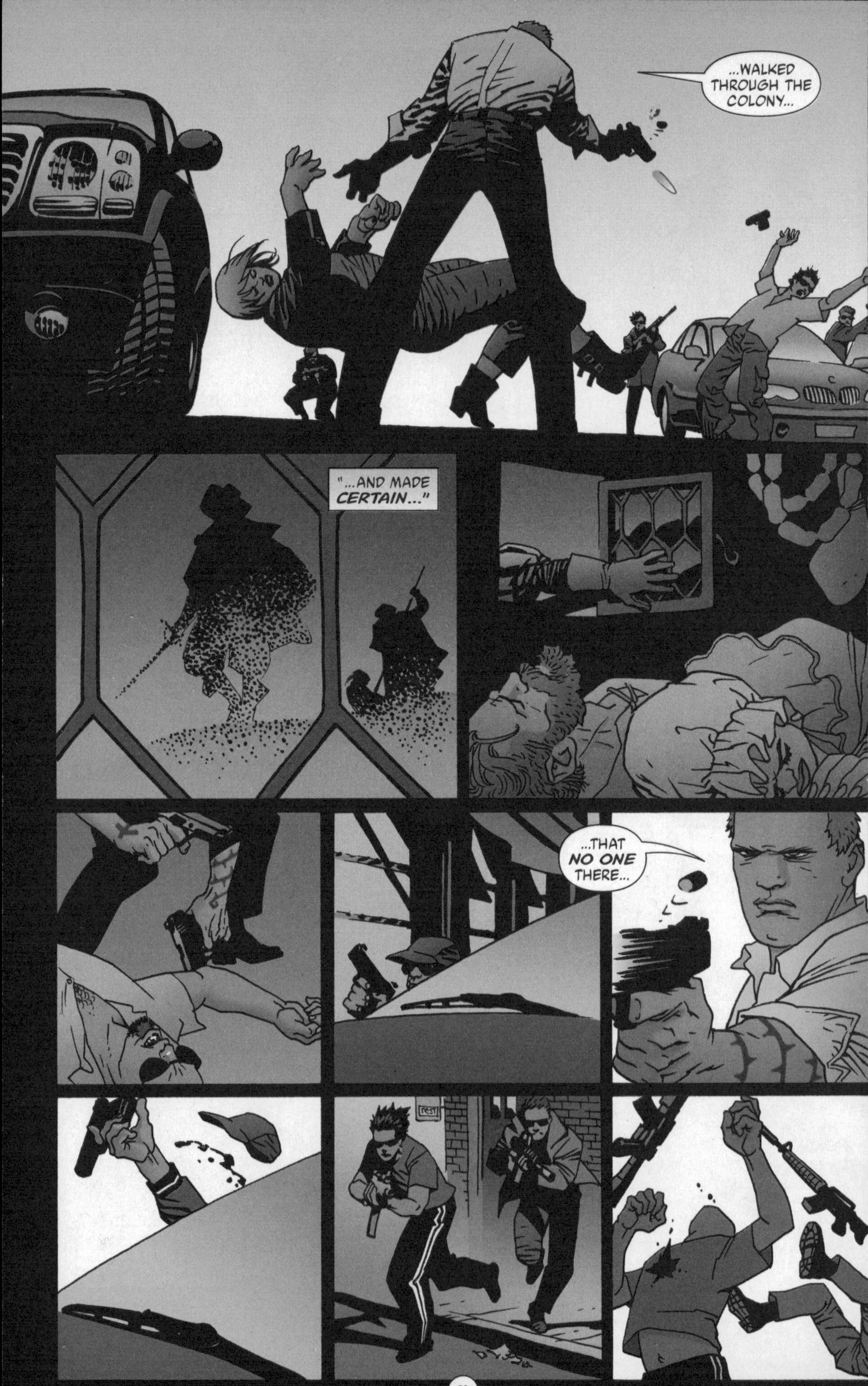
...WALKED THROUGH THE COLONY...
"...AND MADE CERTAIN..."
...THAT NO ONE THERE...

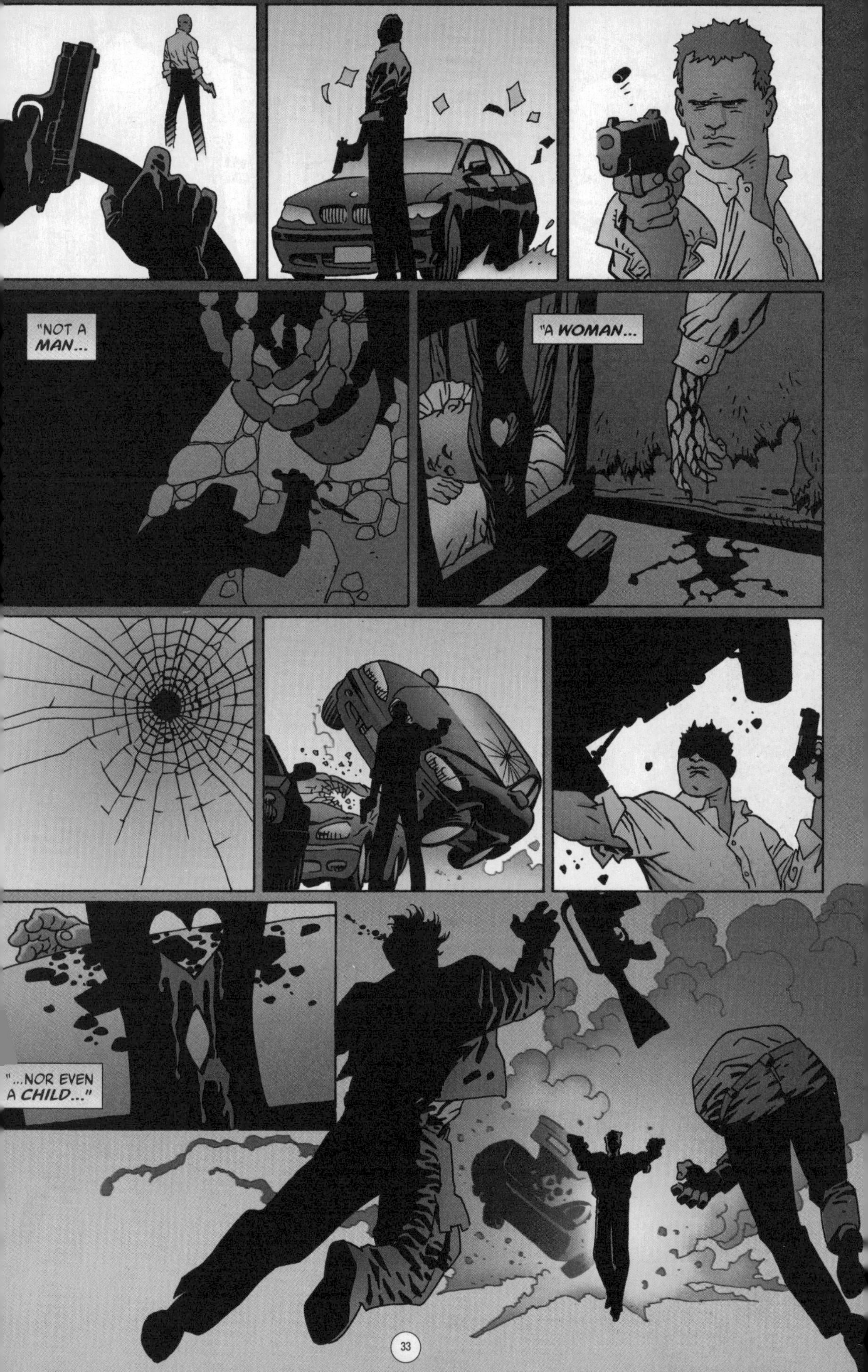
"NOT A
MAN...
"A WOMAN...
"...NOR EVEN
A CHILD..."

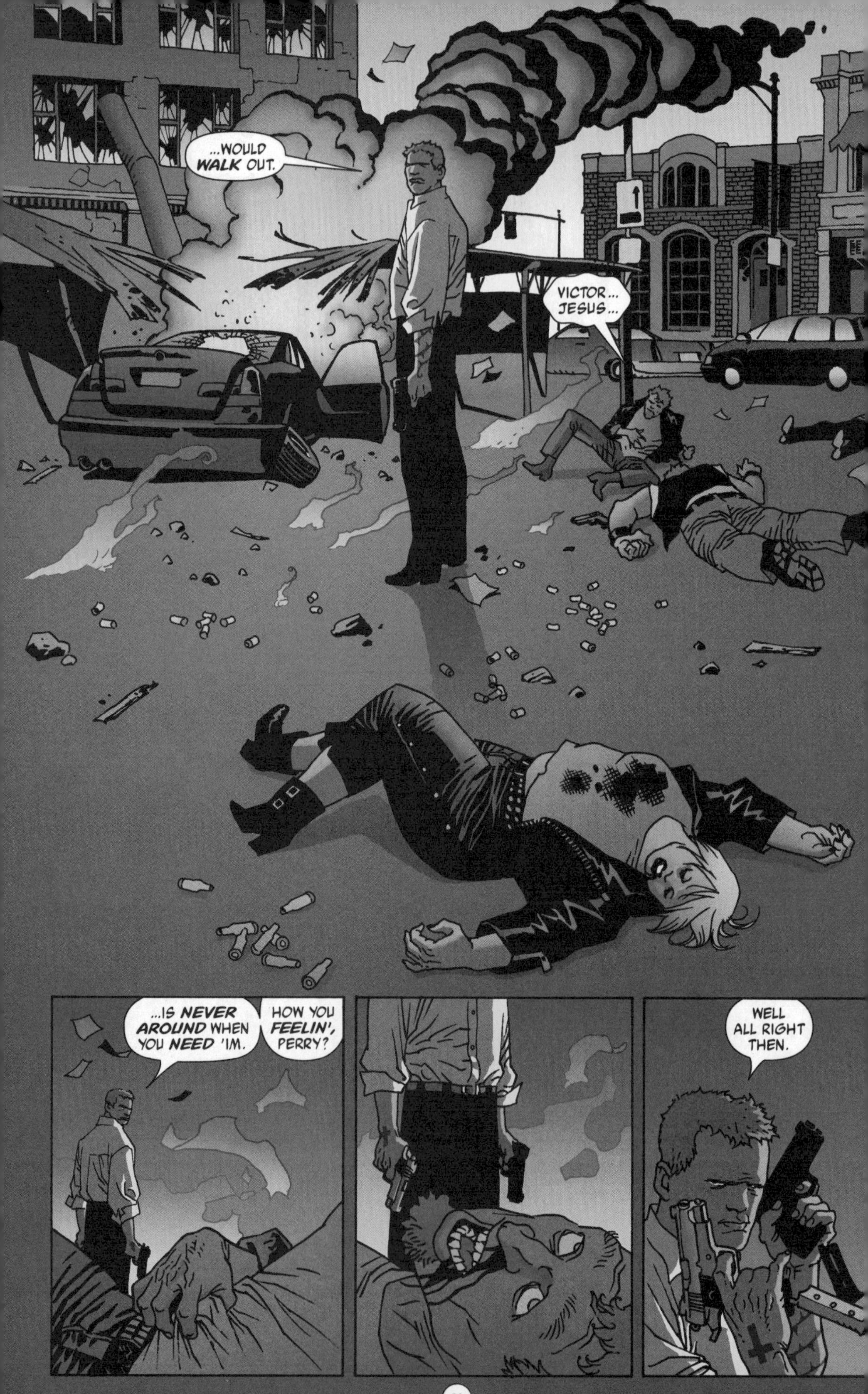
...WOULD WALK OUT.
VICTOR... JESUS...
...IS NEVER AROUND WHEN YOU NEED 'IM.
HOW YOU FEELIN', PERRY?
WELL ALL RIGHT THEN.

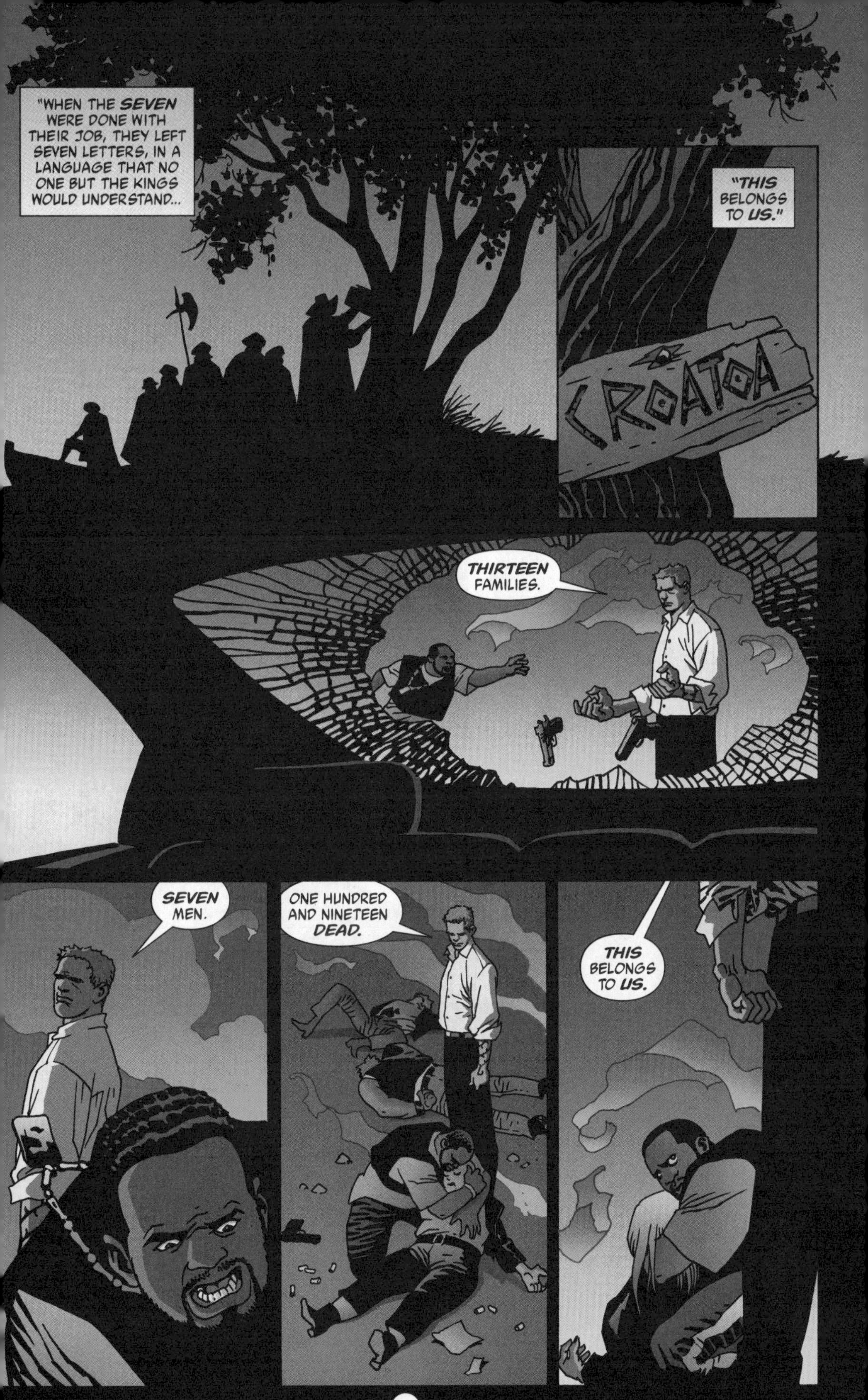
"WHEN THE SEVEN WERE DONE WITH THEIR JOB, THEY LEFT SEVEN LETTERS, IN A LANGUAGE THAT NO ONE BUT THE KINGS WOULD UNDERSTAND...
"THIS BELONGS TO US."
CROATOA
THIRTEEN FAMILIES.
SEVEN MEN.
ONE HUNDRED AND NINETEEN DEAD.
THIS BELONGS TO US.

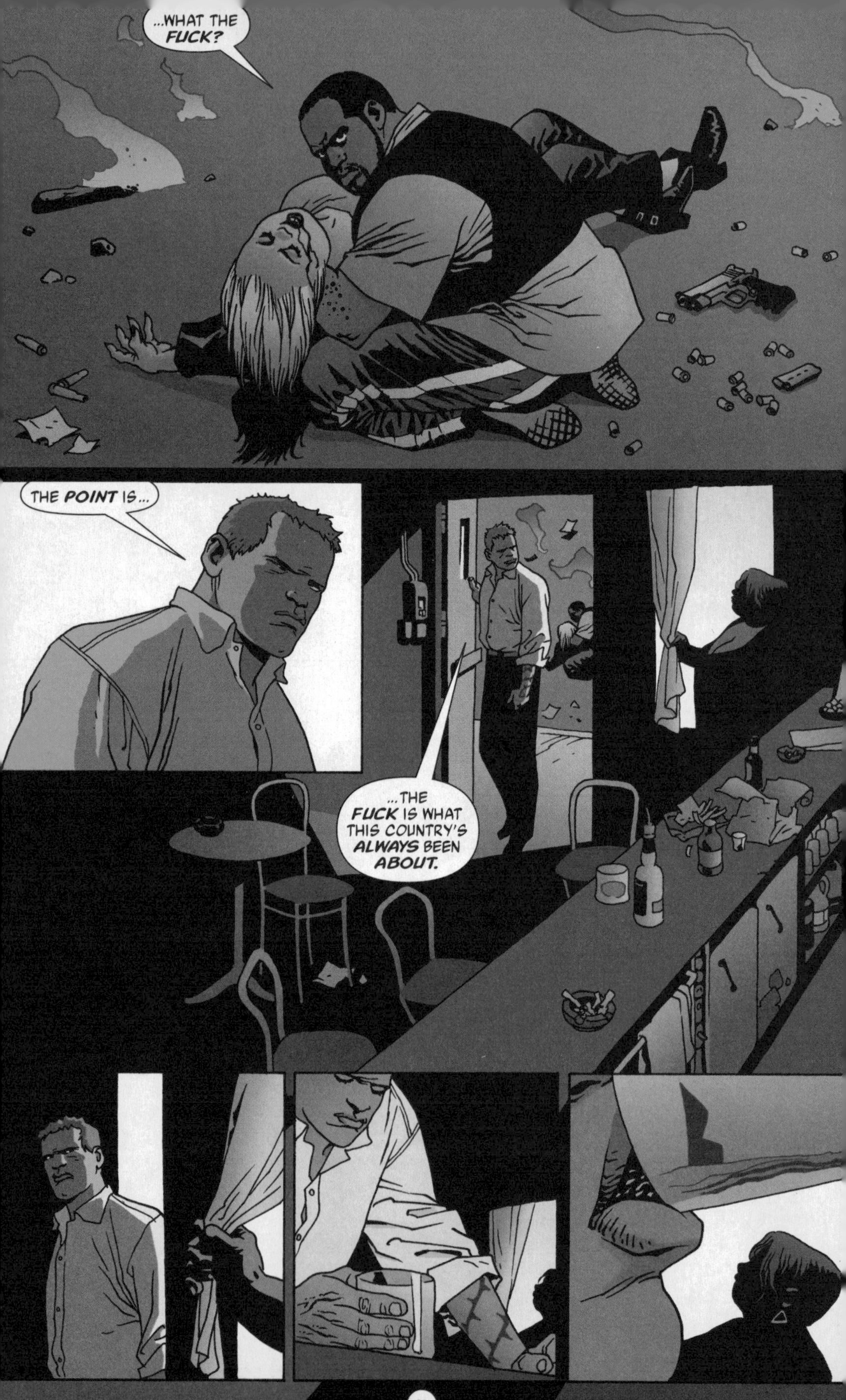

...WHAT THE FUCK?
THE POINT IS...
...THE FUCK IS WHAT THIS COUNTRY'S ALWAYS BEEN ABOUT.

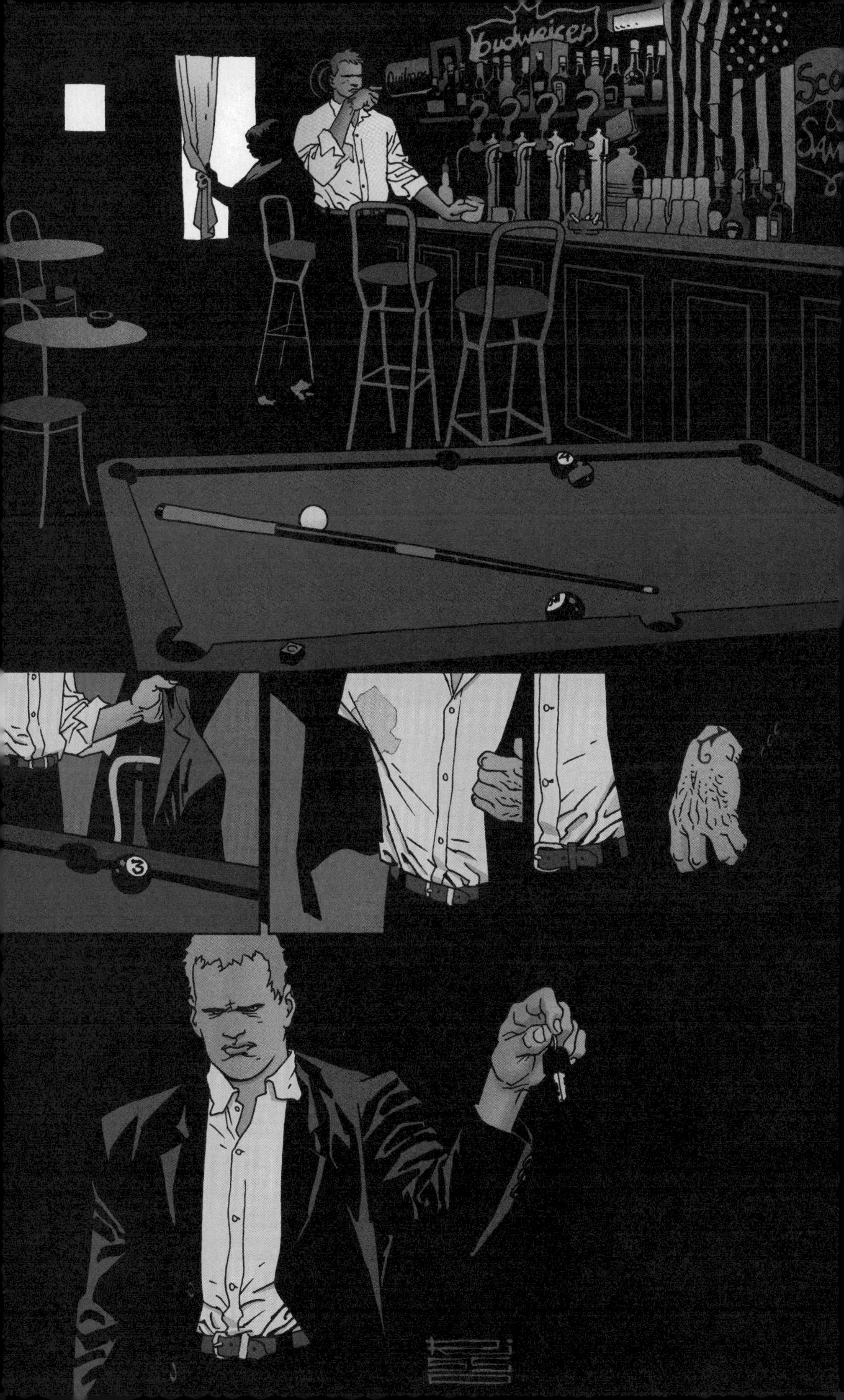
Budweiser

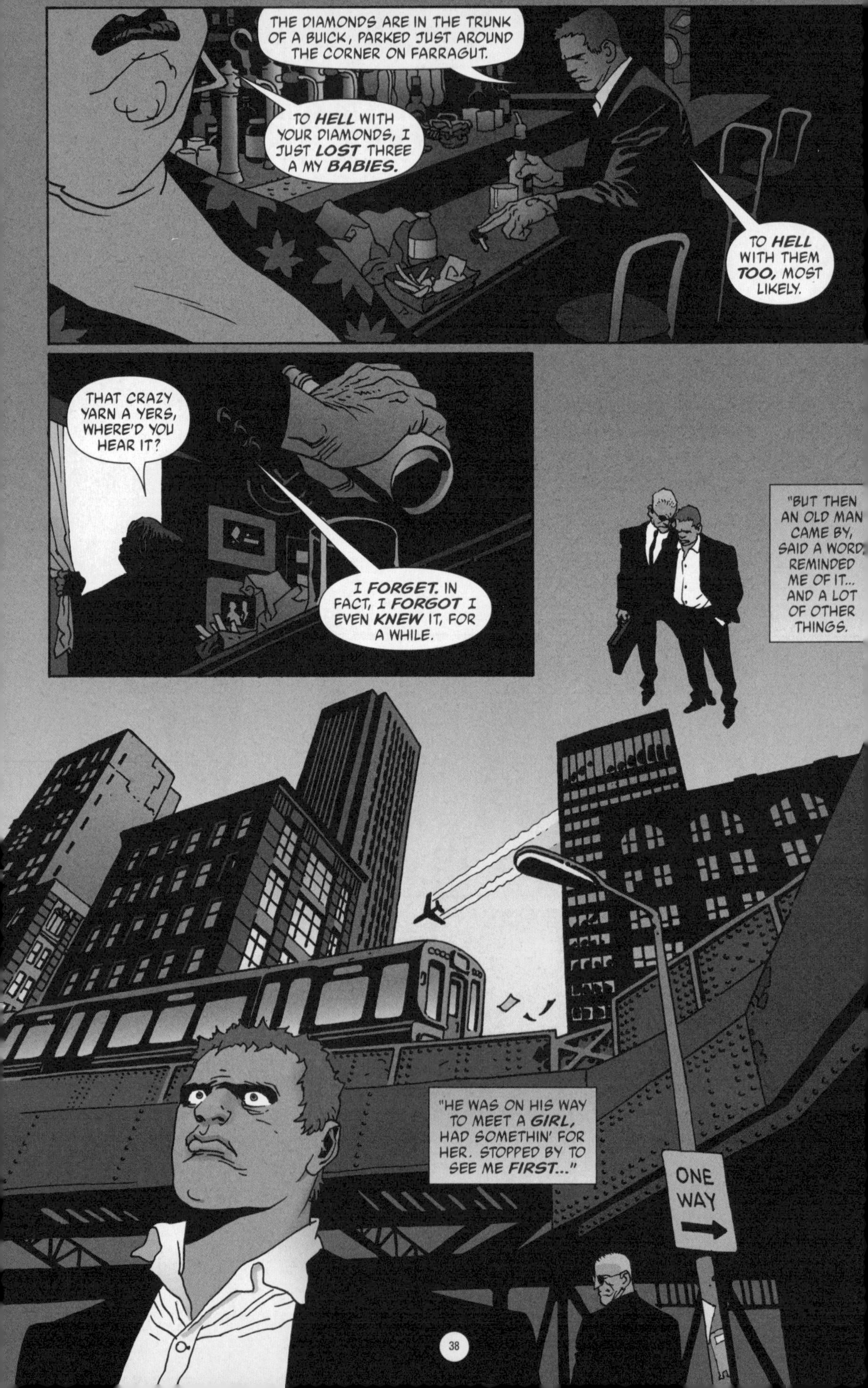
THE DIAMONDS ARE IN THE TRUNK OF A BUICK, PARKED JUST AROUND THE CORNER ON FARRAGUT.
TO HELL WITH YOUR DIAMONDS, I JUST LOST THREE A MY BABIES.
TO HELL WITH THEM TOO, MOST LIKELY.
THAT CRAZY YARN A YERS, WHERE'D YOU HEAR IT?
I FORGET. IN FACT, I FORGOT I EVEN KNEW IT, FOR A WHILE.
"BUT THEN AN OLD MAN CAME BY, SAID A WORD, REMINDED ME OF IT... AND A LOT OF OTHER THINGS.
"HE WAS ON HIS WAY TO MEET A GIRL, HAD SOMETHIN' FOR HER. STOPPED BY TO SEE ME FIRST..."
ONE WAY

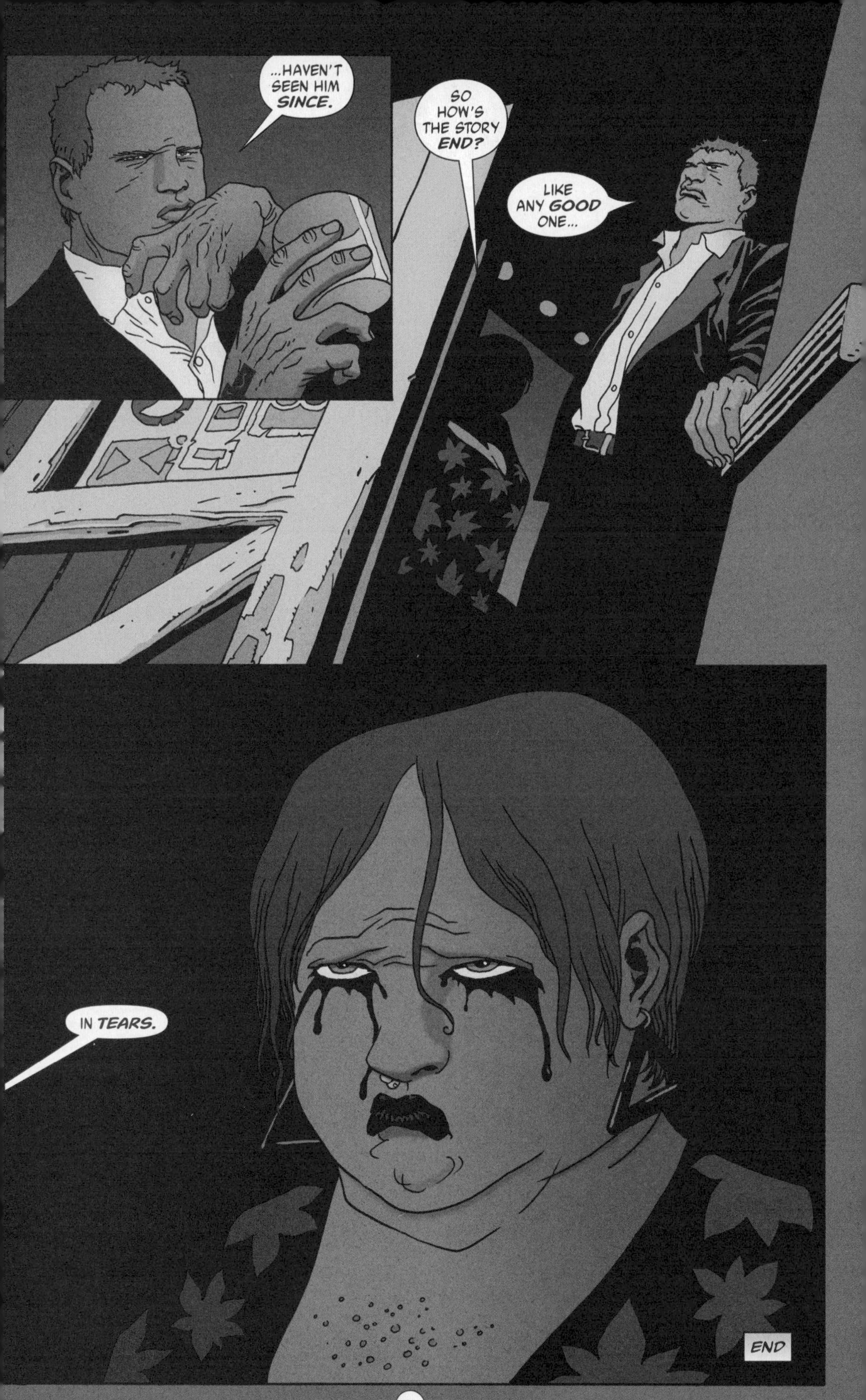
...HAVEN'T SEEN HIM SINCE.
SO HOW'S THE STORY END?
LIKE ANY GOOD ONE...
IN TEARS.
END

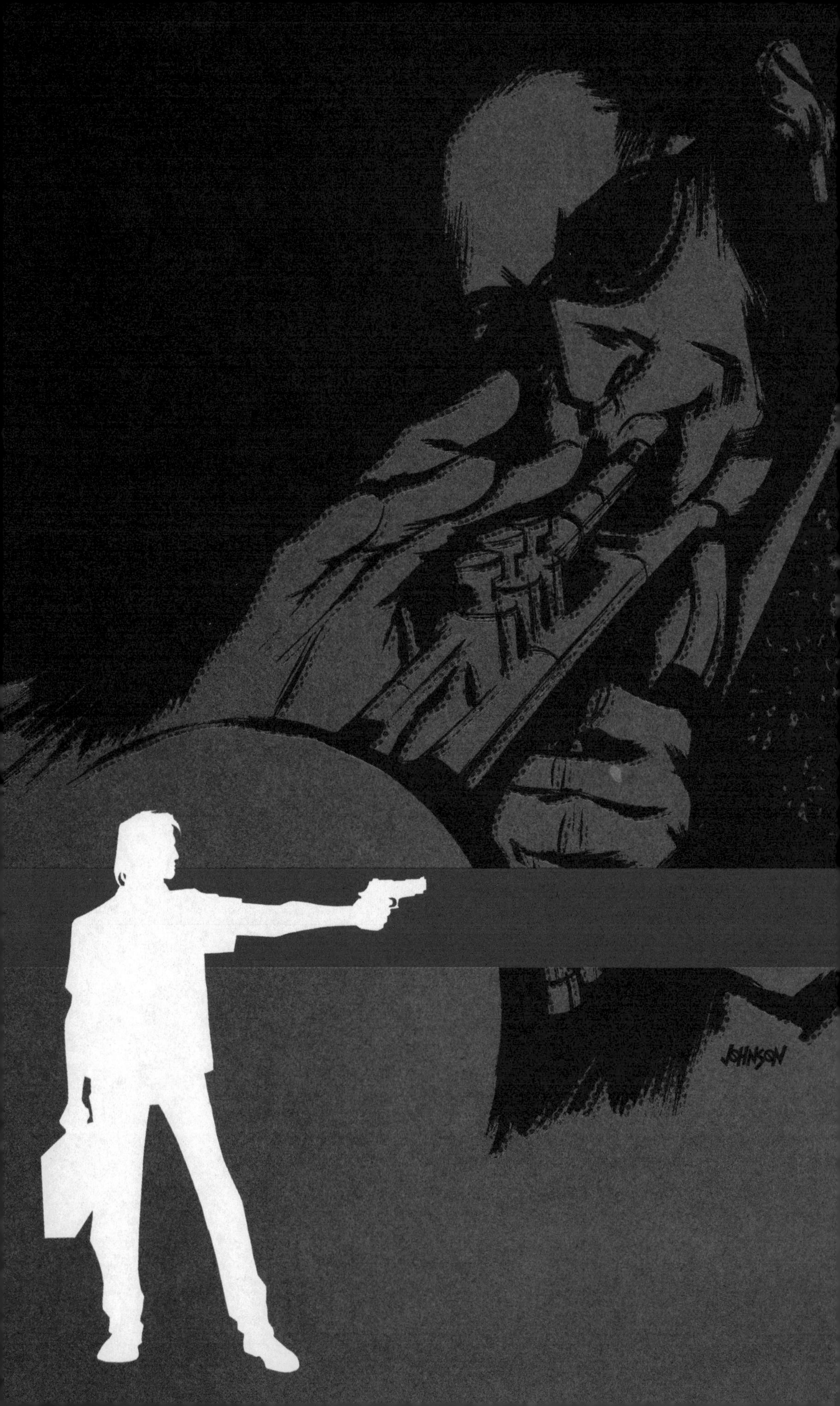

JOHNSON

YOU WANNA KNOW SOMETHIN' 'BOUT ME I NEVER TOL' ANYONE?
I FUCKIN' HATE GUNS.
FUNNY, HUH? A DAMN RIDICULOUS THING FOR ME TO HATE, I MEAN, CONSIDERING...
...YEAH.
IT'S NOT THE GUNS I HATE...
...BUT WHAT THEY DO.

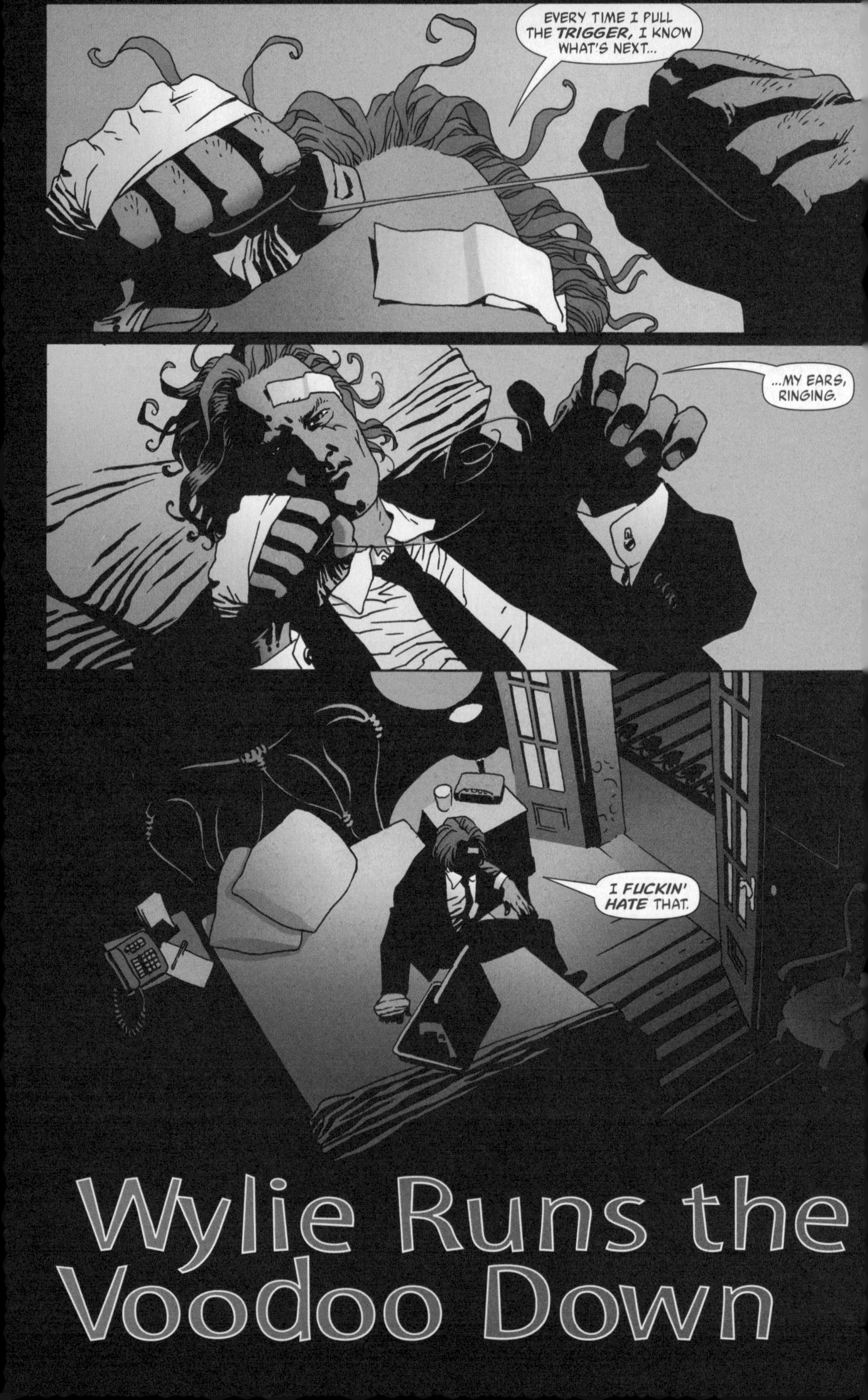
EVERY TIME I PULL THE TRIGGER, I KNOW WHAT'S NEXT...
...MY EARS, RINGING.
I FUCKIN' HATE THAT.

Wylie Runs the Voodoo Down

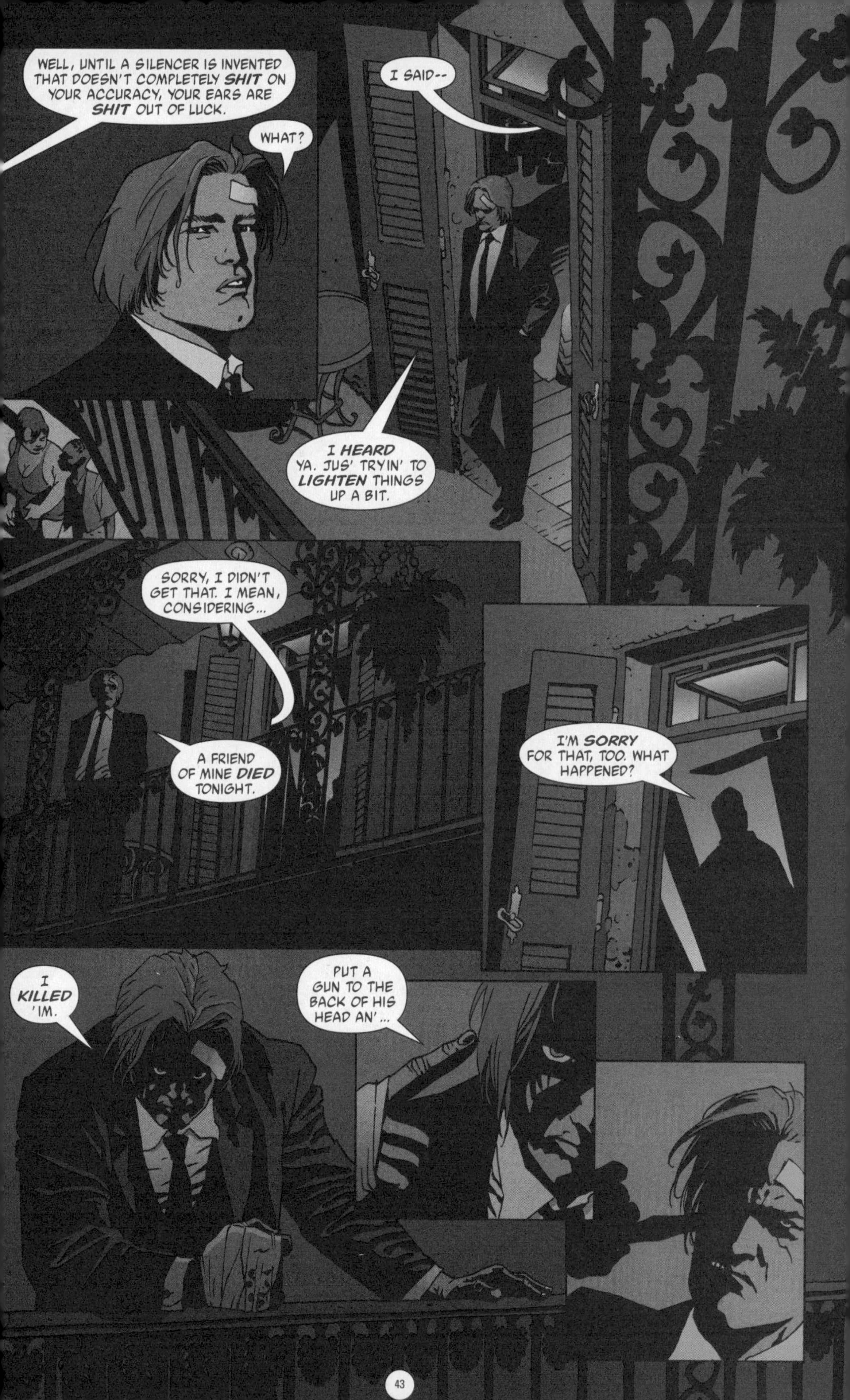

WELL, UNTIL A SILENCER IS INVENTED THAT DOESN'T COMPLETELY SHIT ON YOUR ACCURACY, YOUR EARS ARE SHIT OUT OF LUCK.
I SAID--
WHAT?
I HEARD YA. JUS' TRYIN' TO LIGHTEN THINGS UP A BIT.
SORRY, I DIDN'T GET THAT. I MEAN, CONSIDERING...
A FRIEND OF MINE DIED TONIGHT.
I'M SORRY FOR THAT, TOO. WHAT HAPPENED?
I KILLED 'IM.
PUT A GUN TO THE BACK OF HIS HEAD AN'...

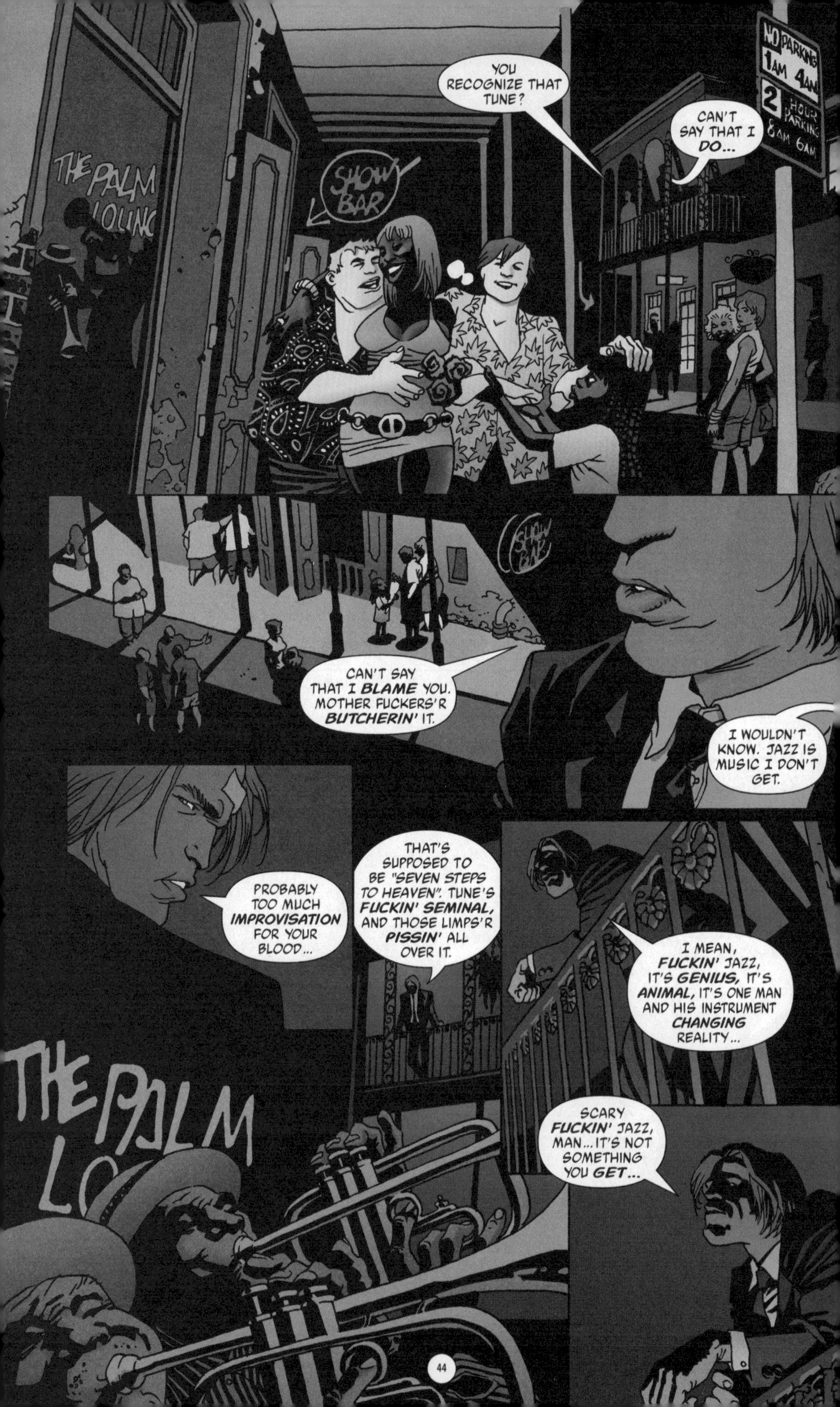
THE PALM LOUNG
SHOW BAR
NO PARKING 1AM 4AM
2 HOUR PARKING 8AM 6AM
YOU RECOGNIZE THAT TUNE?
CAN'T SAY THAT I DO...
CAN'T SAY THAT I BLAME YOU. MOTHER FUCKERS'R BUTCHERIN' IT.
I WOULDN'T KNOW. JAZZ IS MUSIC I DON'T GET.
PROBABLY TOO MUCH IMPROVISATION FOR YOUR BLOOD...
THAT'S SUPPOSED TO BE "SEVEN STEPS TO HEAVEN". TUNE'S FUCKIN' SEMINAL, AND THOSE LIMPS'R PISSIN' ALL OVER IT.
I MEAN, FUCKIN' JAZZ, IT'S GENIUS, IT'S ANIMAL, IT'S ONE MAN AND HIS INSTRUMENT CHANGING REALITY...
THE PALM LO
SCARY FUCKIN' JAZZ, MAN... IT'S NOT SOMETHING YOU GET...

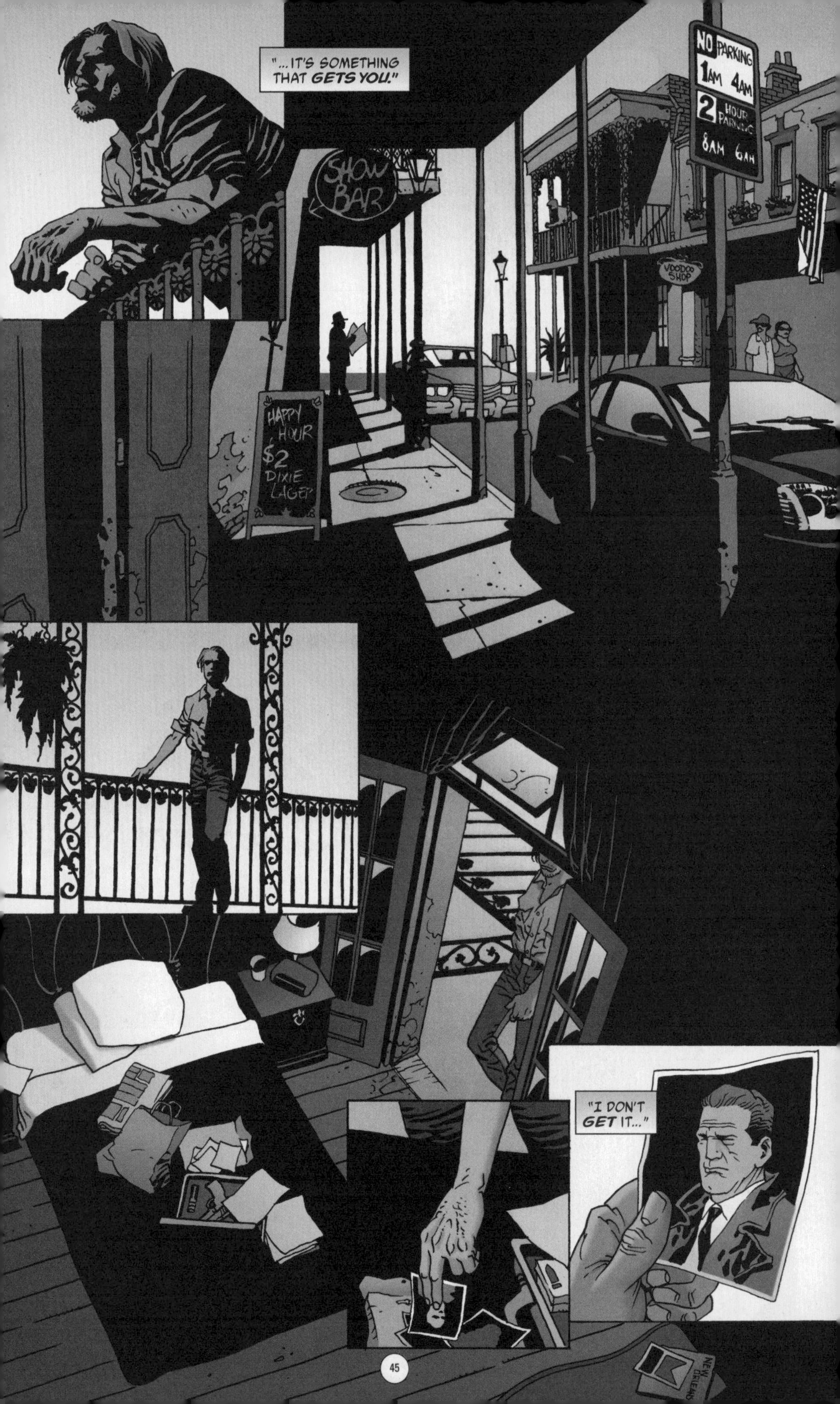
"...IT'S SOMETHING THAT GETS YOU."
NO PARKING
1AM 4AM
2 HOUR PARKING
8AM 6AM
SHOW BAR
VOODOO SHOP
HAPPY HOUR
$2
DIXIE LAGER
"I DON'T GET IT..."
NEW ORLEANS

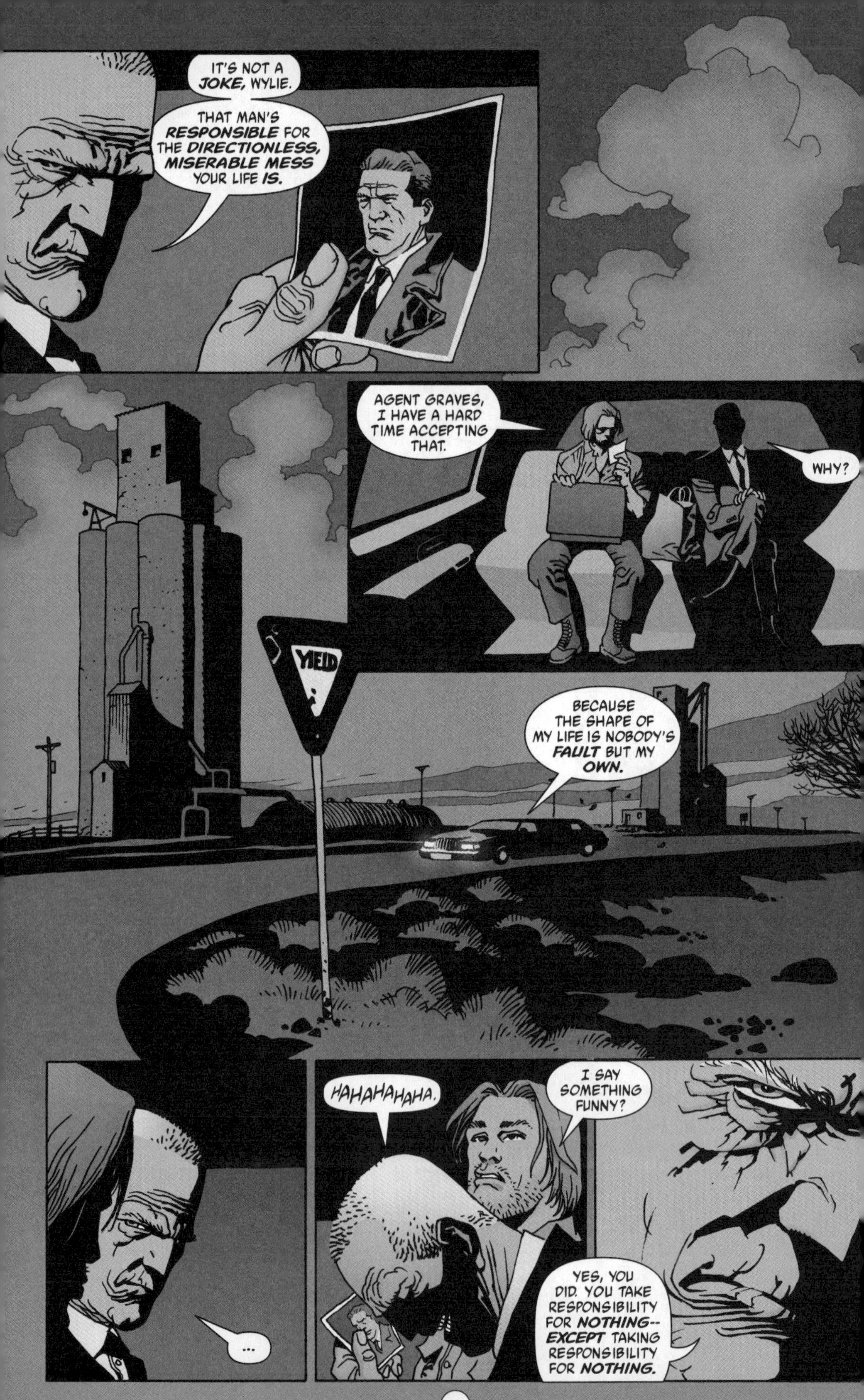

IT'S NOT A JOKE, WYLIE.
THAT MAN'S RESPONSIBLE FOR THE DIRECTIONLESS, MISERABLE MESS YOUR LIFE IS.
AGENT GRAVES, I HAVE A HARD TIME ACCEPTING THAT.
WHY?
YIELD
BECAUSE THE SHAPE OF MY LIFE IS NOBODY'S FAULT BUT MY OWN.
...
HAHAHAHAHAHA.
I SAY SOMETHING FUNNY?
YES, YOU DID. YOU TAKE RESPONSIBILITY FOR NOTHING-- EXCEPT TAKING RESPONSIBILITY FOR NOTHING.

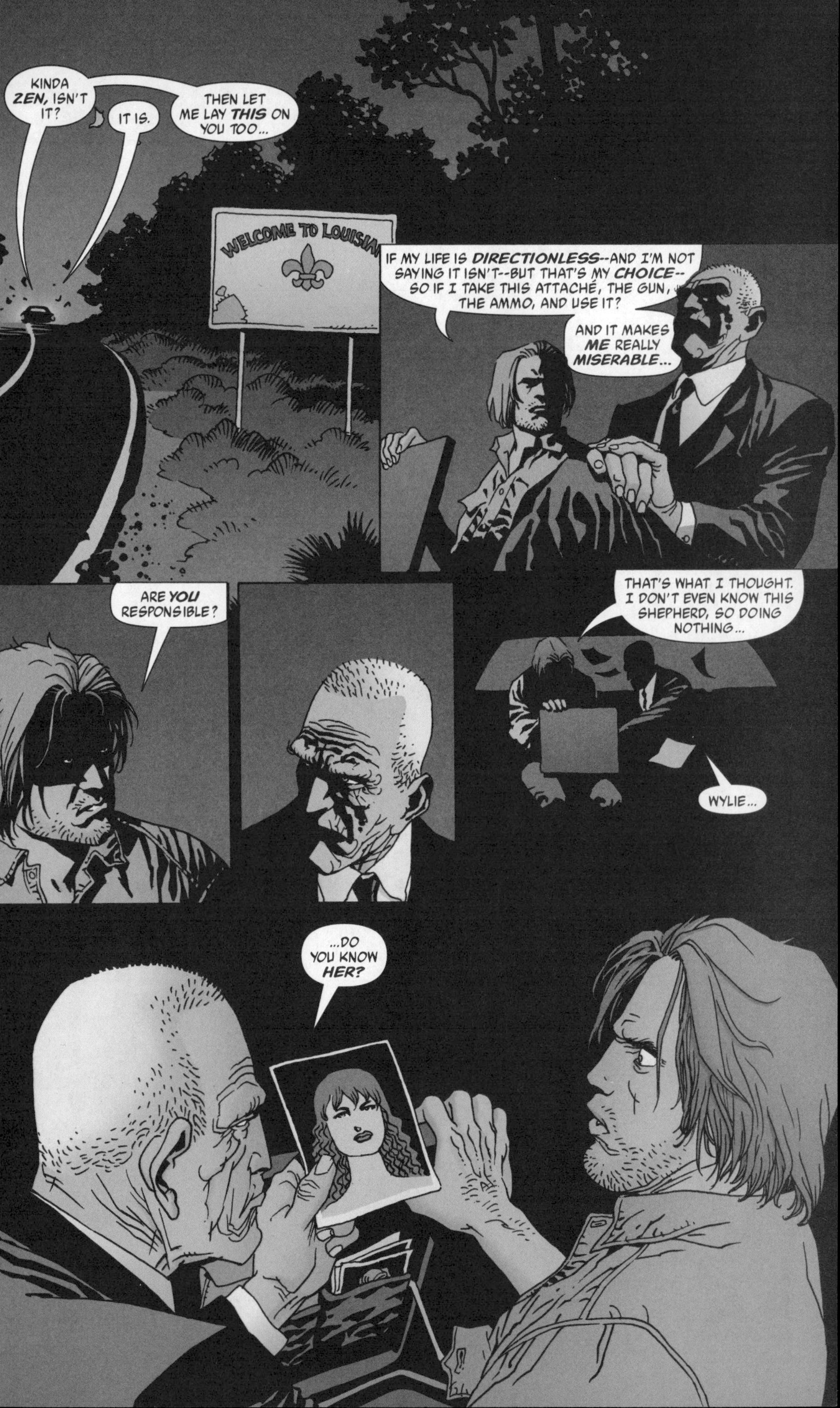
KINDA ZEN, ISN'T IT?
IT IS.
THEN LET ME LAY THIS ON YOU TOO...
WELCOME TO LOUISIAN
IF MY LIFE IS DIRECTIONLESS--AND I'M NOT SAYING IT ISN'T--BUT THAT'S MY CHOICE--SO IF I TAKE THIS ATTACHÉ, THE GUN, THE AMMO, AND USE IT?
AND IT MAKES ME REALLY MISERABLE...
ARE YOU RESPONSIBLE?
THAT'S WHAT I THOUGHT. I DON'T EVEN KNOW THIS SHEPHERD, SO DOING NOTHING...
WYLIE...
...DO YOU KNOW HER?

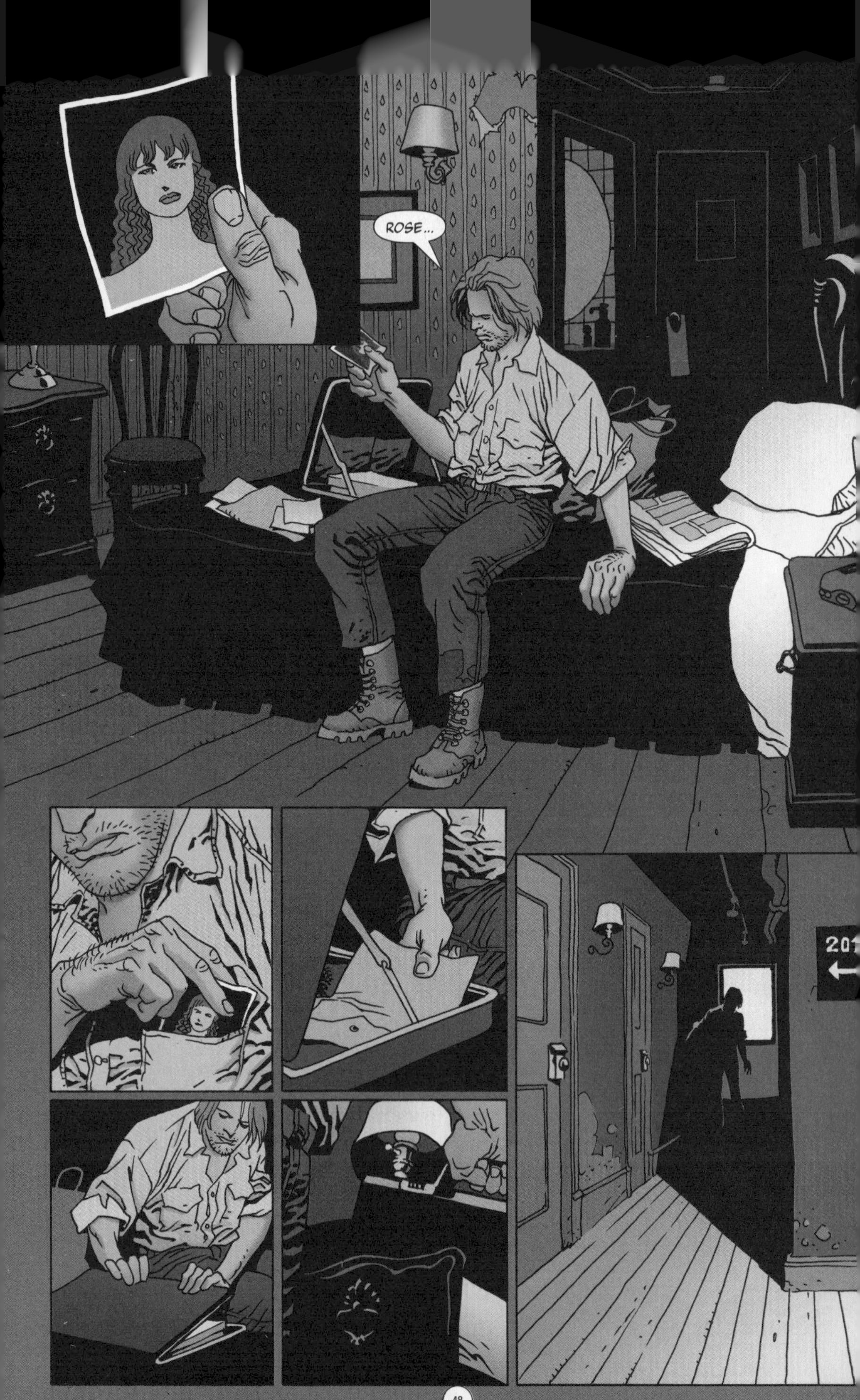
ROSE...
201

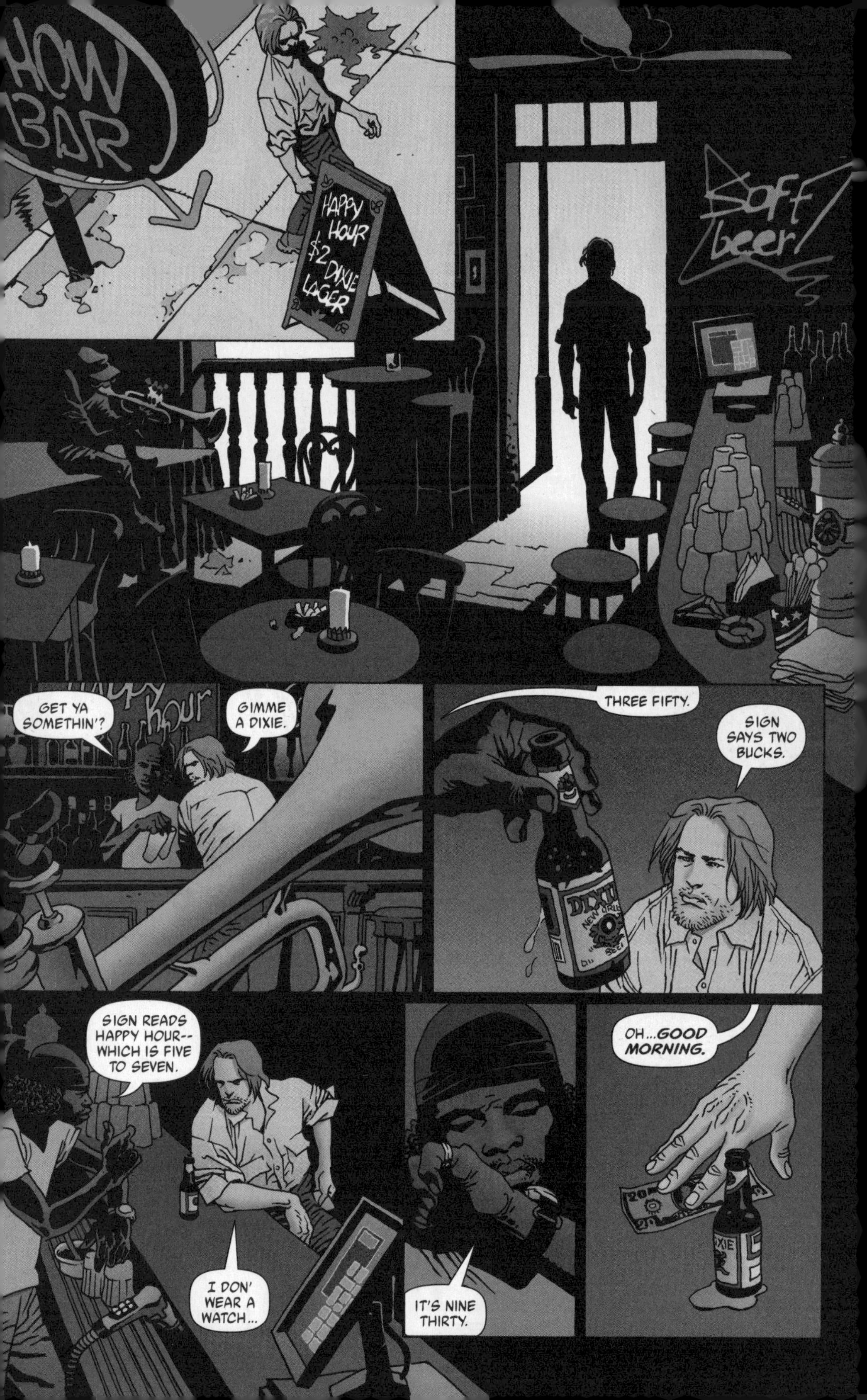
HOW BAR
HAPPY HOUR $2 DIXIE LAGER
Soft beer
GET YA SOMETHIN'?
GIMME A DIXIE.
THREE FIFTY.
SIGN SAYS TWO BUCKS.
SIGN READS HAPPY HOUR-- WHICH IS FIVE TO SEVEN.
I DON' WEAR A WATCH...
IT'S NINE THIRTY.
OH...GOOD MORNING.

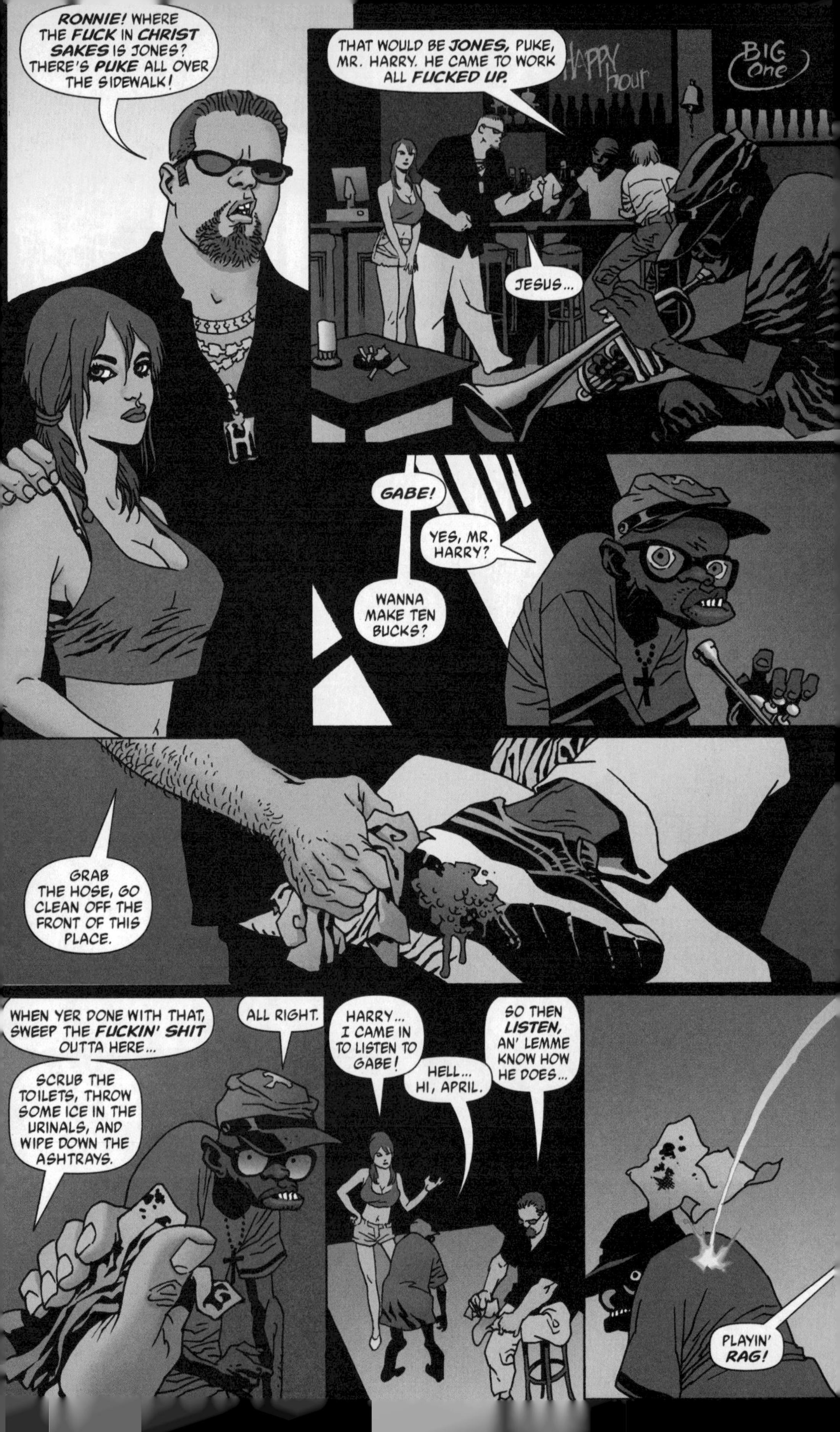

RONNIE! WHERE THE FUCK IN CHRIST SAKES IS JONES? THERE'S PUKE ALL OVER THE SIDEWALK!
THAT WOULD BE JONES, PUKE, MR. HARRY. HE CAME TO WORK ALL FUCKED UP.
HAPPY hour
BIG One
JESUS...
GABE!
YES, MR. HARRY?
WANNA MAKE TEN BUCKS?
GRAB THE HOSE, GO CLEAN OFF THE FRONT OF THIS PLACE.
WHEN YER DONE WITH THAT, SWEEP THE FUCKIN' SHIT OUTTA HERE...
SCRUB THE TOILETS, THROW SOME ICE IN THE URINALS, AND WIPE DOWN THE ASHTRAYS.
ALL RIGHT.
HARRY... I CAME IN TO LISTEN TO GABE!
HELL... HI, APRIL.
SO THEN LISTEN, AN' LEMME KNOW HOW HE DOES...
PLAYIN' RAG!

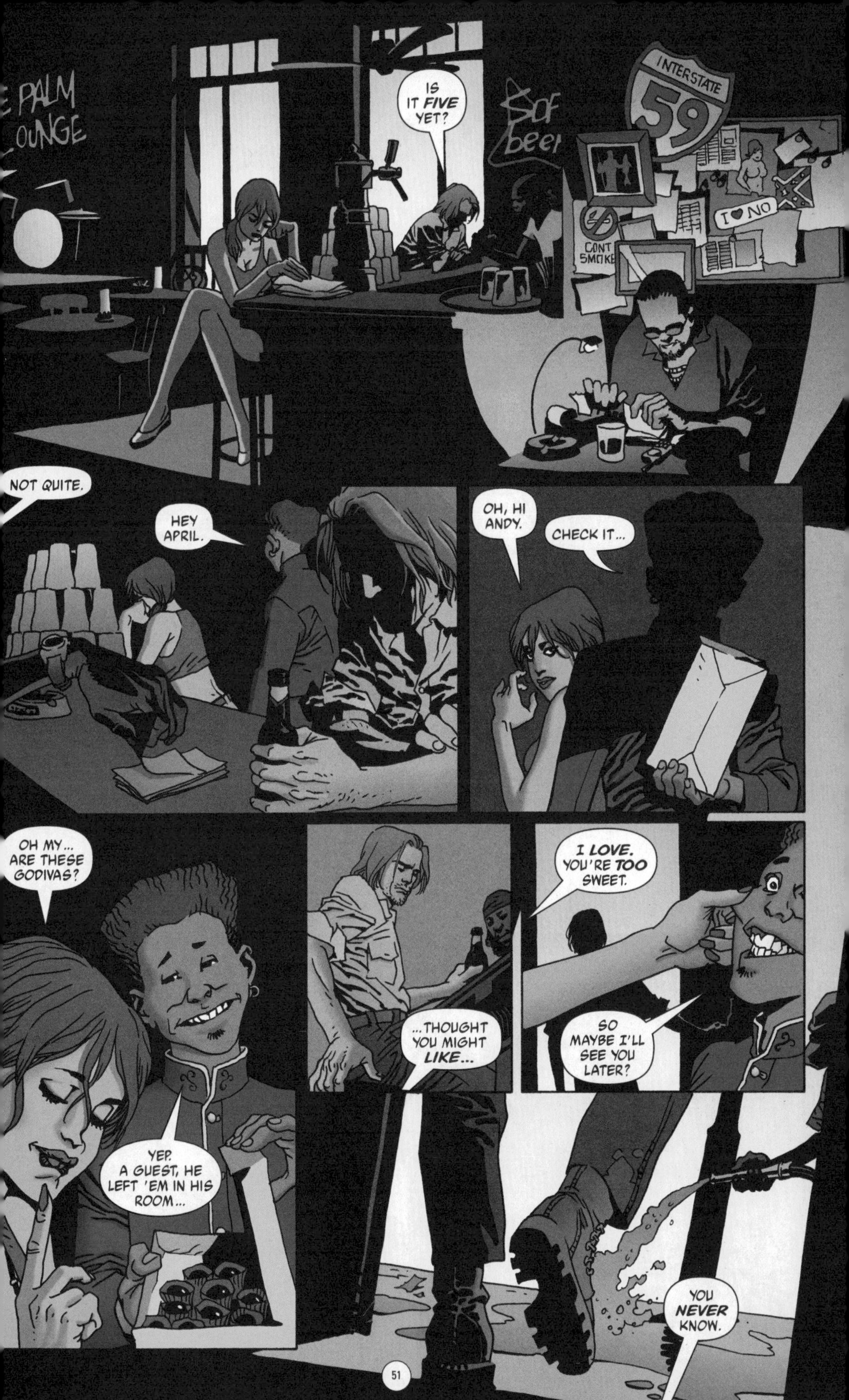
PALM
LOUNGE
IS IT FIVE YET?
INTERSTATE
59
I ♥ NO
CONT SMOKE
NOT QUITE.
HEY APRIL.
OH, HI ANDY.
CHECK IT...
OH MY... ARE THESE GODIVAS?
YEP. A GUEST, HE LEFT 'EM IN HIS ROOM...
...THOUGHT YOU MIGHT LIKE...
I LOVE. YOU'RE TOO SWEET.
SO MAYBE I'LL SEE YOU LATER?
YOU NEVER KNOW.

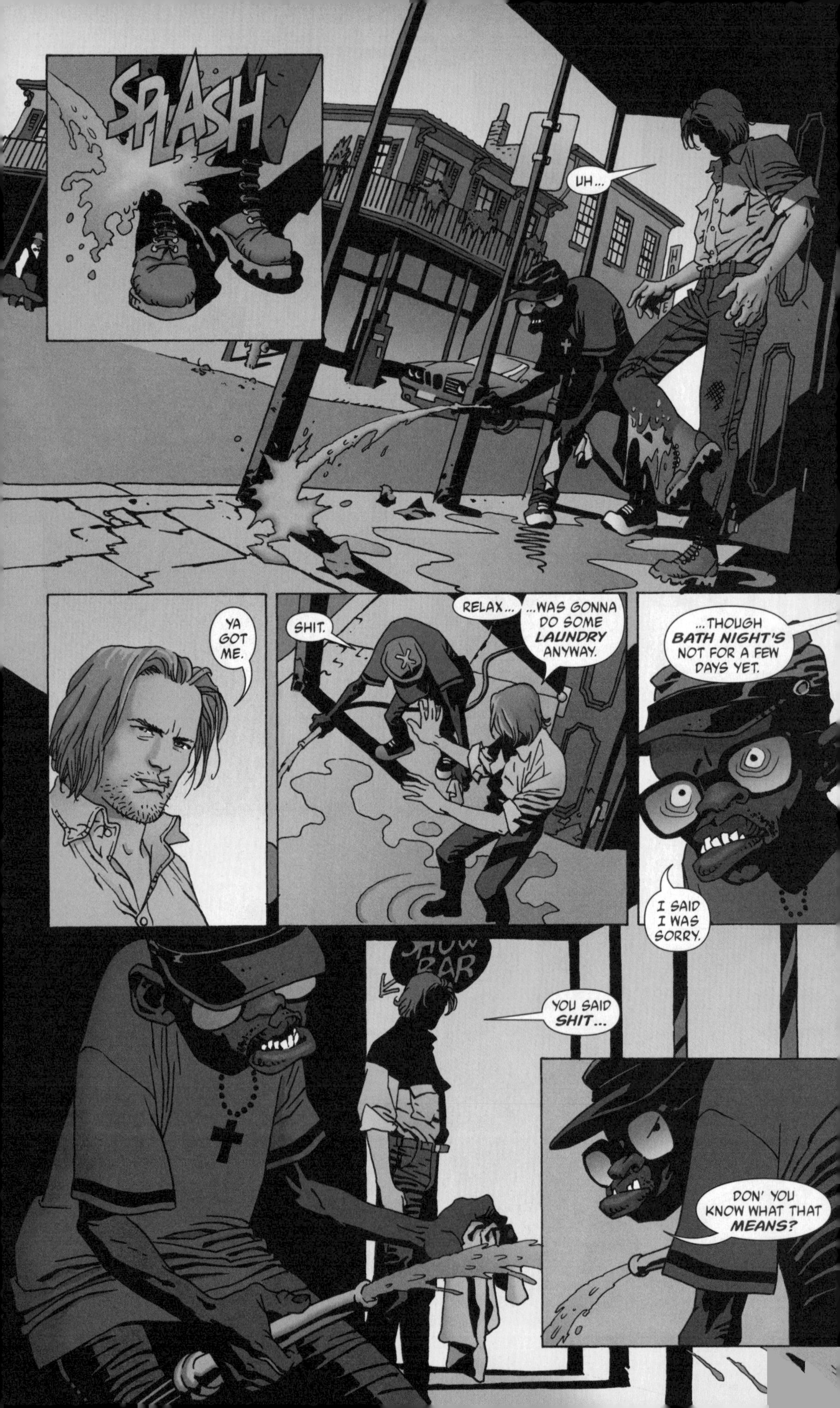

SPLASH
UH...
YA GOT ME.
SHIT.
RELAX...
...WAS GONNA DO SOME LAUNDRY ANYWAY.
...THOUGH BATH NIGHT'S NOT FOR A FEW DAYS YET.
I SAID I WAS SORRY.
YOU SAID SHIT...
DON' YOU KNOW WHAT THAT MEANS?

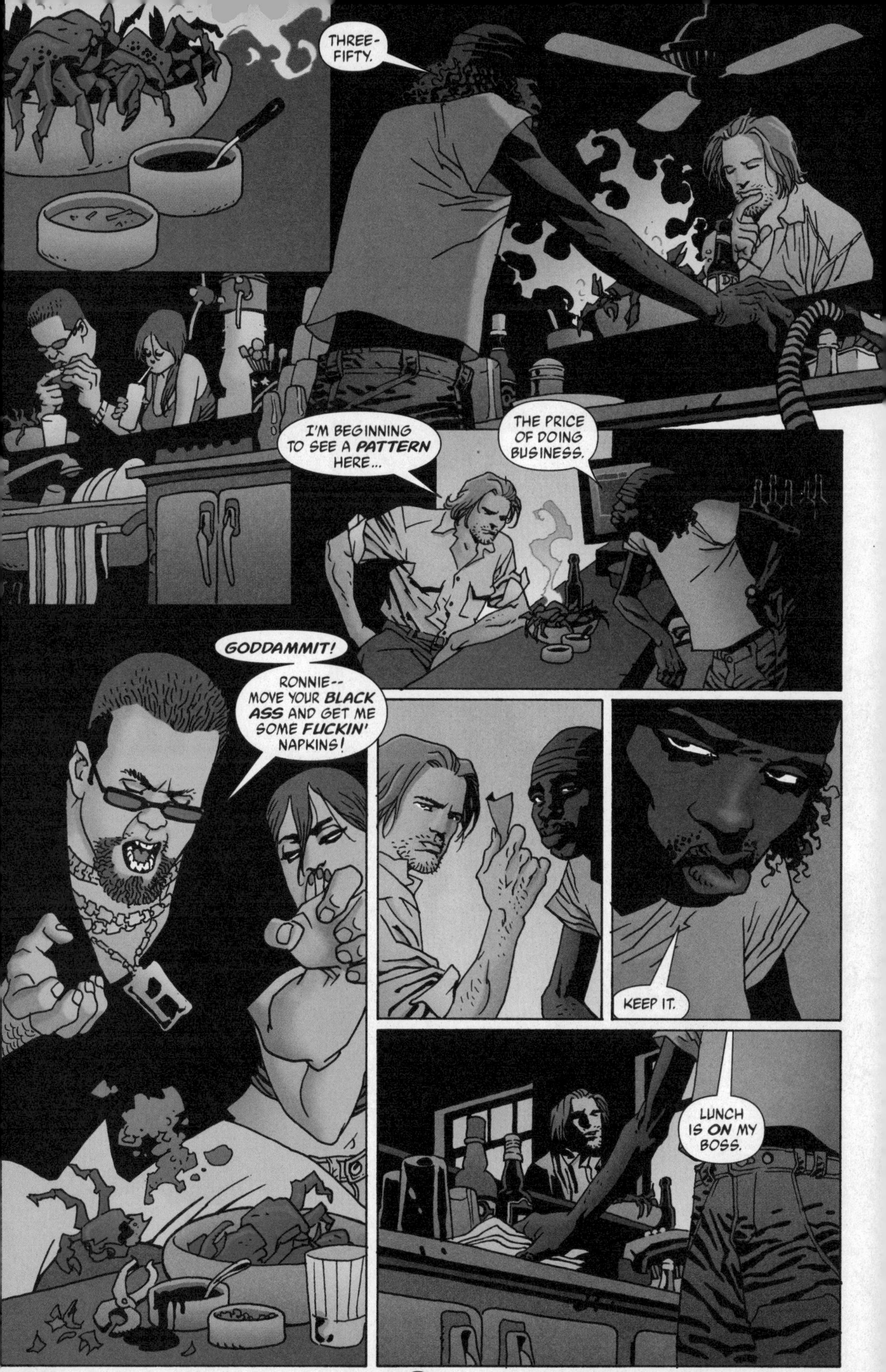
THREE-FIFTY.
I'M BEGINNING TO SEE A PATTERN HERE...
THE PRICE OF DOING BUSINESS.
GODDAMMIT!
RONNIE-- MOVE YOUR BLACK ASS AND GET ME SOME FUCKIN' NAPKINS!
KEEP IT.
LUNCH IS ON MY BOSS.

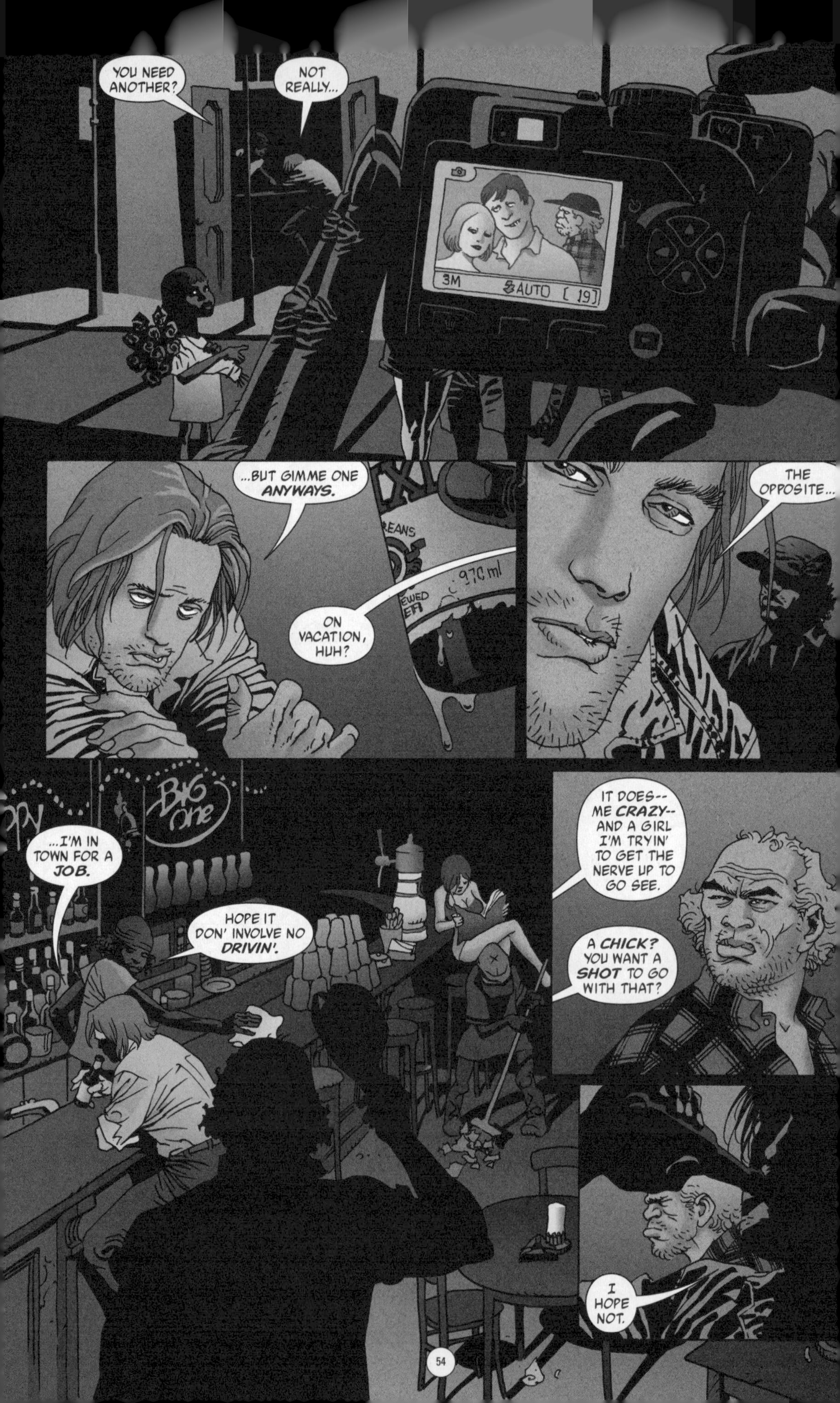

YOU NEED ANOTHER?
NOT REALLY...
3M
AUTO [19]
...BUT GIMME ONE ANYWAYS.
970 ml
ON VACATION, HUH?
THE OPPOSITE...
BIG One
...I'M IN TOWN FOR A JOB.
HOPE IT DON' INVOLVE NO DRIVIN'.
IT DOES-- ME CRAZY-- AND A GIRL I'M TRYIN' TO GET THE NERVE UP TO GO SEE.
A CHICK? YOU WANT A SHOT TO GO WITH THAT?
I HOPE NOT.

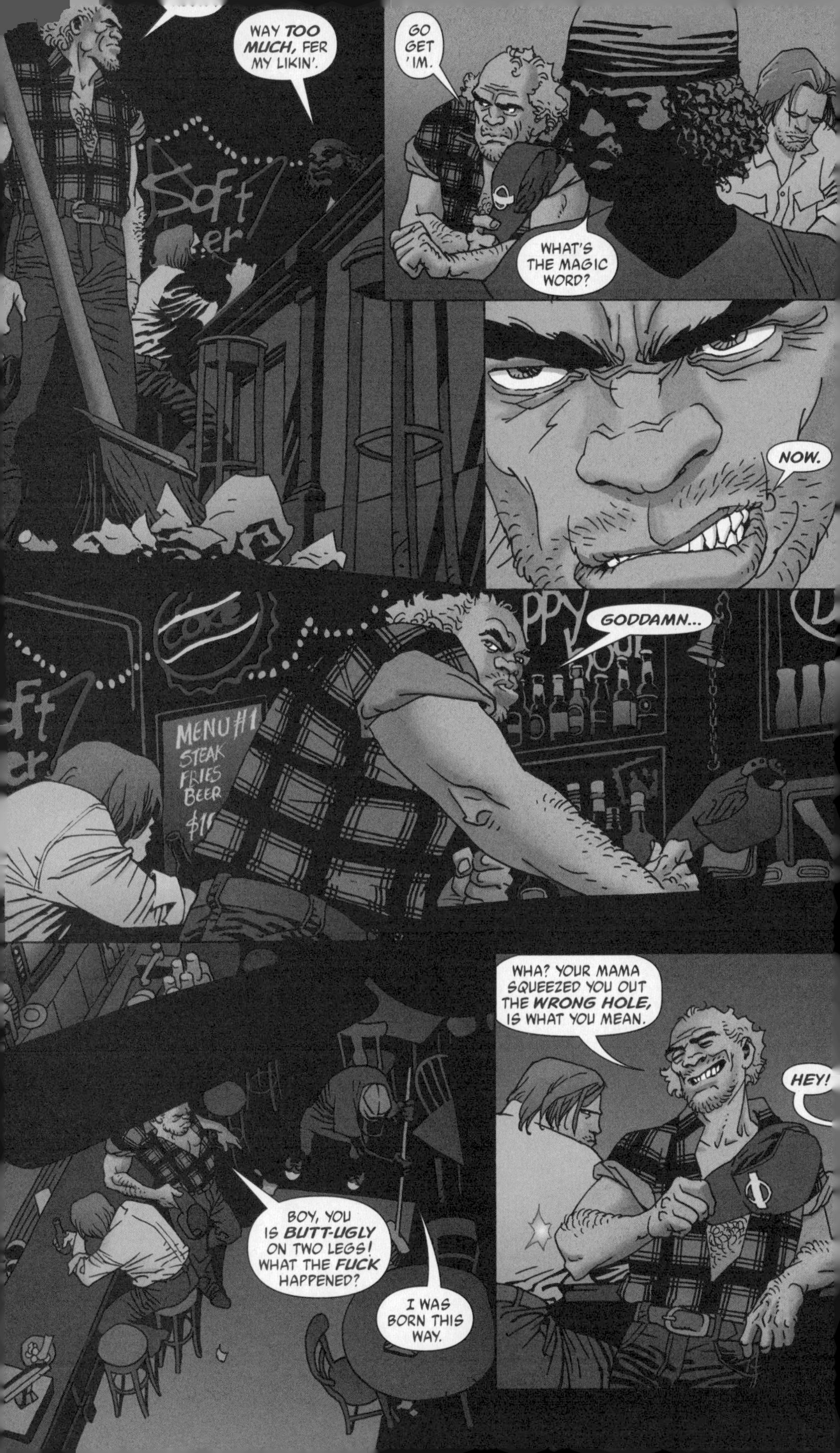
WAY TOO MUCH, FER MY LIKIN'.
GO GET 'IM.
WHAT'S THE MAGIC WORD?
NOW.
GODDAMN...
MENU #1 STEAK FRIES BEER
WHA? YOUR MAMA SQUEEZED YOU OUT THE WRONG HOLE, IS WHAT YOU MEAN.
HEY!
BOY, YOU IS BUTT-UGLY ON TWO LEGS! WHAT THE FUCK HAPPENED?
I WAS BORN THIS WAY.

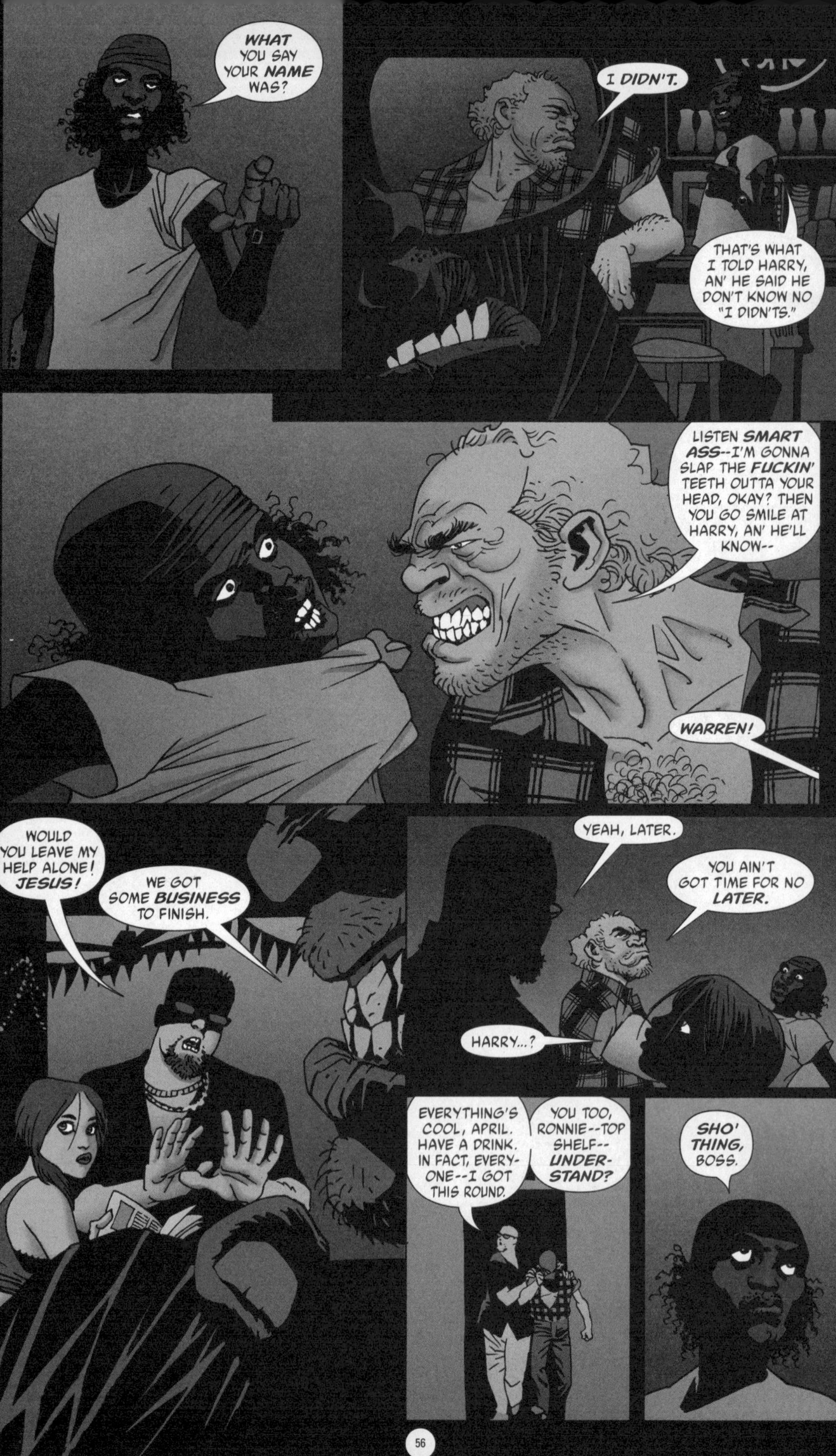
WHAT YOU SAY YOUR NAME WAS?
I DIDN'T.
THAT'S WHAT I TOLD HARRY, AN' HE SAID HE DON'T KNOW NO "I DIDN'TS."
LISTEN SMART ASS--I'M GONNA SLAP THE FUCKIN' TEETH OUTTA YOUR HEAD, OKAY? THEN YOU GO SMILE AT HARRY, AN' HE'LL KNOW--
WARREN!
WOULD YOU LEAVE MY HELP ALONE! JESUS!
WE GOT SOME BUSINESS TO FINISH.
YEAH, LATER.
YOU AIN'T GOT TIME FOR NO LATER.
HARRY...?
EVERYTHING'S COOL, APRIL. HAVE A DRINK. IN FACT, EVERY-ONE--I GOT THIS ROUND.
YOU TOO, RONNIE--TOP SHELF--UNDER-STAND?
SHO' THING, BOSS.

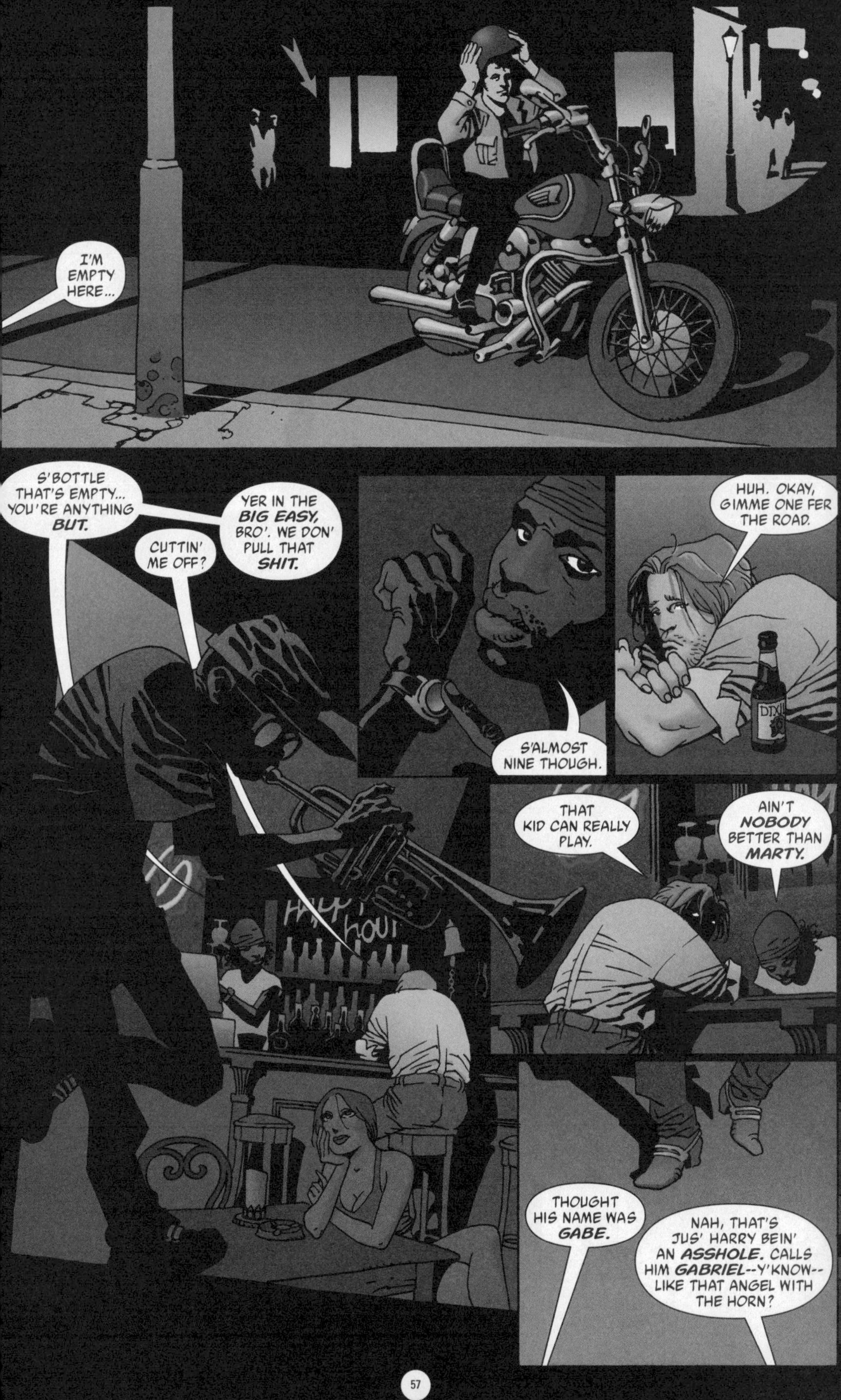
I'M EMPTY HERE...
S'BOTTLE THAT'S EMPTY... YOU'RE ANYTHING BUT.
CUTTIN' ME OFF?
YER IN THE BIG EASY, BRO'. WE DON' PULL THAT SHIT.
S'ALMOST NINE THOUGH.
HUH. OKAY, GIMME ONE FER THE ROAD.
DIXI
HAPP HOUR
THAT KID CAN REALLY PLAY.
AIN'T NOBODY BETTER THAN MARTY.
THOUGHT HIS NAME WAS GABE.
NAH, THAT'S JUS' HARRY BEIN' AN ASSHOLE. CALLS HIM GABRIEL--Y'KNOW--LIKE THAT ANGEL WITH THE HORN?

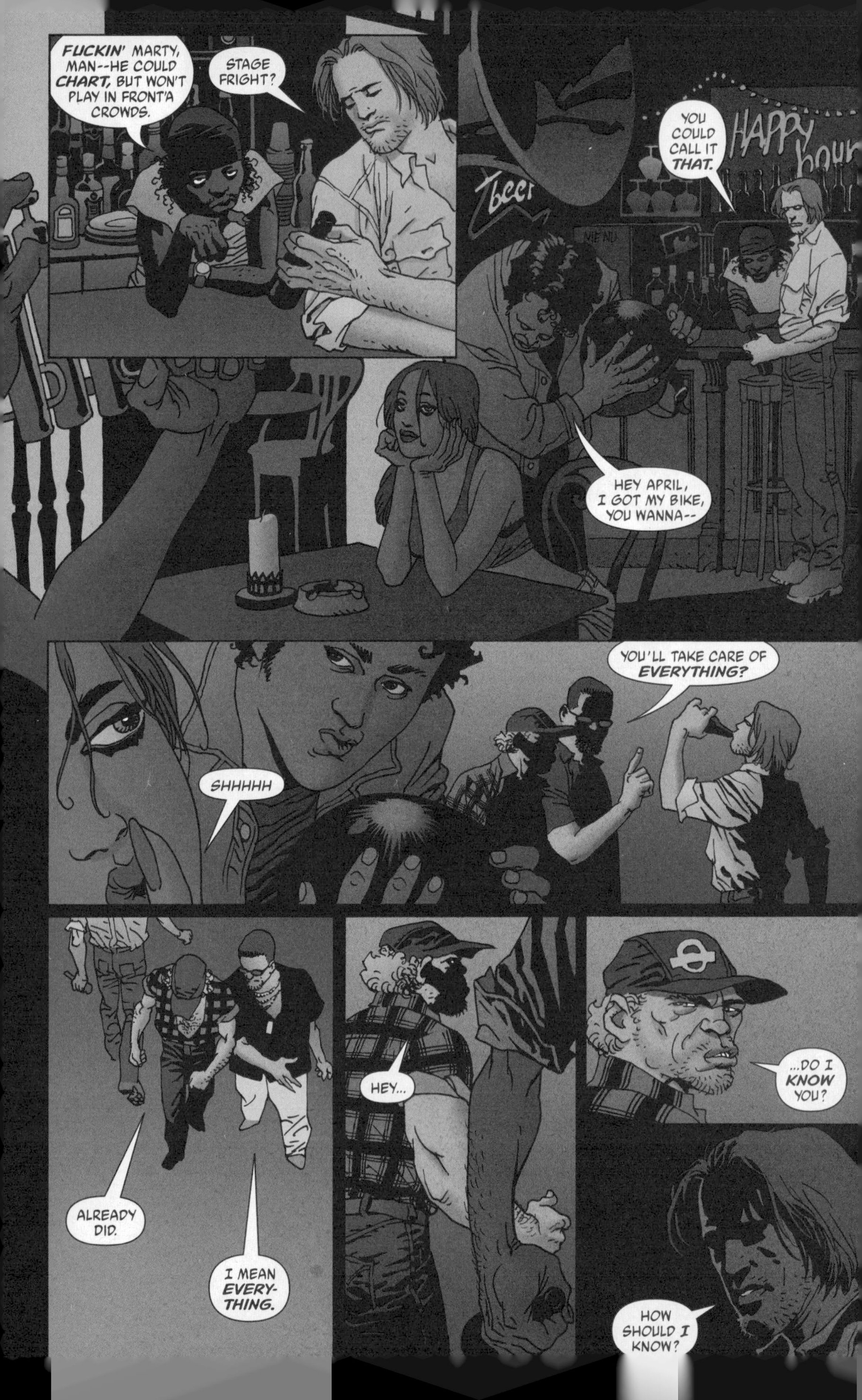
FUCKIN' MARTY, MAN--HE COULD CHART, BUT WON'T PLAY IN FRONT'A CROWDS.
STAGE FRIGHT?
YOU COULD CALL IT THAT.
HAPPY hour
beer
HEY APRIL, I GOT MY BIKE, YOU WANNA--
YOU'LL TAKE CARE OF EVERYTHING?
SHHHHH
ALREADY DID.
I MEAN EVERY-THING.
HEY...
...DO I KNOW YOU?
HOW SHOULD I KNOW?

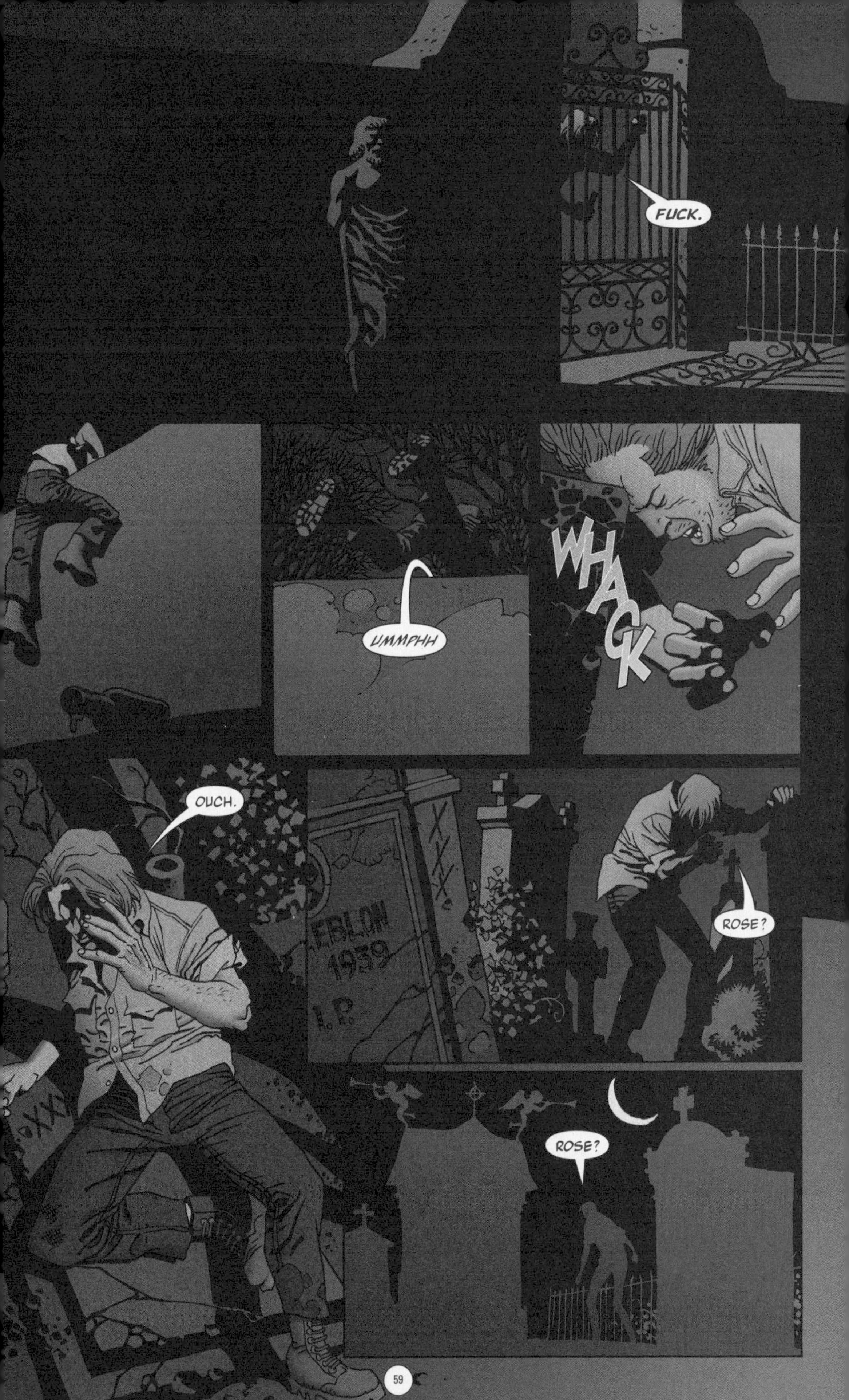
FUCK.
UMMPHH
WHACK
OUCH.
ROSE?
ROSE?

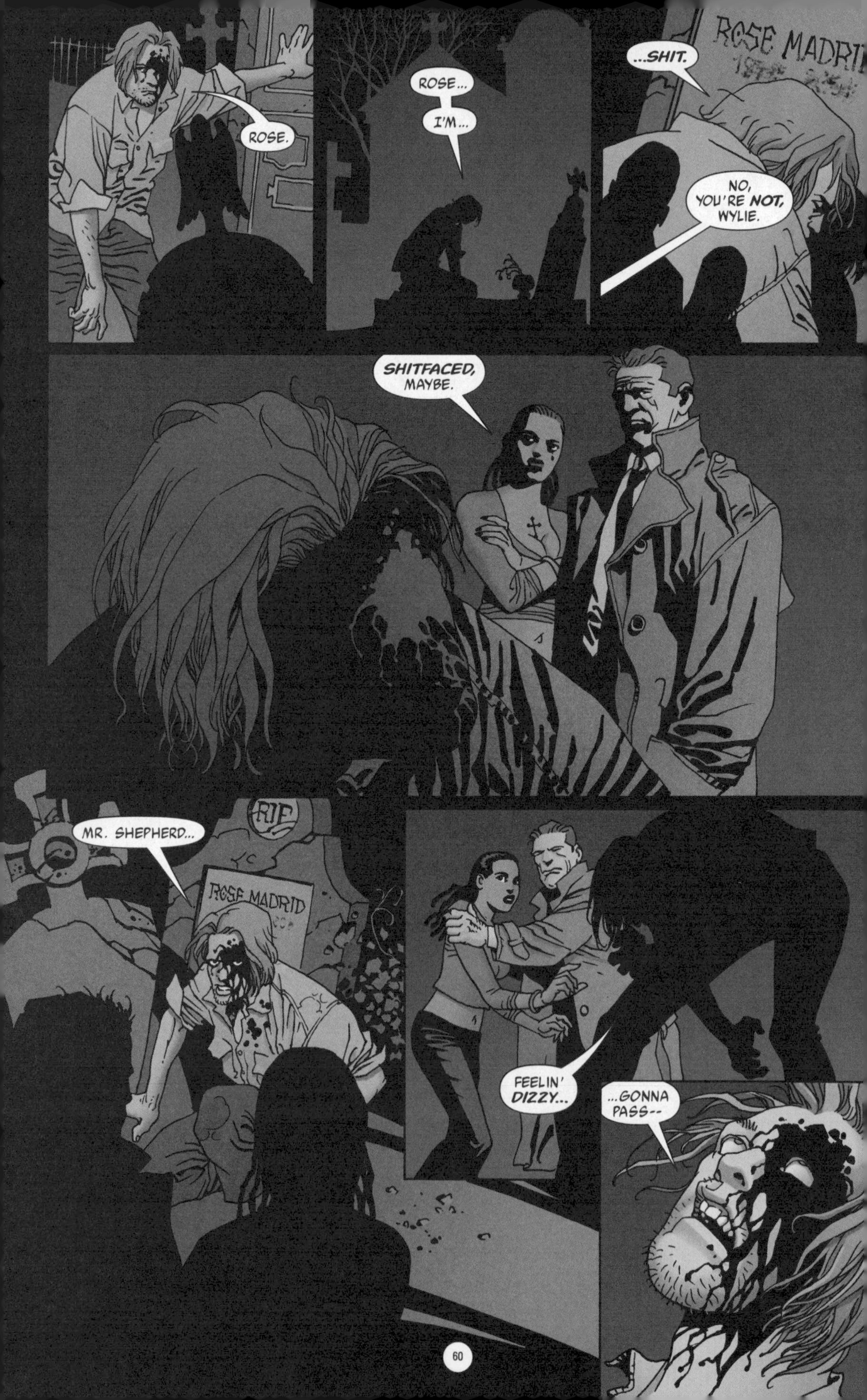
ROSE.
ROSE...
I'M...
...SHIT.
NO, YOU'RE NOT, WYLIE.
SHITFACED, MAYBE.
MR. SHEPHERD...
FEELIN' DIZZY...
...GONNA PASS--

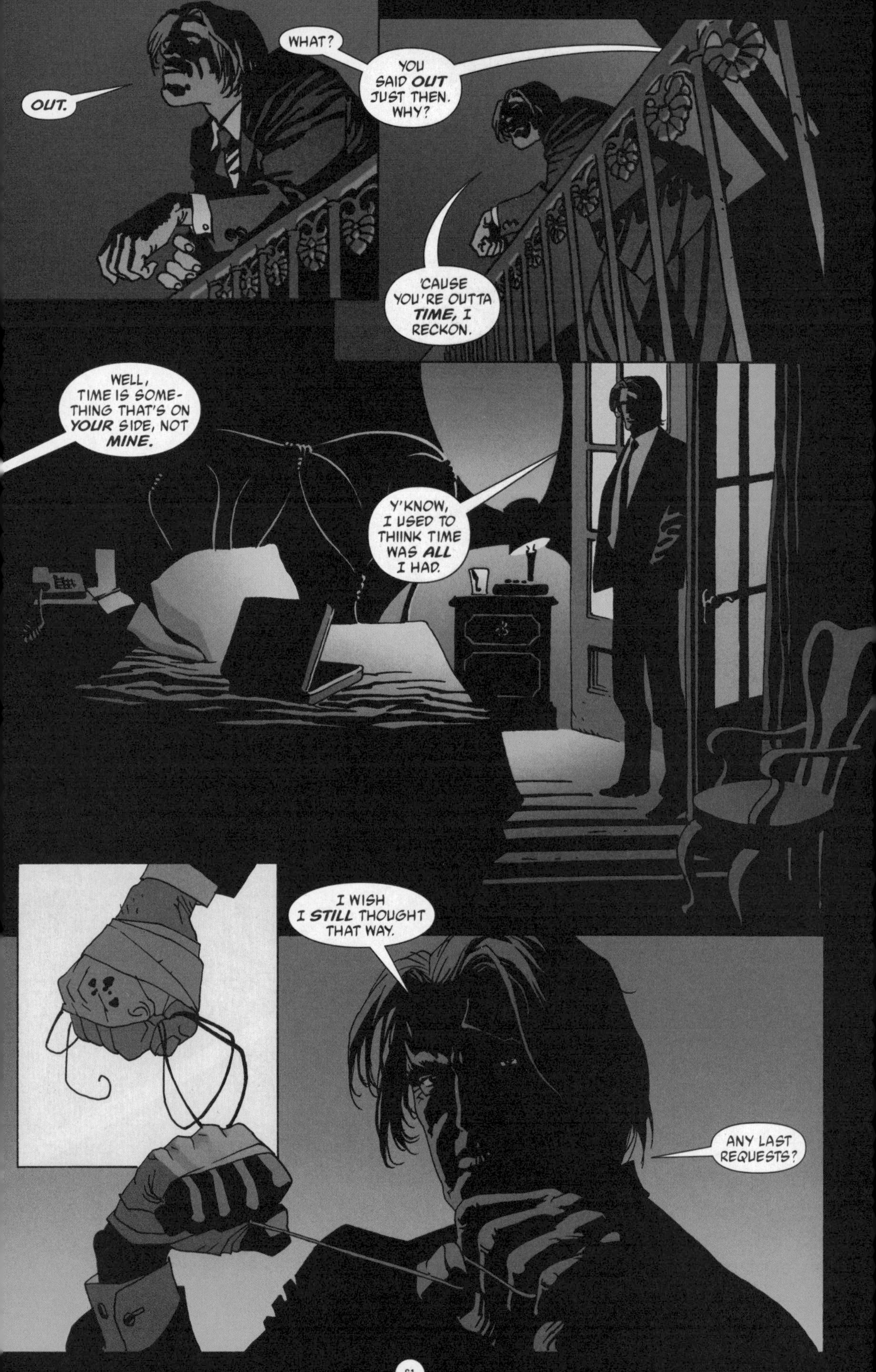
OUT.
WHAT?
YOU SAID **OUT** JUST THEN. WHY?
'CAUSE YOU'RE OUTTA **TIME,** I RECKON.
WELL, TIME IS SOMETHING THAT'S ON **YOUR** SIDE, NOT **MINE.**
Y'KNOW, I USED TO THIINK TIME WAS **ALL** I HAD.
I WISH I **STILL** THOUGHT THAT WAY.
ANY LAST REQUESTS?

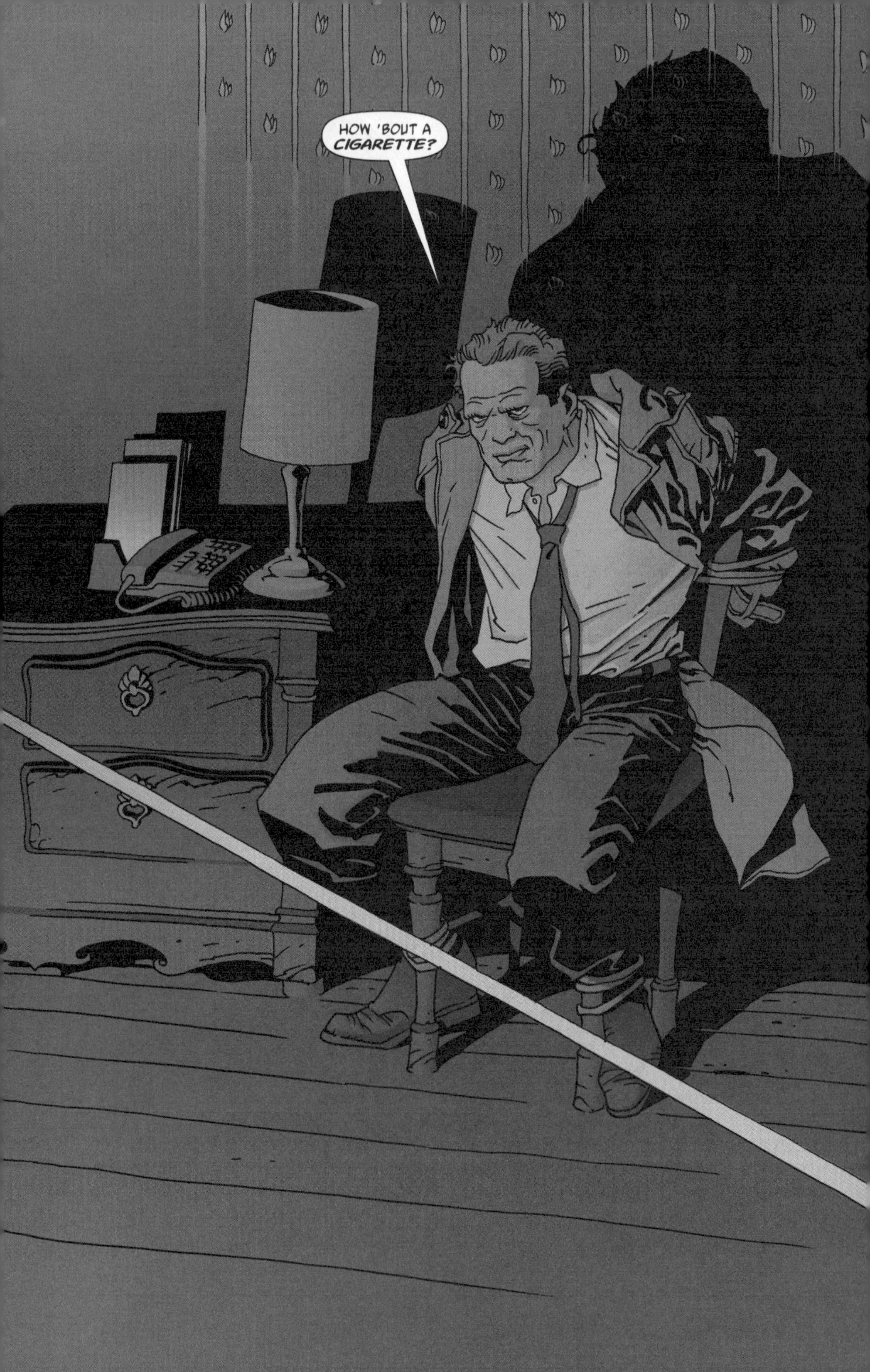
HOW 'BOUT A CIGARETTE?

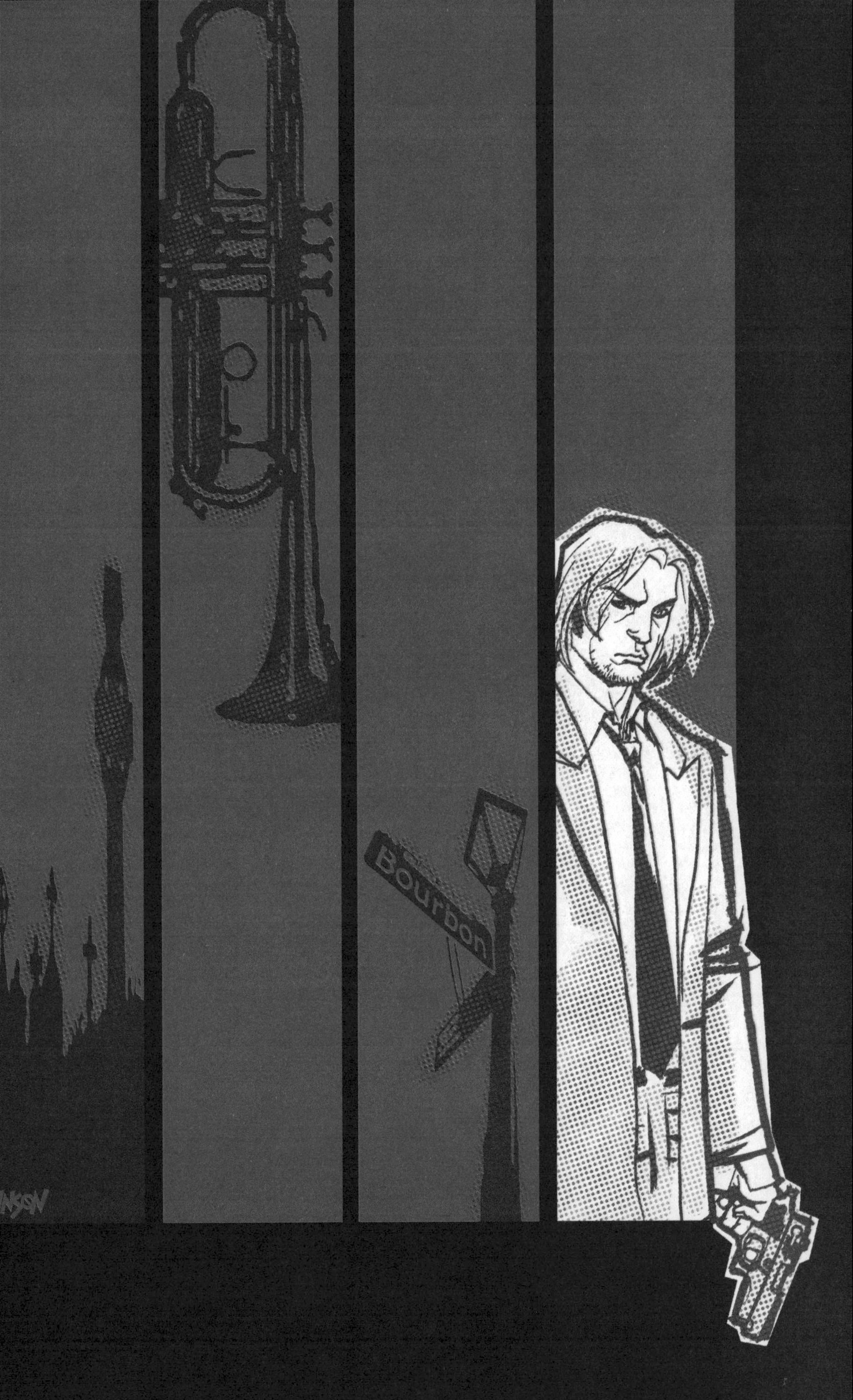
Bourbon

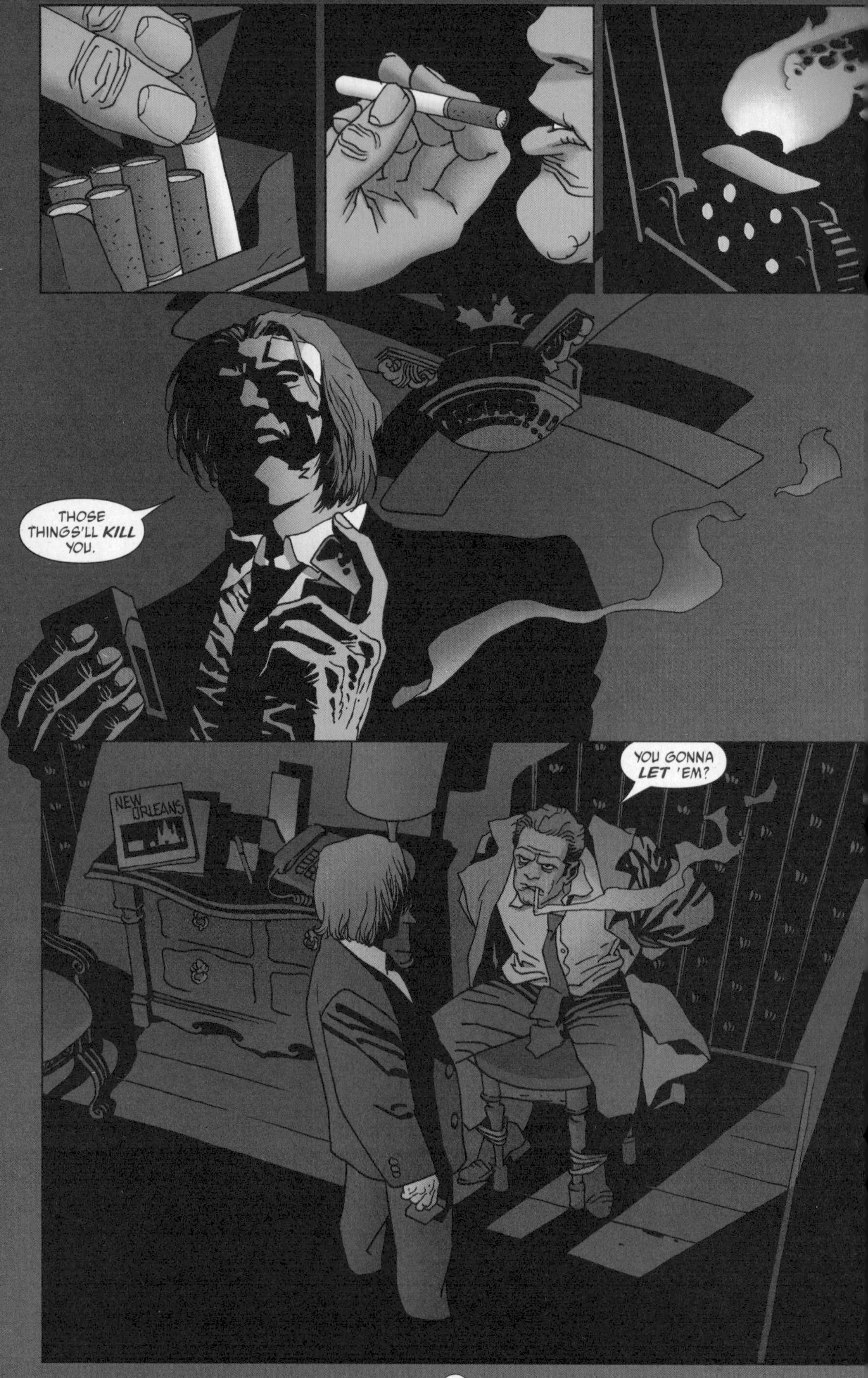
THOSE THINGS'LL **KILL** YOU.
YOU GONNA **LET** 'EM?
NEW ORLEANS

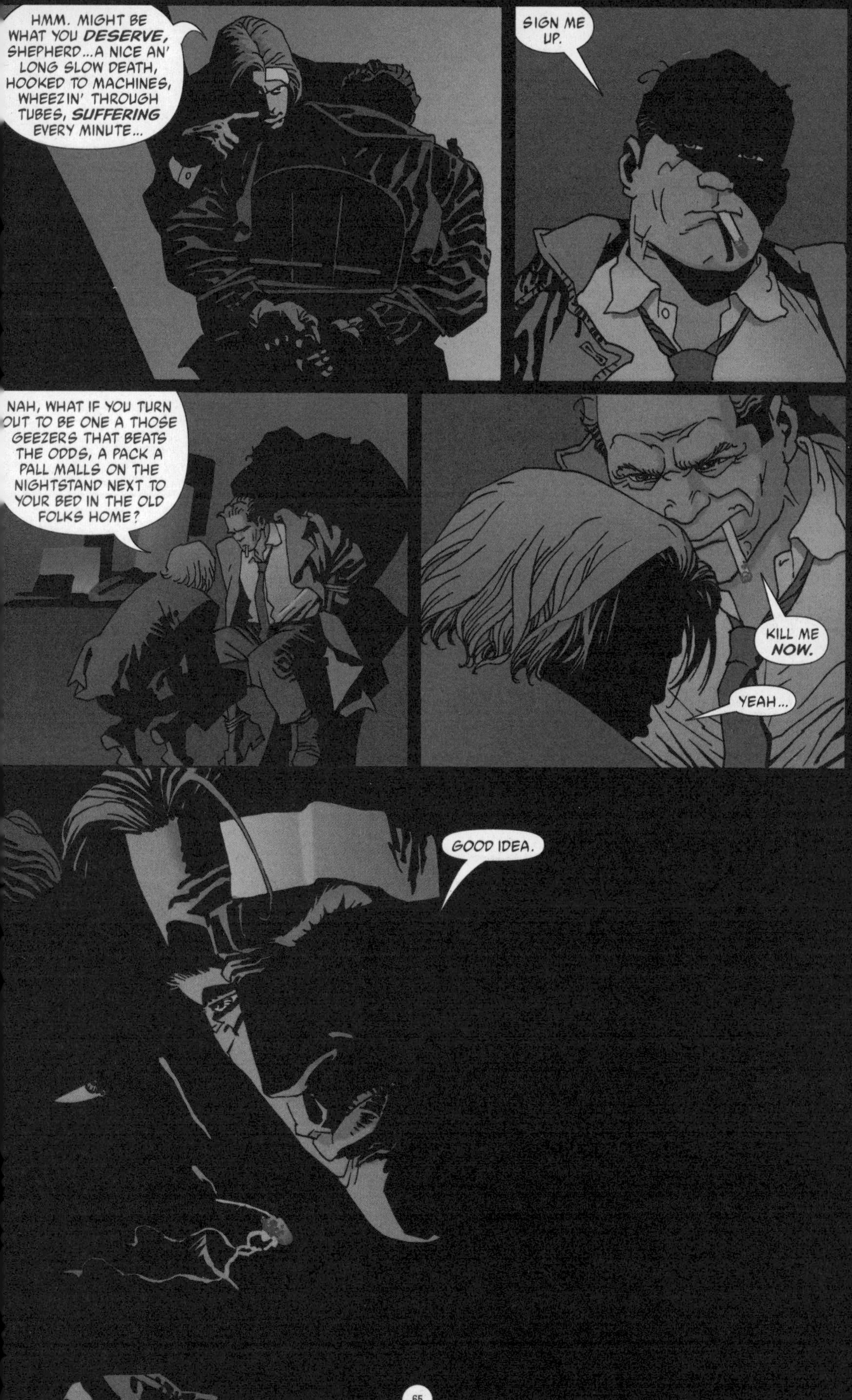
HMM. MIGHT BE WHAT YOU DESERVE, SHEPHERD...A NICE AN' LONG SLOW DEATH, HOOKED TO MACHINES, WHEEZIN' THROUGH TUBES, SUFFERING EVERY MINUTE...
SIGN ME UP.
NAH, WHAT IF YOU TURN OUT TO BE ONE A THOSE GEEZERS THAT BEATS THE ODDS, A PACK A PALL MALLS ON THE NIGHTSTAND NEXT TO YOUR BED IN THE OLD FOLKS HOME?
KILL ME NOW.
YEAH...
GOOD IDEA.

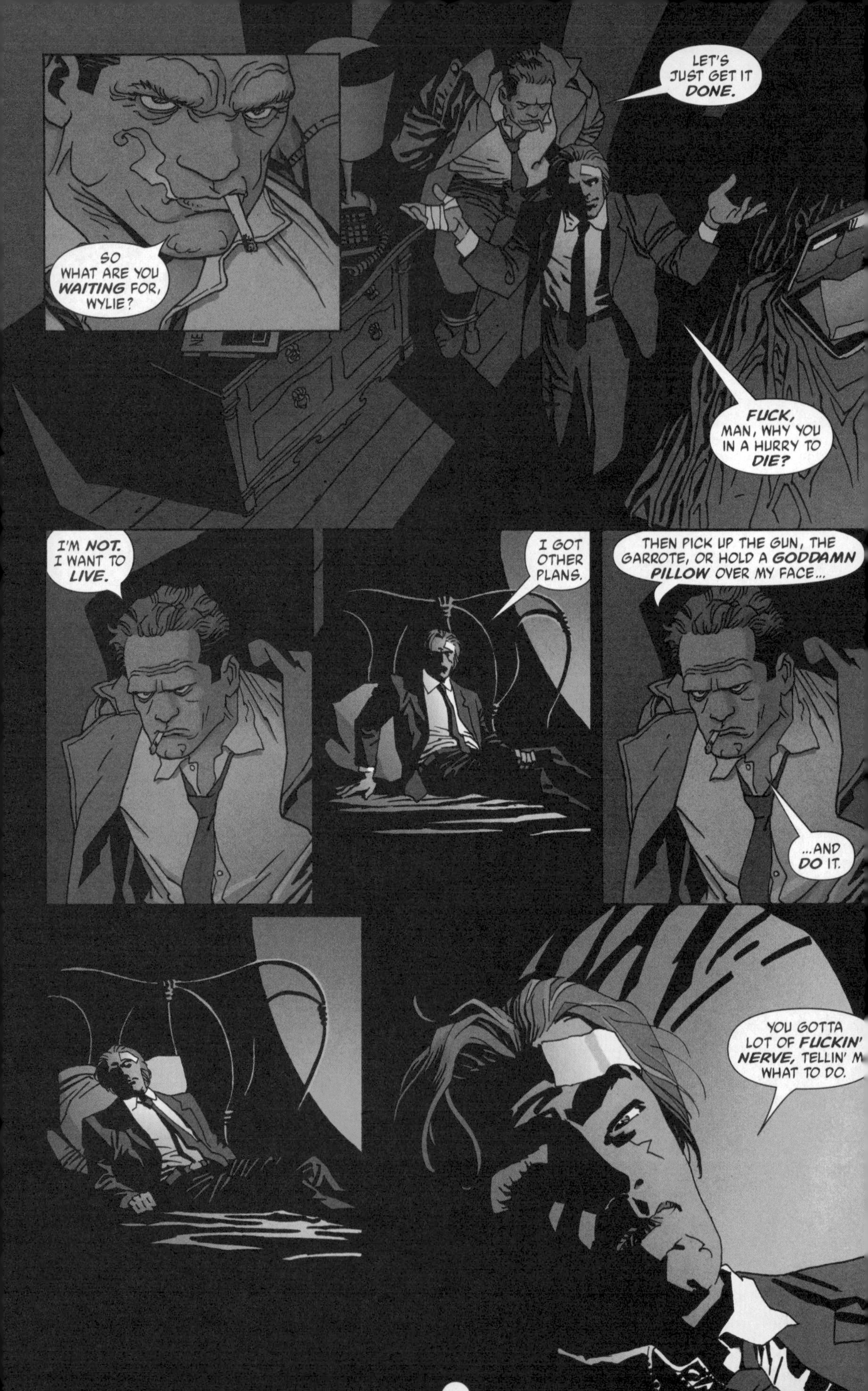
SO WHAT ARE YOU WAITING FOR, WYLIE?
LET'S JUST GET IT DONE.
FUCK, MAN, WHY YOU IN A HURRY TO DIE?
I'M NOT. I WANT TO LIVE.
I GOT OTHER PLANS.
THEN PICK UP THE GUN, THE GARROTE, OR HOLD A GODDAMN PILLOW OVER MY FACE...
...AND DO IT.
YOU GOTTA LOT OF FUCKIN' NERVE, TELLIN' M WHAT TO DO.

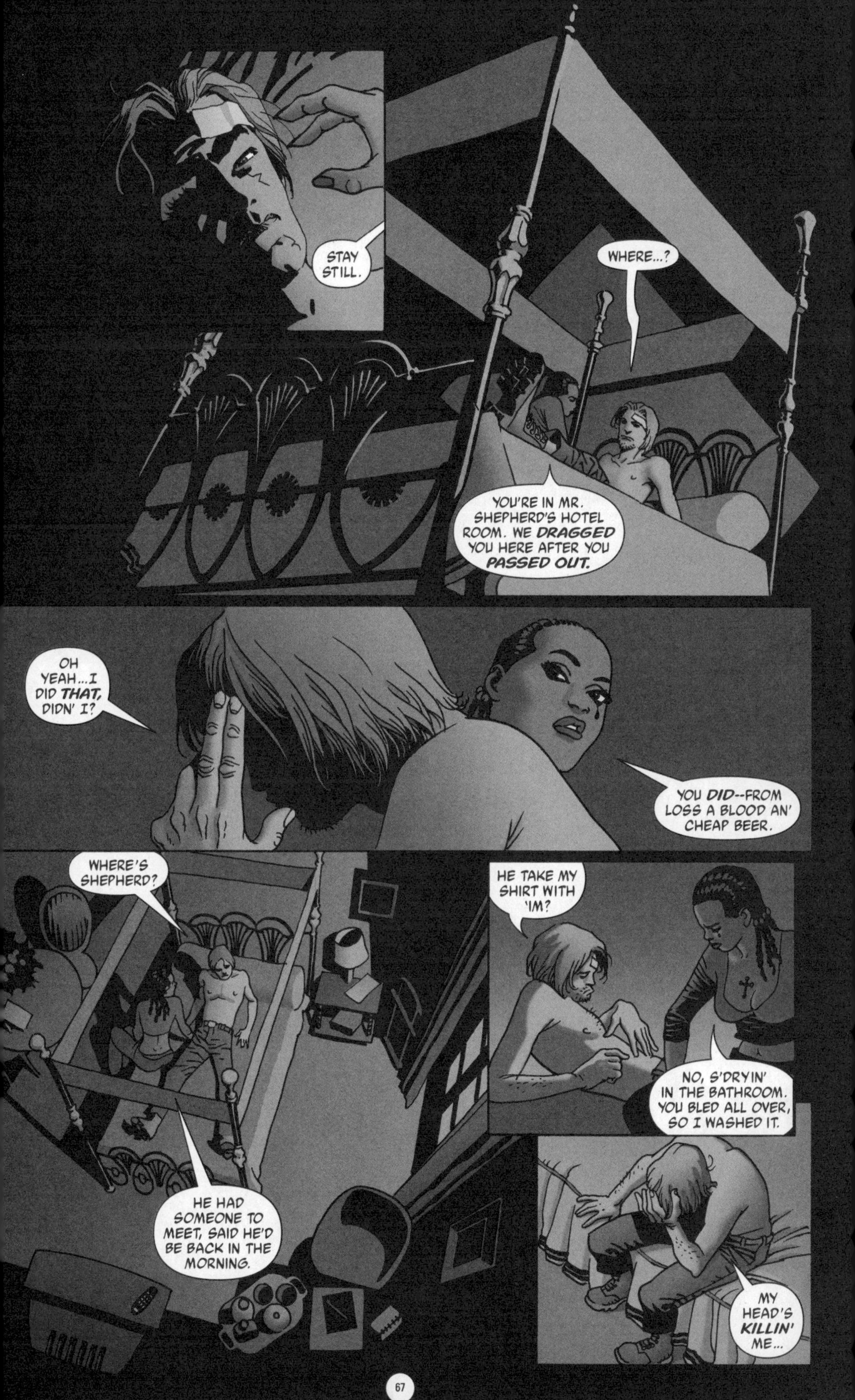
STAY STILL.
WHERE...?
YOU'RE IN MR. SHEPHERD'S HOTEL ROOM. WE DRAGGED YOU HERE AFTER YOU PASSED OUT.
OH YEAH...I DID THAT, DIDN' I?
YOU DID--FROM LOSS A BLOOD AN' CHEAP BEER.
WHERE'S SHEPHERD?
HE HAD SOMEONE TO MEET, SAID HE'D BE BACK IN THE MORNING.
HE TAKE MY SHIRT WITH 'IM?
NO, S'DRYIN' IN THE BATHROOM. YOU BLED ALL OVER, SO I WASHED IT.
MY HEAD'S KILLIN' ME...

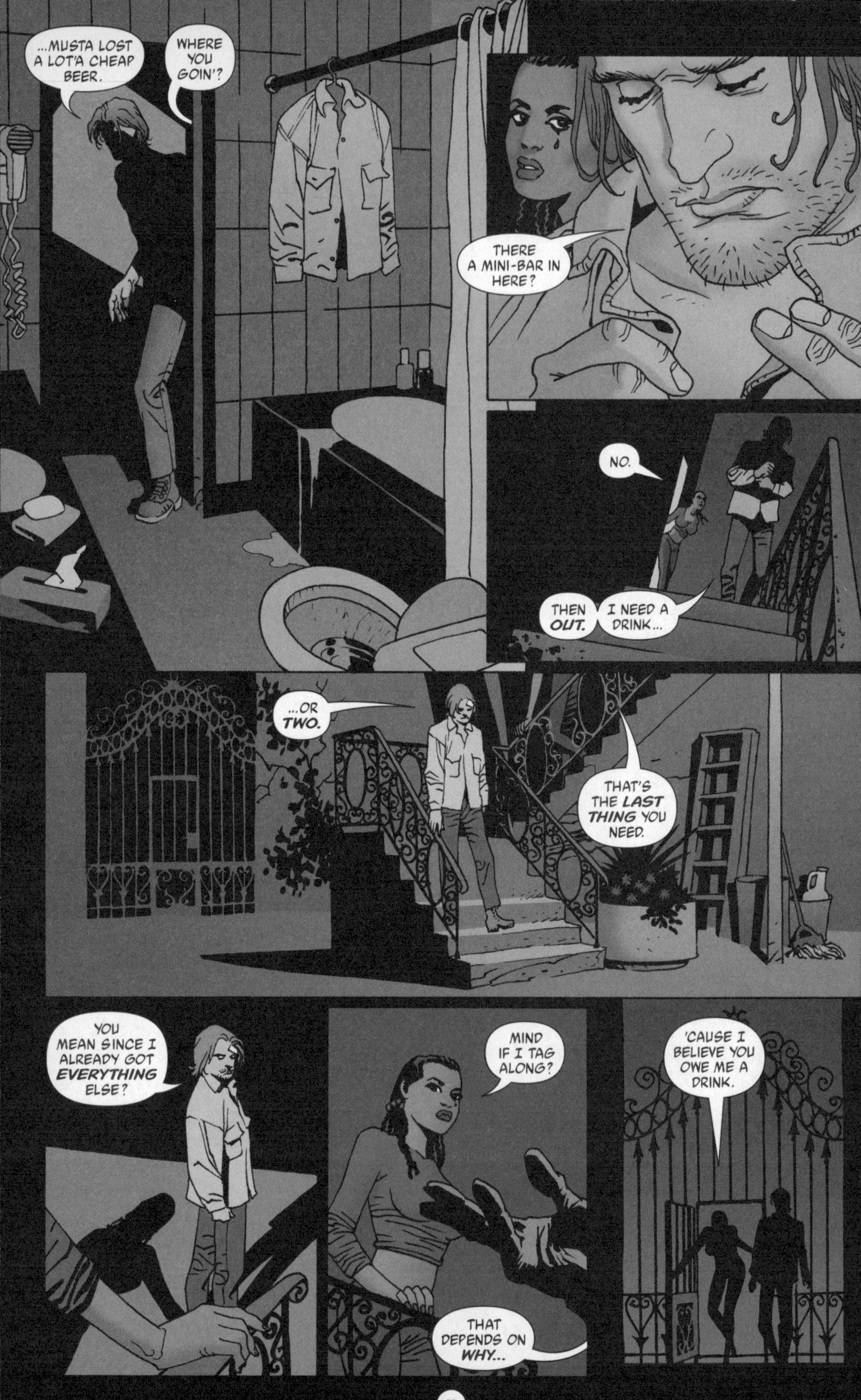
...MUSTA LOST A LOT'A CHEAP BEER.
WHERE YOU GOIN'?
THERE A MINI-BAR IN HERE?
NO.
THEN OUT.
I NEED A DRINK...
...OR TWO.
THAT'S THE LAST THING YOU NEED.
YOU MEAN SINCE I ALREADY GOT EVERYTHING ELSE?
MIND IF I TAG ALONG?
THAT DEPENDS ON WHY...
'CAUSE I BELIEVE YOU OWE ME A DRINK.

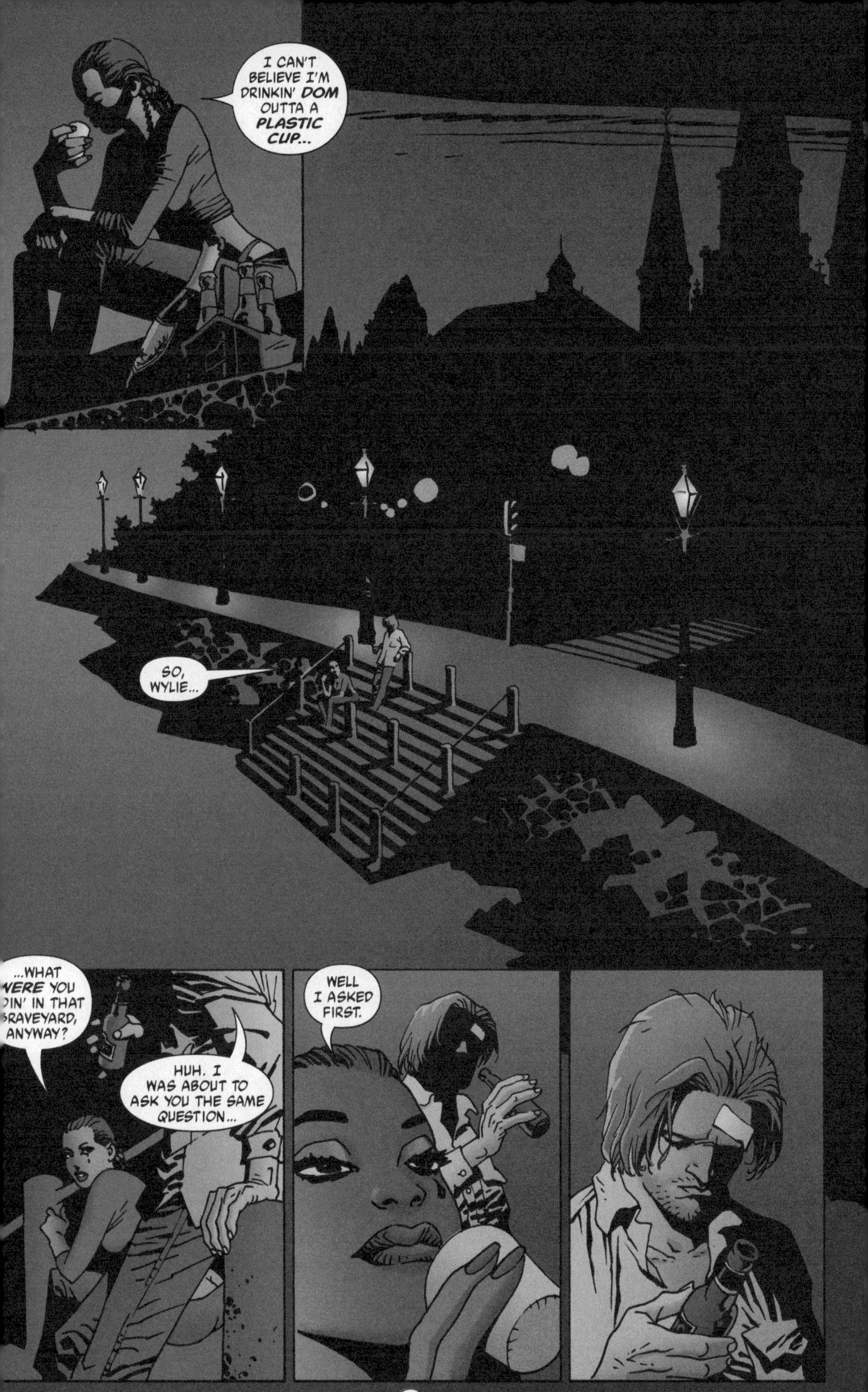
I CAN'T BELIEVE I'M DRINKIN' **DOM** OUTTA A **PLASTIC CUP...**
SO, WYLIE...
...WHAT **WERE** YOU DOIN' IN THAT GRAVEYARD, ANYWAY?
HUH. I WAS ABOUT TO ASK YOU THE SAME QUESTION...
WELL I ASKED FIRST.

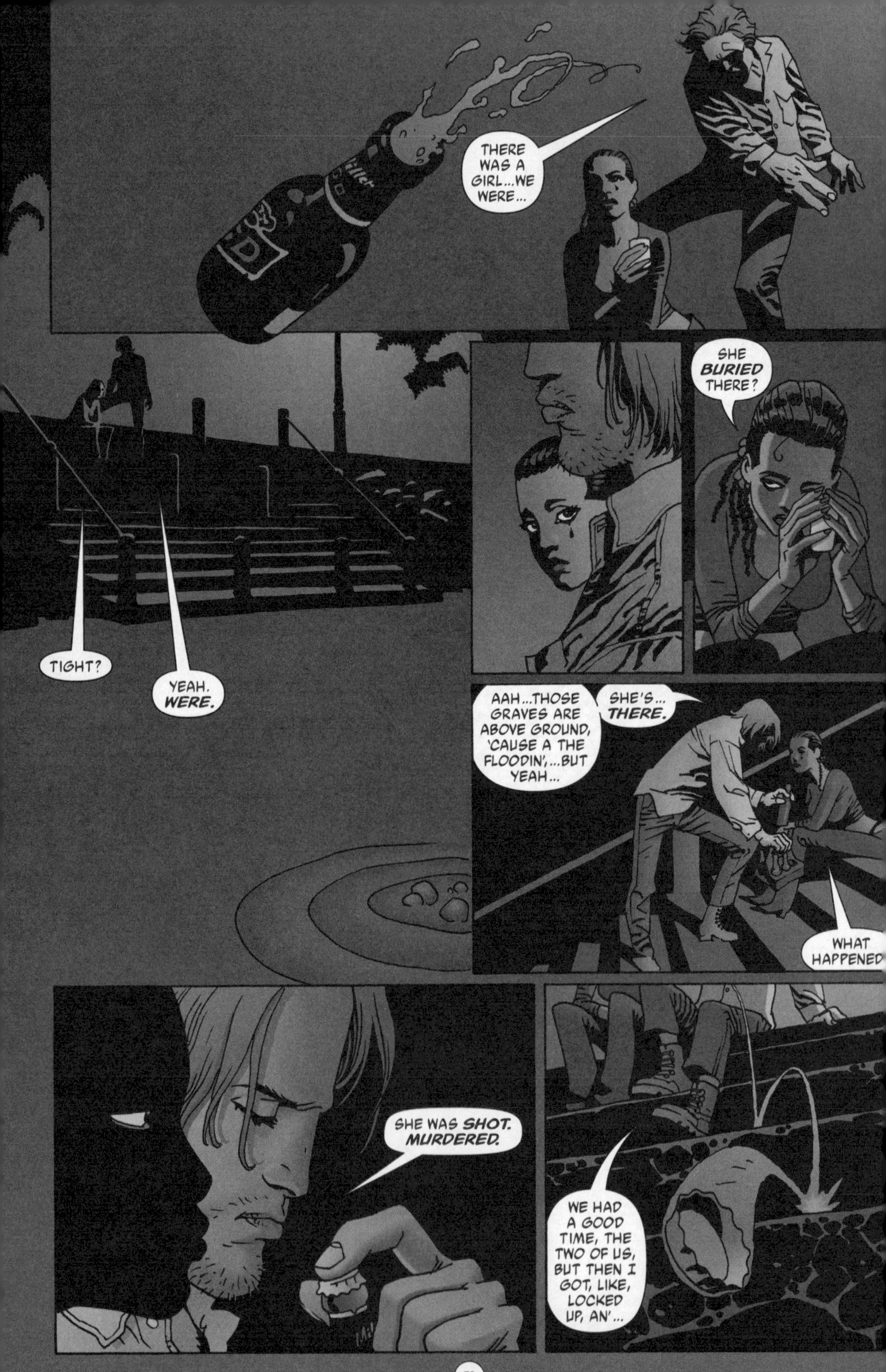
THERE WAS A GIRL... WE WERE...
TIGHT?
YEAH. WERE.
SHE BURIED THERE?
AAH... THOSE GRAVES ARE ABOVE GROUND, 'CAUSE A THE FLOODIN', ...BUT YEAH...
SHE'S... THERE.
WHAT HAPPENED
SHE WAS SHOT. MURDERED.
WE HAD A GOOD TIME, THE TWO OF US, BUT THEN I GOT, LIKE, LOCKED UP, AN'...

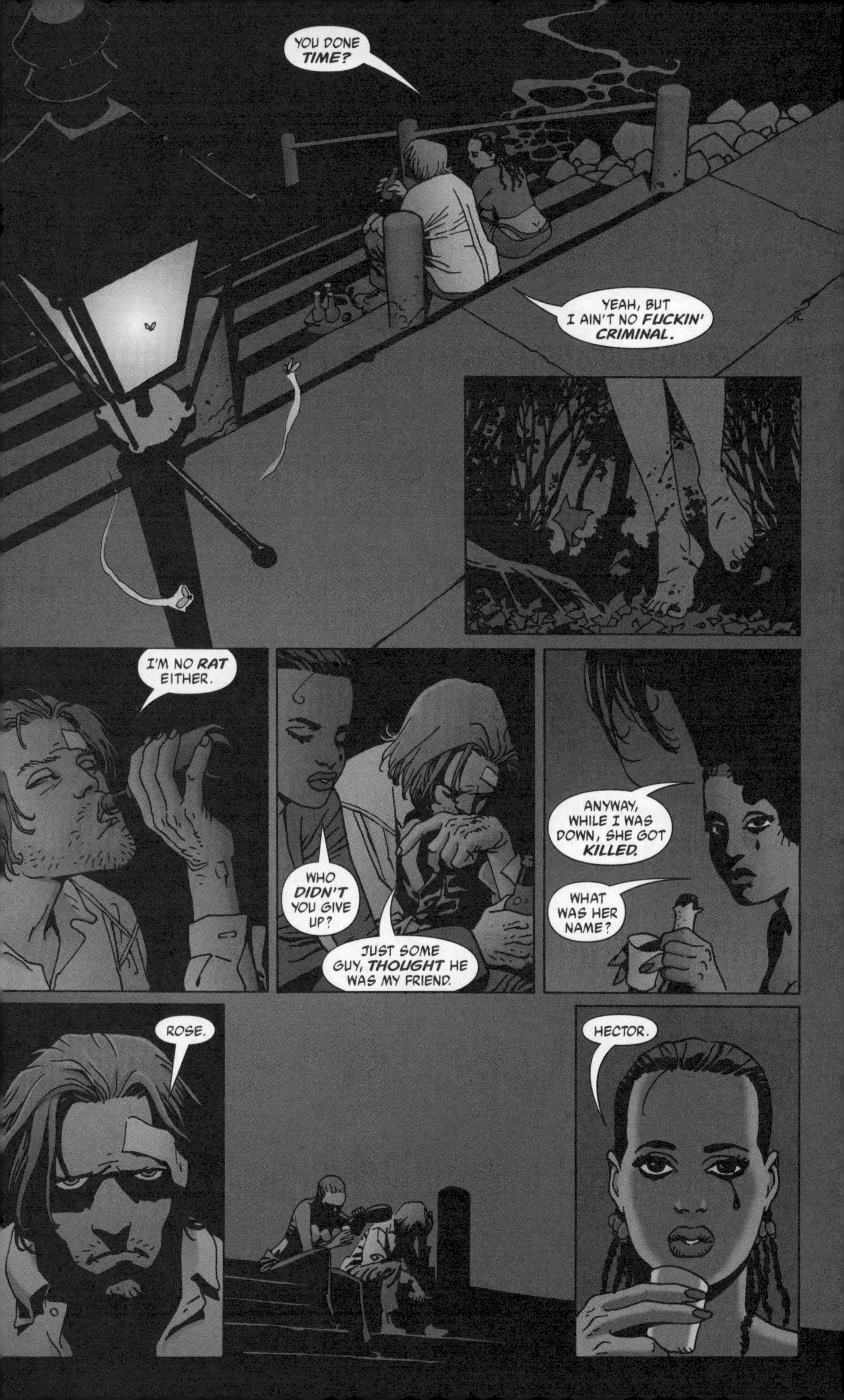
YOU DONE TIME?
YEAH, BUT I AIN'T NO FUCKIN' CRIMINAL.
I'M NO RAT EITHER.
WHO DIDN'T YOU GIVE UP?
JUST SOME GUY, THOUGHT HE WAS MY FRIEND.
ANYWAY, WHILE I WAS DOWN, SHE GOT KILLED.
WHAT WAS HER NAME?
ROSE.
HECTOR.

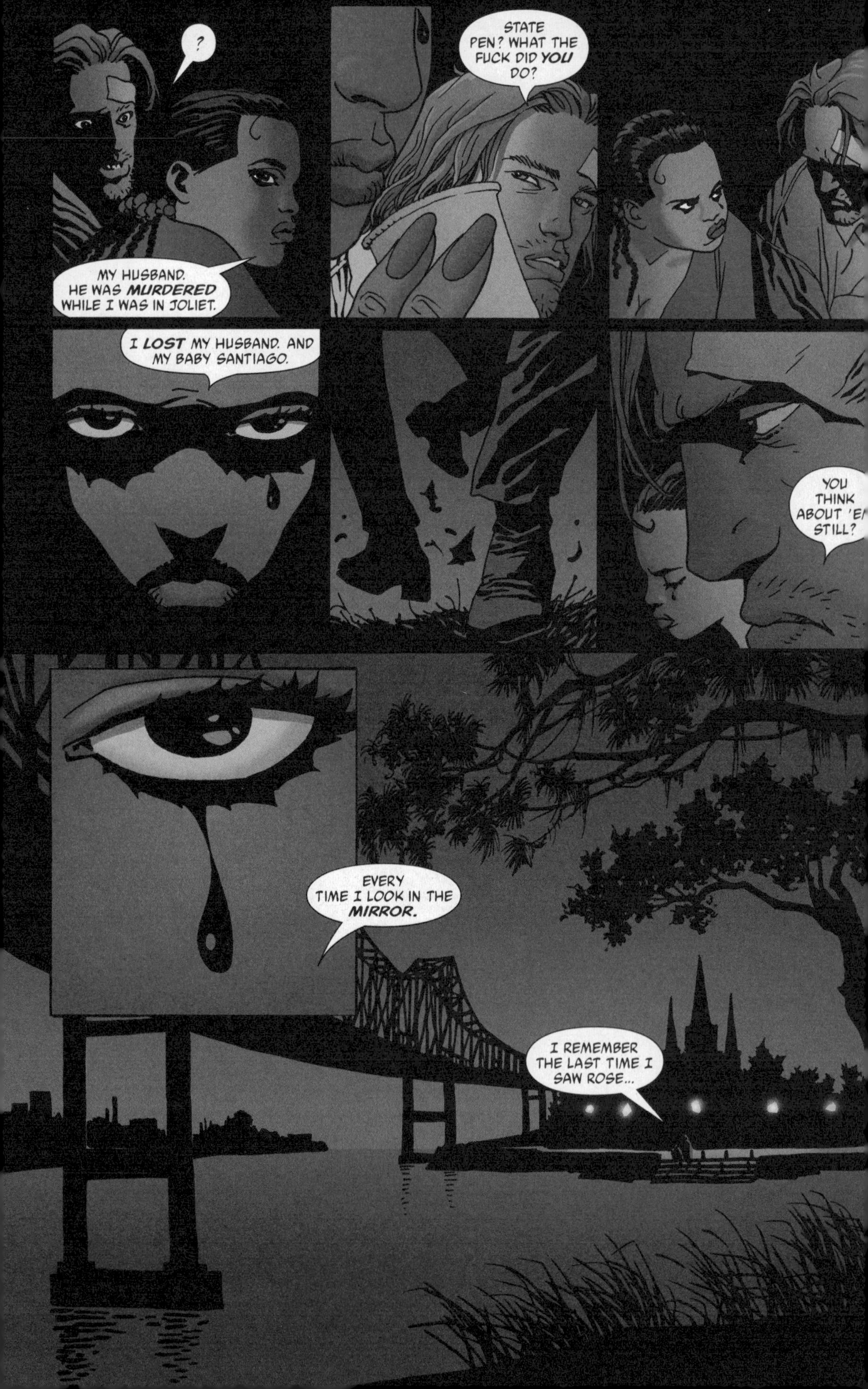
?
MY HUSBAND. HE WAS MURDERED WHILE I WAS IN JOLIET.
STATE PEN? WHAT THE FUCK DID YOU DO?
I LOST MY HUSBAND. AND MY BABY SANTIAGO.
YOU THINK ABOUT 'EM STILL?
EVERY TIME I LOOK IN THE MIRROR.
I REMEMBER THE LAST TIME I SAW ROSE...

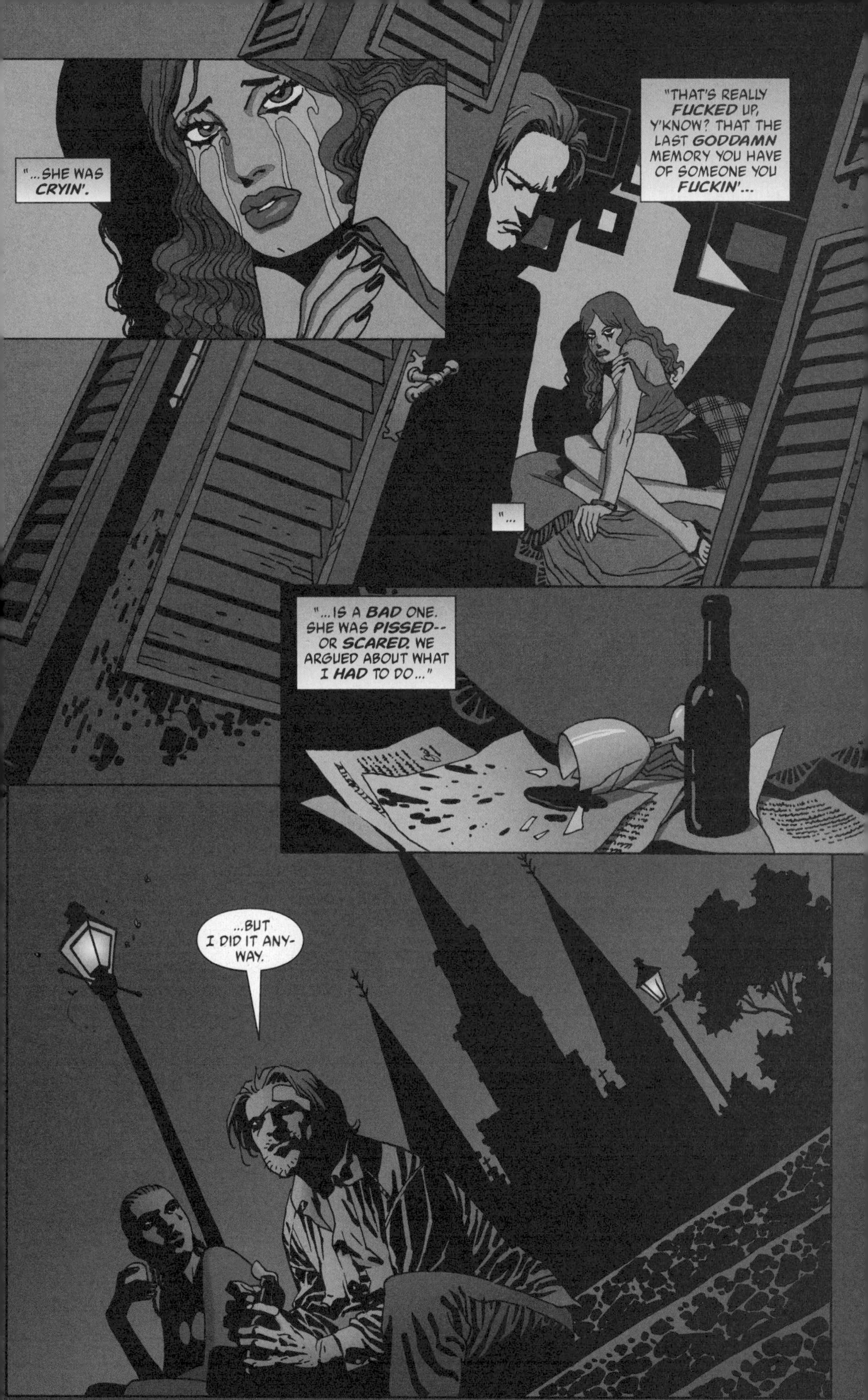
"...SHE WAS CRYIN'.
"THAT'S REALLY FUCKED UP, Y'KNOW? THAT THE LAST GODDAMN MEMORY YOU HAVE OF SOMEONE YOU FUCKIN'...
"...
"...IS A BAD ONE. SHE WAS PISSED-- OR SCARED. WE ARGUED ABOUT WHAT I HAD TO DO..."
...BUT I DID IT ANYWAY.

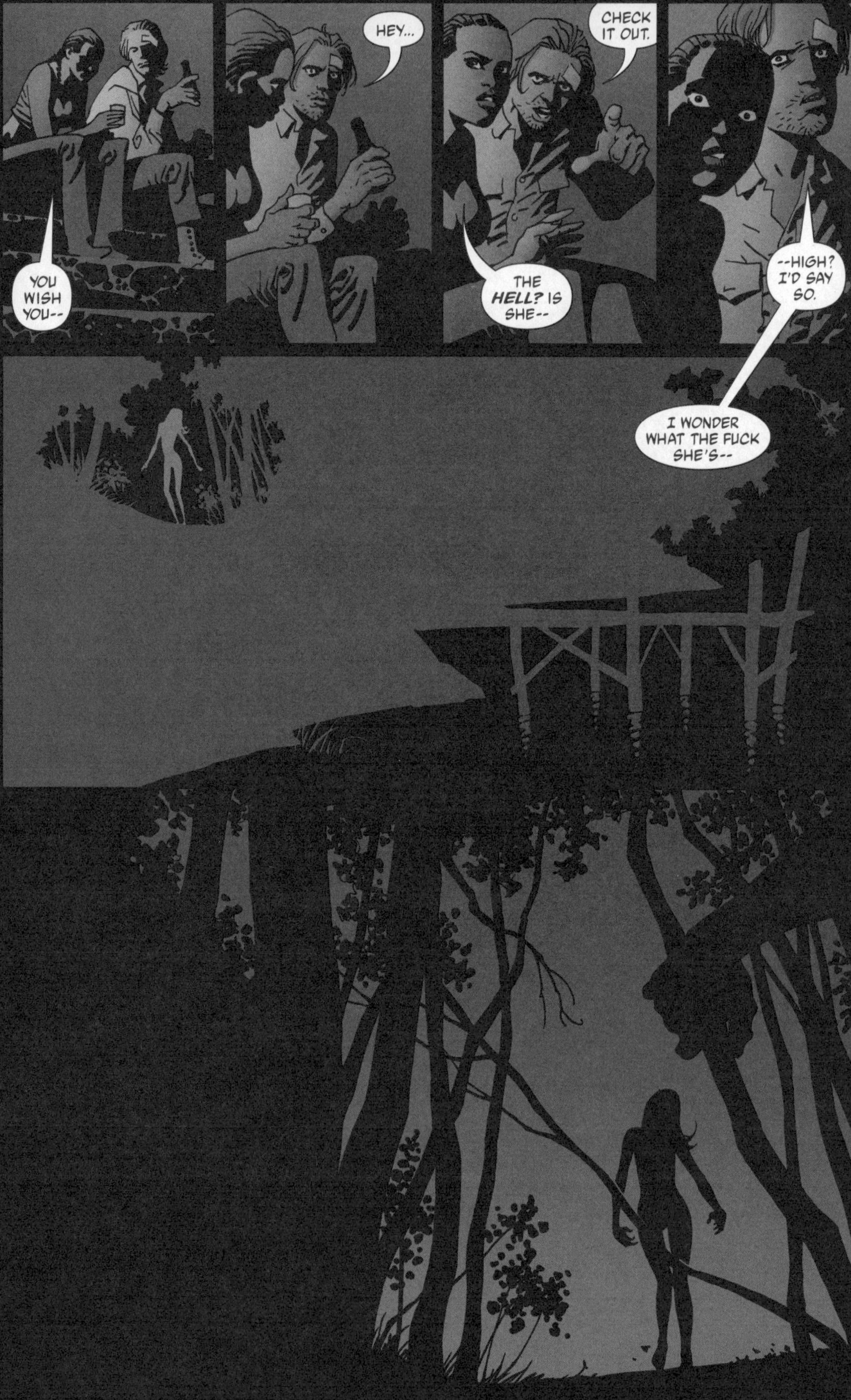
YOU WISH YOU--
HEY...
CHECK IT OUT.
THE HELL? IS SHE--
--HIGH? I'D SAY SO.
I WONDER WHAT THE FUCK SHE'S--

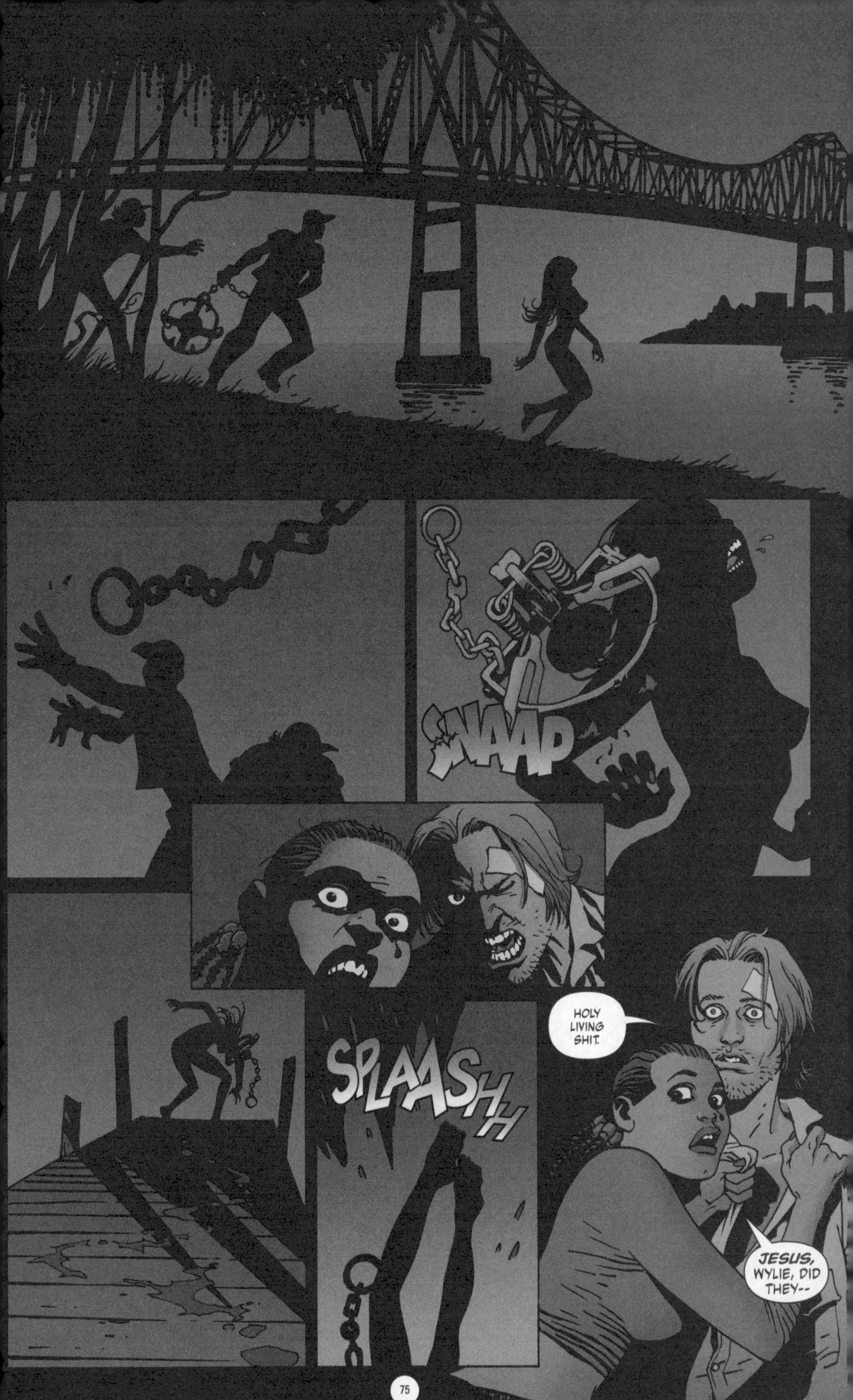
SNAAP
SPLAASHH
HOLY LIVING SHIT.
JESUS, WYLIE, DID THEY--

--A MOTHERFUCKIN' *BEAR TRAP!* FUCKIN' *COCKSUCKER* THREW A MOTHERFUCKIN'--

FUCK!

BANG BANG BANG

FUCK!

GET DOWN!

BANG BANG BANG

WE GOTTA GET *OUTTA* HERE.

NO FUCKIN' *SHIT!*

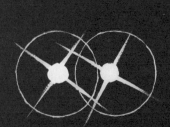

SKREEECH

LIKE RIGHT THE FUCK *NOW!*

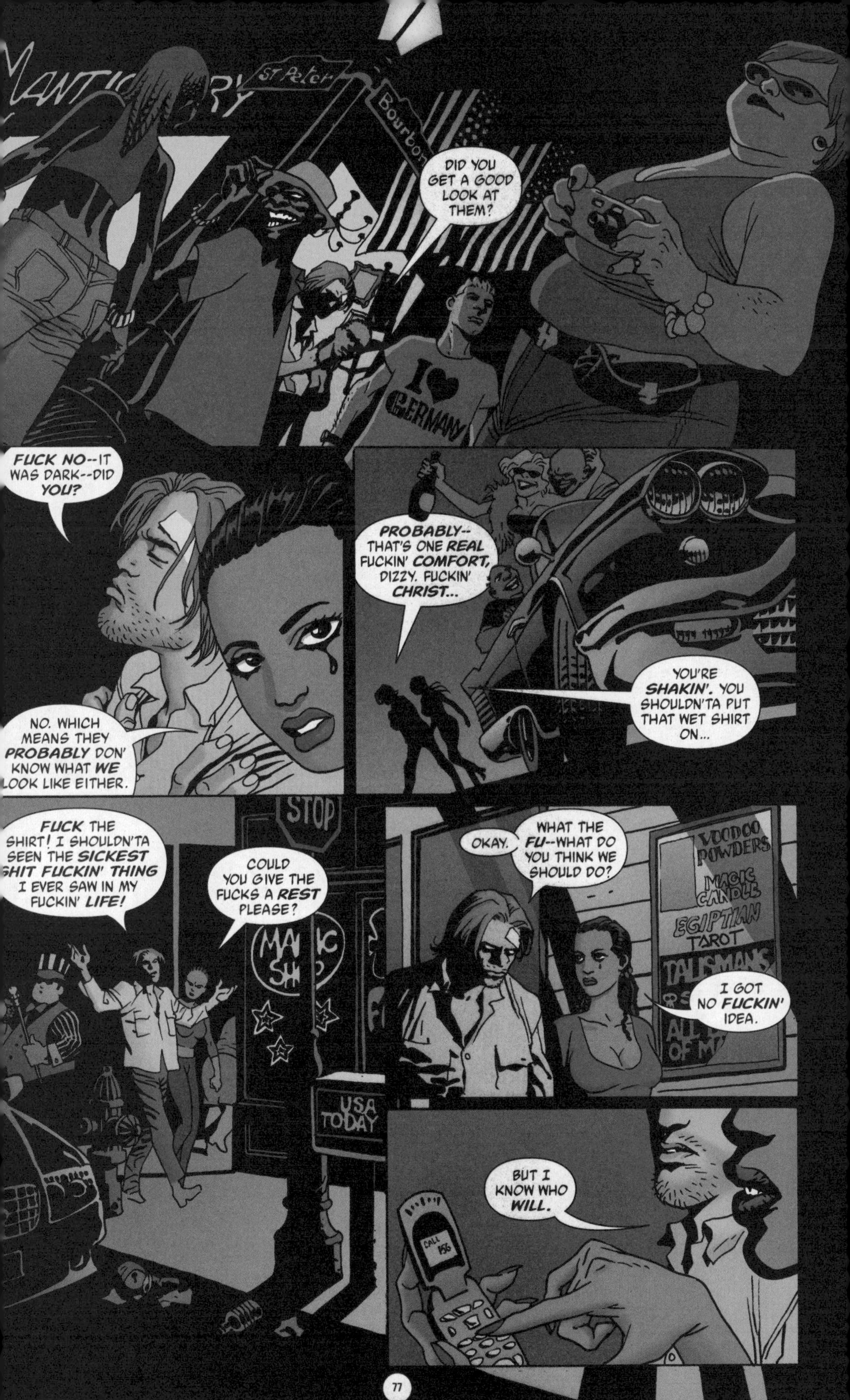

St Peter
Bourbon
DID YOU GET A GOOD LOOK AT THEM?
I ♥ GERMANY
FUCK NO--IT WAS DARK--DID YOU?
NO. WHICH MEANS THEY PROBABLY DON' KNOW WHAT WE LOOK LIKE EITHER.
PROBABLY--THAT'S ONE REAL FUCKIN' COMFORT, DIZZY. FUCKIN' CHRIST...
YOU'RE SHAKIN'. YOU SHOULDN'TA PUT THAT WET SHIRT ON...
STOP
FUCK THE SHIRT! I SHOULDN'TA SEEN THE SICKEST SHIT FUCKIN' THING I EVER SAW IN MY FUCKIN' LIFE!
COULD YOU GIVE THE FUCKS A REST PLEASE?
USA TODAY
OKAY.
WHAT THE FU--WHAT DO YOU THINK WE SHOULD DO?
VOODOO POWDERS
MAGIC CANDLE
EGIPTIAN TAROT
TALISMANS
I GOT NO FUCKIN' IDEA.
BUT I KNOW WHO WILL.

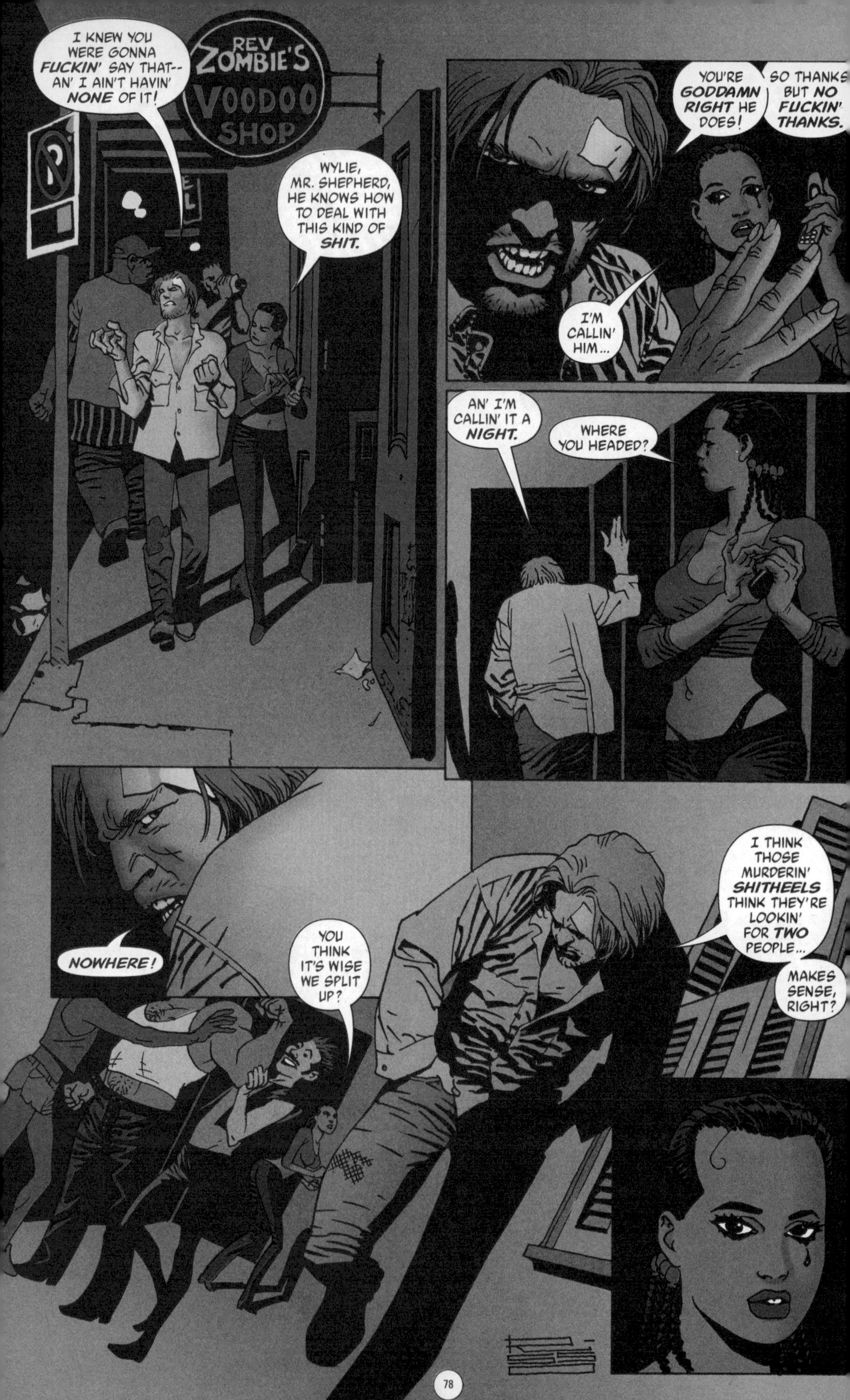
I KNEW YOU WERE GONNA FUCKIN' SAY THAT-- AN' I AIN'T HAVIN' NONE OF IT!
REV ZOMBIE'S VOODOO SHOP
WYLIE, MR. SHEPHERD, HE KNOWS HOW TO DEAL WITH THIS KIND OF SHIT.
I'M CALLIN' HIM...
YOU'RE GODDAMN RIGHT HE DOES!
SO THANKS BUT NO FUCKIN' THANKS.
AN' I'M CALLIN' IT A NIGHT.
WHERE YOU HEADED?
NOWHERE!
YOU THINK IT'S WISE WE SPLIT UP?
I THINK THOSE MURDERIN' SHITHEELS THINK THEY'RE LOOKIN' FOR TWO PEOPLE...
MAKES SENSE, RIGHT?

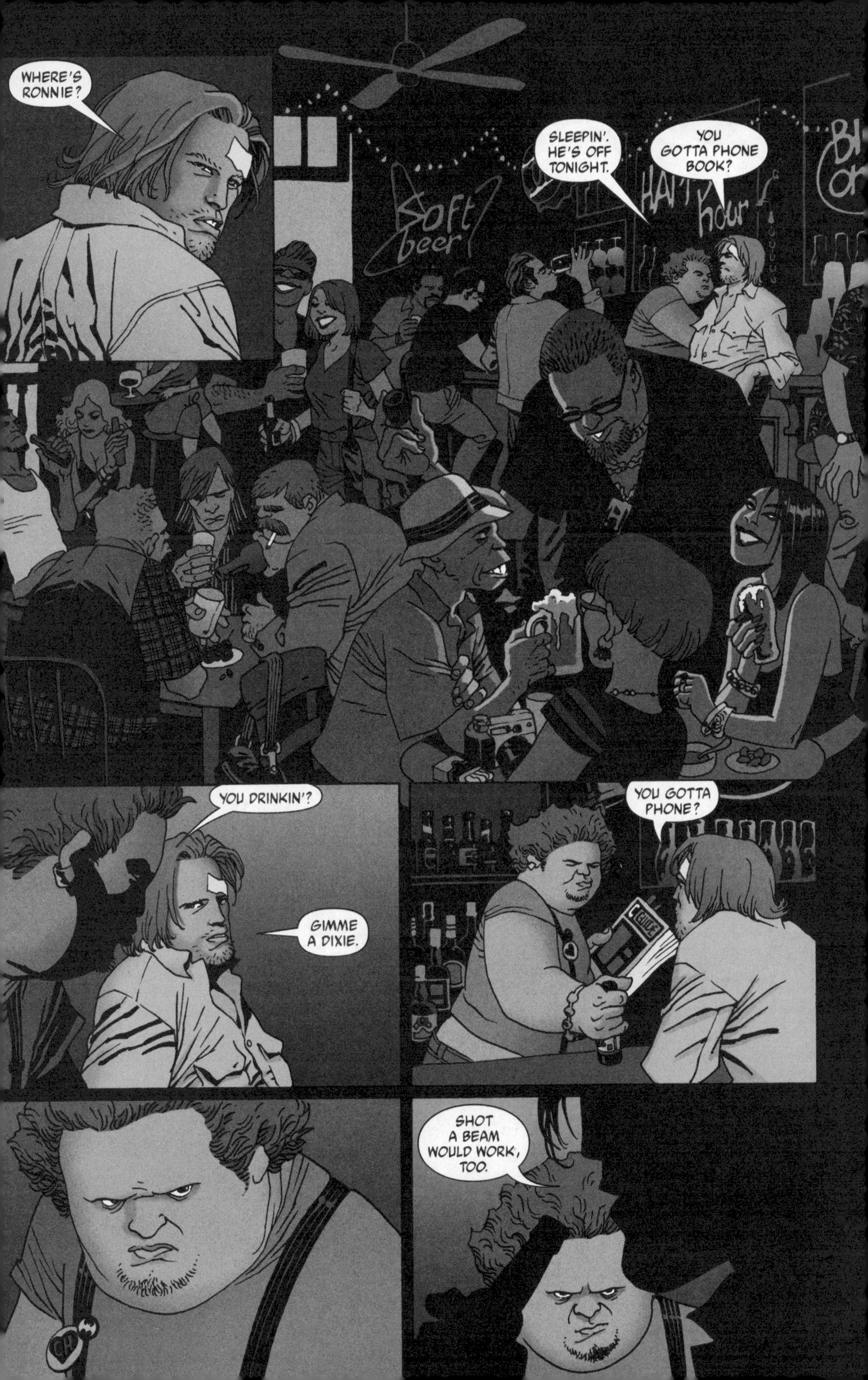
WHERE'S RONNIE?
SLEEPIN'. HE'S OFF TONIGHT.
YOU GOTTA PHONE BOOK?
YOU DRINKIN'?
GIMME A DIXIE.
YOU GOTTA PHONE?
SHOT A BEAM WOULD WORK, TOO.

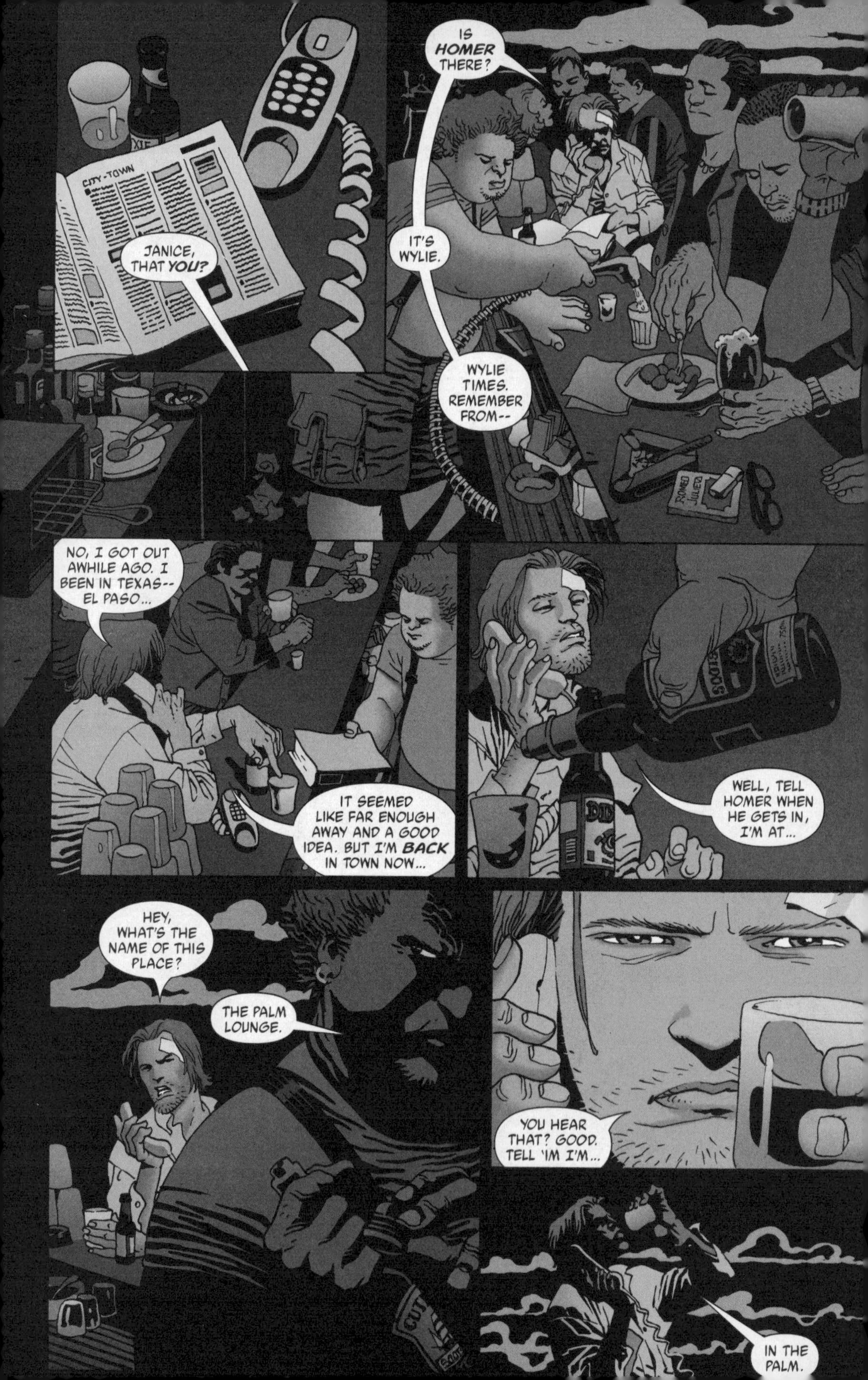
JANICE, THAT YOU?
IS HOMER THERE?
IT'S WYLIE.
WYLIE TIMES. REMEMBER FROM--
NO, I GOT OUT AWHILE AGO. I BEEN IN TEXAS-- EL PASO...
IT SEEMED LIKE FAR ENOUGH AWAY AND A GOOD IDEA. BUT I'M BACK IN TOWN NOW...
WELL, TELL HOMER WHEN HE GETS IN, I'M AT...
HEY, WHAT'S THE NAME OF THIS PLACE?
THE PALM LOUNGE.
YOU HEAR THAT? GOOD. TELL 'IM I'M...
IN THE PALM.
CITY-TOWN
ROMEO JULIETO

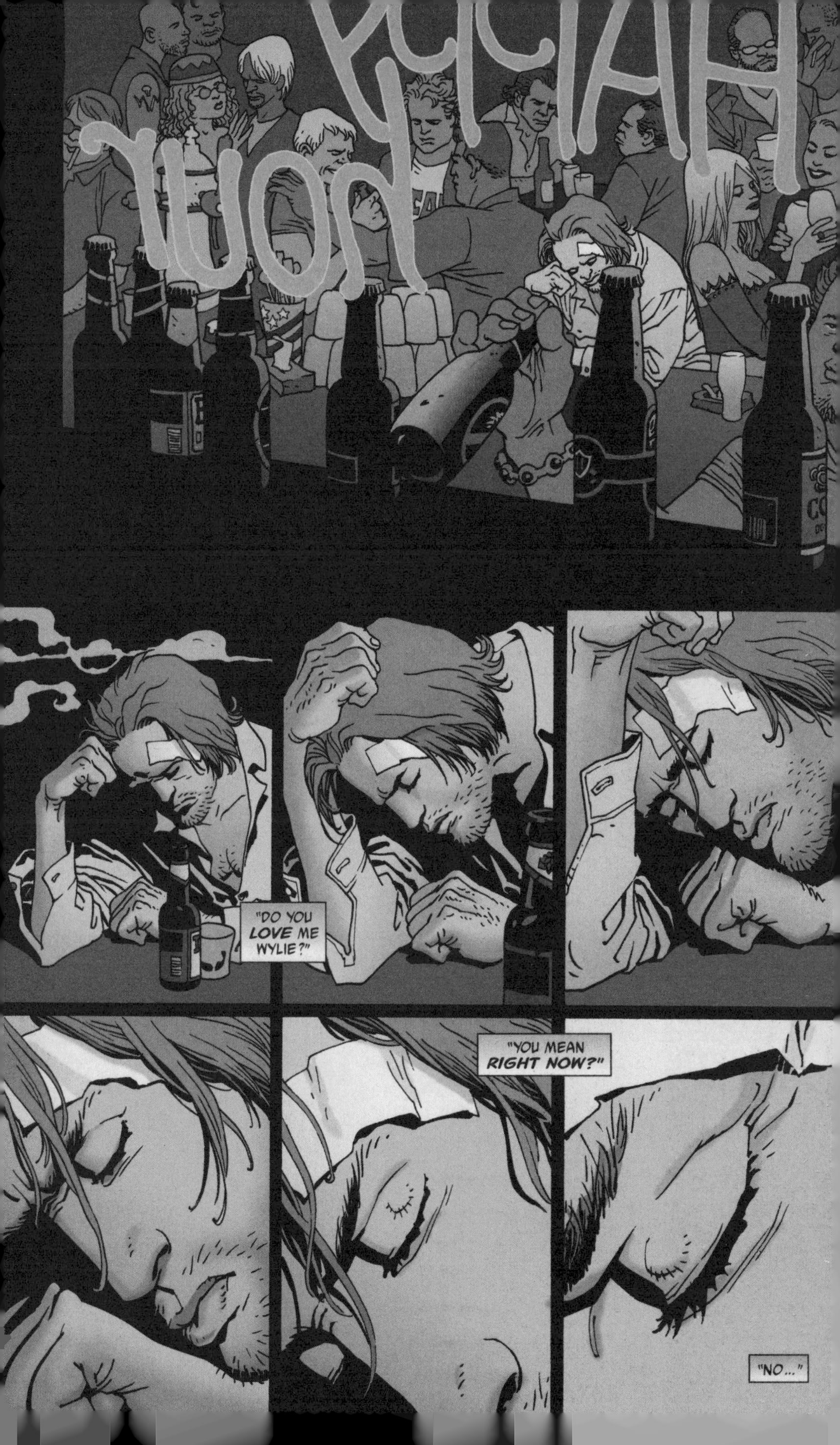
"DO YOU LOVE ME WYLIE?"
"YOU MEAN RIGHT NOW?"
"NO..."

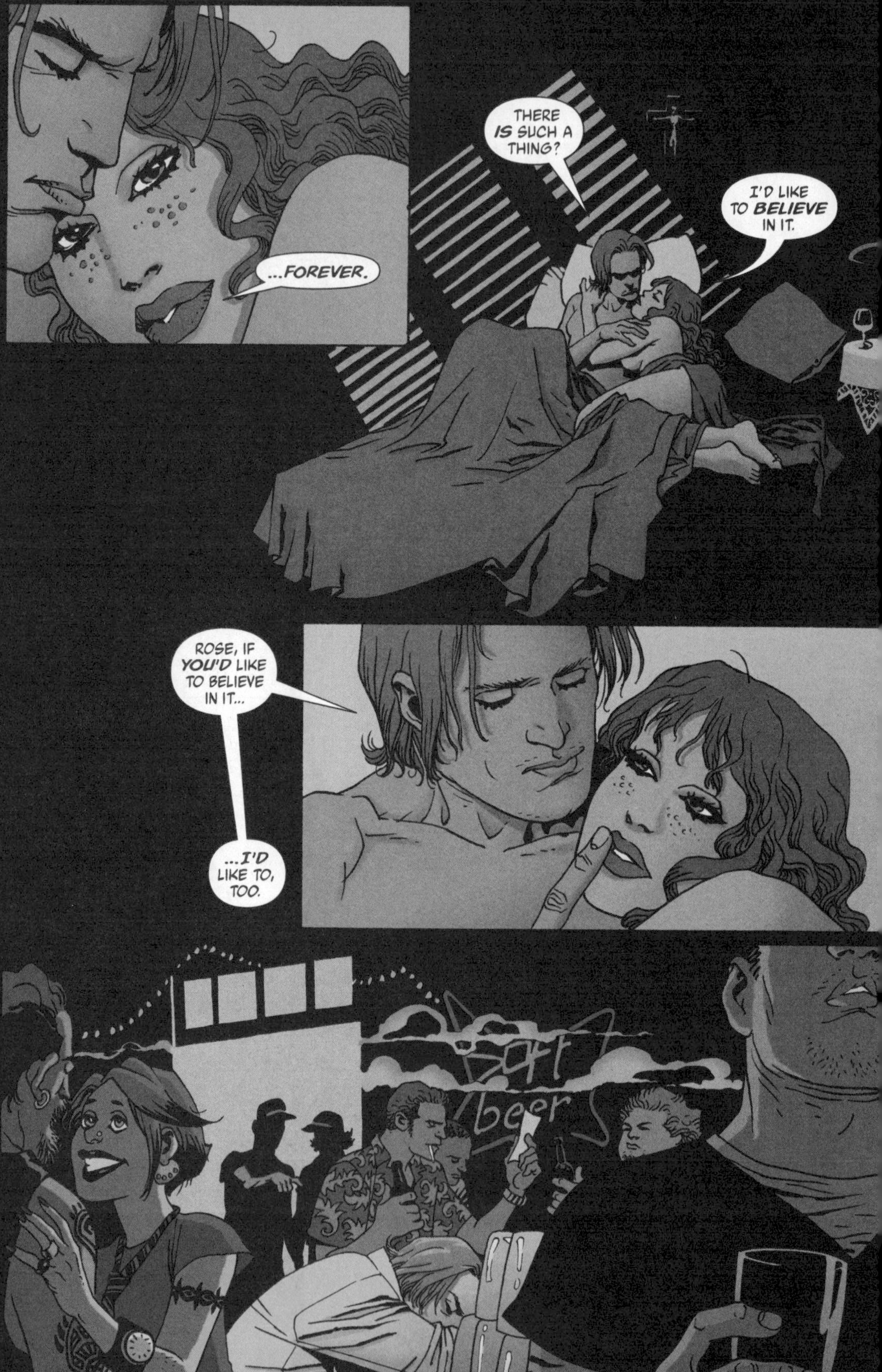
...FOREVER.
THERE IS SUCH A THING?
I'D LIKE TO BELIEVE IN IT.
ROSE, IF YOU'D LIKE TO BELIEVE IN IT...
...I'D LIKE TO, TOO.
Soft beer

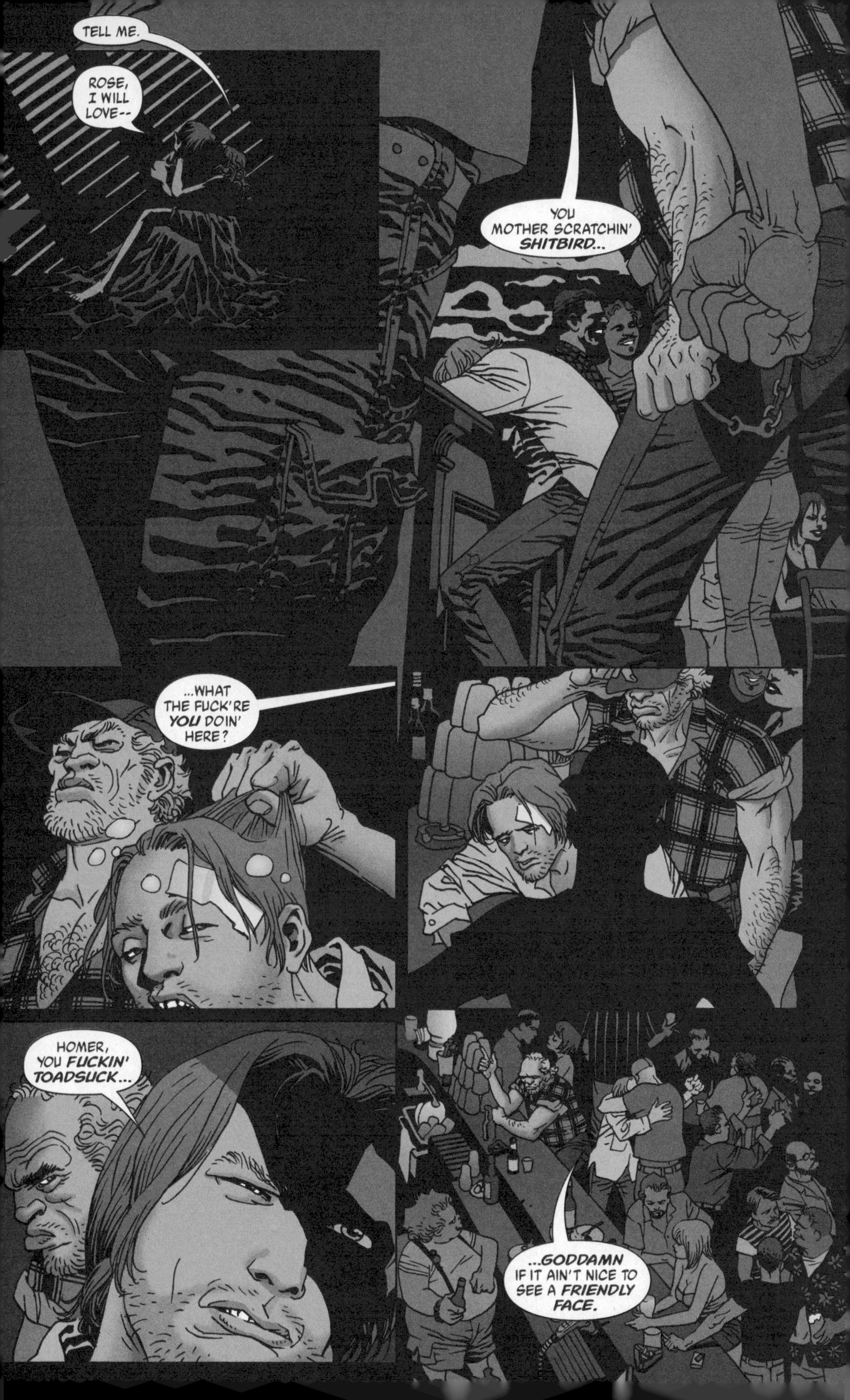
TELL ME.
ROSE, I WILL LOVE--
YOU MOTHER SCRATCHIN' SHITBIRD...
...WHAT THE FUCK'RE YOU DOIN' HERE?
HOMER, YOU FUCKIN' TOADSUCK...
...GODDAMN IF IT AIN'T NICE TO SEE A FRIENDLY FACE.

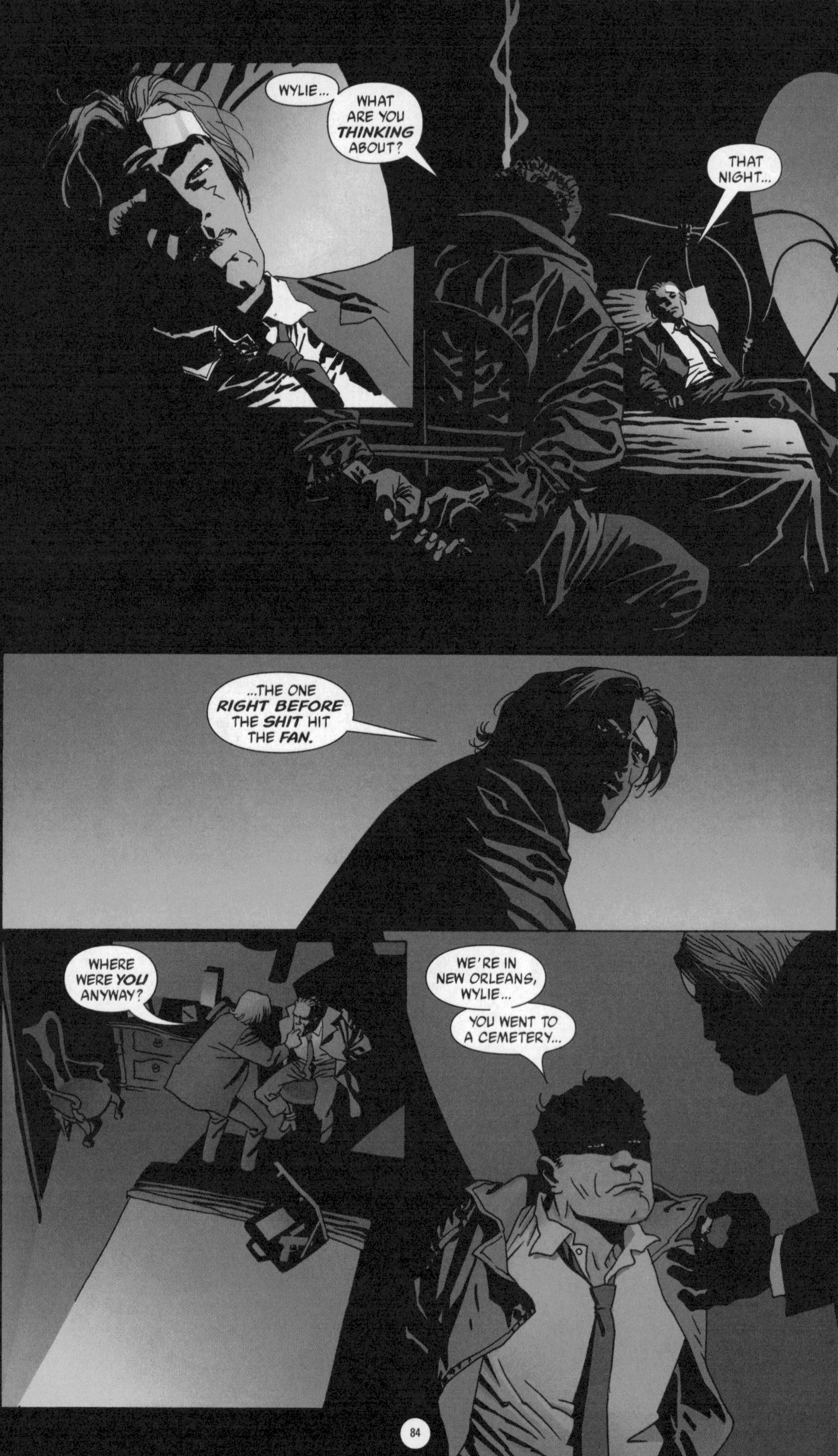

WYLIE...
WHAT ARE YOU THINKING ABOUT?
THAT NIGHT...
...THE ONE RIGHT BEFORE THE SHIT HIT THE FAN.
WHERE WERE YOU ANYWAY?
WE'RE IN NEW ORLEANS, WYLIE...
YOU WENT TO A CEMETERY...

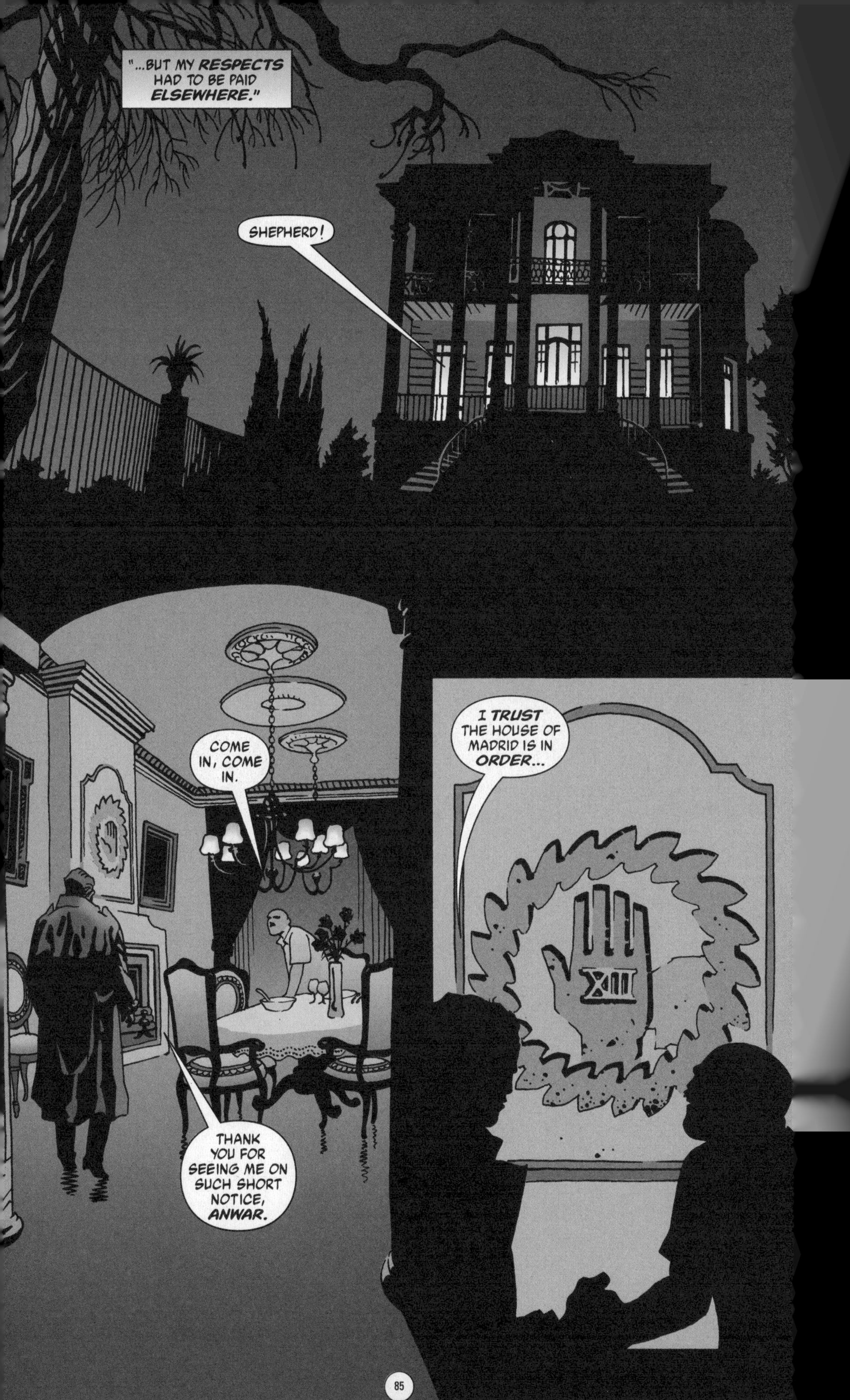
"...BUT MY RESPECTS HAD TO BE PAID ELSEWHERE."
SHEPHERD!
COME IN, COME IN.
THANK YOU FOR SEEING ME ON SUCH SHORT NOTICE, ANWAR.
I TRUST THE HOUSE OF MADRID IS IN ORDER...

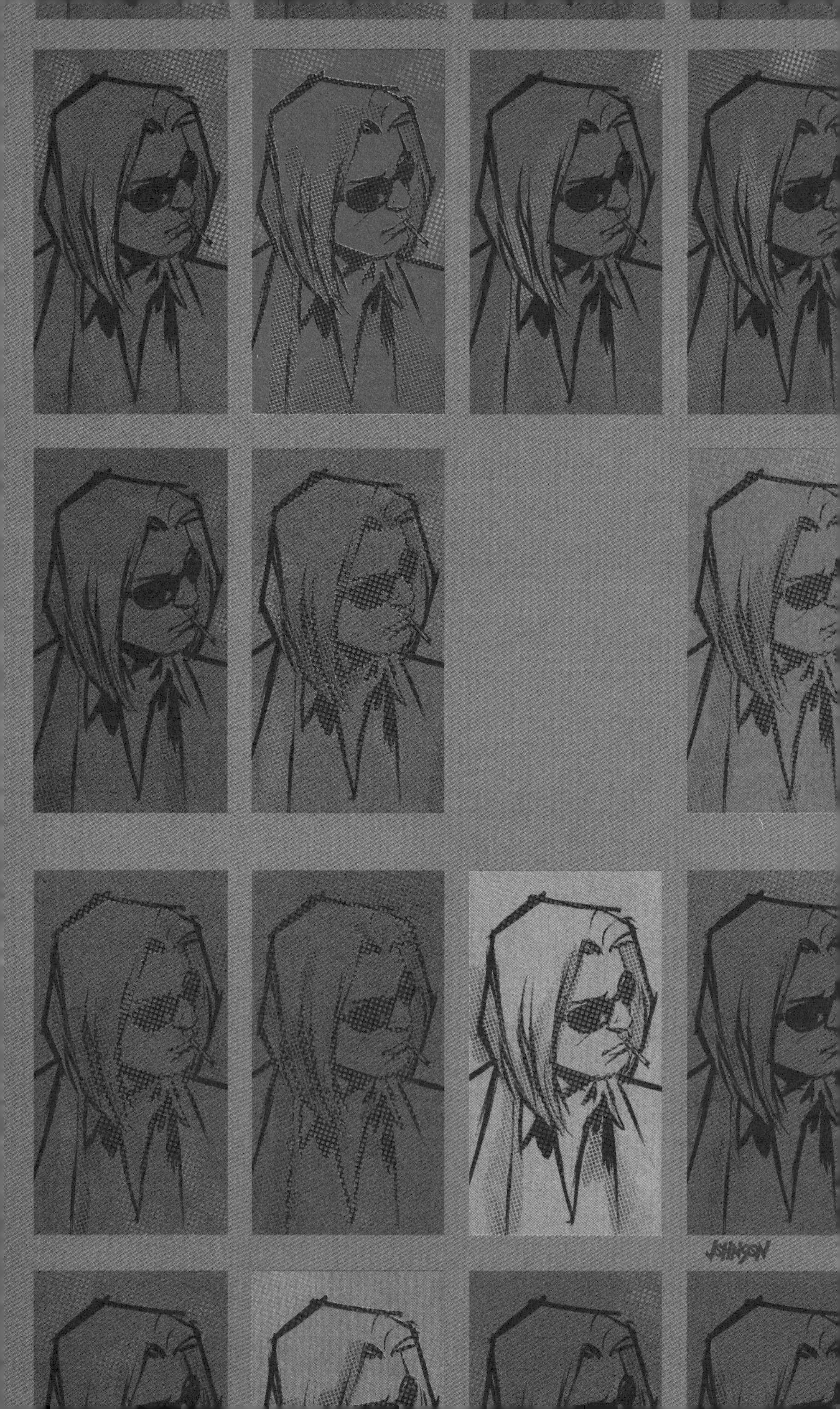
JOHNSON

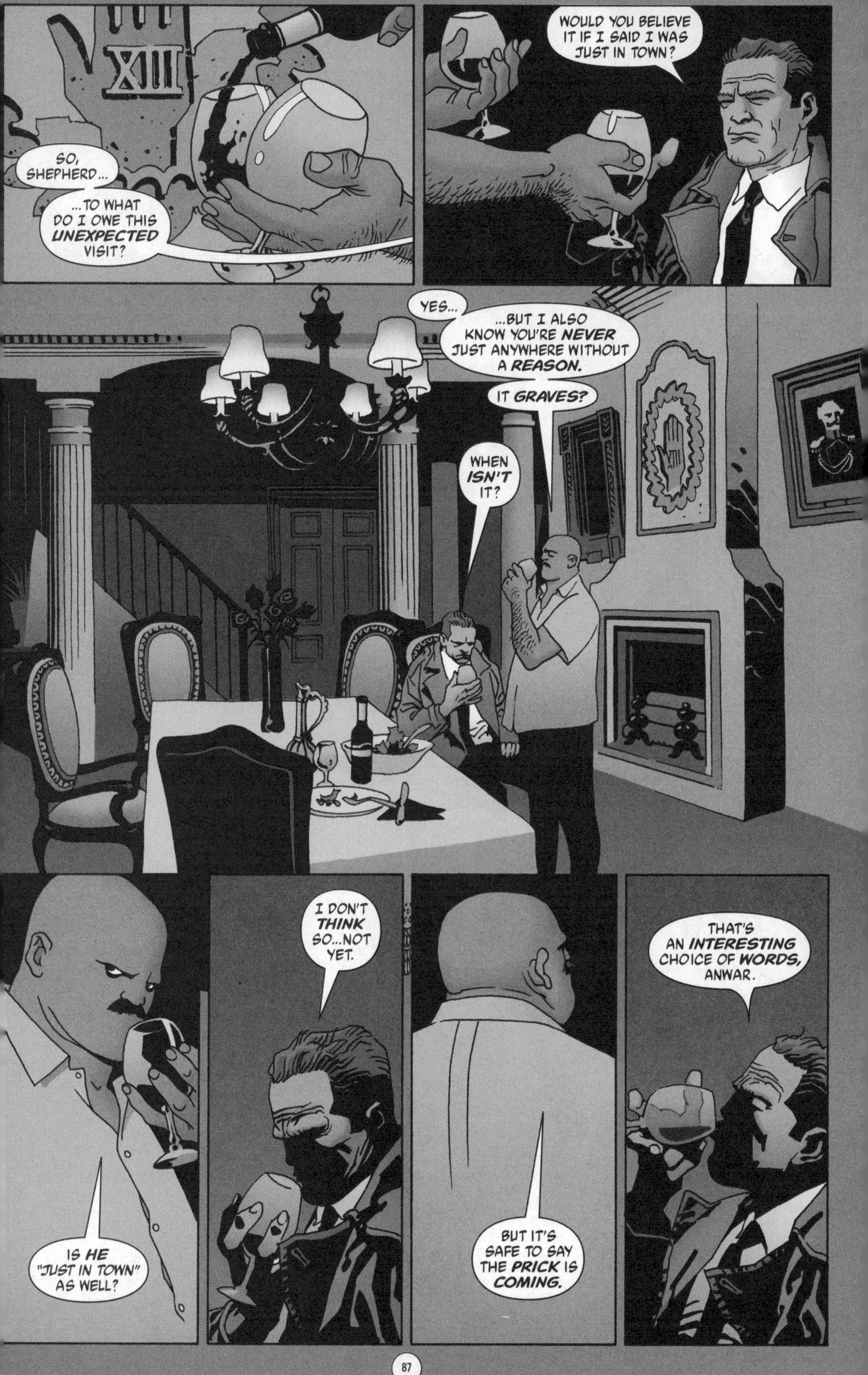
XIII
SO, SHEPHERD...
...TO WHAT DO I OWE THIS UNEXPECTED VISIT?
WOULD YOU BELIEVE IT IF I SAID I WAS JUST IN TOWN?
YES...
...BUT I ALSO KNOW YOU'RE NEVER JUST ANYWHERE WITHOUT A REASON.
IT GRAVES?
WHEN ISN'T IT?
IS HE "JUST IN TOWN" AS WELL?
I DON'T THINK SO...NOT YET.
BUT IT'S SAFE TO SAY THE PRICK IS COMING.
THAT'S AN INTERESTING CHOICE OF WORDS, ANWAR.

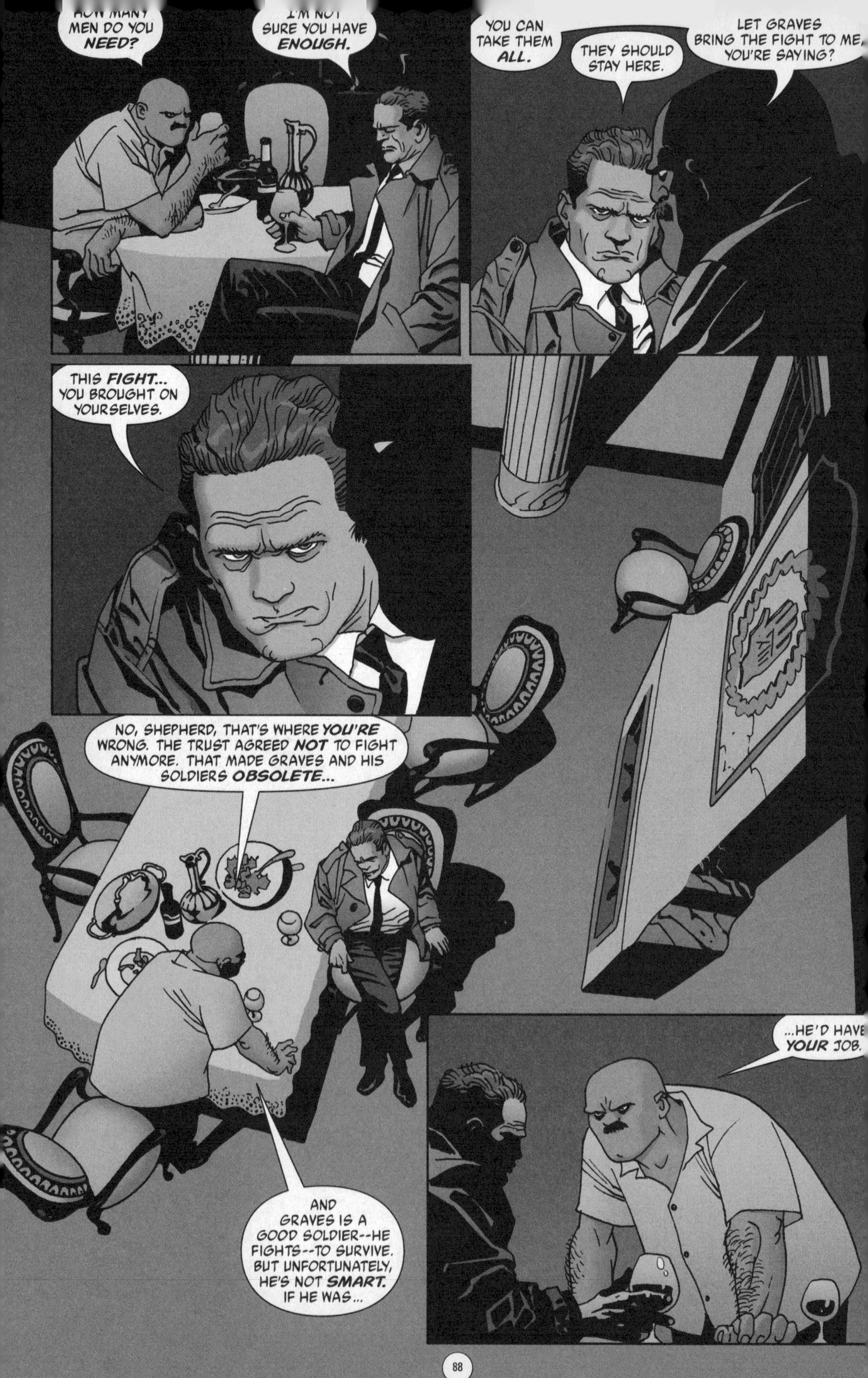

MEN DO YOU NEED?
SURE YOU HAVE ENOUGH.
YOU CAN TAKE THEM ALL.
THEY SHOULD STAY HERE.
LET GRAVES BRING THE FIGHT TO ME, YOU'RE SAYING?
THIS FIGHT... YOU BROUGHT ON YOURSELVES.
NO, SHEPHERD, THAT'S WHERE YOU'RE WRONG. THE TRUST AGREED NOT TO FIGHT ANYMORE. THAT MADE GRAVES AND HIS SOLDIERS OBSOLETE...
AND GRAVES IS A GOOD SOLDIER--HE FIGHTS--TO SURVIVE. BUT UNFORTUNATELY, HE'S NOT SMART. IF HE WAS...
...HE'D HAVE YOUR JOB.

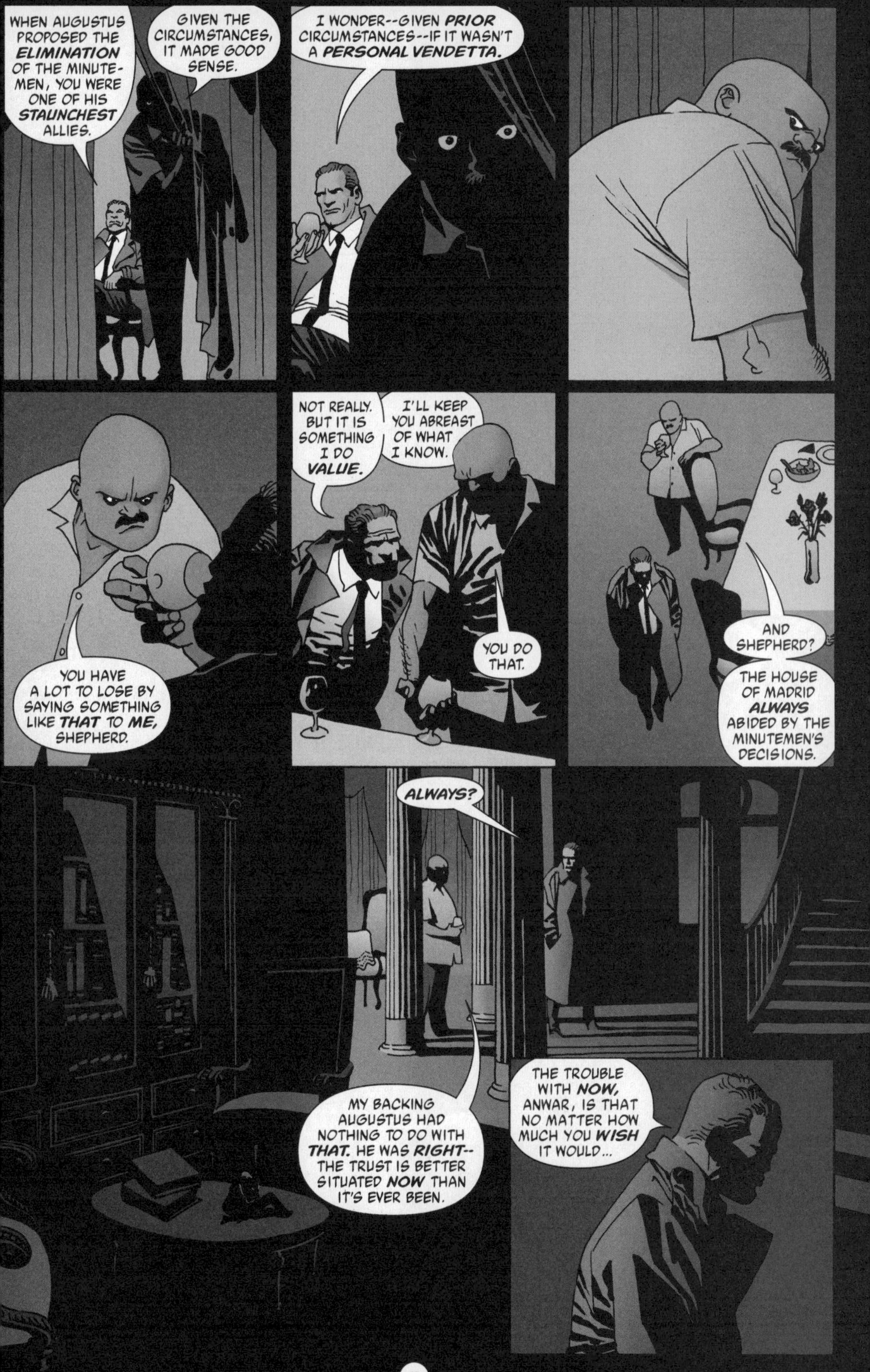

WHEN AUGUSTUS PROPOSED THE ELIMINATION OF THE MINUTEMEN, YOU WERE ONE OF HIS STAUNCHEST ALLIES.
GIVEN THE CIRCUMSTANCES, IT MADE GOOD SENSE.
I WONDER--GIVEN PRIOR CIRCUMSTANCES--IF IT WASN'T A PERSONAL VENDETTA.
YOU HAVE A LOT TO LOSE BY SAYING SOMETHING LIKE THAT TO ME, SHEPHERD.
NOT REALLY. BUT IT IS SOMETHING I DO VALUE.
I'LL KEEP YOU ABREAST OF WHAT I KNOW.
YOU DO THAT.
AND SHEPHERD?
THE HOUSE OF MADRID ALWAYS ABIDED BY THE MINUTEMEN'S DECISIONS.
ALWAYS?
MY BACKING AUGUSTUS HAD NOTHING TO DO WITH THAT. HE WAS RIGHT-- THE TRUST IS BETTER SITUATED NOW THAN IT'S EVER BEEN.
THE TROUBLE WITH NOW, ANWAR, IS THAT NO MATTER HOW MUCH YOU WISH IT WOULD...

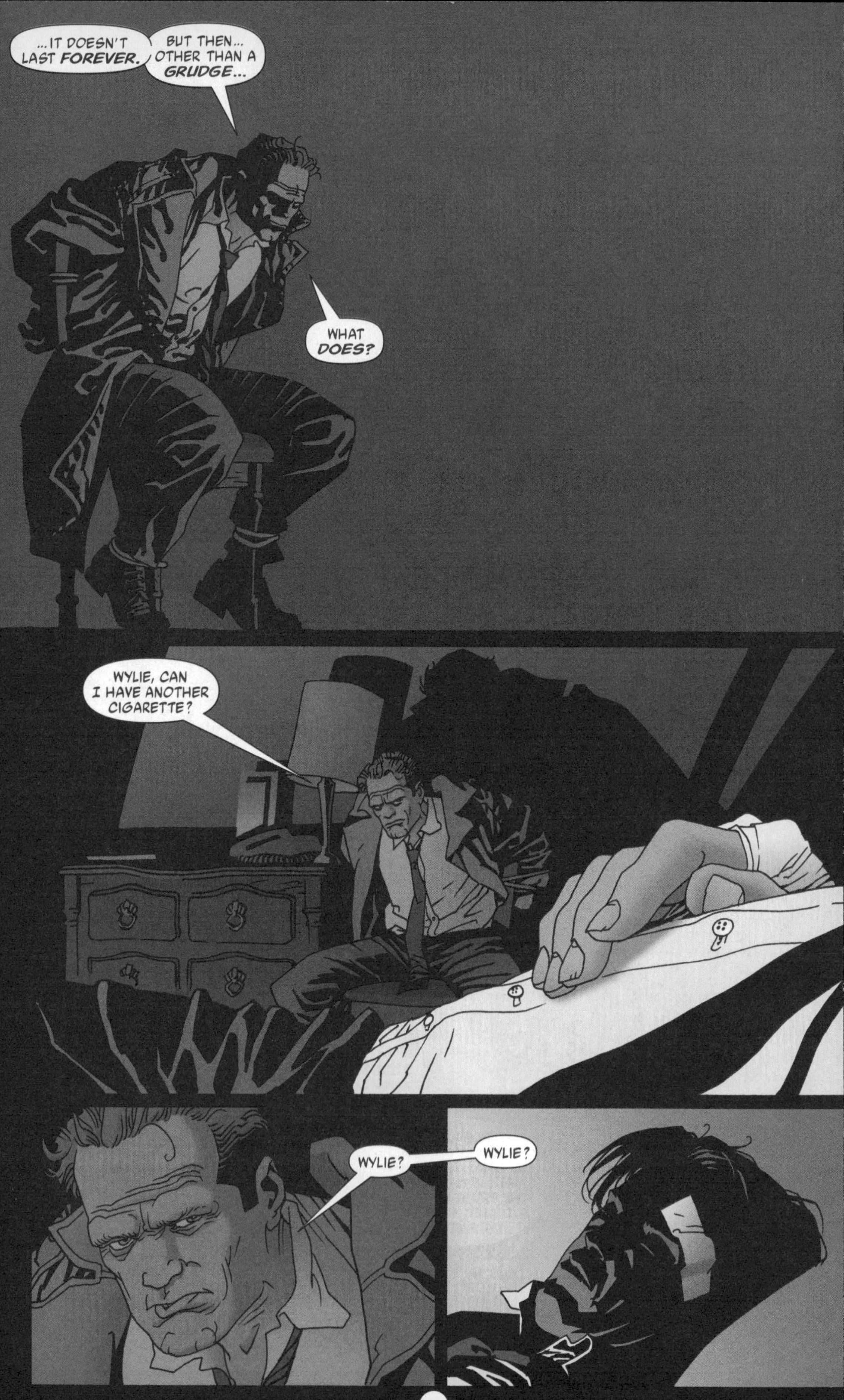
...IT DOESN'T LAST FOREVER.
BUT THEN... OTHER THAN A GRUDGE...
WHAT DOES?
WYLIE, CAN I HAVE ANOTHER CIGARETTE?
WYLIE?
WYLIE?

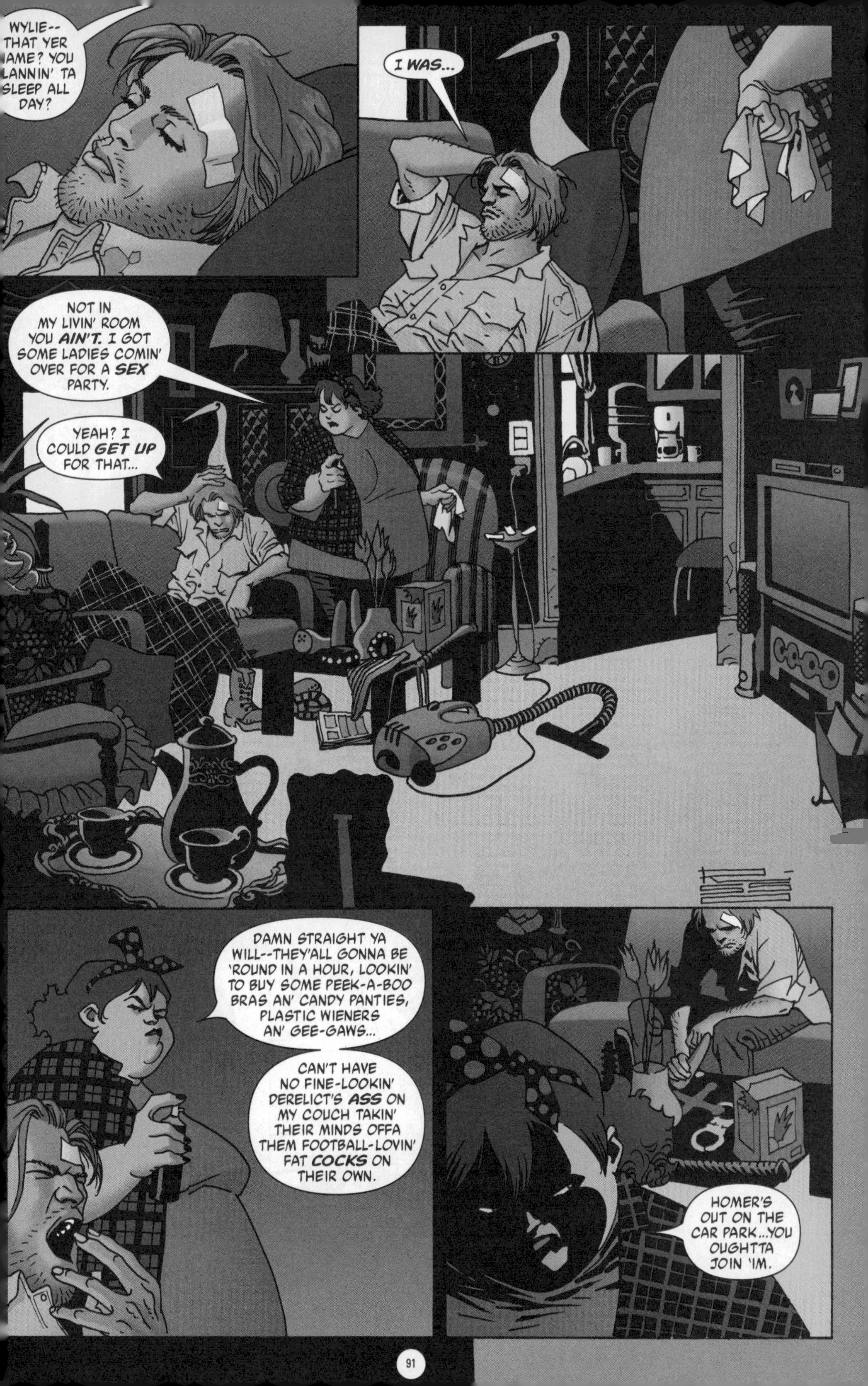
WYLIE-- THAT YER NAME? YOU PLANNIN' TA SLEEP ALL DAY?
I WAS...
NOT IN MY LIVIN' ROOM YOU AIN'T. I GOT SOME LADIES COMIN' OVER FOR A SEX PARTY.
YEAH? I COULD GET UP FOR THAT...
DAMN STRAIGHT YA WILL--THEY'ALL GONNA BE 'ROUND IN A HOUR, LOOKIN' TO BUY SOME PEEK-A-BOO BRAS AN' CANDY PANTIES, PLASTIC WIENERS AN' GEE-GAWS...
CAN'T HAVE NO FINE-LOOKIN' DERELICT'S ASS ON MY COUCH TAKIN' THEIR MINDS OFFA THEM FOOTBALL-LOVIN' FAT COCKS ON THEIR OWN.
HOMER'S OUT ON THE CAR PARK...YOU OUGHTTA JOIN 'IM.

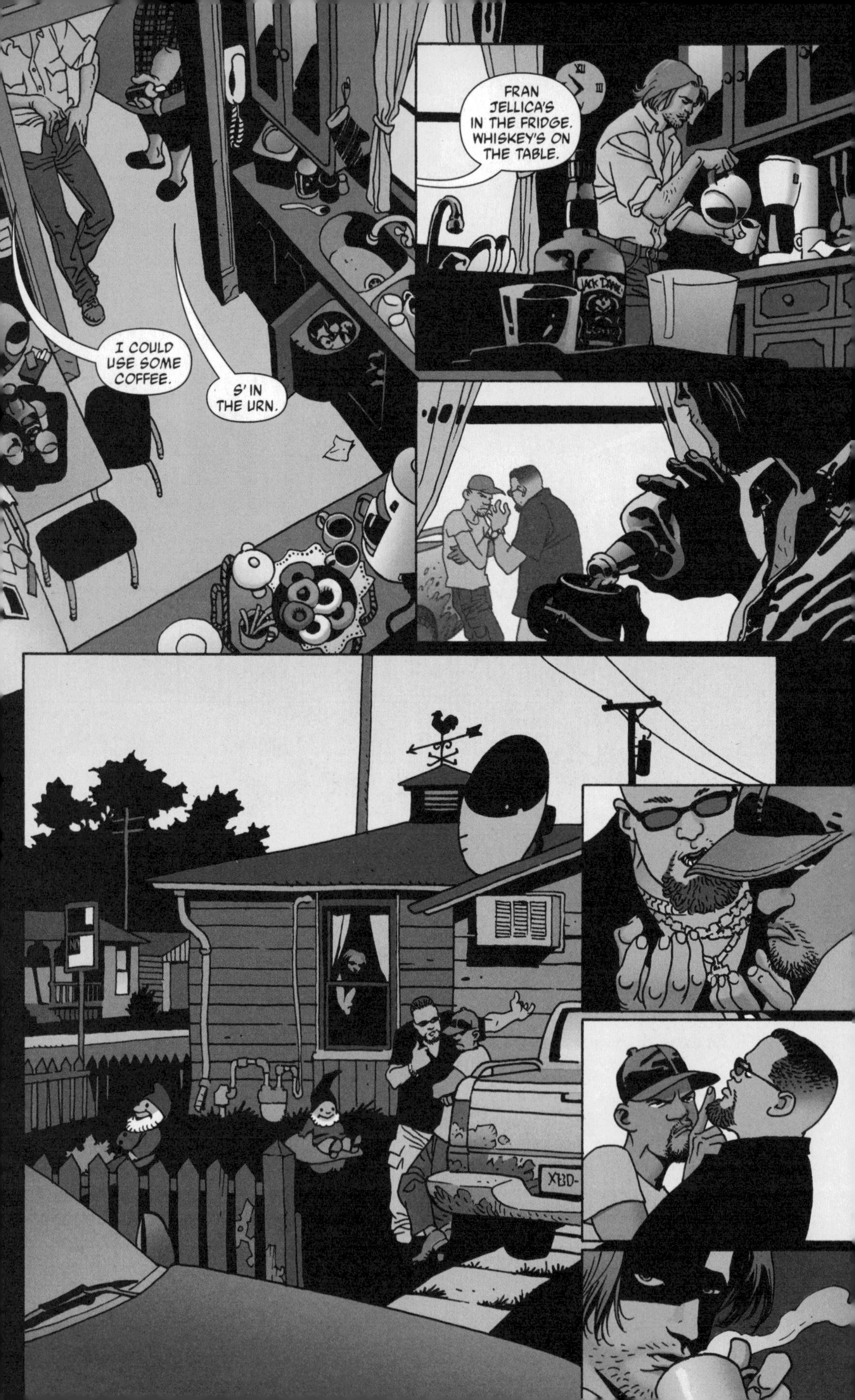
FRAN
JELLICA'S
IN THE FRIDGE.
WHISKEY'S ON
THE TABLE.
I COULD
USE SOME
COFFEE.
S' IN
THE URN.

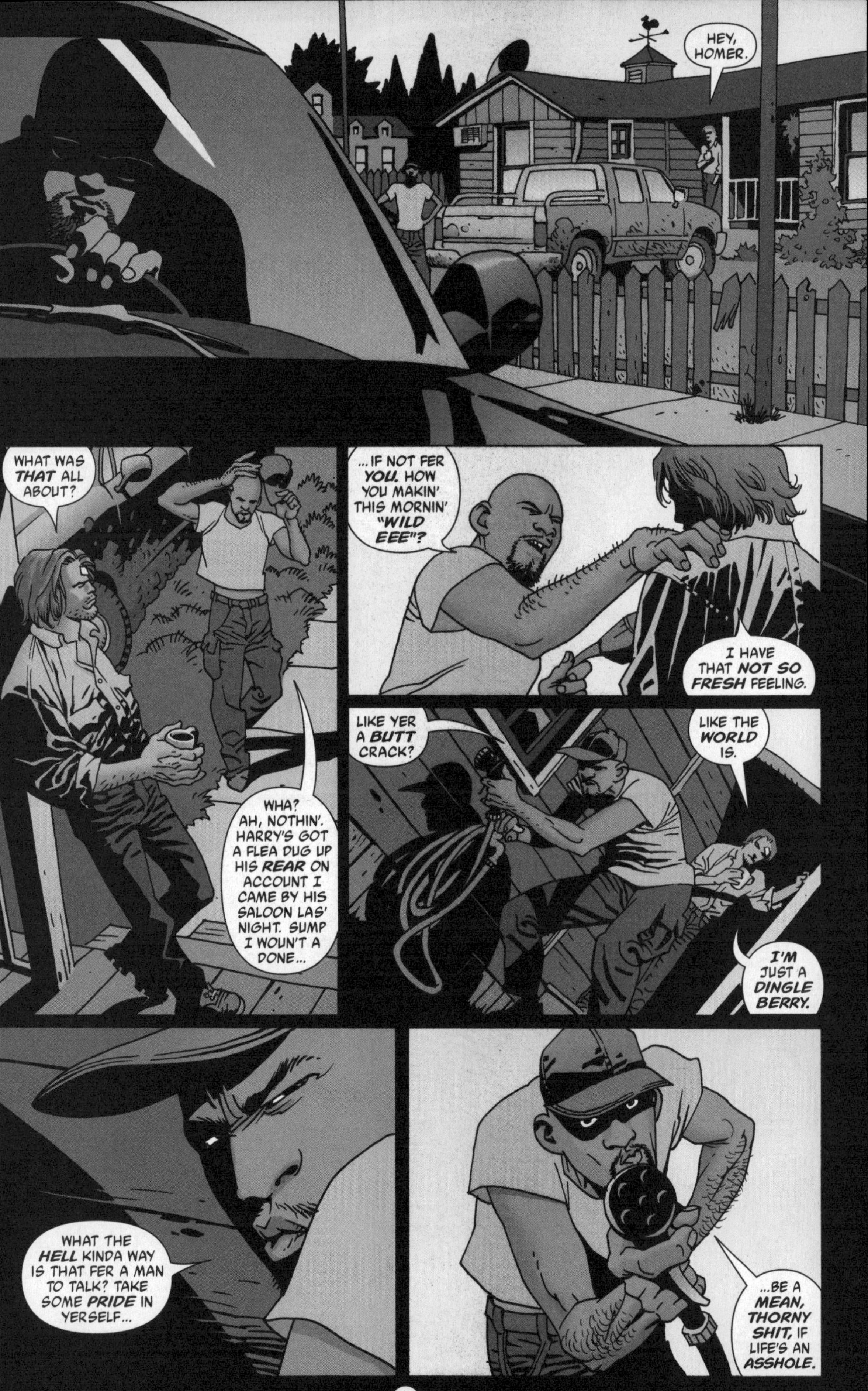

HEY, HOMER.
WHAT WAS THAT ALL ABOUT?
WHA? AH, NOTHIN'. HARRY'S GOT A FLEA DUG UP HIS REAR ON ACCOUNT I CAME BY HIS SALOON LAS' NIGHT. SUMP I WOUN'T A DONE...
...IF NOT FER YOU. HOW YOU MAKIN' THIS MORNIN' "WILD EEE"?
I HAVE THAT NOT SO FRESH FEELING.
LIKE YER A BUTT CRACK?
LIKE THE WORLD IS.
I'M JUST A DINGLE BERRY.
WHAT THE HELL KINDA WAY IS THAT FER A MAN TO TALK? TAKE SOME PRIDE IN YERSELF...
...BE A MEAN, THORNY SHIT, IF LIFE'S AN ASSHOLE.

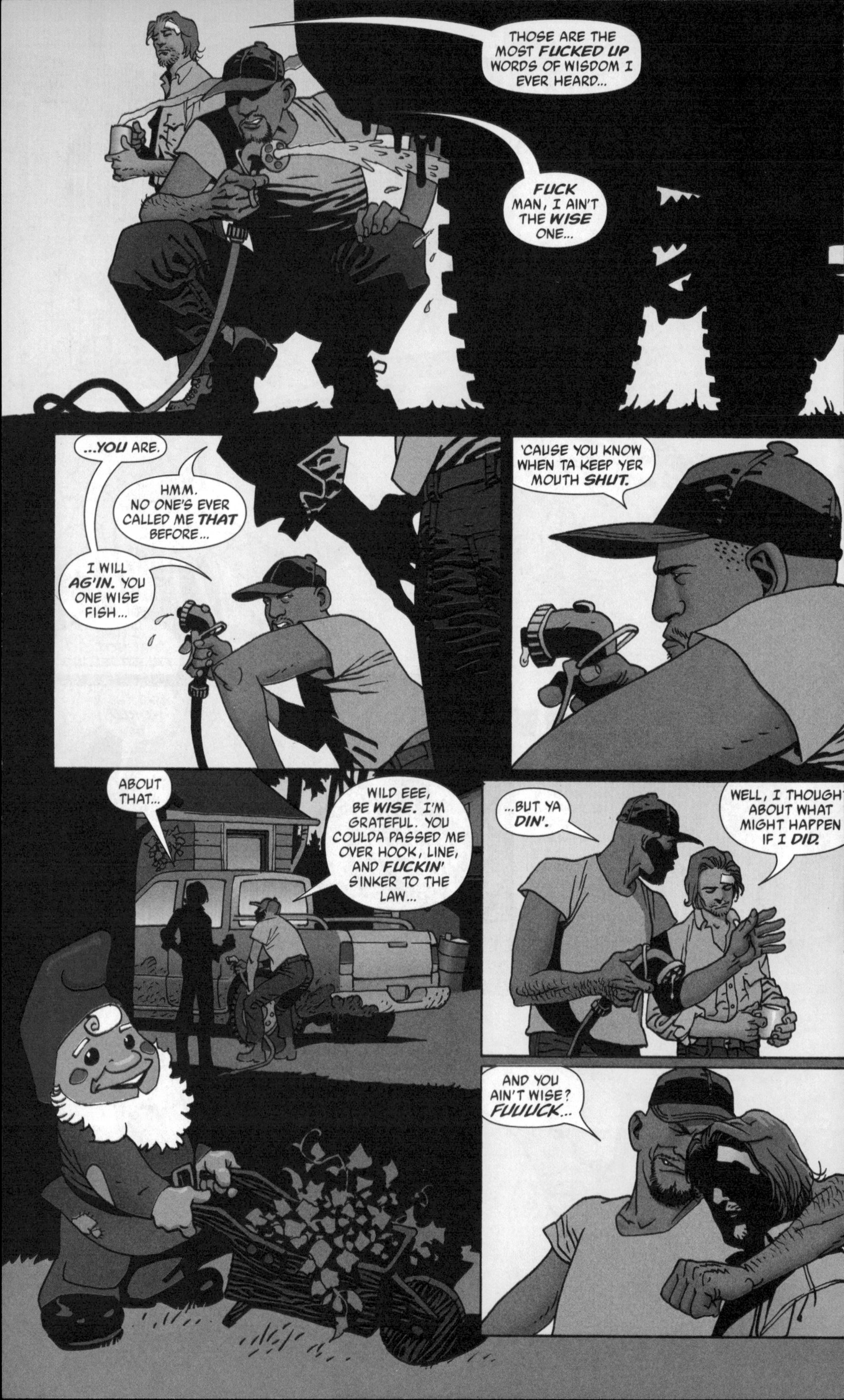
THOSE ARE THE MOST FUCKED UP WORDS OF WISDOM I EVER HEARD...
FUCK MAN, I AIN'T THE WISE ONE...
...YOU ARE.
HMM. NO ONE'S EVER CALLED ME THAT BEFORE...
I WILL AG'IN. YOU ONE WISE FISH...
'CAUSE YOU KNOW WHEN TA KEEP YER MOUTH SHUT.
ABOUT THAT...
WILD EEE, BE WISE. I'M GRATEFUL. YOU COULDA PASSED ME OVER HOOK, LINE, AND FUCKIN' SINKER TO THE LAW...
...BUT YA DIN'.
WELL, I THOUGHT ABOUT WHAT MIGHT HAPPEN IF I DID.
AND YOU AIN'T WISE? FUUUCK...

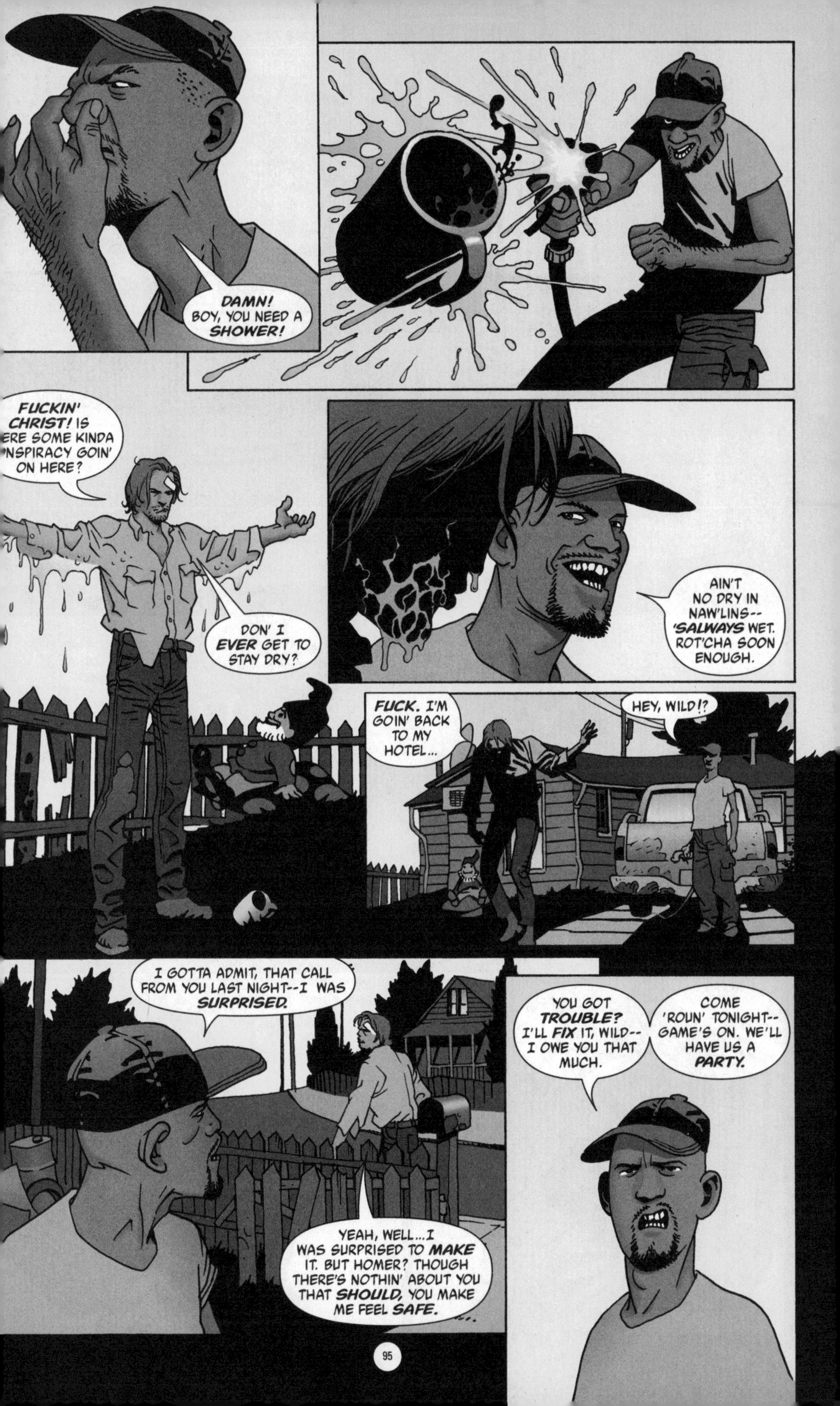

DAMN! BOY, YOU NEED A SHOWER!
FUCKIN' CHRIST! IS ERE SOME KINDA NSPIRACY GOIN' ON HERE?
DON' I EVER GET TO STAY DRY?
AIN'T NO DRY IN NAW'LINS-- 'SALWAYS WET. ROT'CHA SOON ENOUGH.
FUCK. I'M GOIN' BACK TO MY HOTEL...
HEY, WILD!?
I GOTTA ADMIT, THAT CALL FROM YOU LAST NIGHT--I WAS SURPRISED.
YEAH, WELL...I WAS SURPRISED TO MAKE IT. BUT HOMER? THOUGH THERE'S NOTHIN' ABOUT YOU THAT SHOULD, YOU MAKE ME FEEL SAFE.
YOU GOT TROUBLE? I'LL FIX IT, WILD-- I OWE YOU THAT MUCH.
COME 'ROUN' TONIGHT-- GAME'S ON. WE'LL HAVE US A PARTY.

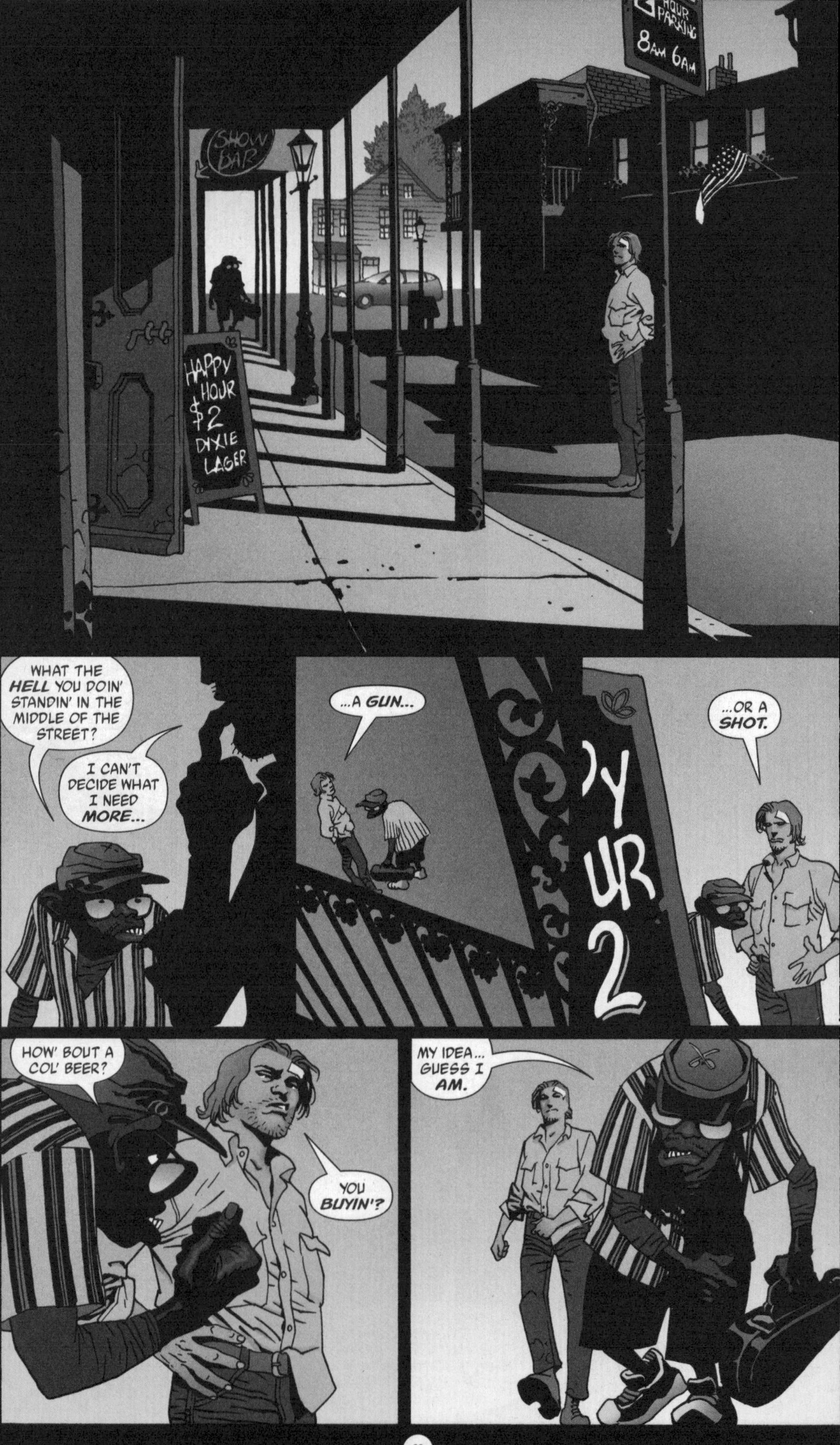
HOUR PARKING
8AM 6AM
SHOW BAR
HAPPY HOUR $2 DIXIE LAGER
WHAT THE HELL YOU DOIN' STANDIN' IN THE MIDDLE OF THE STREET?
I CAN'T DECIDE WHAT I NEED MORE...
...A GUN...
...OR A SHOT.
HOW' BOUT A COL' BEER?
YOU BUYIN'?
MY IDEA... GUESS I AM.

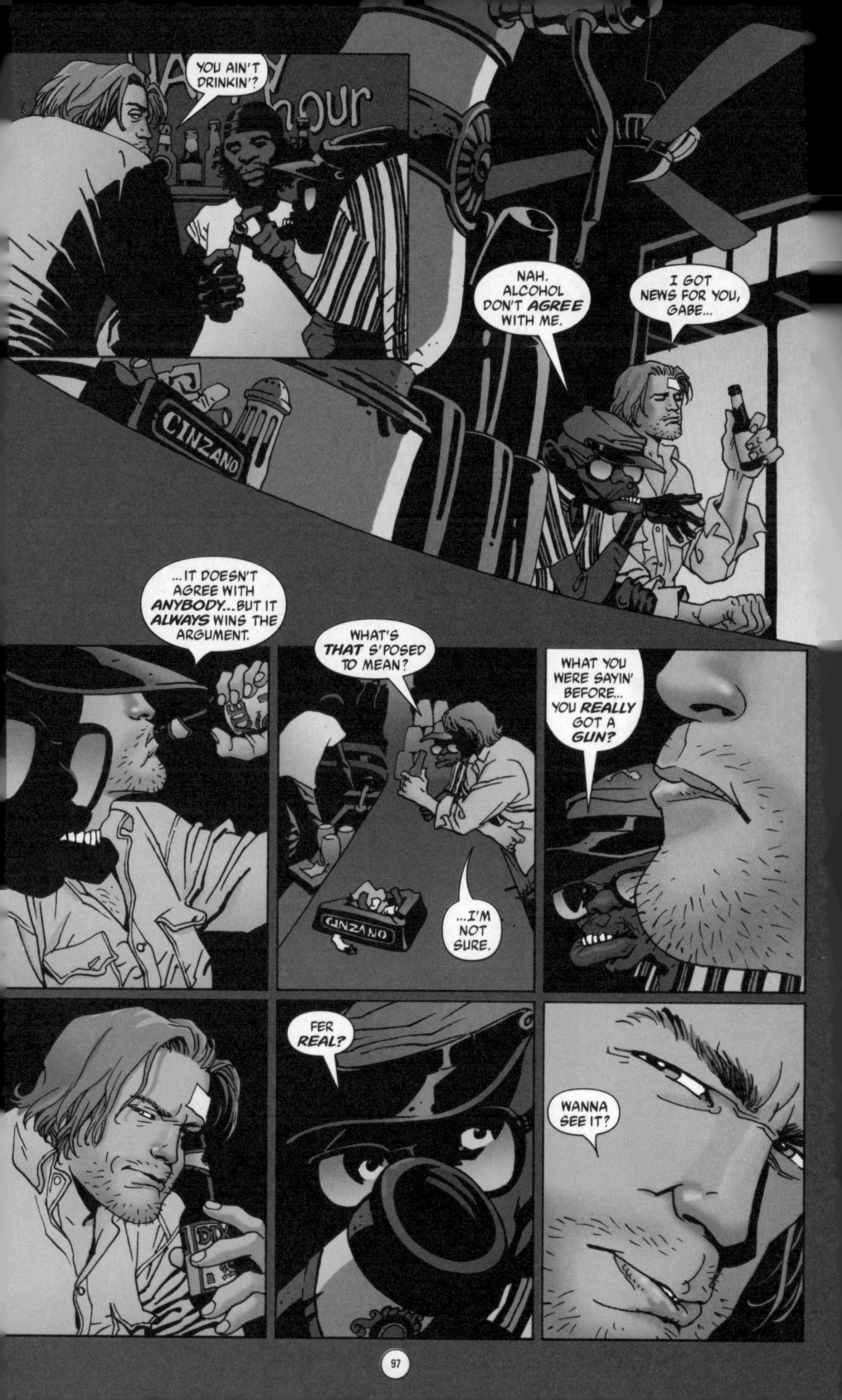

happy hour
YOU AIN'T DRINKIN'?
NAH. ALCOHOL DON'T AGREE WITH ME.
I GOT NEWS FOR YOU, GABE...
CINZANO
...IT DOESN'T AGREE WITH ANYBODY...BUT IT ALWAYS WINS THE ARGUMENT.
WHAT'S THAT S'POSED TO MEAN?
CINZANO
...I'M NOT SURE.
WHAT YOU WERE SAYIN' BEFORE... YOU REALLY GOT A GUN?
FER REAL?
WANNA SEE IT?

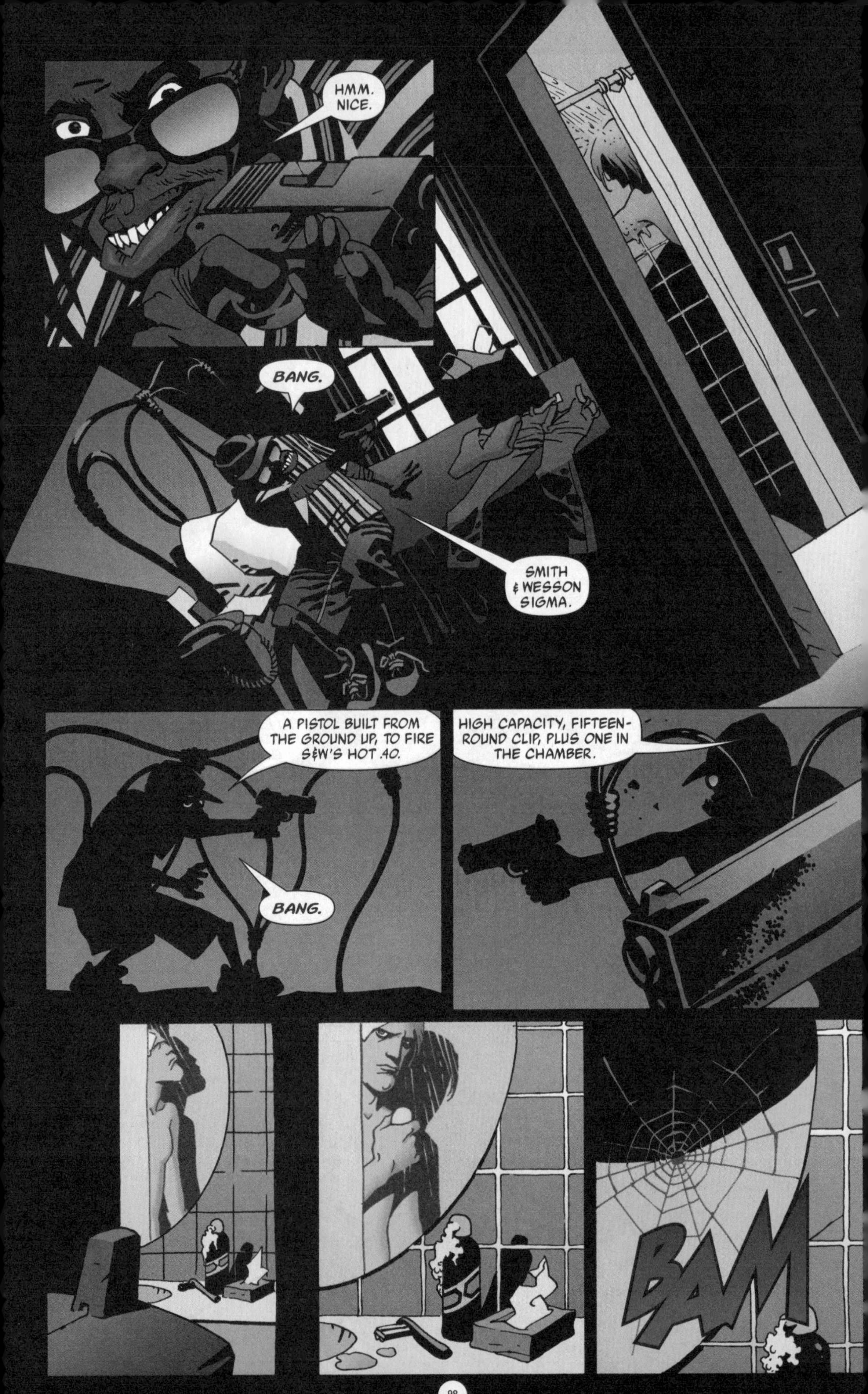
HMM. NICE.
BANG.
SMITH & WESSON SIGMA.
A PISTOL BUILT FROM THE GROUND UP, TO FIRE S&W'S HOT .40.
BANG.
HIGH CAPACITY, FIFTEEN-ROUND CLIP, PLUS ONE IN THE CHAMBER.
BAM

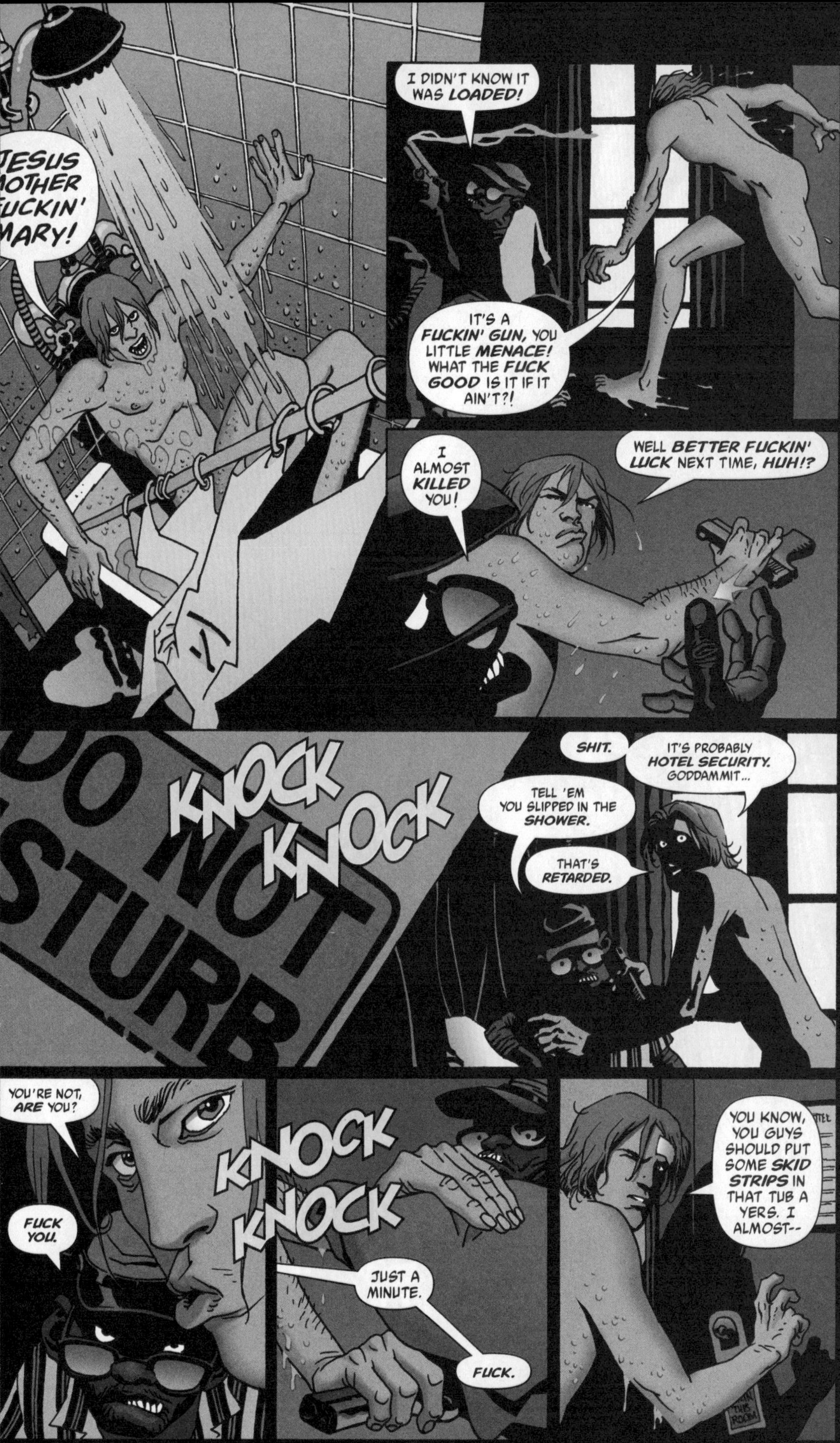

JESUS MOTHER FUCKIN' MARY!
I DIDN'T KNOW IT WAS **LOADED!**
IT'S A **FUCKIN' GUN**, YOU LITTLE **MENACE!** WHAT THE **FUCK GOOD** IS IT IF IT AIN'T?!
I ALMOST **KILLED** YOU!
WELL **BETTER FUCKIN' LUCK** NEXT TIME, **HUH!?**
DO NOT
STURB
KNOCK KNOCK
SHIT.
IT'S PROBABLY **HOTEL SECURITY.** GODDAMMIT...
TELL 'EM YOU SLIPPED IN THE **SHOWER.**
THAT'S **RETARDED.**
YOU'RE NOT, **ARE** YOU?
FUCK YOU.
KNOCK KNOCK
JUST A MINUTE.
FUCK.
YOU KNOW, YOU GUYS SHOULD PUT SOME **SKID STRIPS** IN THAT TUB A YERS. I ALMOST--

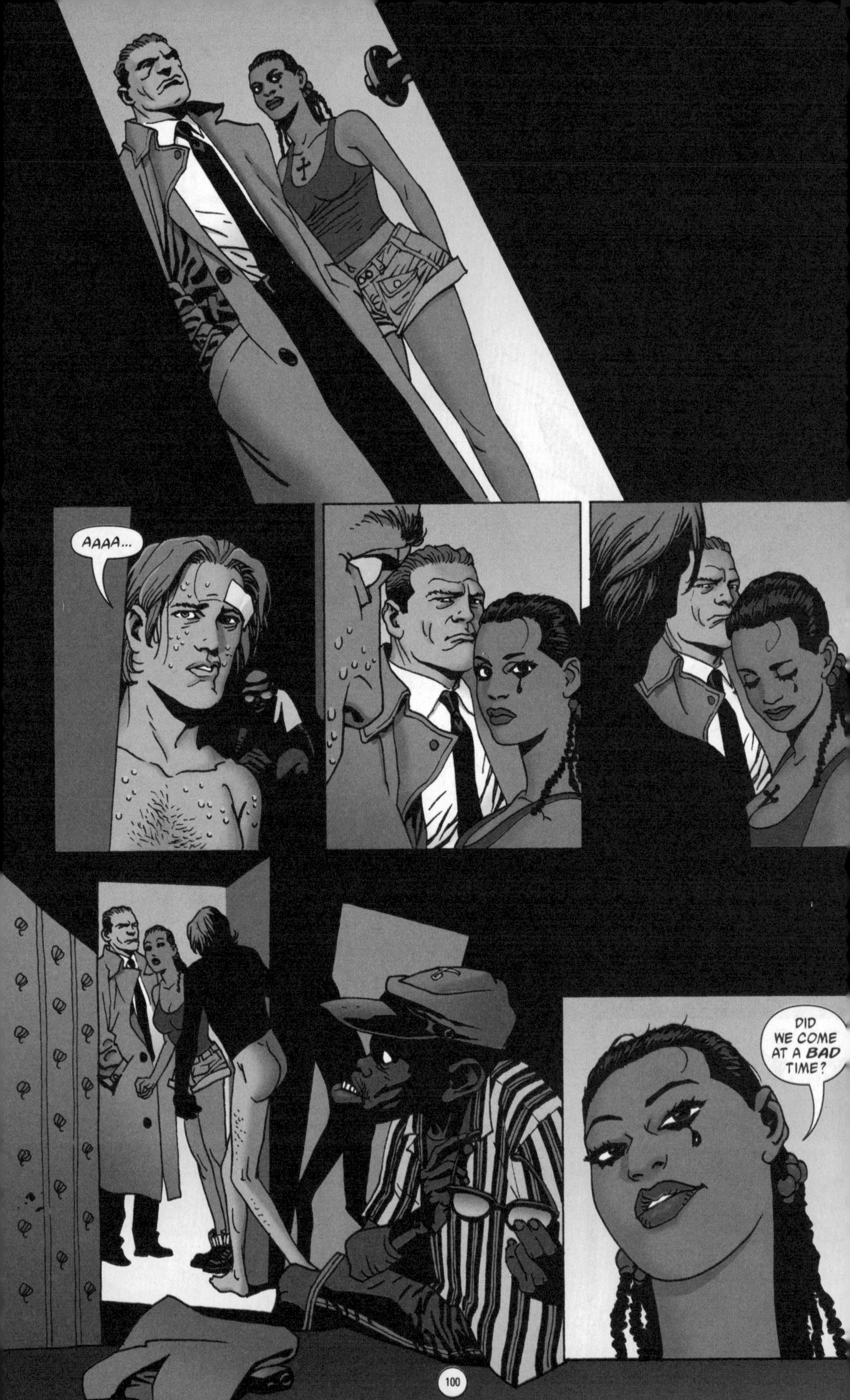
AAAA...
DID WE COME AT A *BAD* TIME?

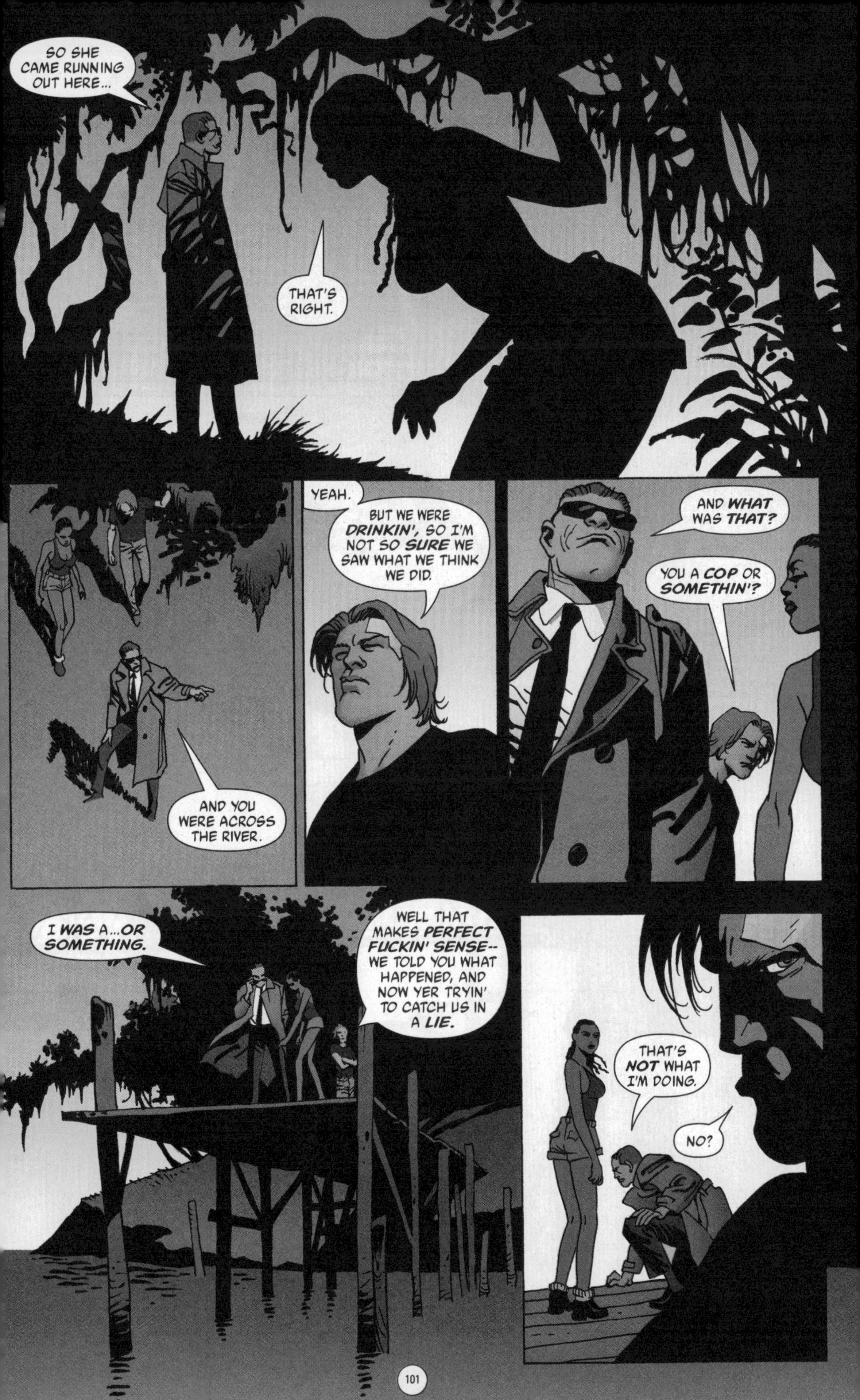
SO SHE CAME RUNNING OUT HERE...
THAT'S RIGHT.
AND YOU WERE ACROSS THE RIVER.
YEAH.
BUT WE WERE DRINKIN', SO I'M NOT SO SURE WE SAW WHAT WE THINK WE DID.
AND WHAT WAS THAT?
YOU A COP OR SOMETHIN'?
I WAS A...OR SOMETHING.
WELL THAT MAKES PERFECT FUCKIN' SENSE-- WE TOLD YOU WHAT HAPPENED, AND NOW YER TRYIN' TO CATCH US IN A LIE.
THAT'S NOT WHAT I'M DOING.
NO?

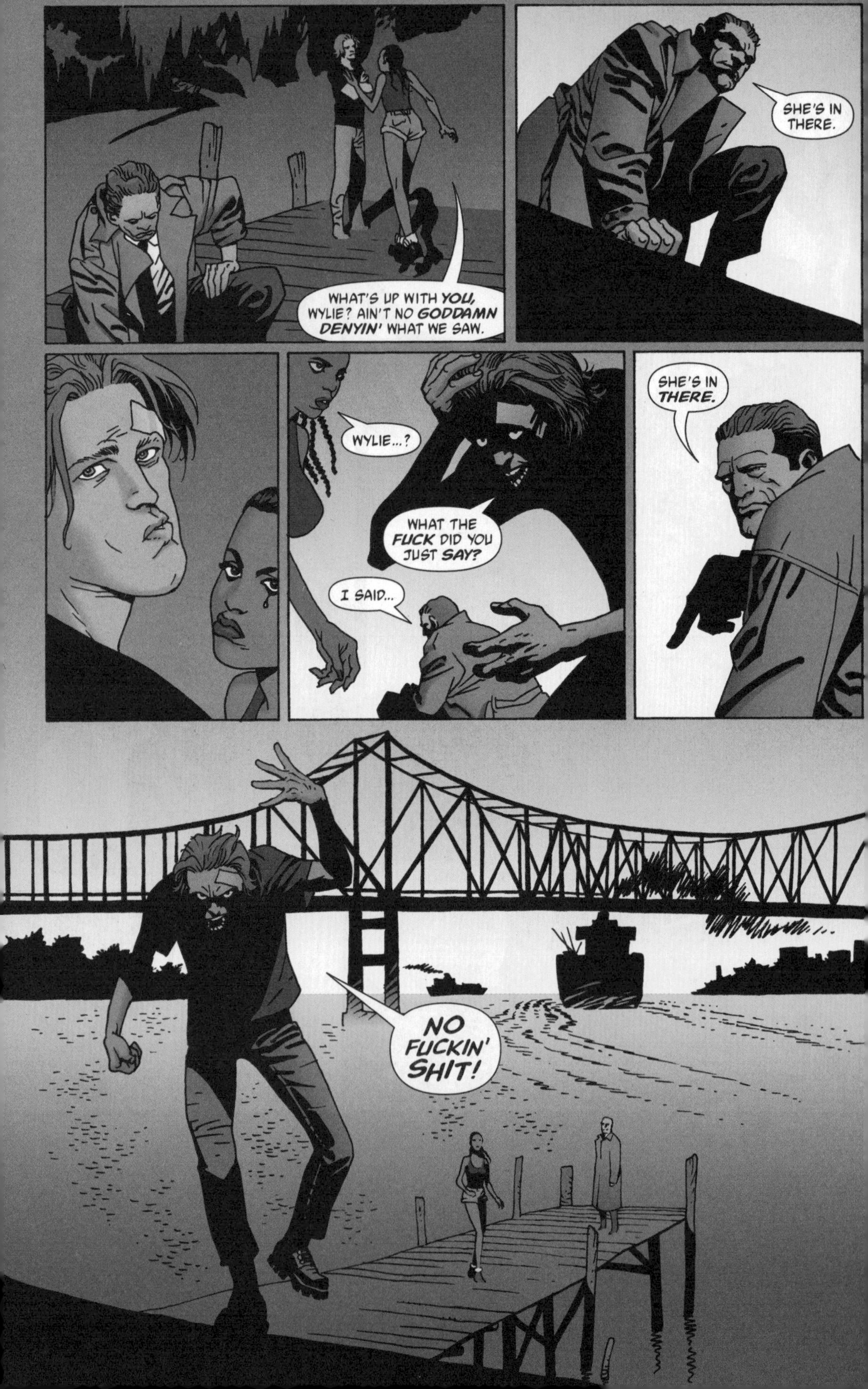
WHAT'S UP WITH YOU, WYLIE? AIN'T NO GODDAMN DENYIN' WHAT WE SAW.
SHE'S IN THERE.
WYLIE...?
WHAT THE FUCK DID YOU JUST SAY?
I SAID...
SHE'S IN THERE.
NO FUCKIN' SHIT!

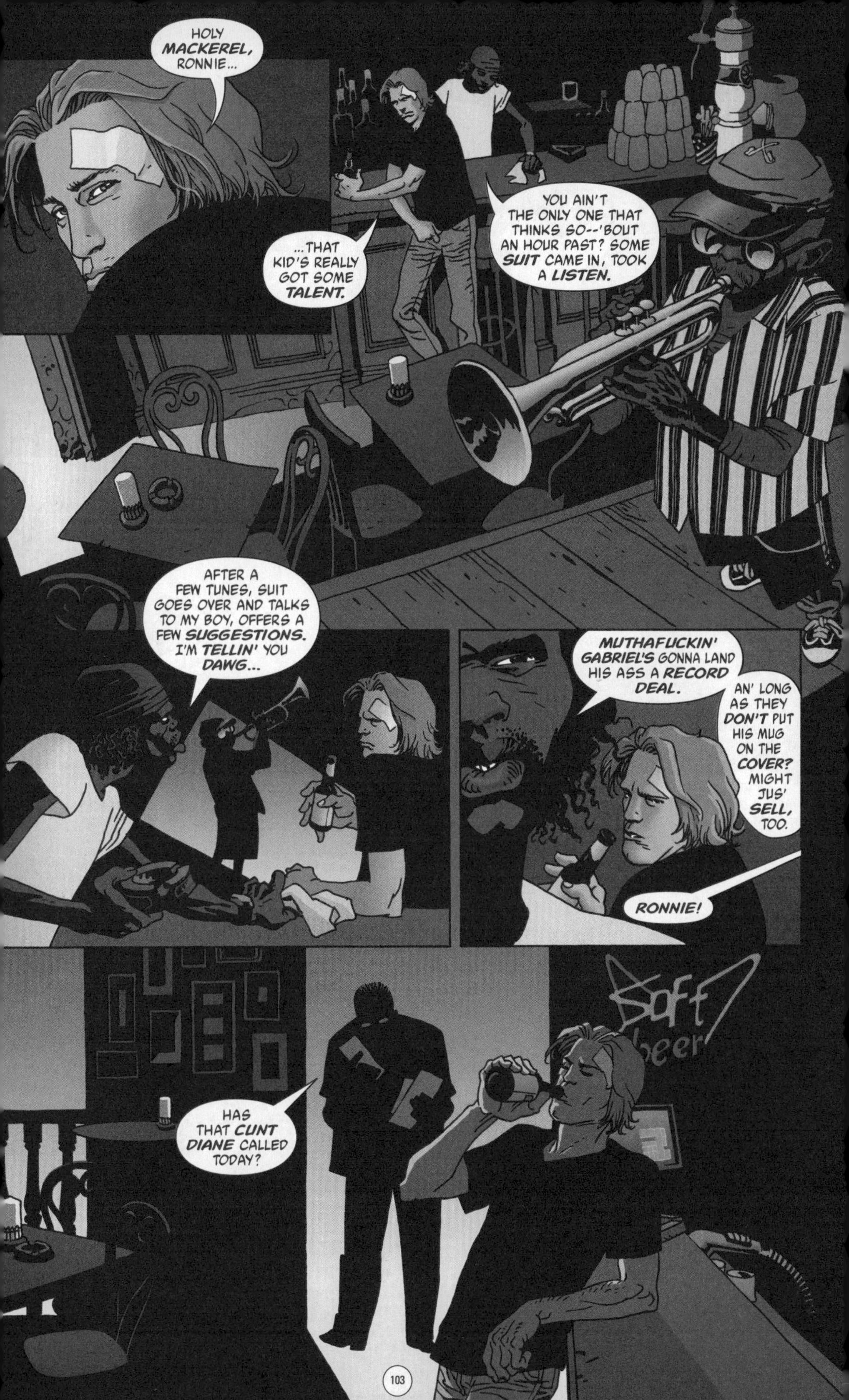
HOLY MACKEREL, RONNIE...
...THAT KID'S REALLY GOT SOME TALENT.
YOU AIN'T THE ONLY ONE THAT THINKS SO--'BOUT AN HOUR PAST? SOME SUIT CAME IN, TOOK A LISTEN.
AFTER A FEW TUNES, SUIT GOES OVER AND TALKS TO MY BOY, OFFERS A FEW SUGGESTIONS. I'M TELLIN' YOU DAWG...
MUTHAFUCKIN' GABRIEL'S GONNA LAND HIS ASS A RECORD DEAL.
AN' LONG AS THEY DON'T PUT HIS MUG ON THE COVER? MIGHT JUS' SELL, TOO.
RONNIE!
HAS THAT CUNT DIANE CALLED TODAY?
Soft beer

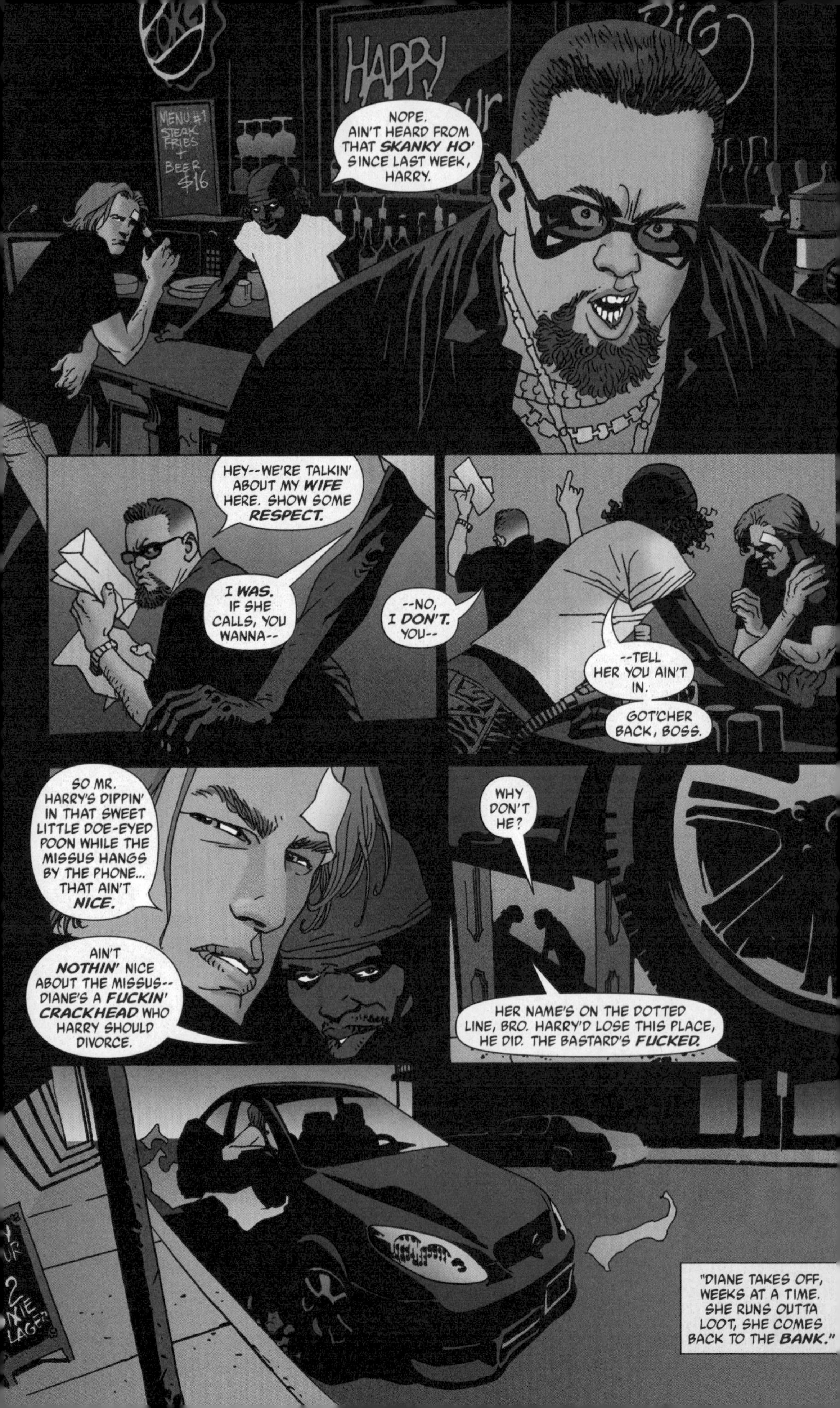
HAPPY
MENU #1 STEAK FRIES + BEER $16
NOPE. AIN'T HEARD FROM THAT SKANKY HO' SINCE LAST WEEK, HARRY.
HEY--WE'RE TALKIN' ABOUT MY WIFE HERE. SHOW SOME RESPECT.
I WAS. IF SHE CALLS, YOU WANNA--
--NO, I DON'T. YOU--
--TELL HER YOU AIN'T IN.
GOT'CHER BACK, BOSS.
SO MR. HARRY'S DIPPIN' IN THAT SWEET LITTLE DOE-EYED POON WHILE THE MISSUS HANGS BY THE PHONE... THAT AIN'T NICE.
AIN'T NOTHIN' NICE ABOUT THE MISSUS--DIANE'S A FUCKIN' CRACKHEAD WHO HARRY SHOULD DIVORCE.
WHY DON'T HE?
HER NAME'S ON THE DOTTED LINE, BRO. HARRY'D LOSE THIS PLACE, HE DID. THE BASTARD'S FUCKED.
"DIANE TAKES OFF, WEEKS AT A TIME. SHE RUNS OUTTA LOOT, SHE COMES BACK TO THE BANK."

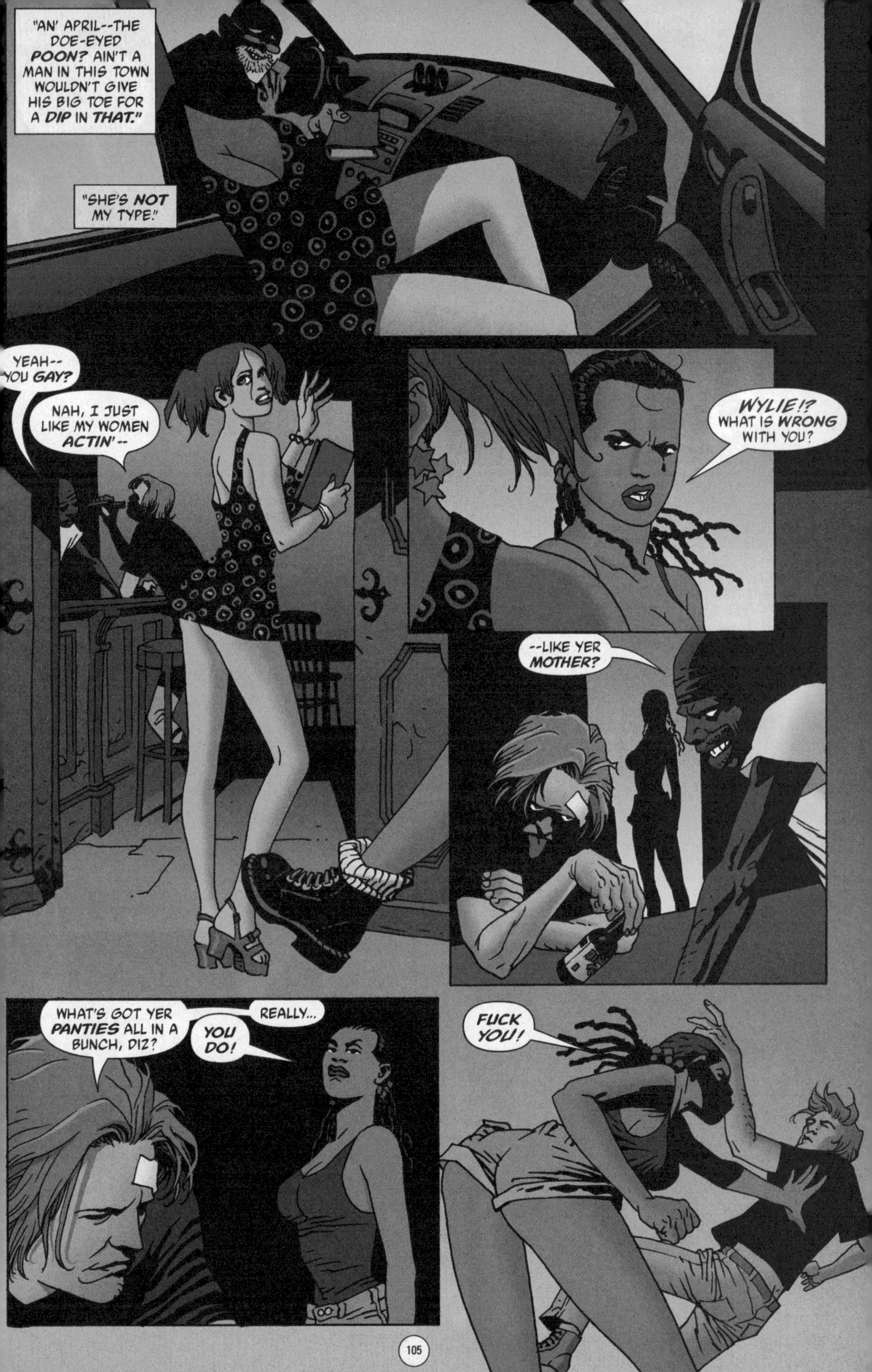
"AN' APRIL--THE DOE-EYED POON? AIN'T A MAN IN THIS TOWN WOULDN'T GIVE HIS BIG TOE FOR A DIP IN THAT."
"SHE'S NOT MY TYPE."
YEAH-- YOU GAY?
NAH, I JUST LIKE MY WOMEN ACTIN'--
WYLIE!? WHAT IS WRONG WITH YOU?
--LIKE YER MOTHER?
WHAT'S GOT YER PANTIES ALL IN A BUNCH, DIZ?
REALLY...
YOU DO!
FUCK YOU!

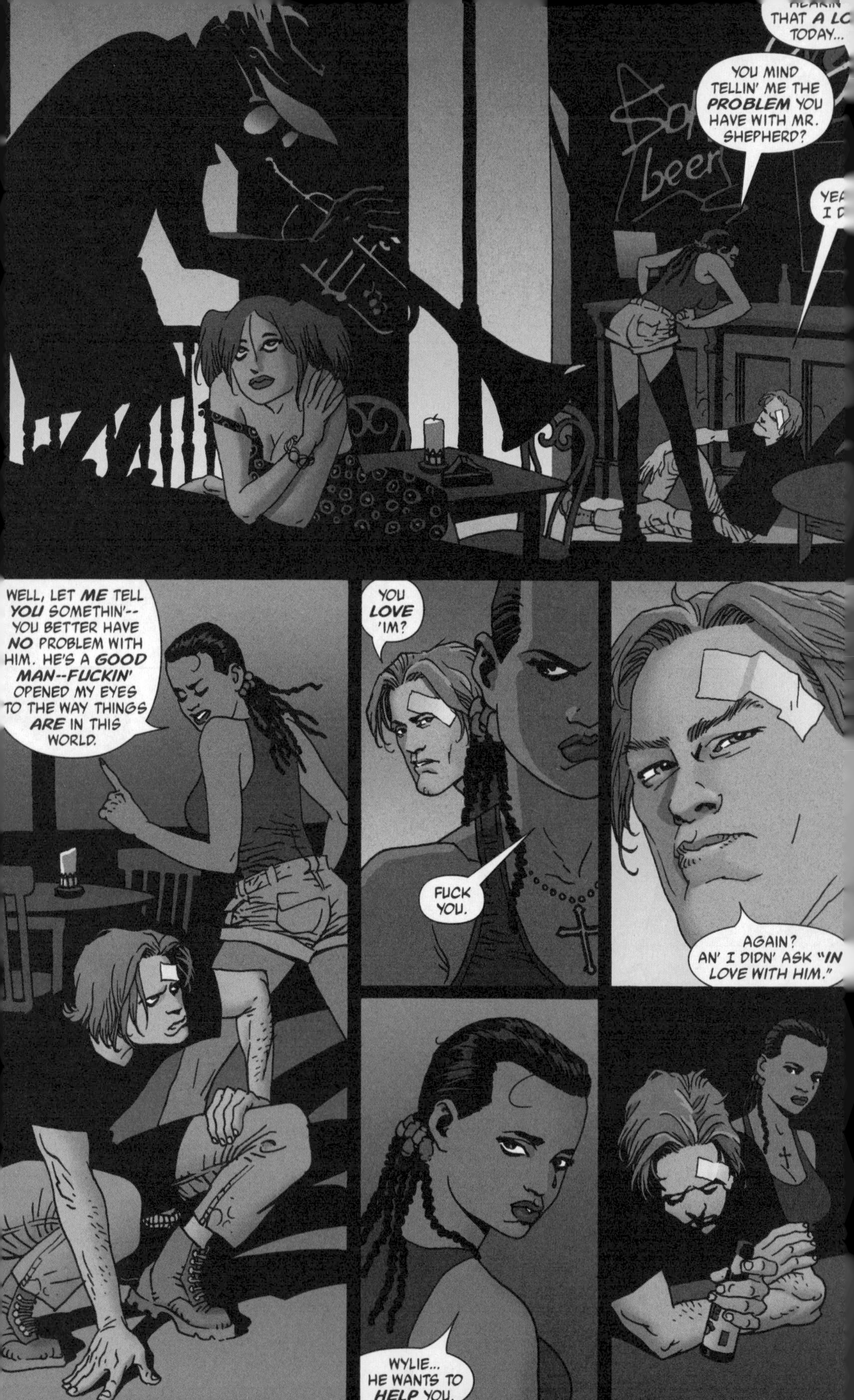
THAT A LO TODAY...
YOU MIND TELLIN' ME THE PROBLEM YOU HAVE WITH MR. SHEPHERD?
beer
WELL, LET ME TELL YOU SOMETHIN'-- YOU BETTER HAVE NO PROBLEM WITH HIM. HE'S A GOOD MAN--FUCKIN' OPENED MY EYES TO THE WAY THINGS ARE IN THIS WORLD.
YOU LOVE 'IM?
FUCK YOU.
AGAIN? AN' I DIDN' ASK "IN LOVE WITH HIM."
WYLIE... HE WANTS TO HELP YOU.

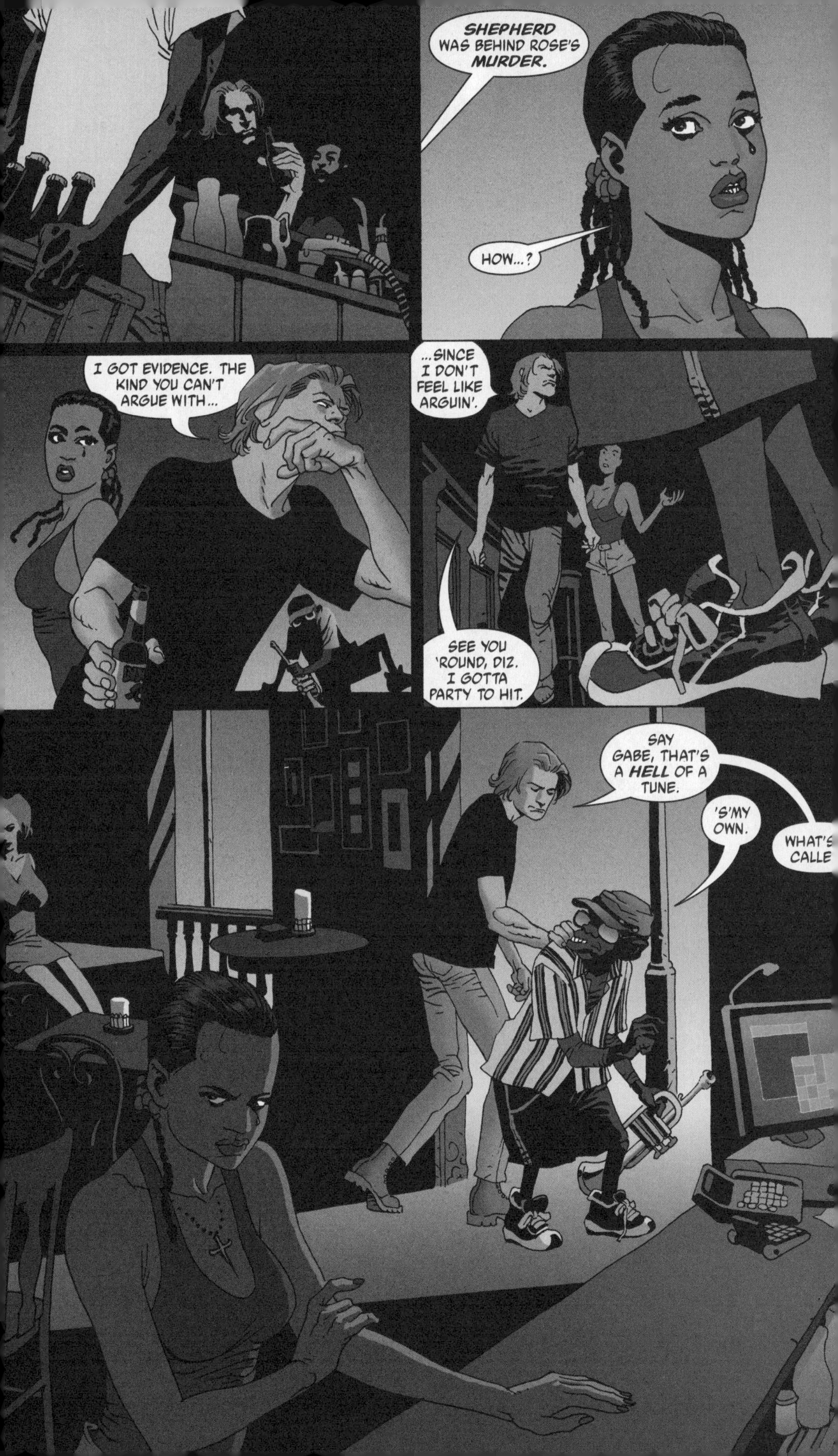
SHEPHERD WAS BEHIND ROSE'S MURDER.
HOW...?
I GOT EVIDENCE. THE KIND YOU CAN'T ARGUE WITH...
...SINCE I DON'T FEEL LIKE ARGUIN'.
SEE YOU 'ROUND, DIZ. I GOTTA PARTY TO HIT.
SAY GABE, THAT'S A HELL OF A TUNE.
'S'MY OWN.
WHAT'S CALLE

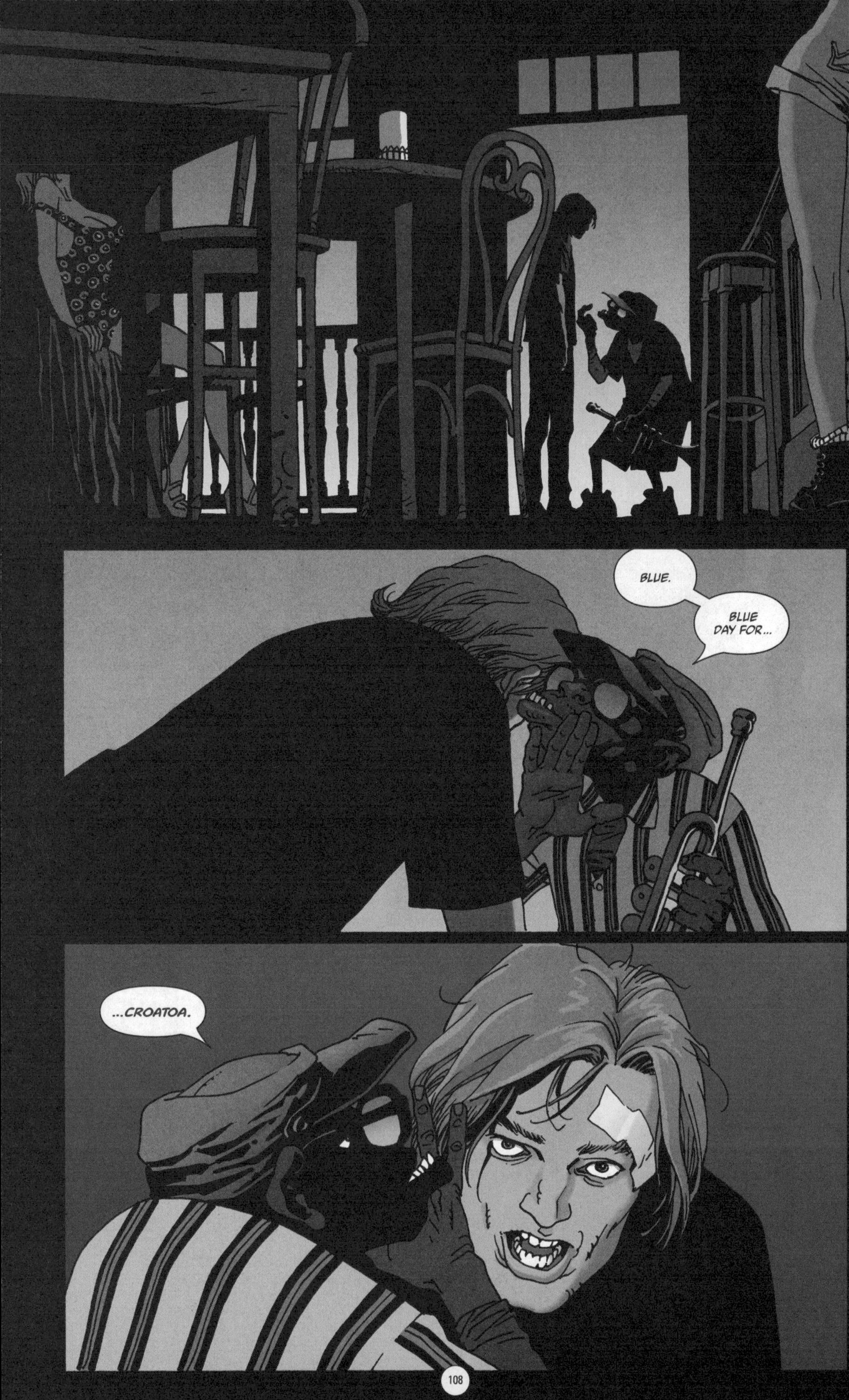
BLUE.
BLUE DAY FOR...
...CROATOA.

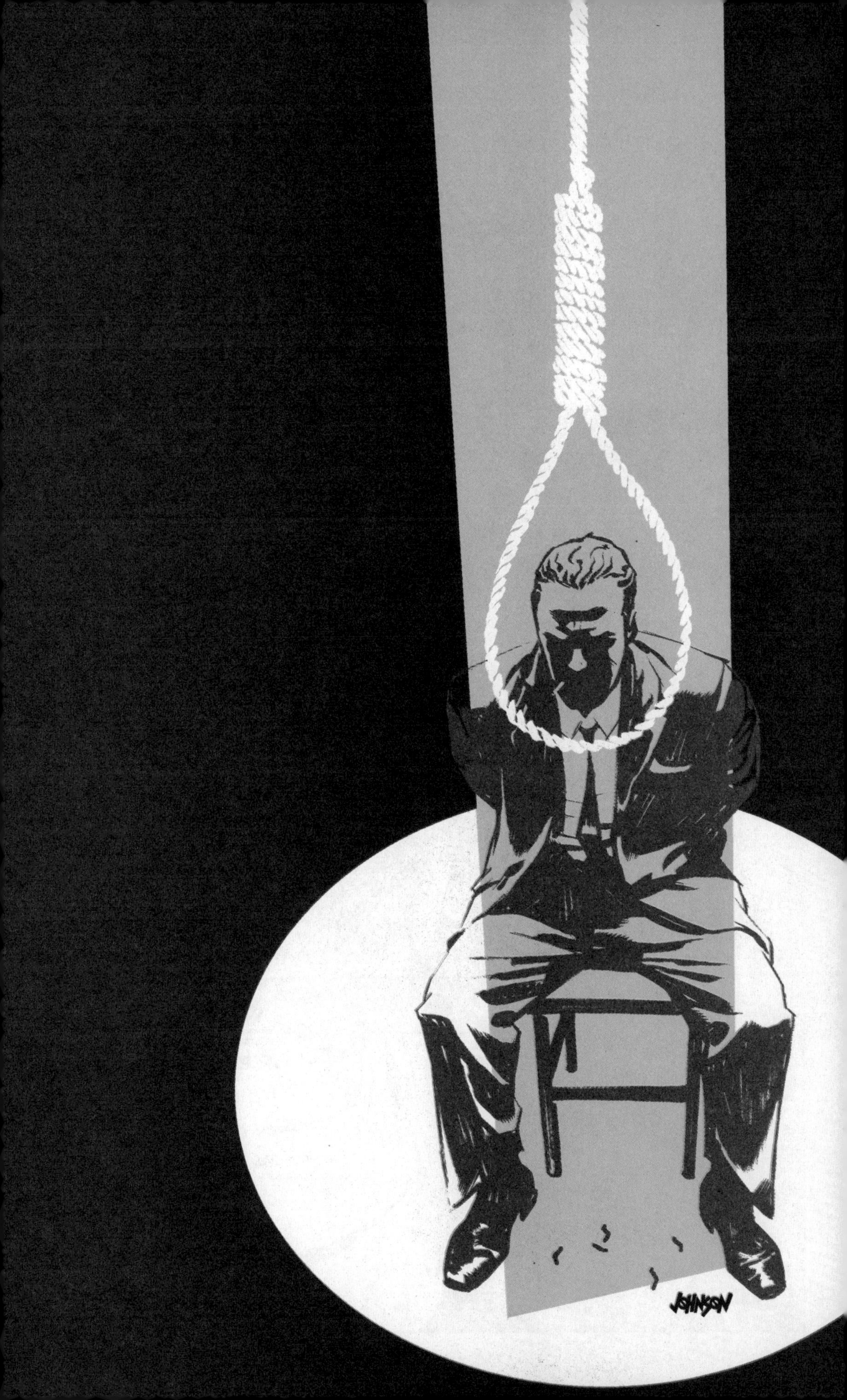
JOHNSON

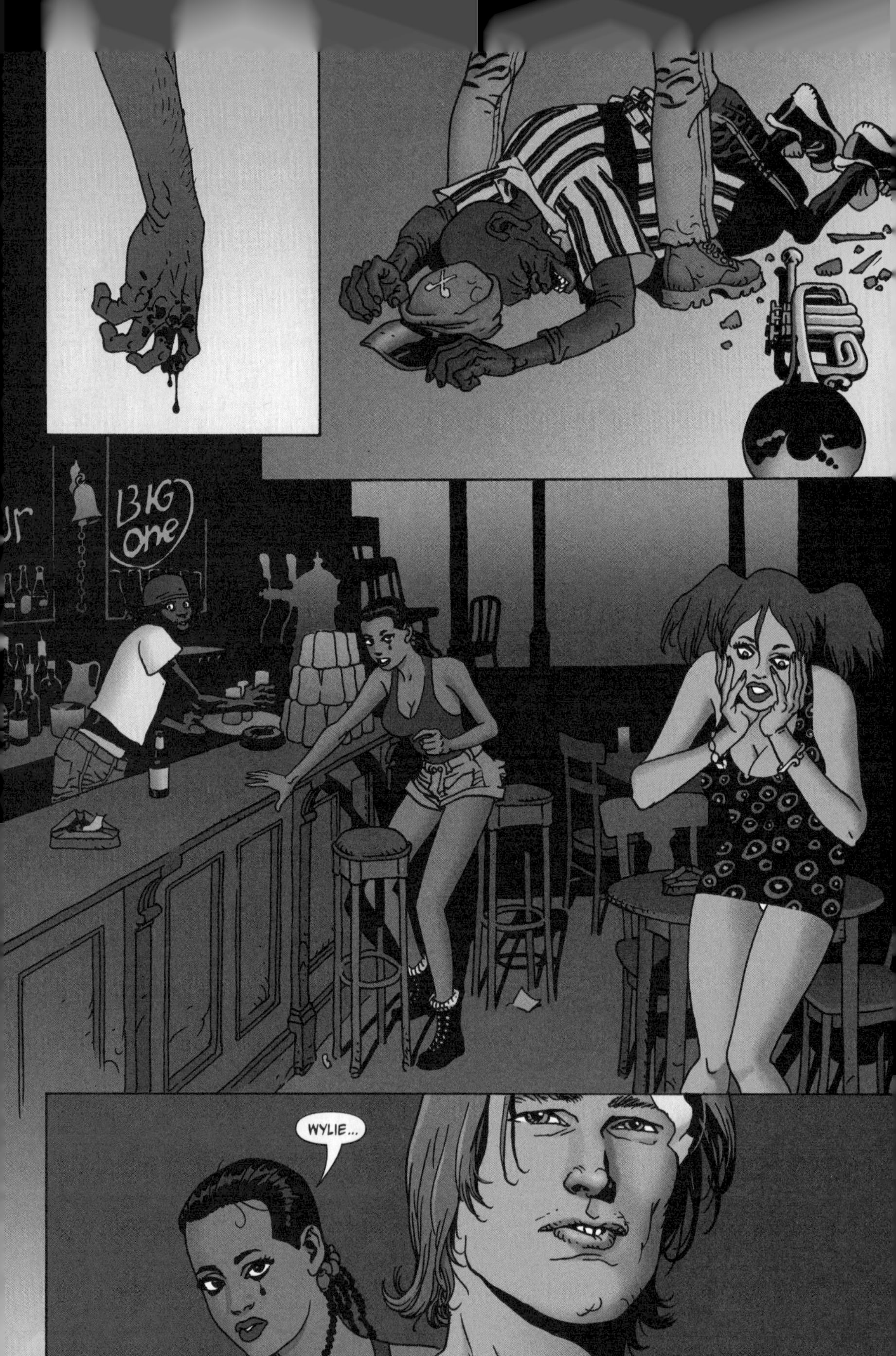
BIG one
WYLIE...

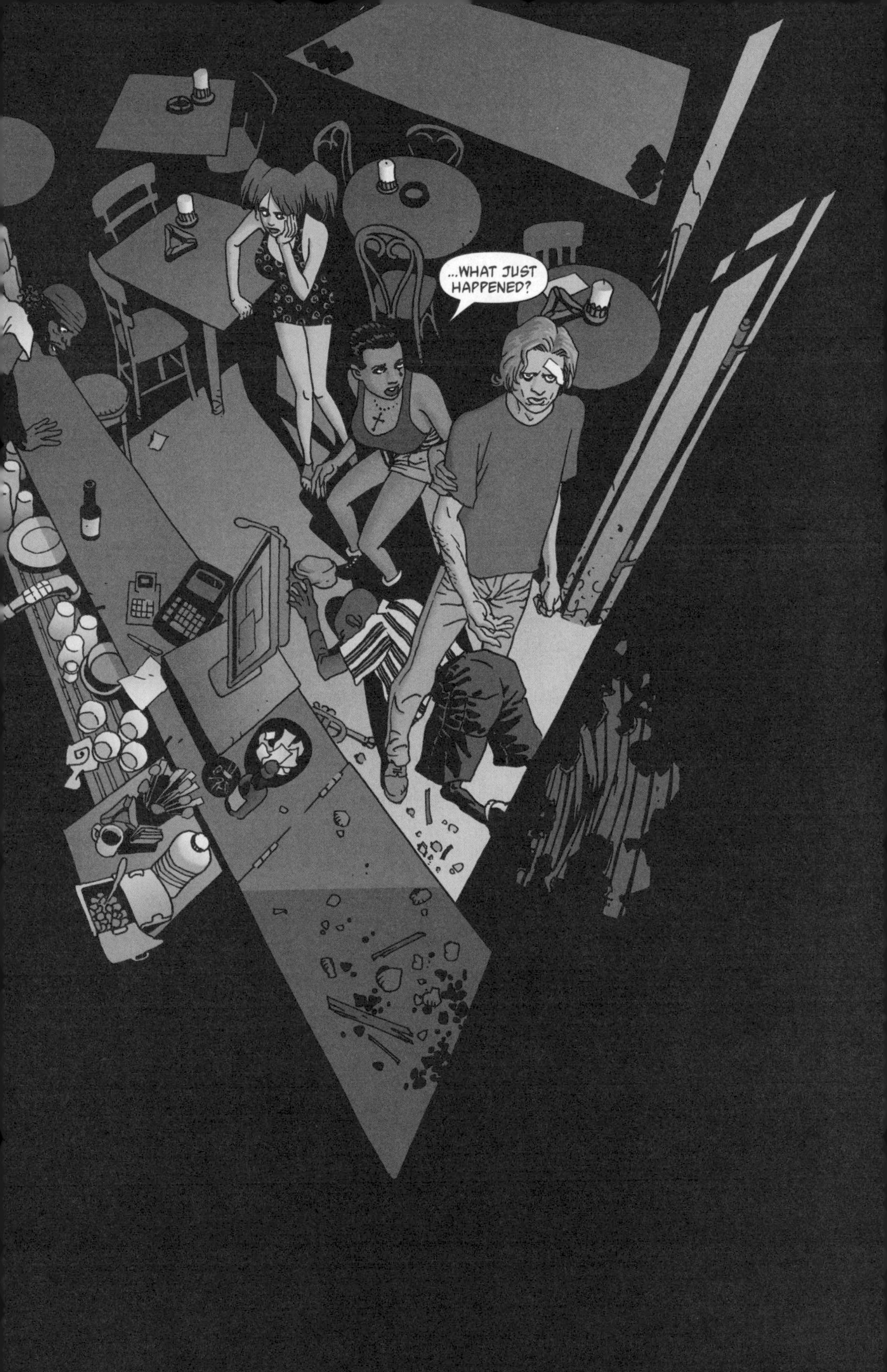
...WHAT JUST HAPPENED?

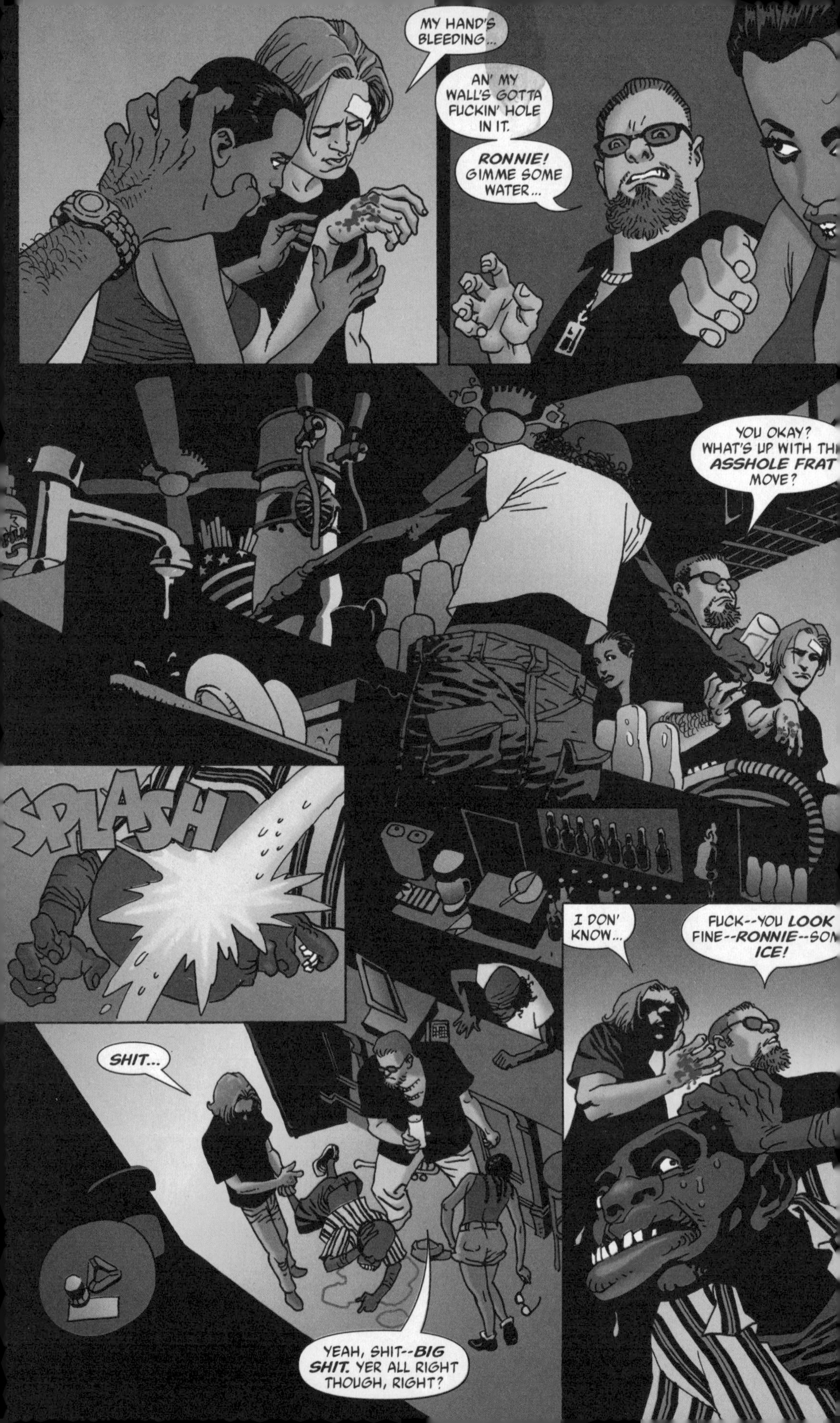

MY HAND'S BLEEDING...
AN' MY WALL'S GOTTA FUCKIN' HOLE IN IT.
RONNIE! GIMME SOME WATER...
YOU OKAY? WHAT'S UP WITH TH ASSHOLE FRAT MOVE?
SPLASH
I DON' KNOW...
FUCK--YOU LOOK FINE--RONNIE--SOM ICE!
SHIT...
YEAH, SHIT--BIG SHIT. YER ALL RIGHT THOUGH, RIGHT?

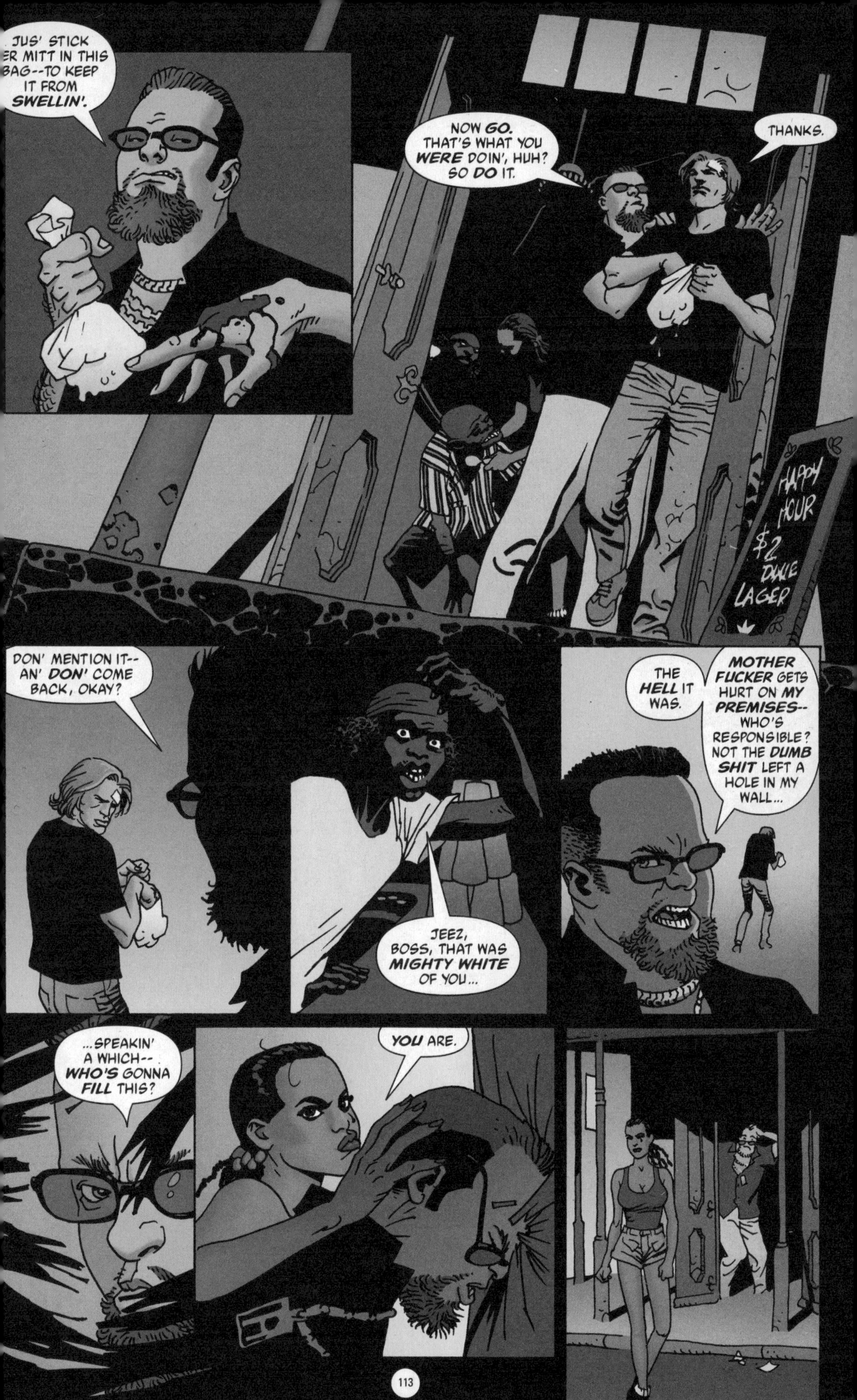
JUS' STICK
ER MITT IN THIS
BAG--TO KEEP
IT FROM
SWELLIN'.
NOW GO. THAT'S WHAT YOU WERE DOIN', HUH? SO DO IT.
THANKS.
HAPPY HOUR $2 DIXIE LAGER
DON' MENTION IT-- AN' DON' COME BACK, OKAY?
JEEZ, BOSS, THAT WAS MIGHTY WHITE OF YOU...
THE HELL IT WAS.
MOTHER FUCKER GETS HURT ON MY PREMISES-- WHO'S RESPONSIBLE? NOT THE DUMB SHIT LEFT A HOLE IN MY WALL...
...SPEAKIN' A WHICH-- WHO'S GONNA FILL THIS?
YOU ARE.

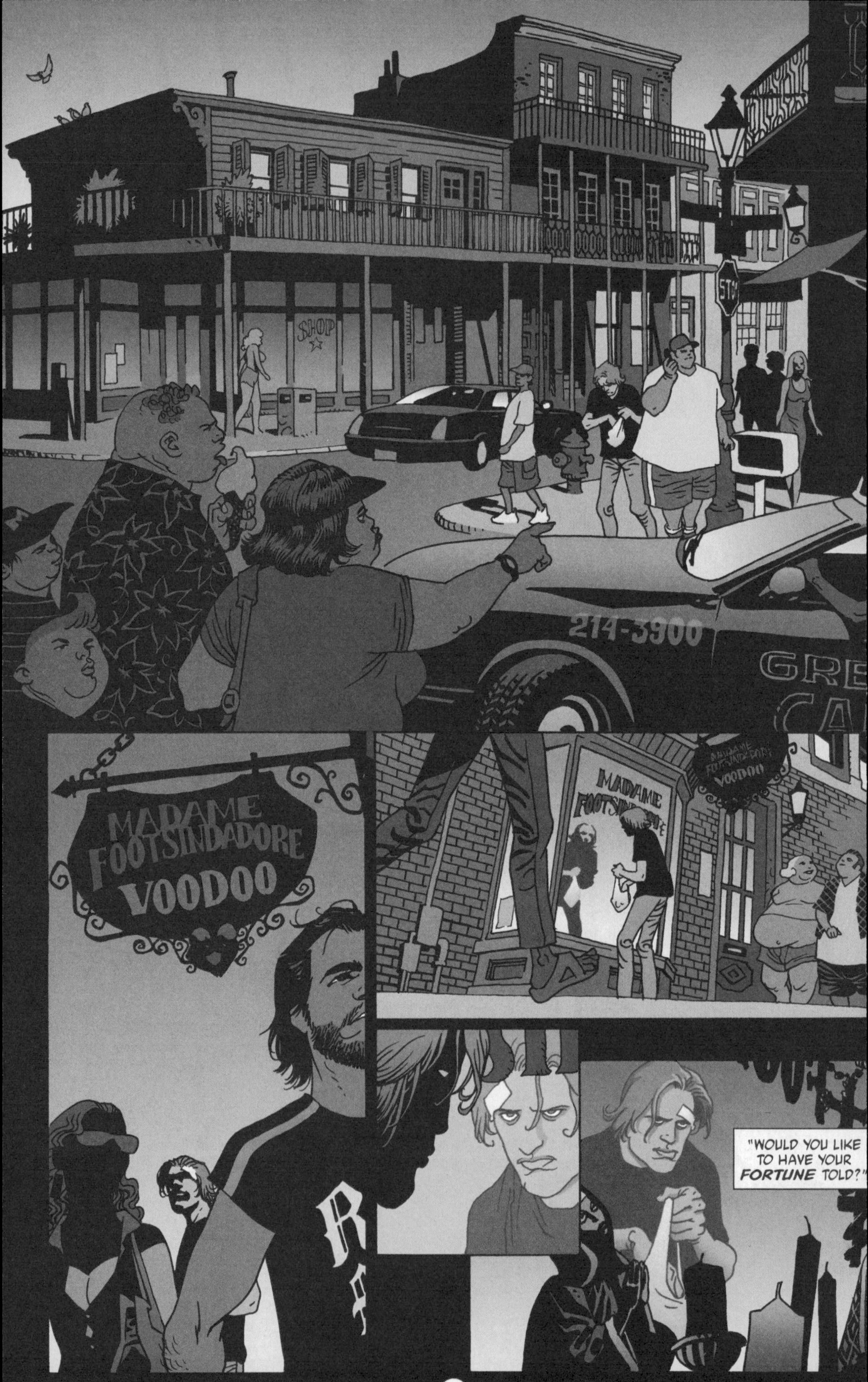

SHOP
214-3900
MADAME FOOTSINDADORE VOODOO
"WOULD YOU LIKE TO HAVE YOUR FORTUNE TOLD?"

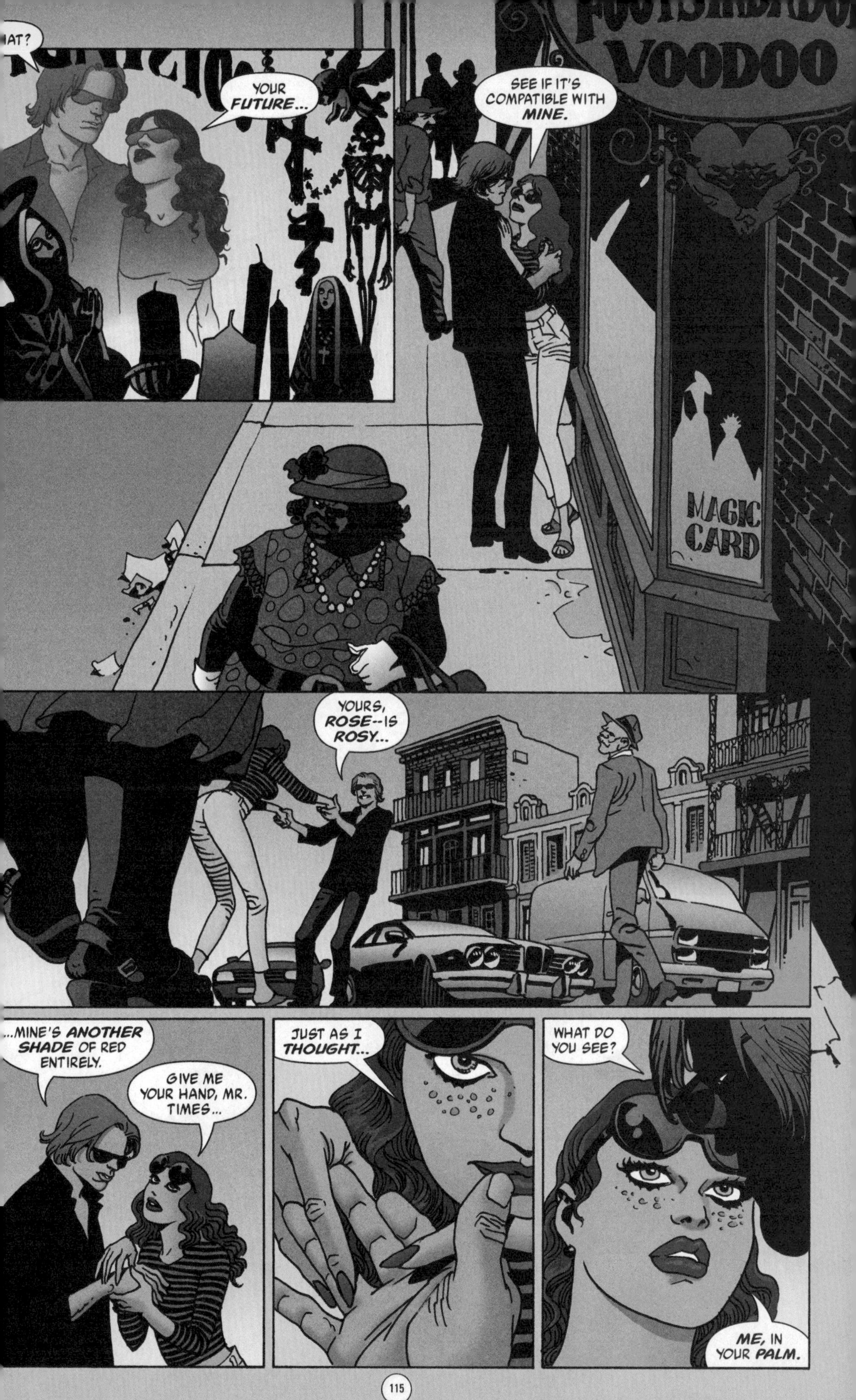

...HAT?
YOUR FUTURE...
SEE IF IT'S COMPATIBLE WITH MINE.
VOODOO
MAGIC CARD
YOURS, ROSE--IS ROSY...
...MINE'S ANOTHER SHADE OF RED ENTIRELY.
GIVE ME YOUR HAND, MR. TIMES...
JUST AS I THOUGHT...
WHAT DO YOU SEE?
ME, IN YOUR PALM.

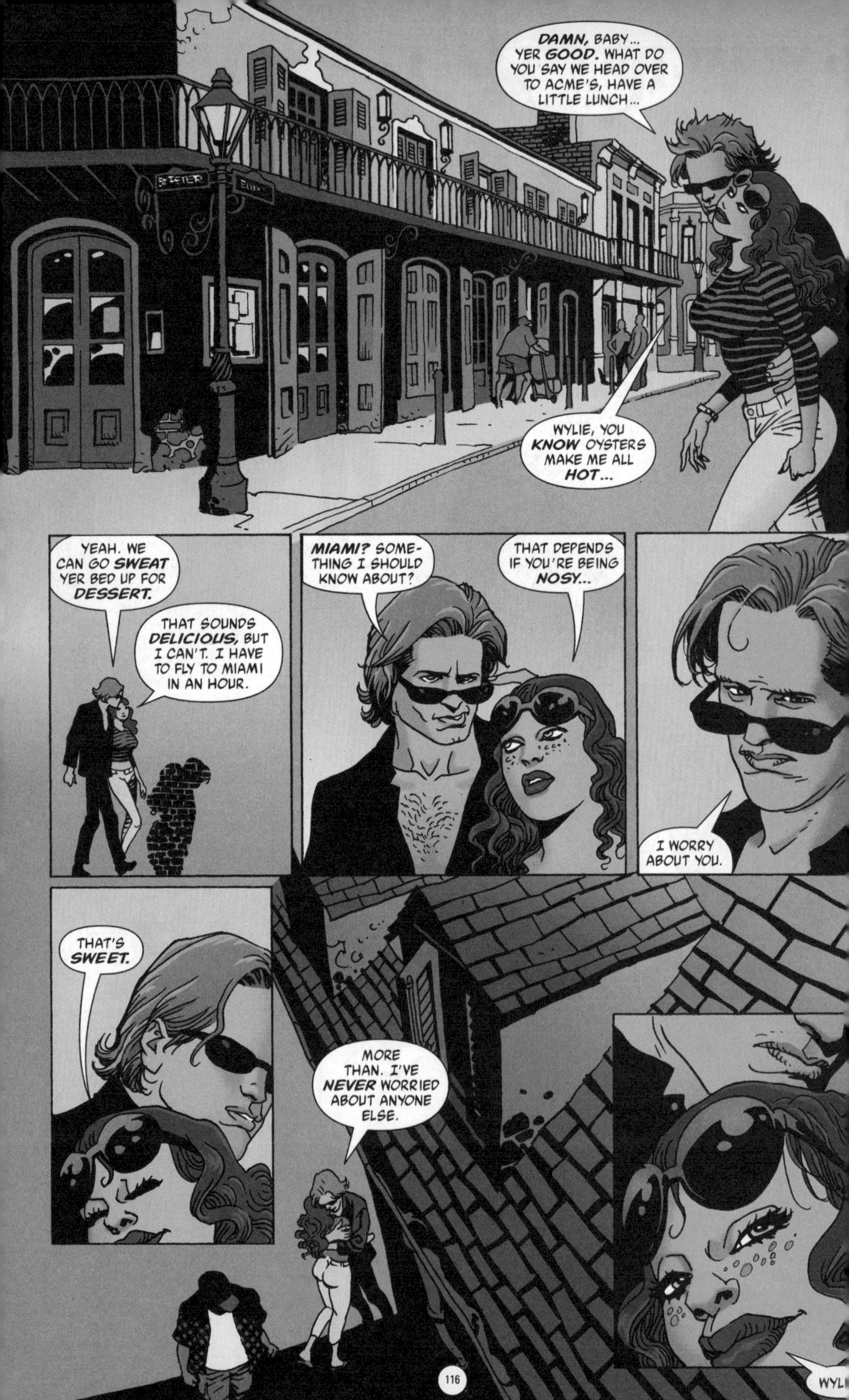

ST PETER
DAMN, BABY... YER GOOD. WHAT DO YOU SAY WE HEAD OVER TO ACME'S, HAVE A LITTLE LUNCH...
WYLIE, YOU KNOW OYSTERS MAKE ME ALL HOT...
YEAH. WE CAN GO SWEAT YER BED UP FOR DESSERT.
THAT SOUNDS DELICIOUS, BUT I CAN'T. I HAVE TO FLY TO MIAMI IN AN HOUR.
MIAMI? SOMETHING I SHOULD KNOW ABOUT?
THAT DEPENDS IF YOU'RE BEING NOSY...
I WORRY ABOUT YOU.
THAT'S SWEET.
MORE THAN. I'VE NEVER WORRIED ABOUT ANYONE ELSE.
WYL

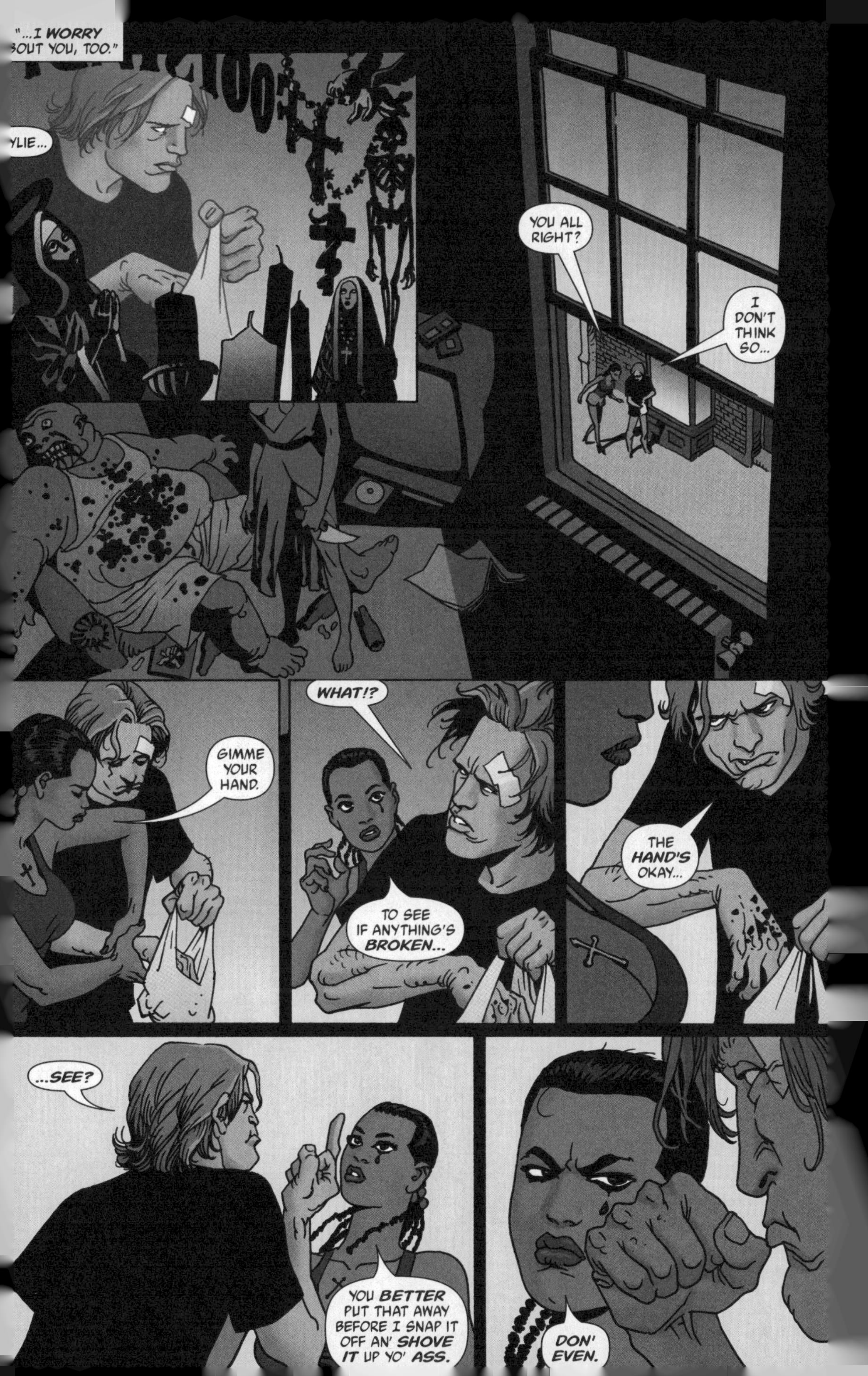
"...I WORRY
BOUT YOU, TOO."
YLIE...
YOU ALL RIGHT?
I DON'T THINK SO...
GIMME YOUR HAND.
WHAT!?
TO SEE IF ANYTHING'S BROKEN...
THE HAND'S OKAY...
...SEE?
YOU BETTER PUT THAT AWAY BEFORE I SNAP IT OFF AN' SHOVE IT UP YO' ASS.
DON' EVEN.

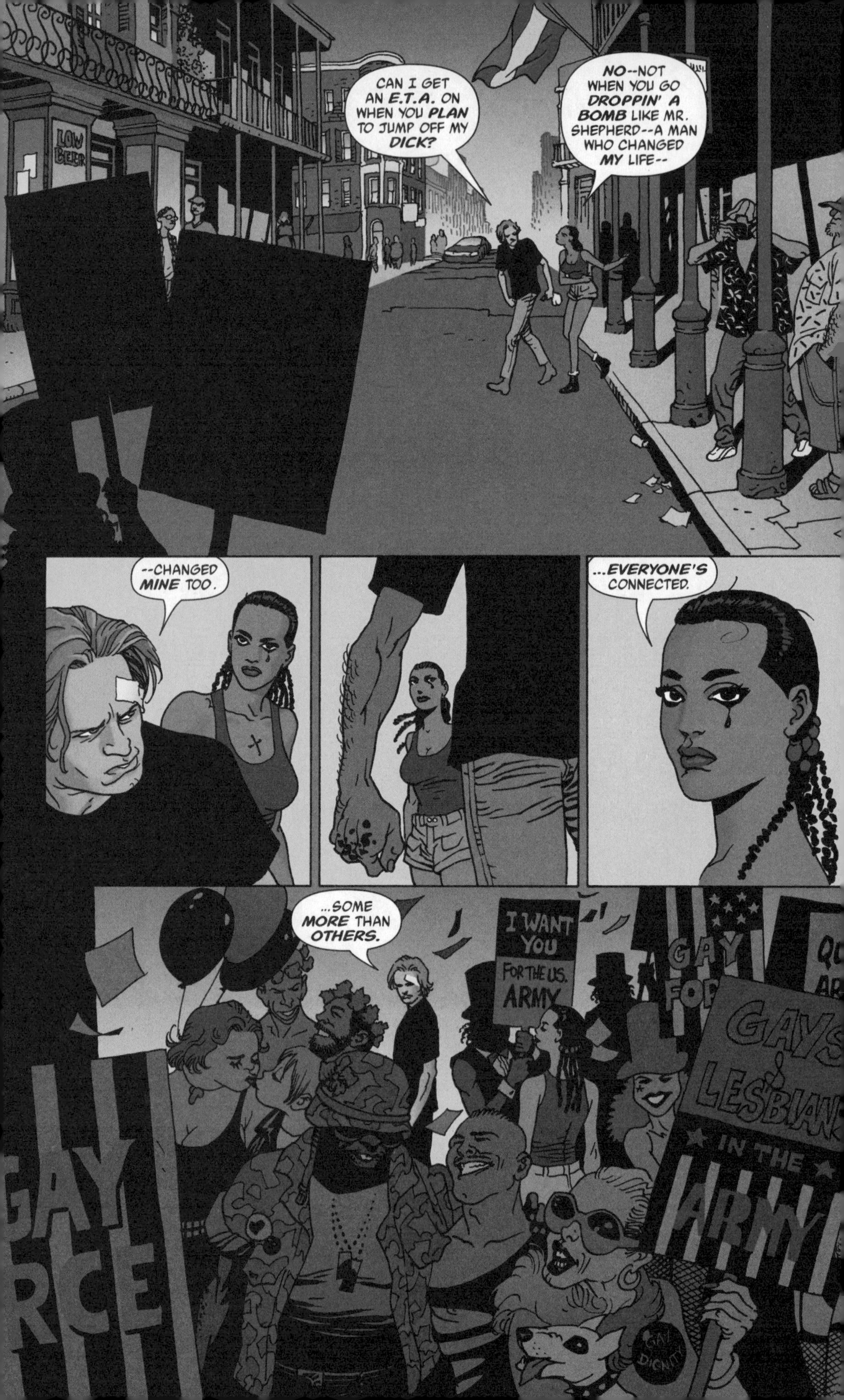
LOW BEER
CAN I GET AN E.T.A. ON WHEN YOU PLAN TO JUMP OFF MY DICK?
NO--NOT WHEN YOU GO DROPPIN' A BOMB LIKE MR. SHEPHERD--A MAN WHO CHANGED MY LIFE--
--CHANGED MINE TOO.
...EVERYONE'S CONNECTED.
...SOME MORE THAN OTHERS.
I WANT YOU FOR THE U.S. ARMY
GAYS & LESBIANS IN THE ARMY
GAY DIGNITY

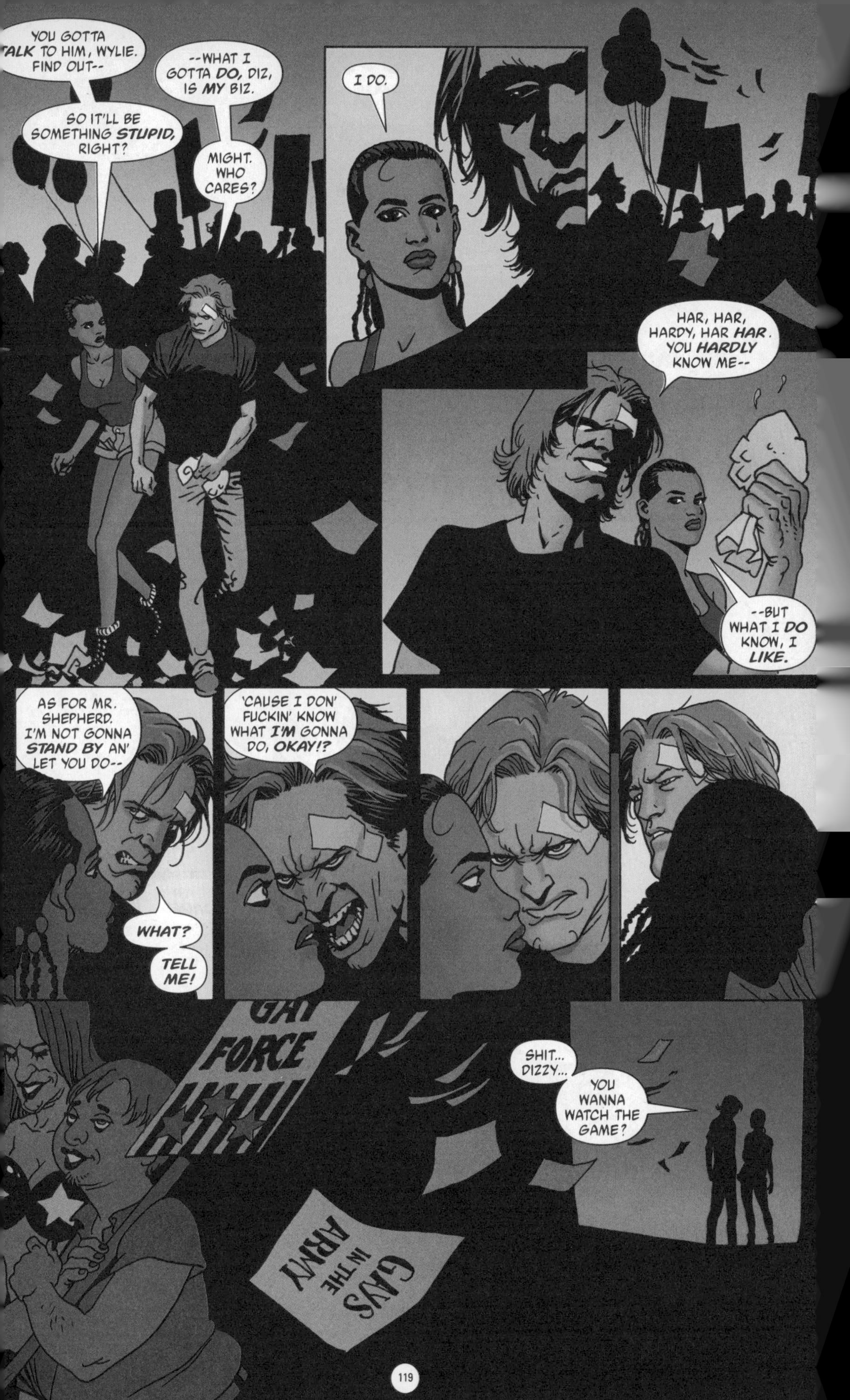

YOU GOTTA TALK TO HIM, WYLIE. FIND OUT--
SO IT'LL BE SOMETHING STUPID, RIGHT?
--WHAT I GOTTA DO, DIZ, IS MY BIZ.
MIGHT. WHO CARES?
I DO.
HAR, HAR, HARDY, HAR HAR. YOU HARDLY KNOW ME--
--BUT WHAT I DO KNOW, I LIKE.
AS FOR MR. SHEPHERD. I'M NOT GONNA STAND BY AN' LET YOU DO--
WHAT?
TELL ME!
'CAUSE I DON' FUCKIN' KNOW WHAT I'M GONNA DO, OKAY!?
GAY FORCE
SHIT... DIZZY...
YOU WANNA WATCH THE GAME?
GAYS IN THE ARMY

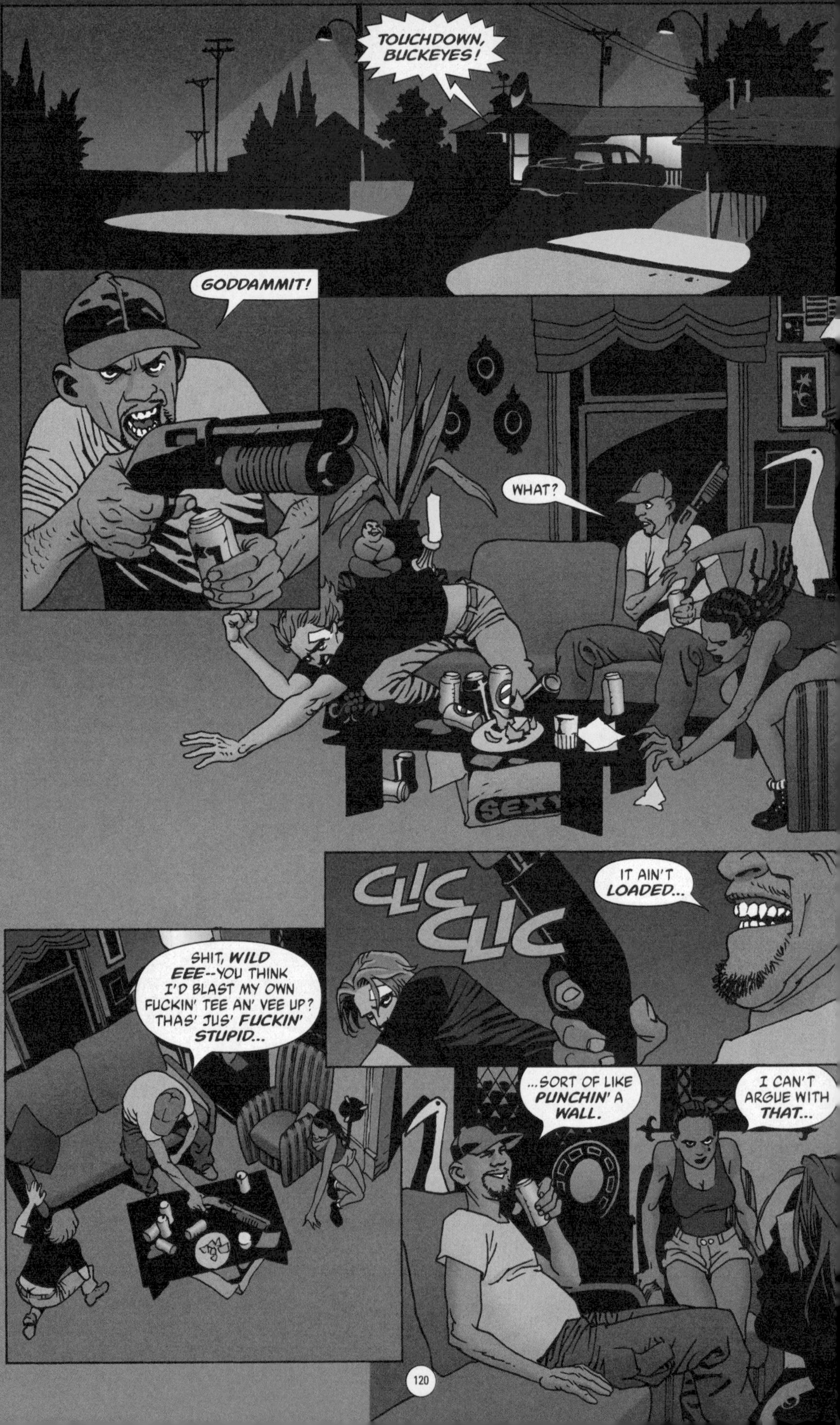
TOUCHDOWN, BUCKEYES!
GODDAMMIT!
WHAT?
CLIC CLIC
IT AIN'T LOADED...
SHIT, WILD EEE--YOU THINK I'D BLAST MY OWN FUCKIN' TEE AN' VEE UP? THAS' JUS' FUCKIN' STUPID...
...SORT OF LIKE PUNCHIN' A WALL.
I CAN'T ARGUE WITH THAT...

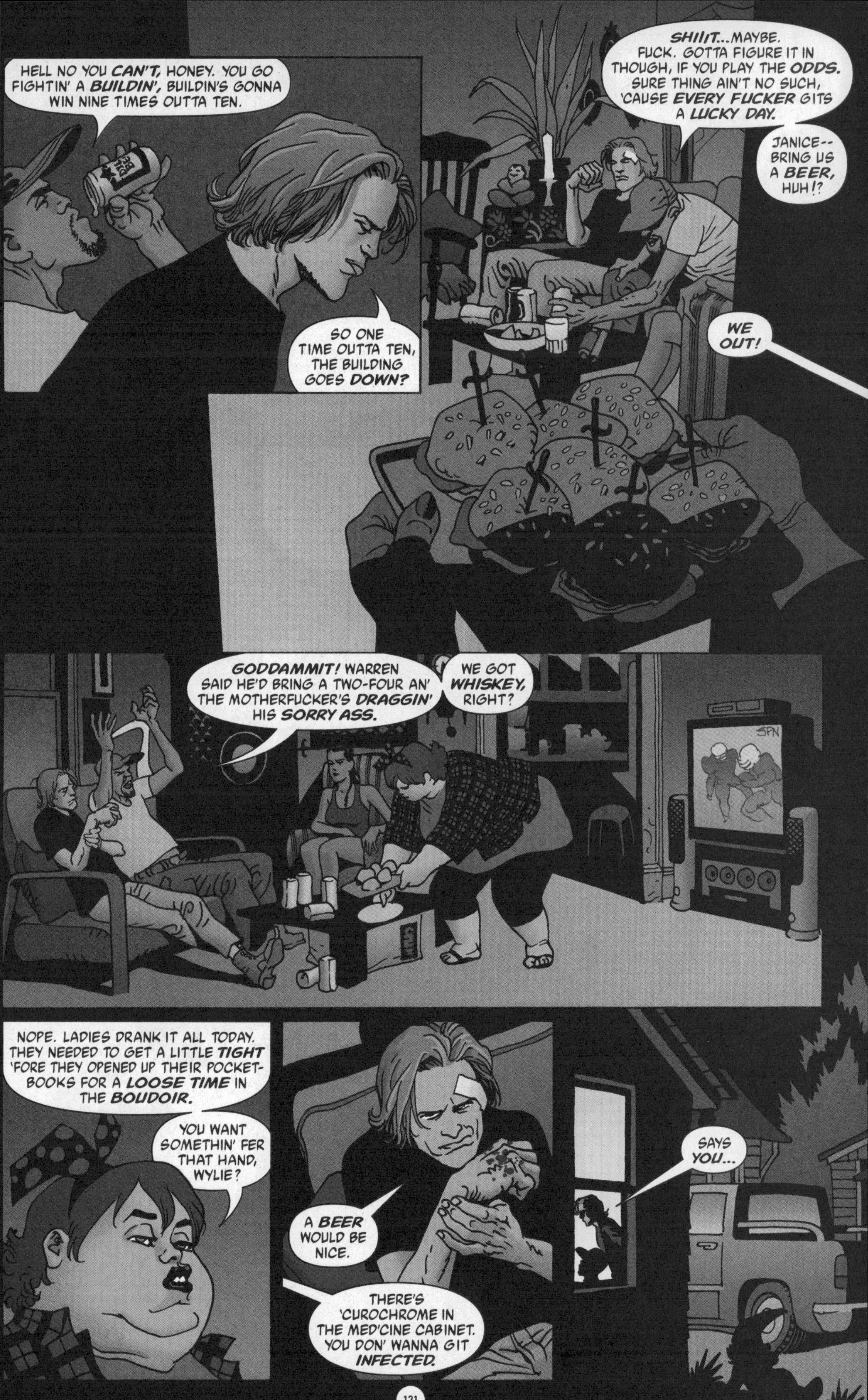
HELL NO YOU CAN'T, HONEY. YOU GO FIGHTIN' A BUILDIN', BUILDIN'S GONNA WIN NINE TIMES OUTTA TEN.
SO ONE TIME OUTTA TEN, THE BUILDING GOES DOWN?
SHII!T... MAYBE. FUCK. GOTTA FIGURE IT IN THOUGH, IF YOU PLAY THE ODDS. SURE THING AIN'T NO SUCH, 'CAUSE EVERY FUCKER GITS A LUCKY DAY.
JANICE-- BRING US A BEER, HUH!?
WE OUT!
GODDAMMIT! WARREN SAID HE'D BRING A TWO-FOUR AN' THE MOTHERFUCKER'S DRAGGIN' HIS SORRY ASS.
WE GOT WHISKEY, RIGHT?
SPN
NOPE. LADIES DRANK IT ALL TODAY. THEY NEEDED TO GET A LITTLE TIGHT 'FORE THEY OPENED UP THEIR POCKETBOOKS FOR A LOOSE TIME IN THE BOUDOIR.
YOU WANT SOMETHIN' FER THAT HAND, WYLIE?
A BEER WOULD BE NICE.
THERE'S 'CUROCHROME IN THE MED'CINE CABINET. YOU DON' WANNA GIT INFECTED.
SAYS YOU...

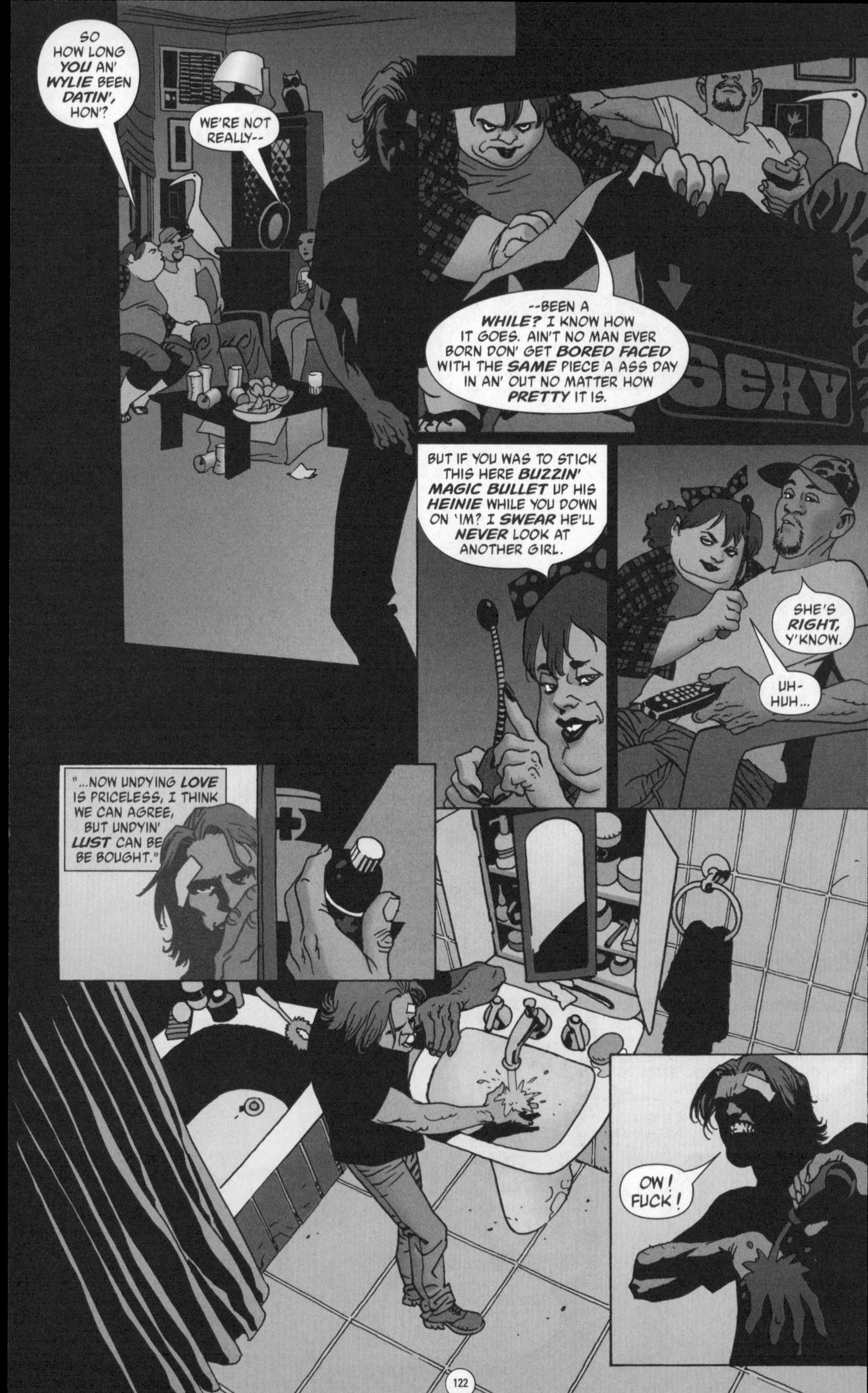

SO HOW LONG YOU AN' WYLIE BEEN DATIN', HON'?
WE'RE NOT REALLY--
--BEEN A WHILE? I KNOW HOW IT GOES. AIN'T NO MAN EVER BORN DON' GET BORED FACED WITH THE SAME PIECE A ASS DAY IN AN' OUT NO MATTER HOW PRETTY IT IS.
SEXY
BUT IF YOU WAS TO STICK THIS HERE BUZZIN' MAGIC BULLET UP HIS HEINIE WHILE YOU DOWN ON 'IM? I SWEAR HE'LL NEVER LOOK AT ANOTHER GIRL.
SHE'S RIGHT, Y'KNOW.
UH-HUH...
"...NOW UNDYING LOVE IS PRICELESS, I THINK WE CAN AGREE, BUT UNDYIN' LUST CAN BE BE BOUGHT."
OW! FUCK!

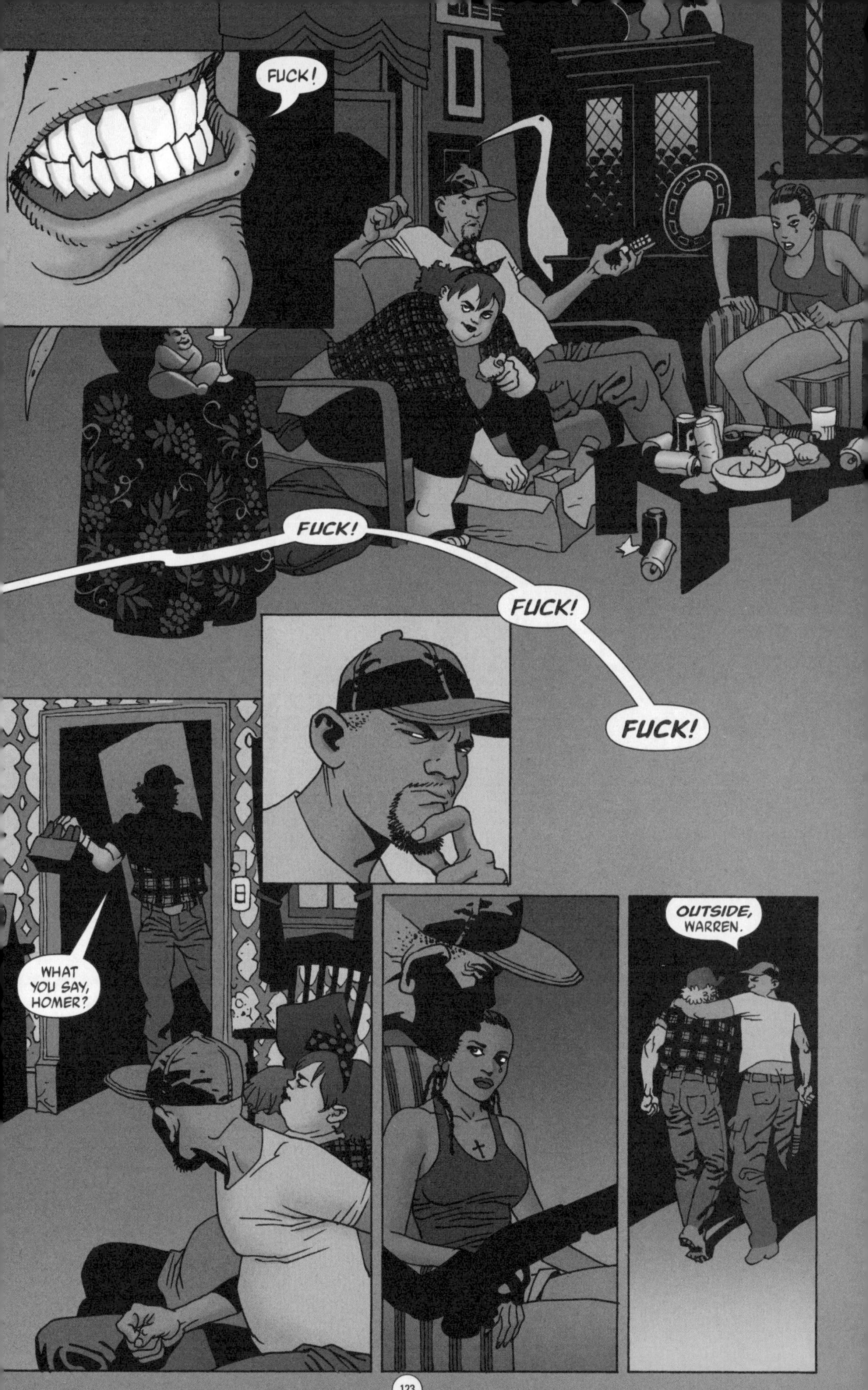
FUCK!
FUCK!
FUCK!
FUCK!
WHAT YOU SAY, HOMER?
OUTSIDE, WARREN.

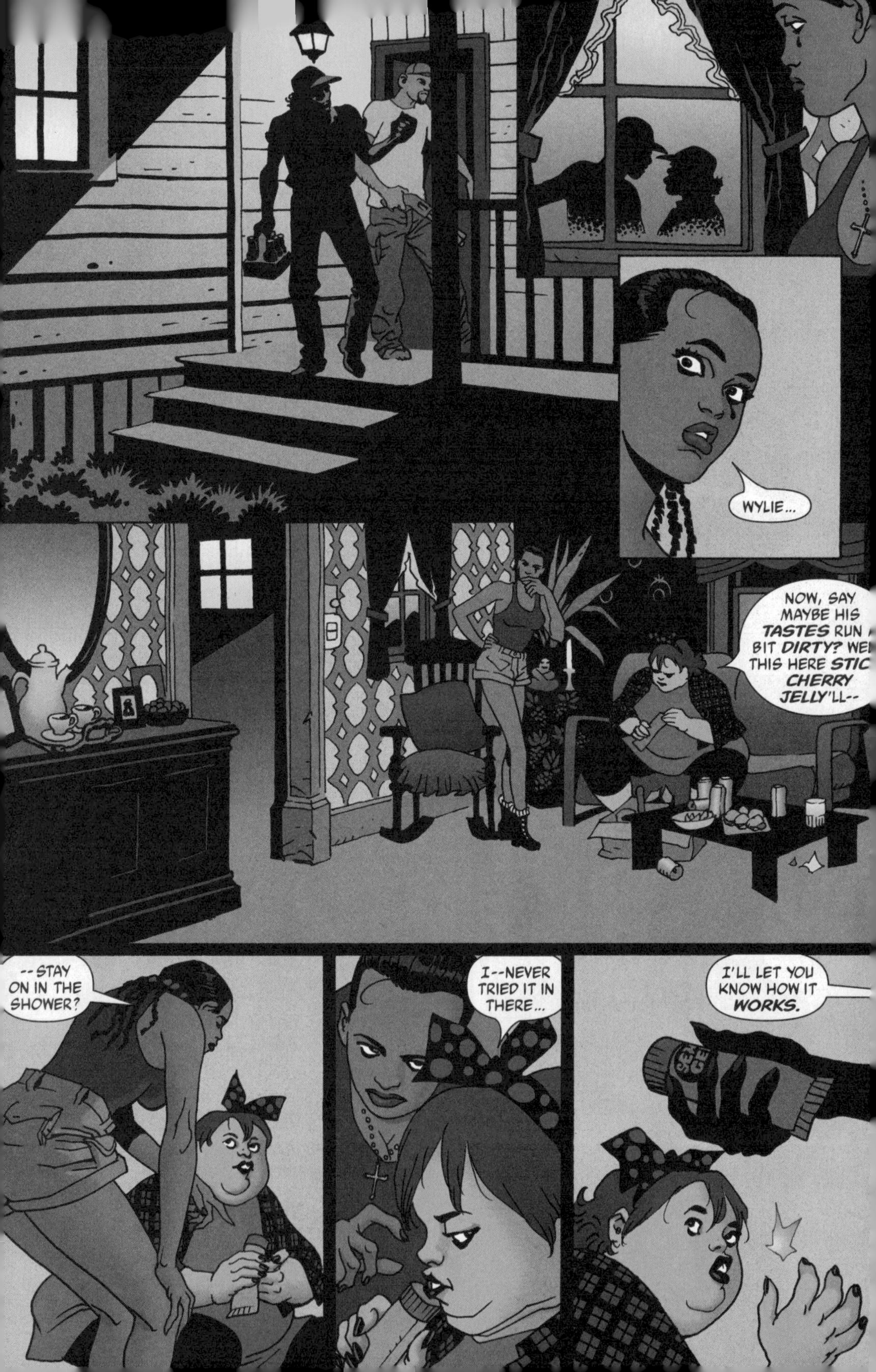
WYLIE...
NOW, SAY MAYBE HIS TASTES RUN A BIT DIRTY? WE THIS HERE STIC CHERRY JELLY'LL--
--STAY ON IN THE SHOWER?
I--NEVER TRIED IT IN THERE...
I'LL LET YOU KNOW HOW IT WORKS.

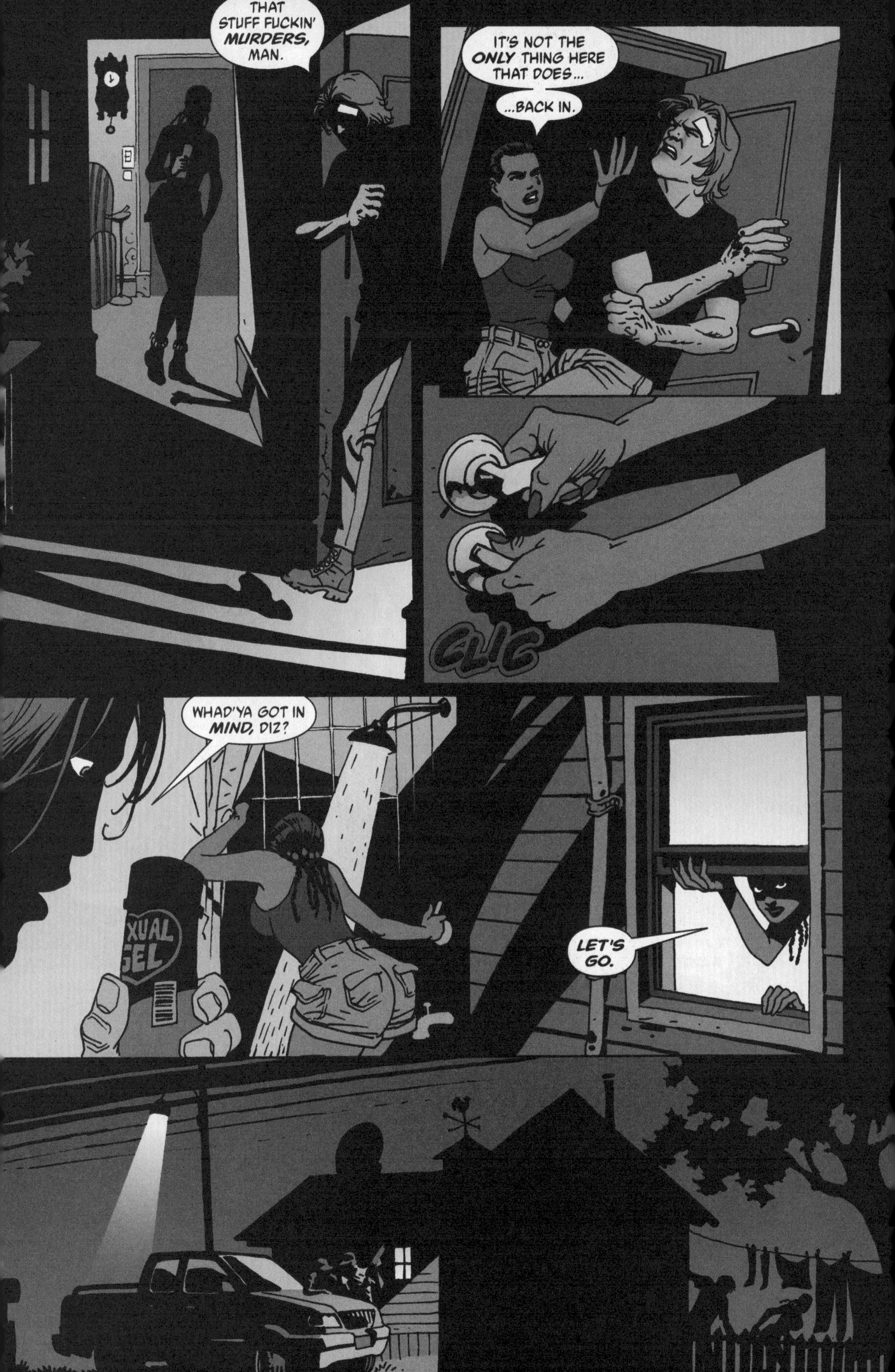
THAT STUFF FUCKIN' MURDERS, MAN.
IT'S NOT THE ONLY THING HERE THAT DOES...
...BACK IN.
CLIC
WHAD'YA GOT IN MIND, DIZ?
XUAL GEL
LET'S GO.

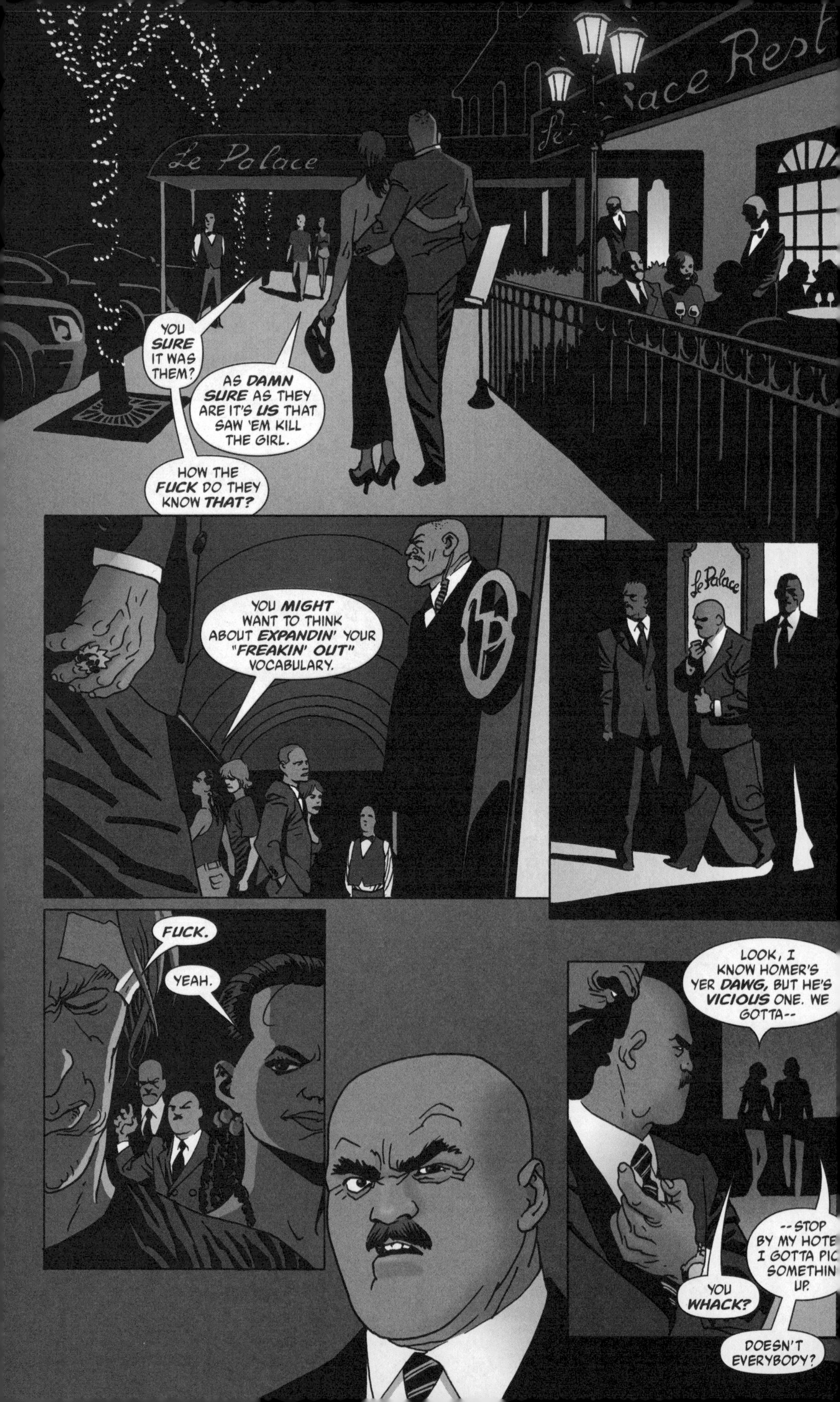
Le Palace
Le Palace Rest
YOU SURE IT WAS THEM?
AS DAMN SURE AS THEY ARE IT'S US THAT SAW 'EM KILL THE GIRL.
HOW THE FUCK DO THEY KNOW THAT?
YOU MIGHT WANT TO THINK ABOUT EXPANDIN' YOUR "FREAKIN' OUT" VOCABULARY.
Le Palace
FUCK.
YEAH.
LOOK, I KNOW HOMER'S YER DAWG, BUT HE'S VICIOUS ONE. WE GOTTA--
--STOP BY MY HOTE I GOTTA PIC SOMETHIN UP.
YOU WHACK?
DOESN'T EVERYBODY?

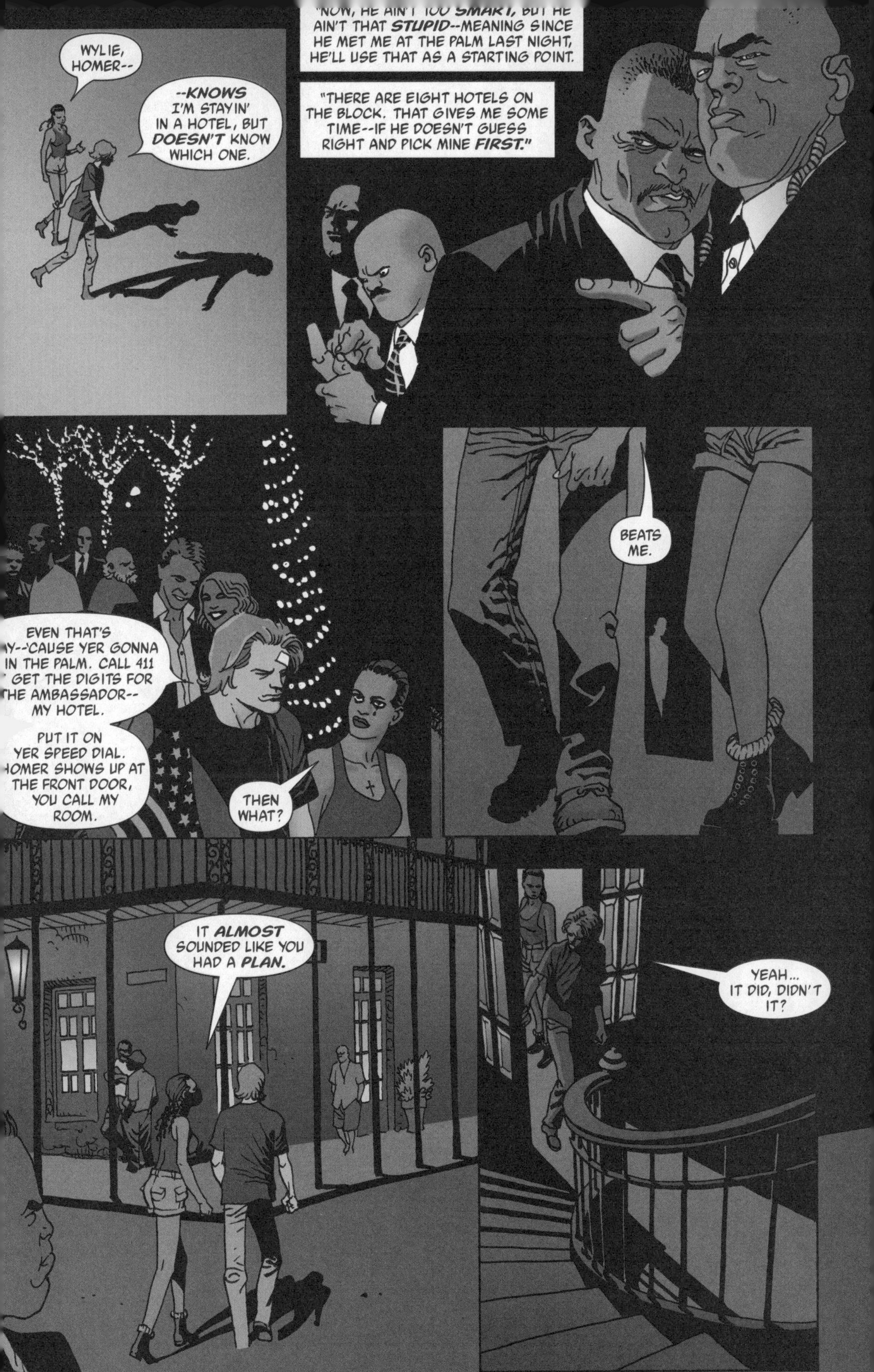

WYLIE, HOMER--
--**KNOWS** I'M STAYIN' IN A HOTEL, BUT **DOESN'T** KNOW WHICH ONE.
"NOW, HE AIN'T TOO **SMART,** BUT HE AIN'T THAT **STUPID**--MEANING SINCE HE MET ME AT THE PALM LAST NIGHT, HE'LL USE THAT AS A STARTING POINT.
"THERE ARE EIGHT HOTELS ON THE BLOCK. THAT GIVES ME SOME TIME--IF HE DOESN'T GUESS RIGHT AND PICK MINE **FIRST.**"
EVEN THAT'S
Y--'CAUSE YER GONNA
IN THE PALM. CALL 411
GET THE DIGITS FOR
HE AMBASSADOR--
MY HOTEL.
PUT IT ON YER SPEED DIAL.
HOMER SHOWS UP AT THE FRONT DOOR, YOU CALL MY ROOM.
THEN WHAT?
BEATS ME.
IT **ALMOST** SOUNDED LIKE YOU HAD A **PLAN.**
YEAH... IT DID, DIDN'T IT?

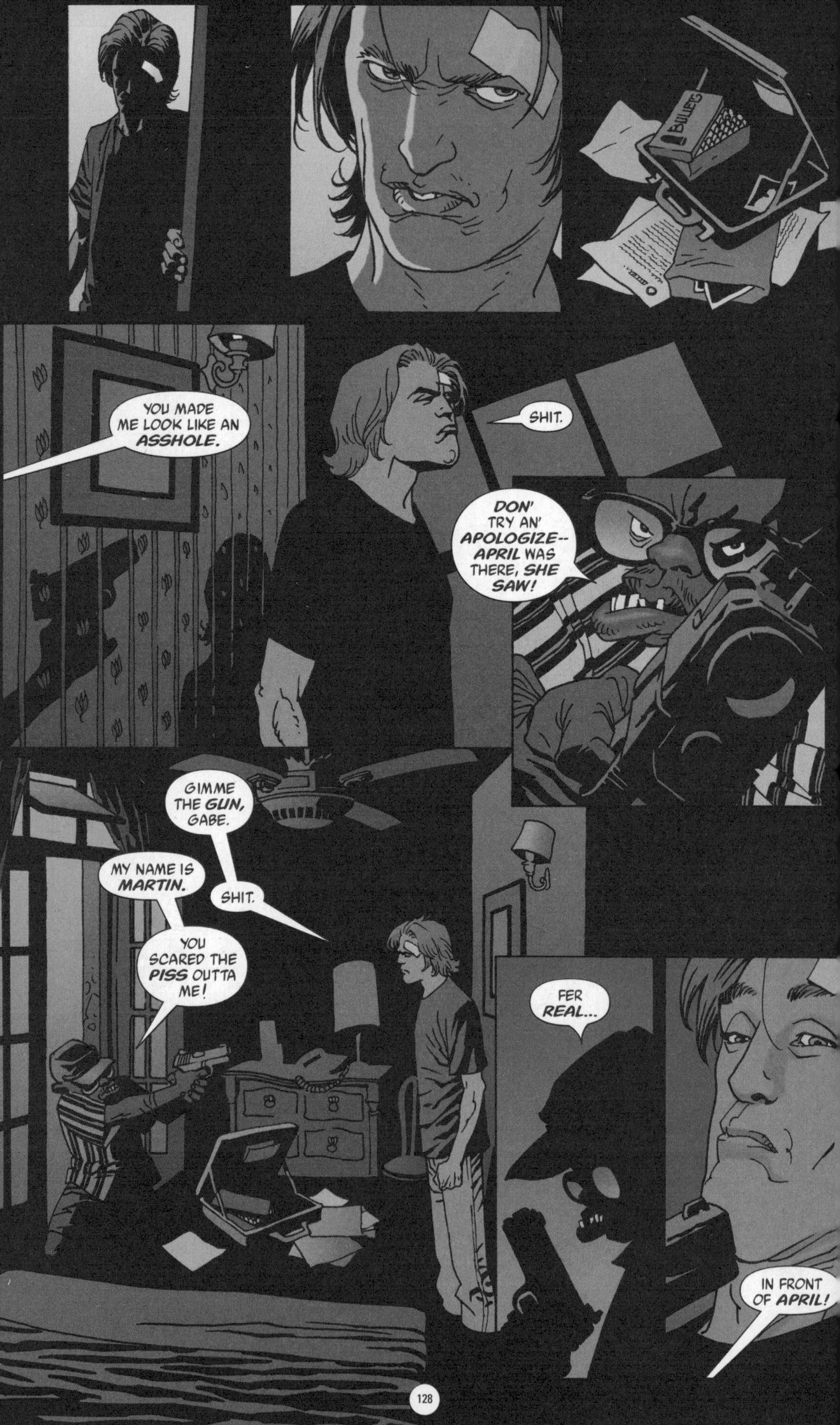
YOU MADE ME LOOK LIKE AN ASSHOLE.
SHIT.
DON' TRY AN' APOLOGIZE-- APRIL WAS THERE, SHE SAW!
GIMME THE GUN, GABE.
MY NAME IS MARTIN.
SHIT.
YOU SCARED THE PISS OUTTA ME!
FER REAL...
IN FRONT OF APRIL!

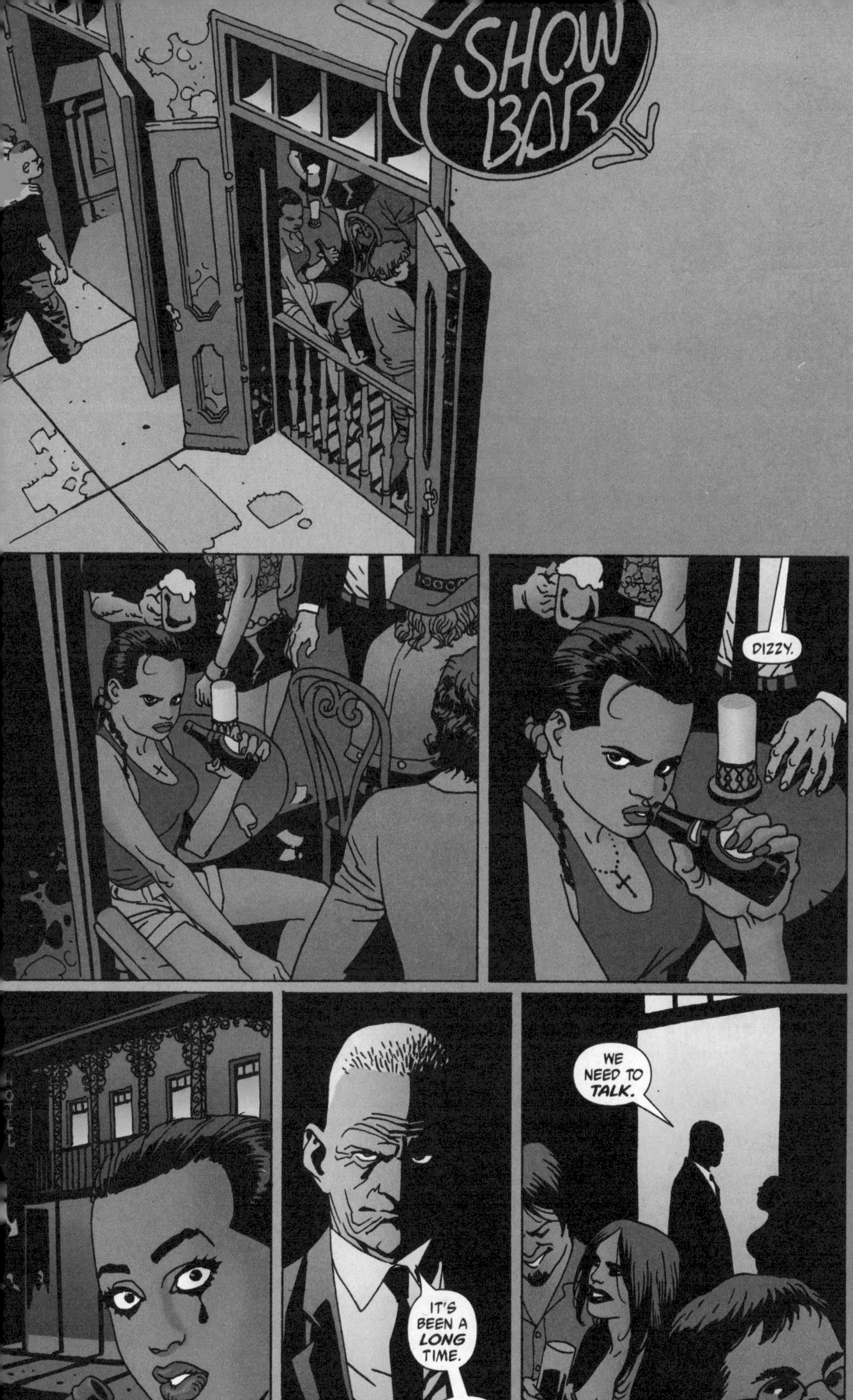
SHOW BAR
DIZZY.
IT'S BEEN A LONG TIME.
TOO LONG.
WE NEED TO TALK.

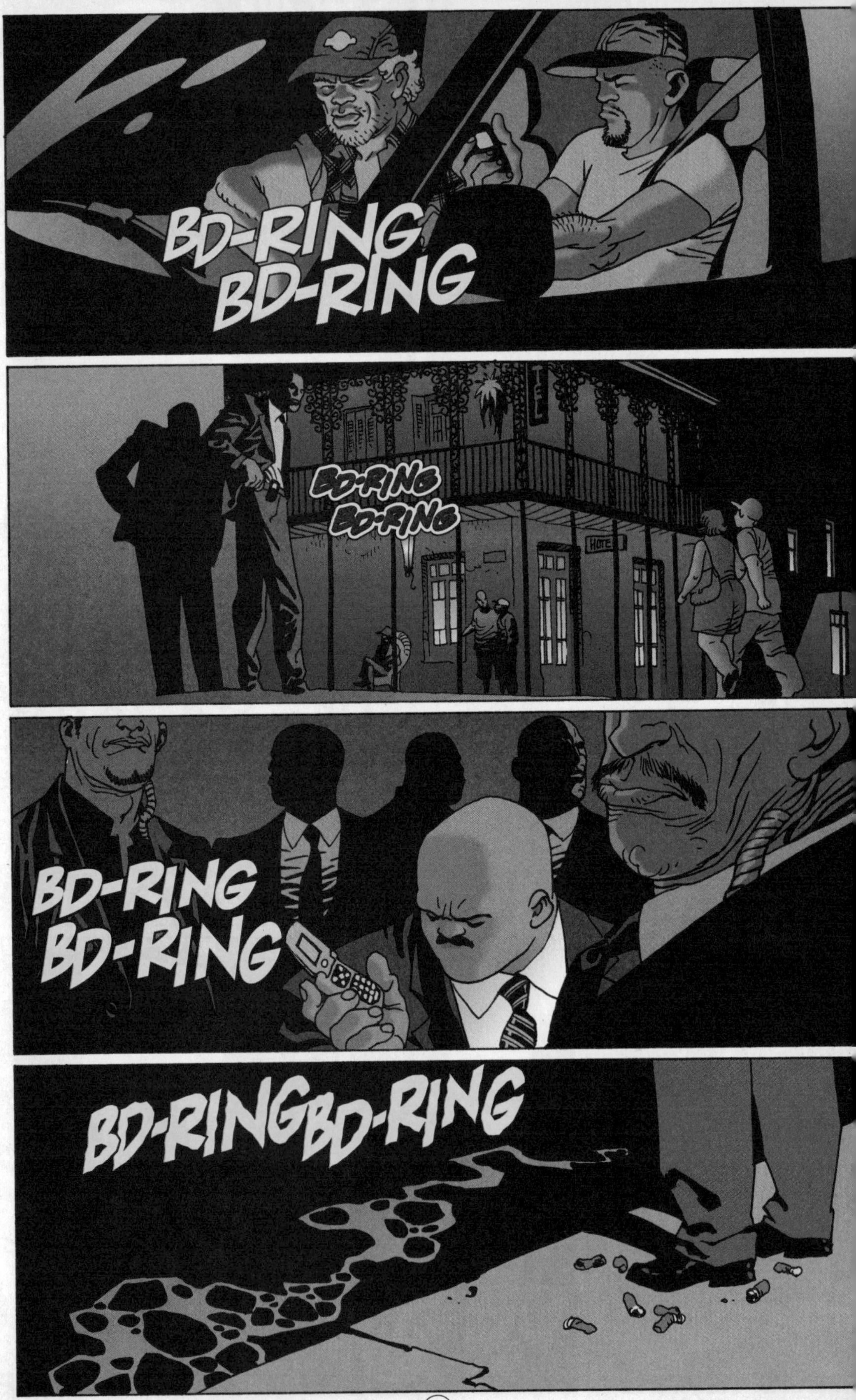
BD-RING
BD-RING
BD-RING
BD-RING
HOTE
BD-RING
BD-RING
BD-RINGBD-RING

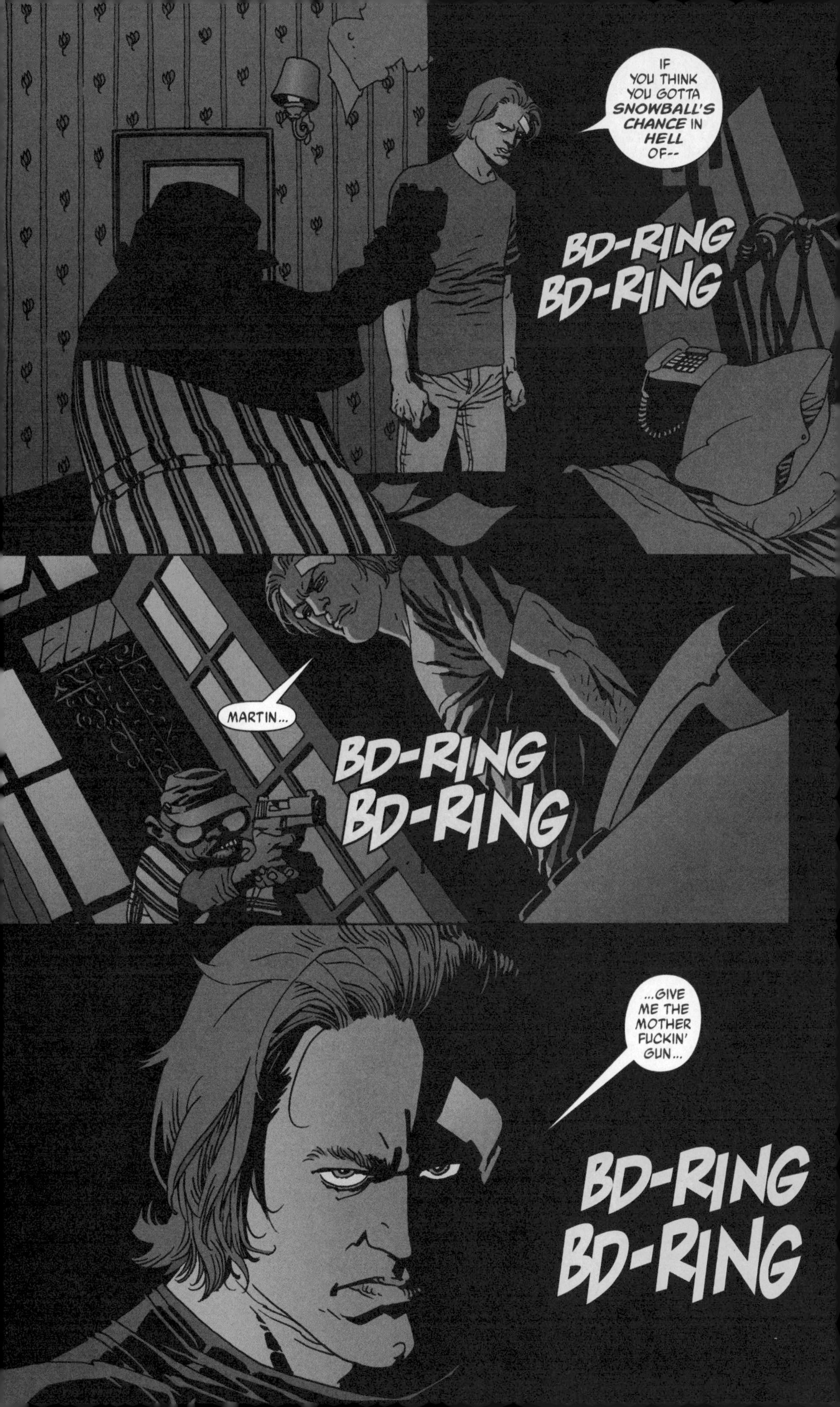
IF YOU THINK YOU GOTTA SNOWBALL'S CHANCE IN HELL OF--
BD-RING BD-RING
MARTIN...
BD-RING BD-RING
...GIVE ME THE MOTHER FUCKIN' GUN...
BD-RING BD-RING

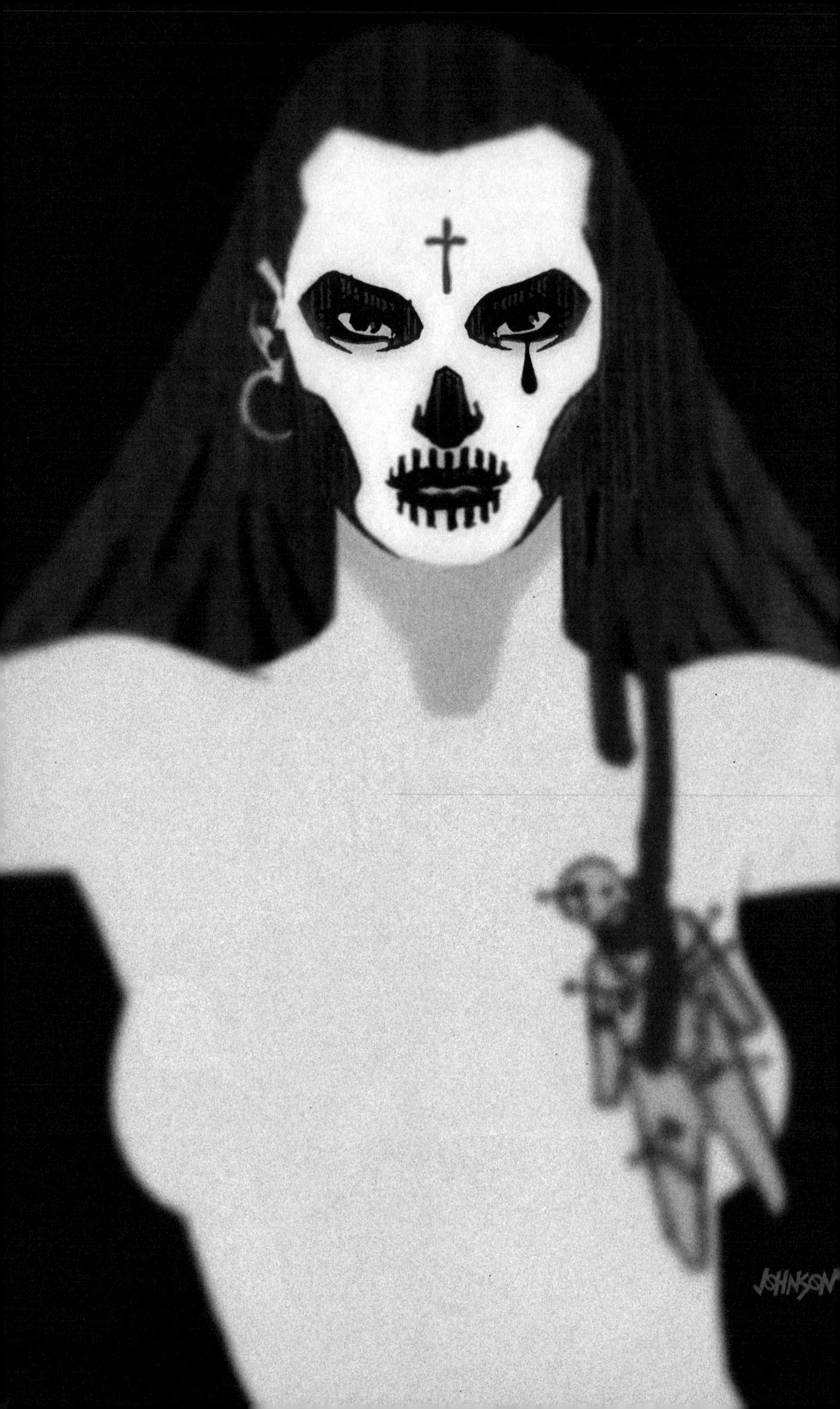
JOHNSON

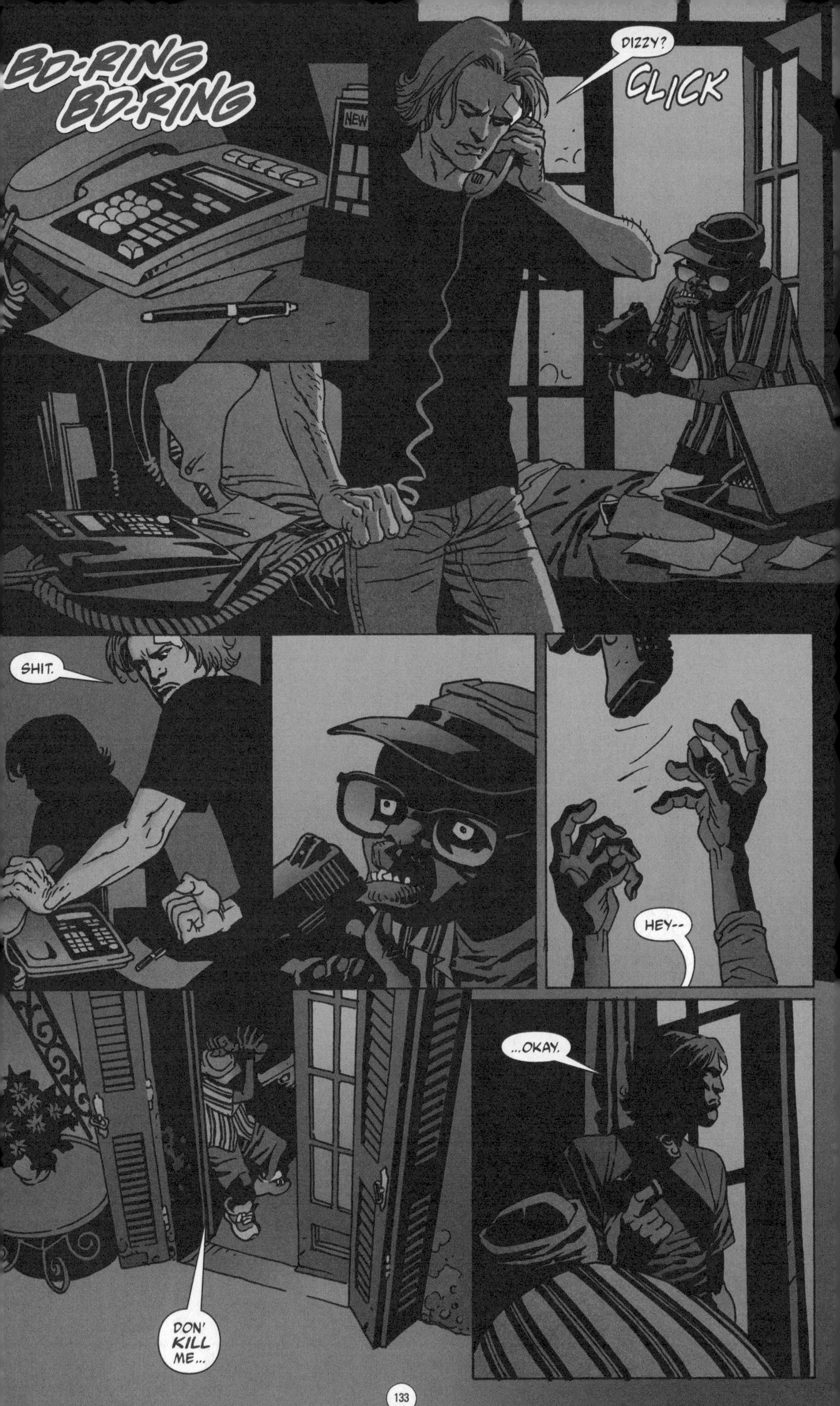
BD-RING
BD-RING
DIZZY?
CLICK
SHIT.
HEY--
DON' KILL ME...
...OKAY.

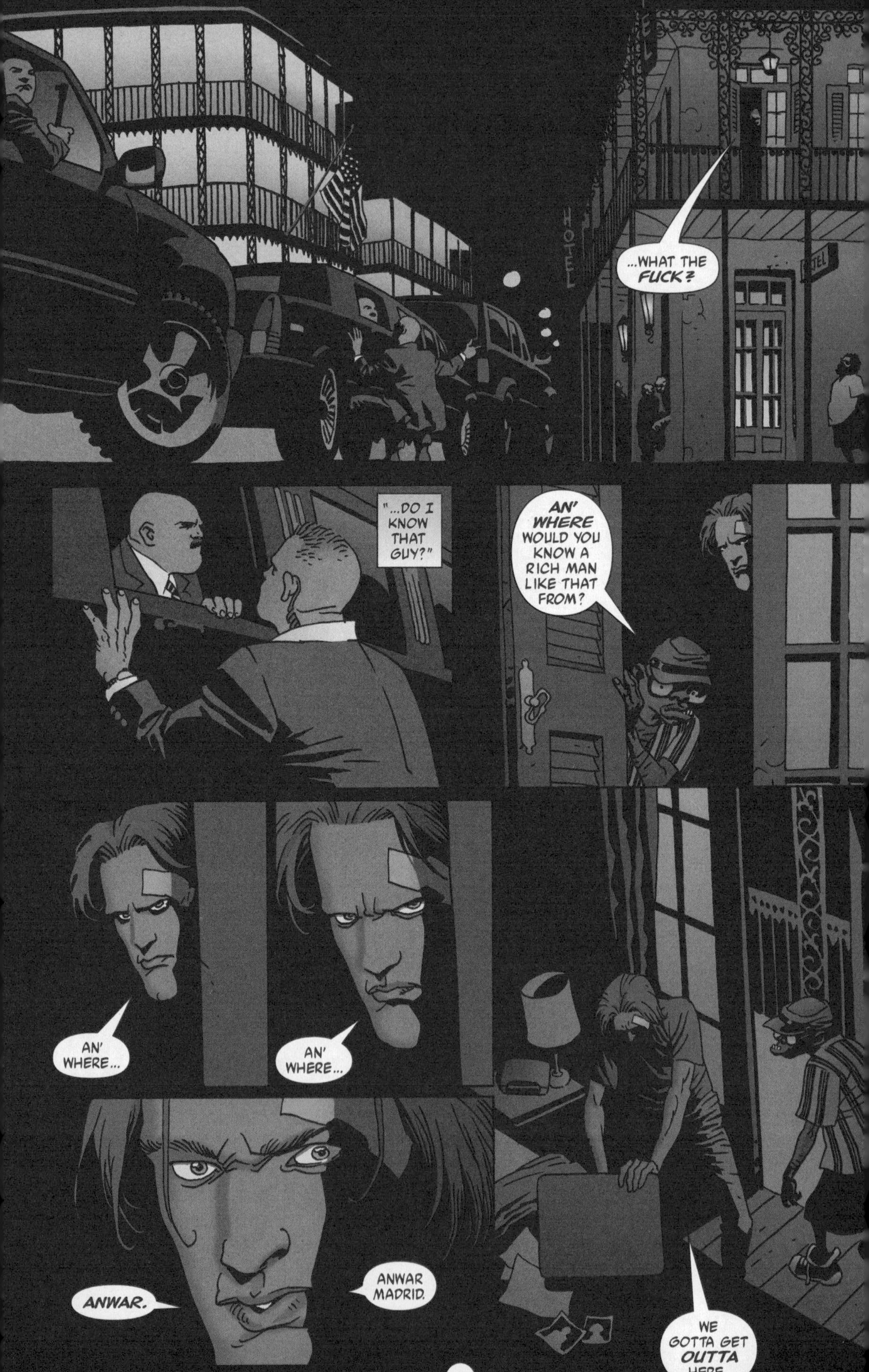
HOTEL
...WHAT THE FUCK?
"...DO I KNOW THAT GUY?"
AN' WHERE WOULD YOU KNOW A RICH MAN LIKE THAT FROM?
AN' WHERE...
AN' WHERE...
ANWAR.
ANWAR MADRID.
WE GOTTA GET OUTTA HERE.

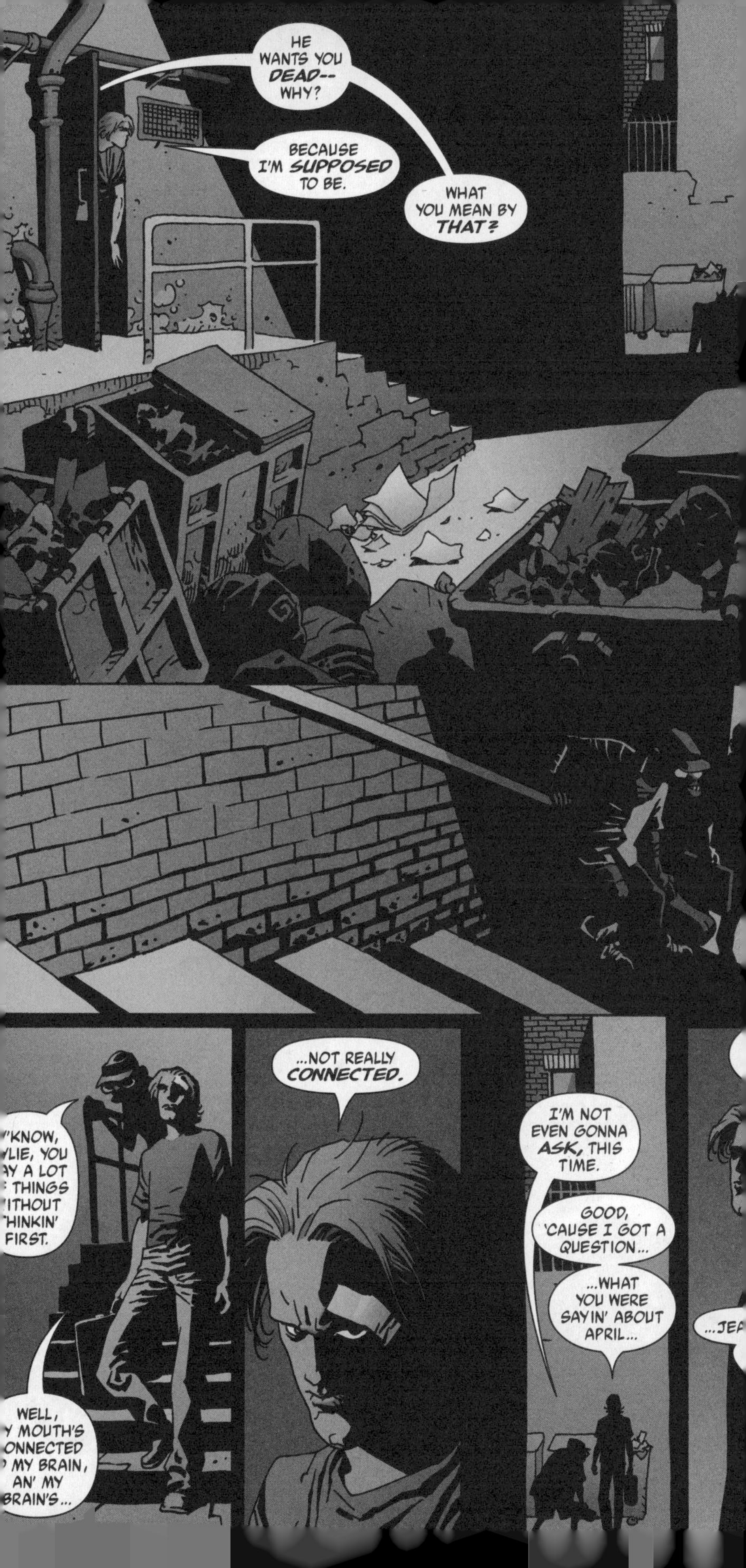
HE WANTS YOU DEAD-- WHY?
BECAUSE I'M SUPPOSED TO BE.
WHAT YOU MEAN BY THAT?
'KNOW, YLIE, YOU AY A LOT F THINGS ITHOUT THINKIN' FIRST.
WELL, Y MOUTH'S ONNECTED D MY BRAIN, AN' MY BRAIN'S...
...NOT REALLY CONNECTED.
I'M NOT EVEN GONNA ASK, THIS TIME.
GOOD, 'CAUSE I GOT A QUESTION...
...WHAT YOU WERE SAYIN' ABOUT APRIL...
...JEA

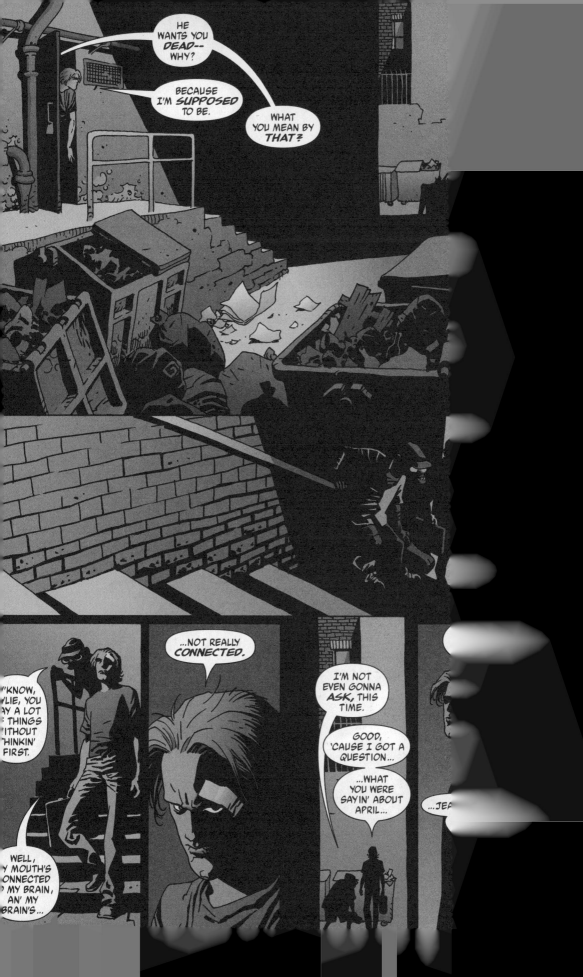

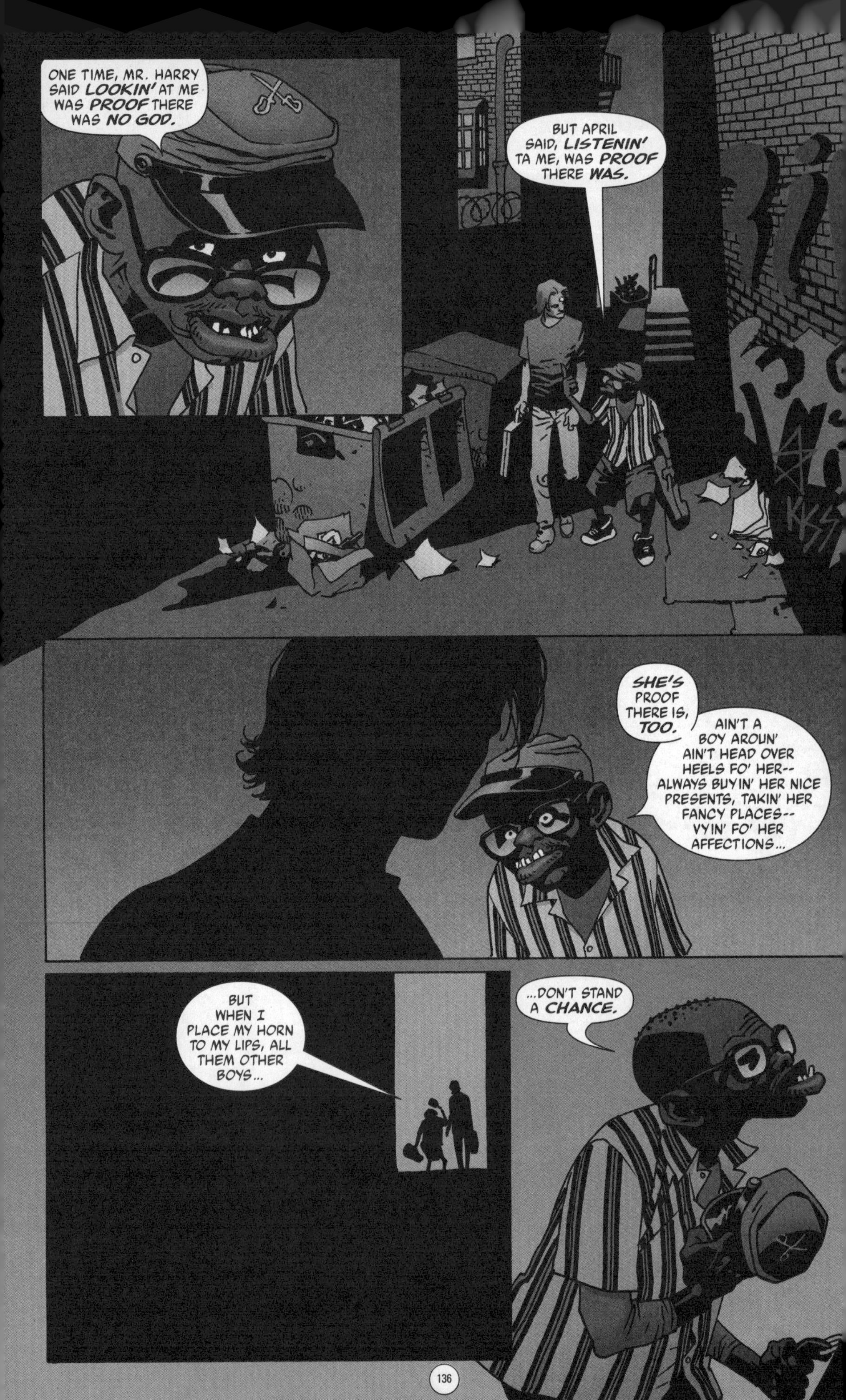
ONE TIME, MR. HARRY SAID LOOKIN' AT ME WAS PROOF THERE WAS NO GOD.
BUT APRIL SAID, LISTENIN' TA ME, WAS PROOF THERE WAS.
SHE'S PROOF THERE IS, TOO.
AIN'T A BOY AROUN' AIN'T HEAD OVER HEELS FO' HER-- ALWAYS BUYIN' HER NICE PRESENTS, TAKIN' HER FANCY PLACES-- VYIN' FO' HER AFFECTIONS...
BUT WHEN I PLACE MY HORN TO MY LIPS, ALL THEM OTHER BOYS...
...DON'T STAND A CHANCE.

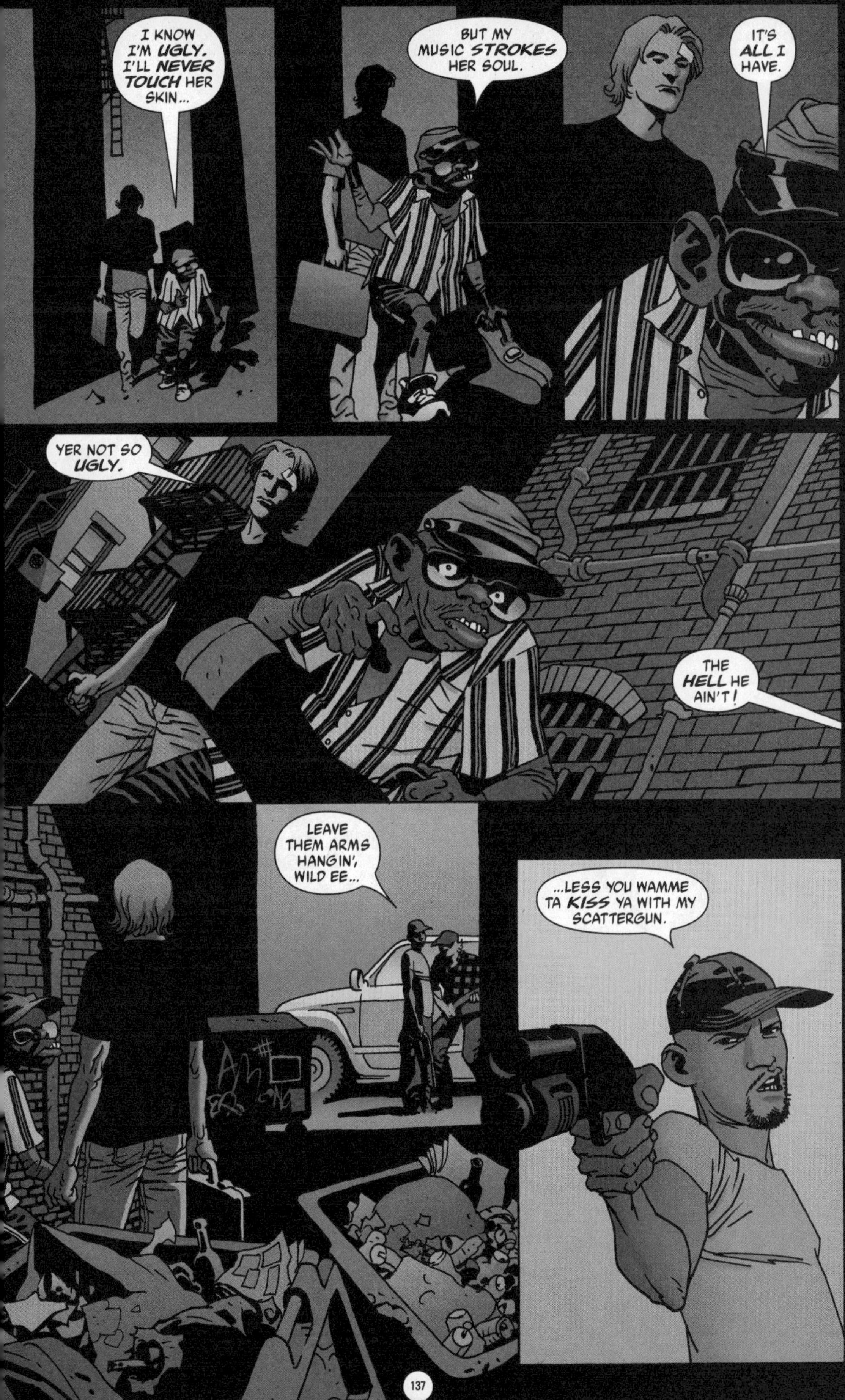
I KNOW I'M UGLY. I'LL NEVER TOUCH HER SKIN...
BUT MY MUSIC STROKES HER SOUL.
IT'S ALL I HAVE.
YER NOT SO UGLY.
THE HELL HE AIN'T!
LEAVE THEM ARMS HANGIN', WILD EE...
...LESS YOU WAMME TA KISS YA WITH MY SCATTERGUN.

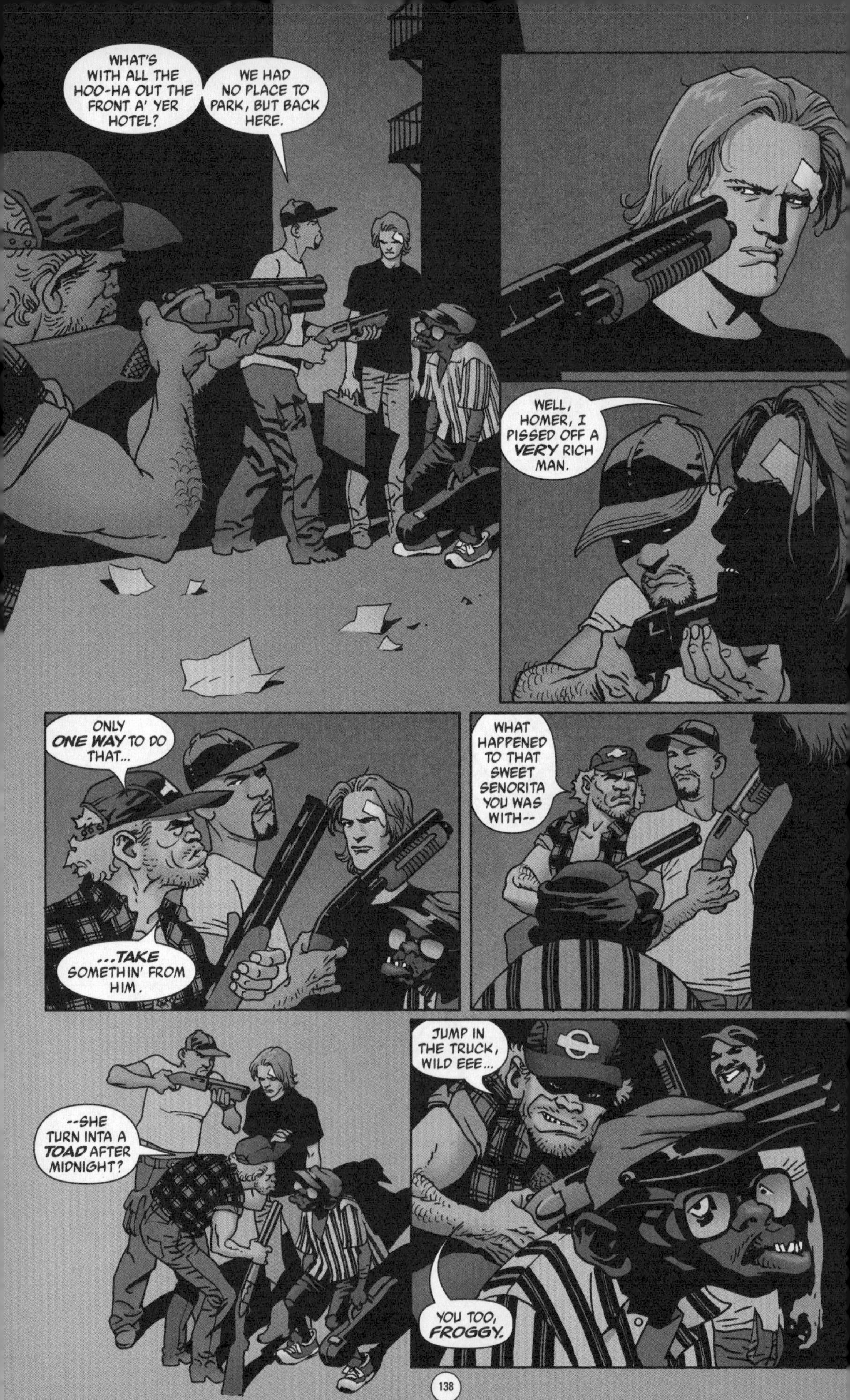
WHAT'S WITH ALL THE HOO-HA OUT THE FRONT A' YER HOTEL?
WE HAD NO PLACE TO PARK, BUT BACK HERE.
WELL, HOMER, I PISSED OFF A VERY RICH MAN.
ONLY ONE WAY TO DO THAT...
...TAKE SOMETHIN' FROM HIM.
WHAT HAPPENED TO THAT SWEET SENORITA YOU WAS WITH--
--SHE TURN INTA A TOAD AFTER MIDNIGHT?
JUMP IN THE TRUCK, WILD EEE...
YOU TOO, FROGGY.

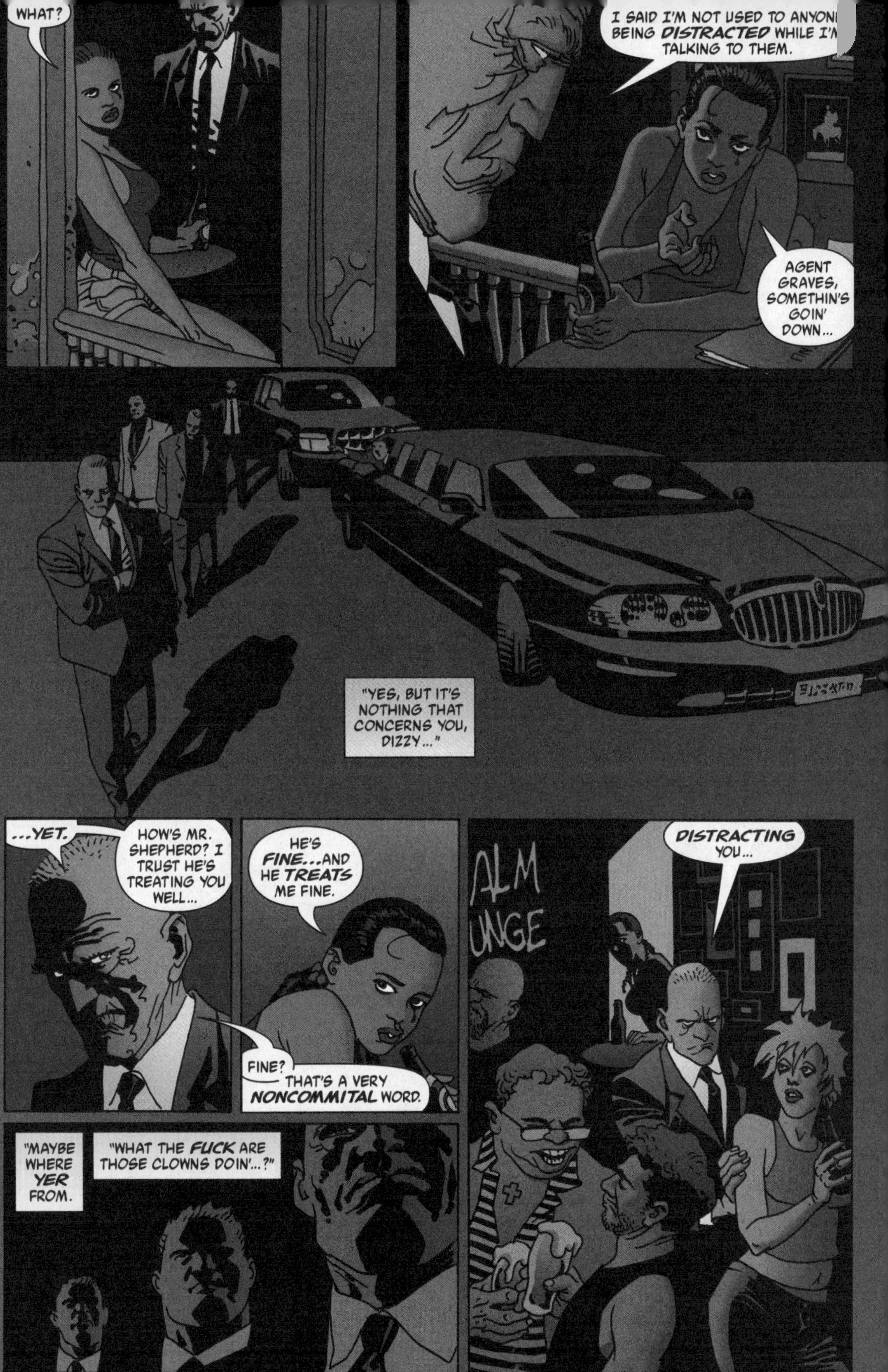
WHAT?
I SAID I'M NOT USED TO ANYONE BEING DISTRACTED WHILE I'M TALKING TO THEM.
AGENT GRAVES, SOMETHIN'S GOIN' DOWN...
"YES, BUT IT'S NOTHING THAT CONCERNS YOU, DIZZY..."
...YET.
HOW'S MR. SHEPHERD? I TRUST HE'S TREATING YOU WELL...
HE'S FINE...AND HE TREATS ME FINE.
FINE? THAT'S A VERY NONCOMMITAL WORD.
DISTRACTING YOU...
"MAYBE WHERE YER FROM.
"WHAT THE FUCK ARE THOSE CLOWNS DOIN'...?"

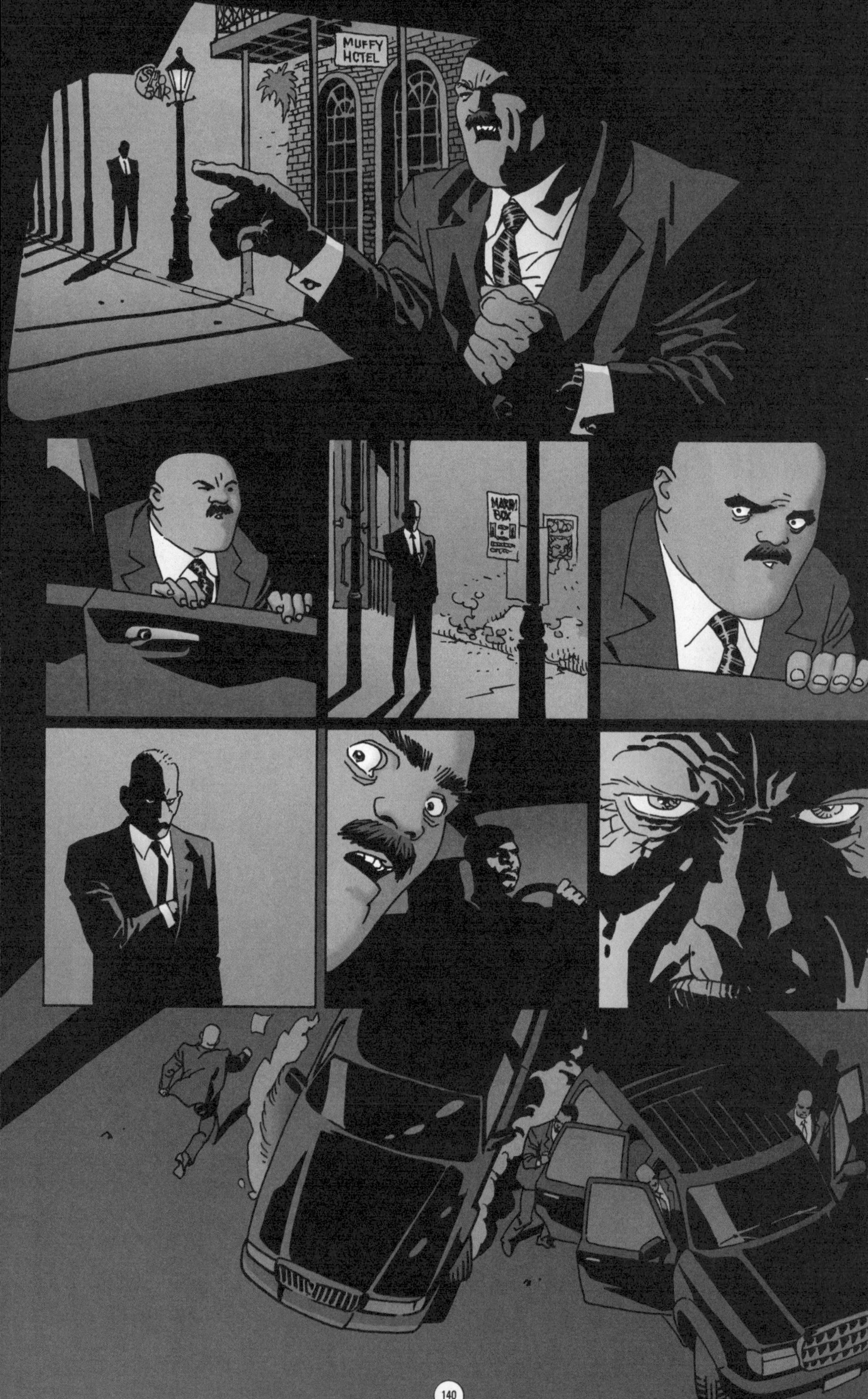
MUFFY
HOTEL

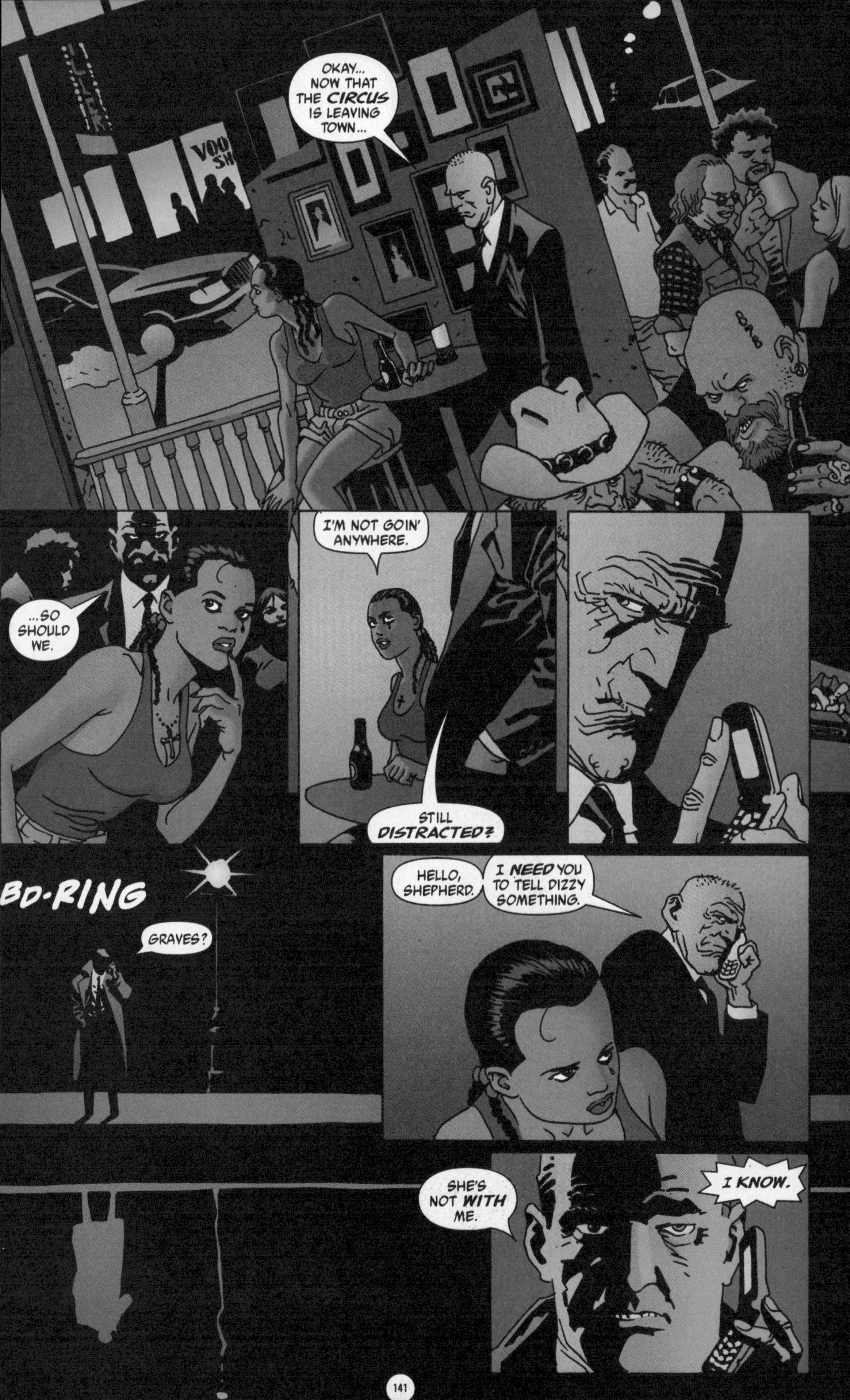
OKAY... NOW THAT THE CIRCUS IS LEAVING TOWN...
...SO SHOULD WE.
I'M NOT GOIN' ANYWHERE.
STILL DISTRACTED?
BD-RING
GRAVES?
HELLO, SHEPHERD.
I NEED YOU TO TELL DIZZY SOMETHING.
SHE'S NOT WITH ME.
I KNOW.

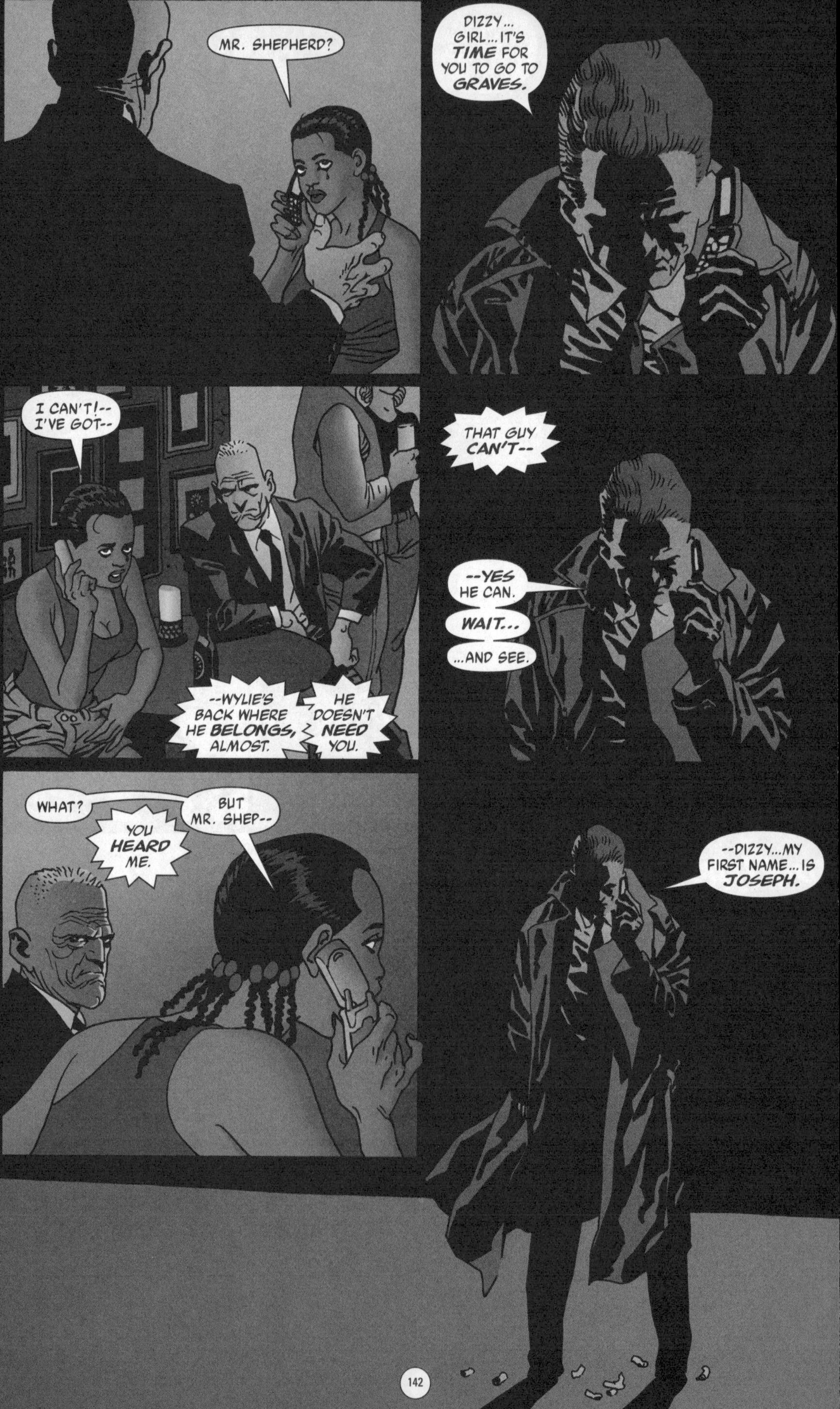
MR. SHEPHERD?
DIZZY... GIRL... IT'S TIME FOR YOU TO GO TO GRAVES.
I CAN'T!-- I'VE GOT--
--WYLIE'S BACK WHERE HE BELONGS, ALMOST.
HE DOESN'T NEED YOU.
THAT GUY CAN'T--
--YES HE CAN.
WAIT...
...AND SEE.
WHAT?
BUT MR. SHEP--
YOU HEARD ME.
--DIZZY...MY FIRST NAME... IS JOSEPH.

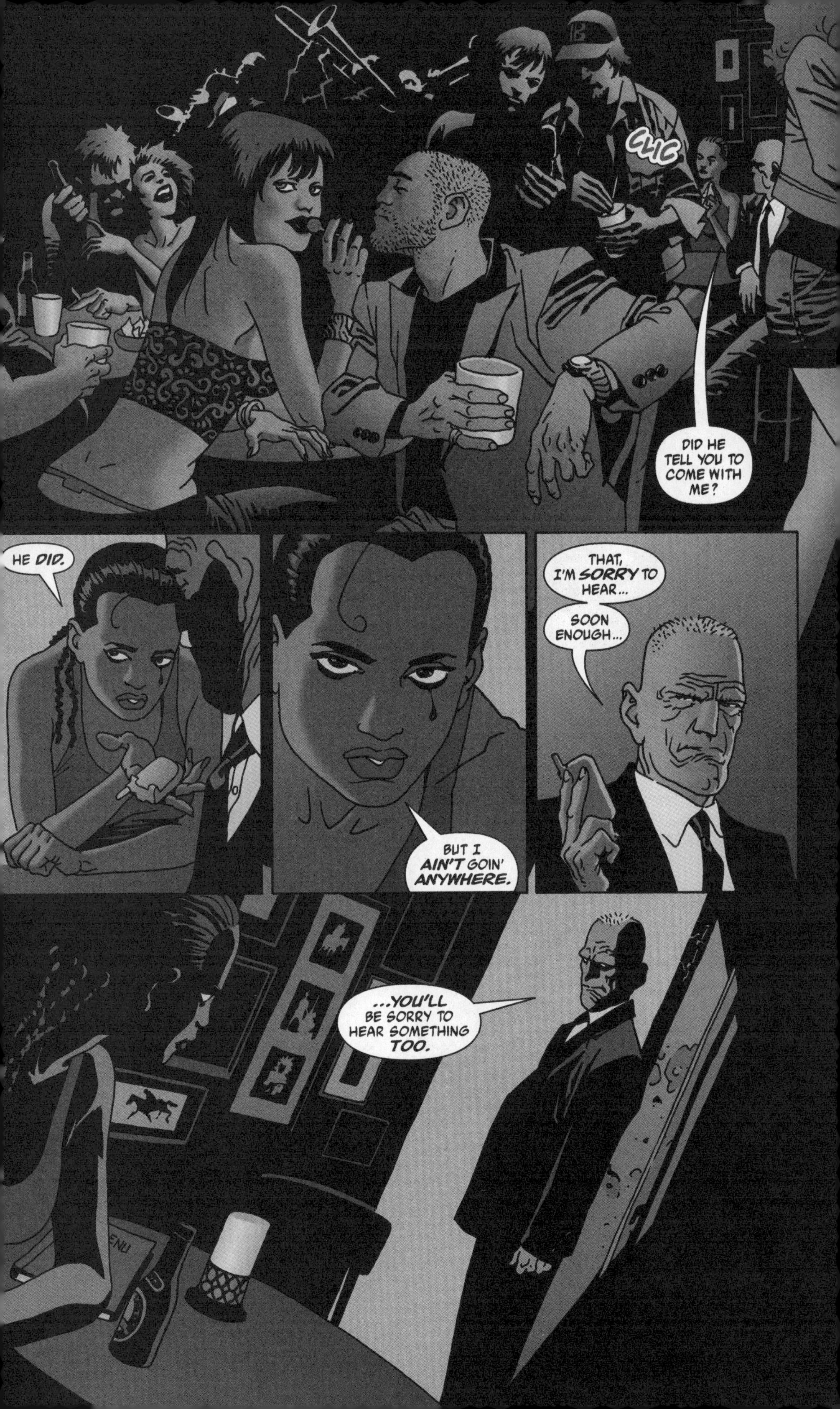
CLIC
DID HE TELL YOU TO COME WITH ME?
HE DID.
BUT I AIN'T GOIN' ANYWHERE.
THAT, I'M SORRY TO HEAR...
SOON ENOUGH...
...YOU'LL BE SORRY TO HEAR SOMETHING TOO.

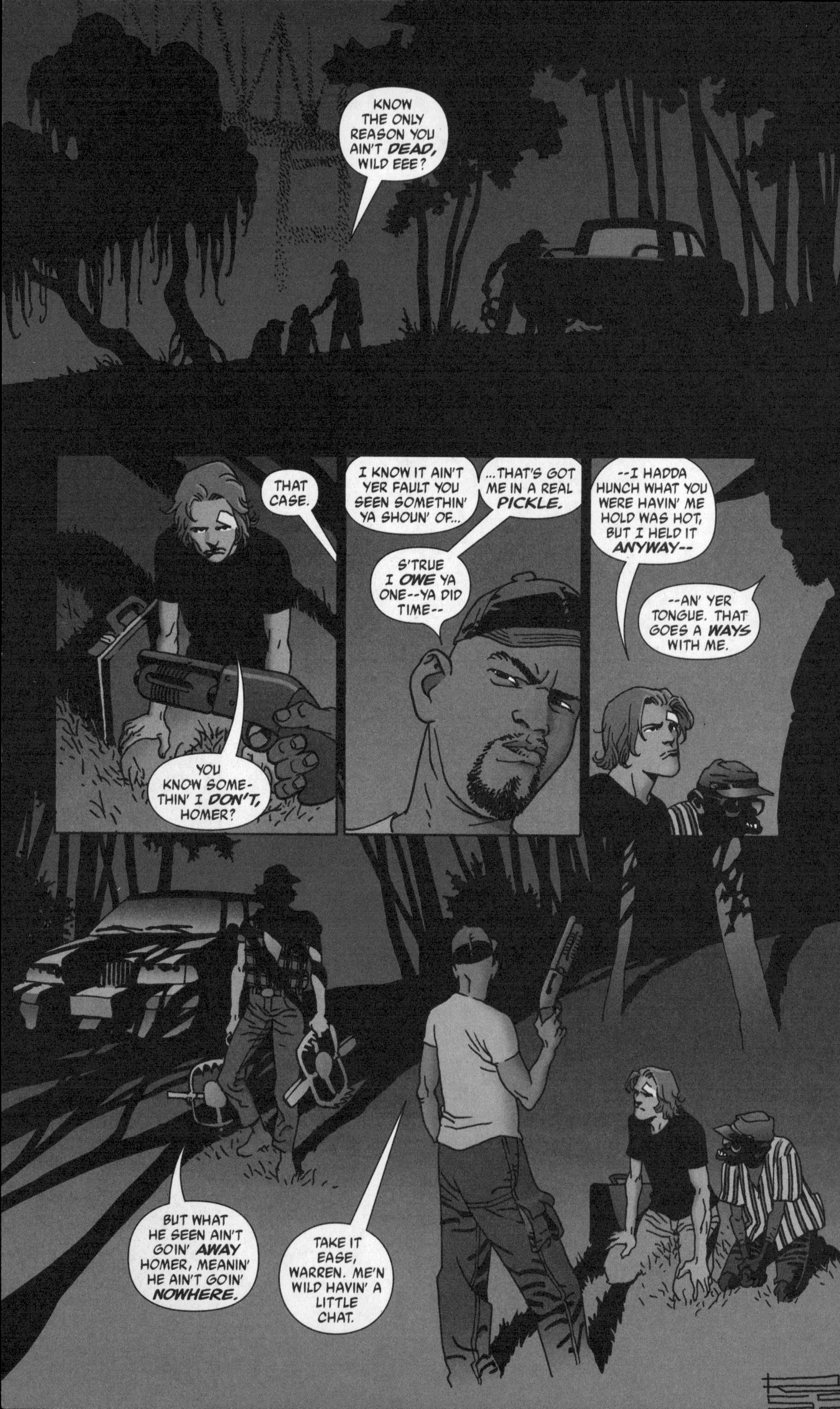
KNOW THE ONLY REASON YOU AIN'T DEAD, WILD EEE?
THAT CASE.
YOU KNOW SOME-THIN' I DON'T, HOMER?
I KNOW IT AIN'T YER FAULT YOU SEEN SOMETHIN' YA SHOUN' OF...
...THAT'S GOT ME IN A REAL PICKLE.
S'TRUE I OWE YA ONE--YA DID TIME--
--I HADDA HUNCH WHAT YOU WERE HAVIN' ME HOLD WAS HOT, BUT I HELD IT ANYWAY--
--AN' YER TONGUE. THAT GOES A WAYS WITH ME.
BUT WHAT HE SEEN AIN'T GOIN' AWAY HOMER, MEANIN' HE AIN'T GOIN' NOWHERE.
TAKE IT EASE, WARREN. ME'N WILD HAVIN' A LITTLE CHAT.

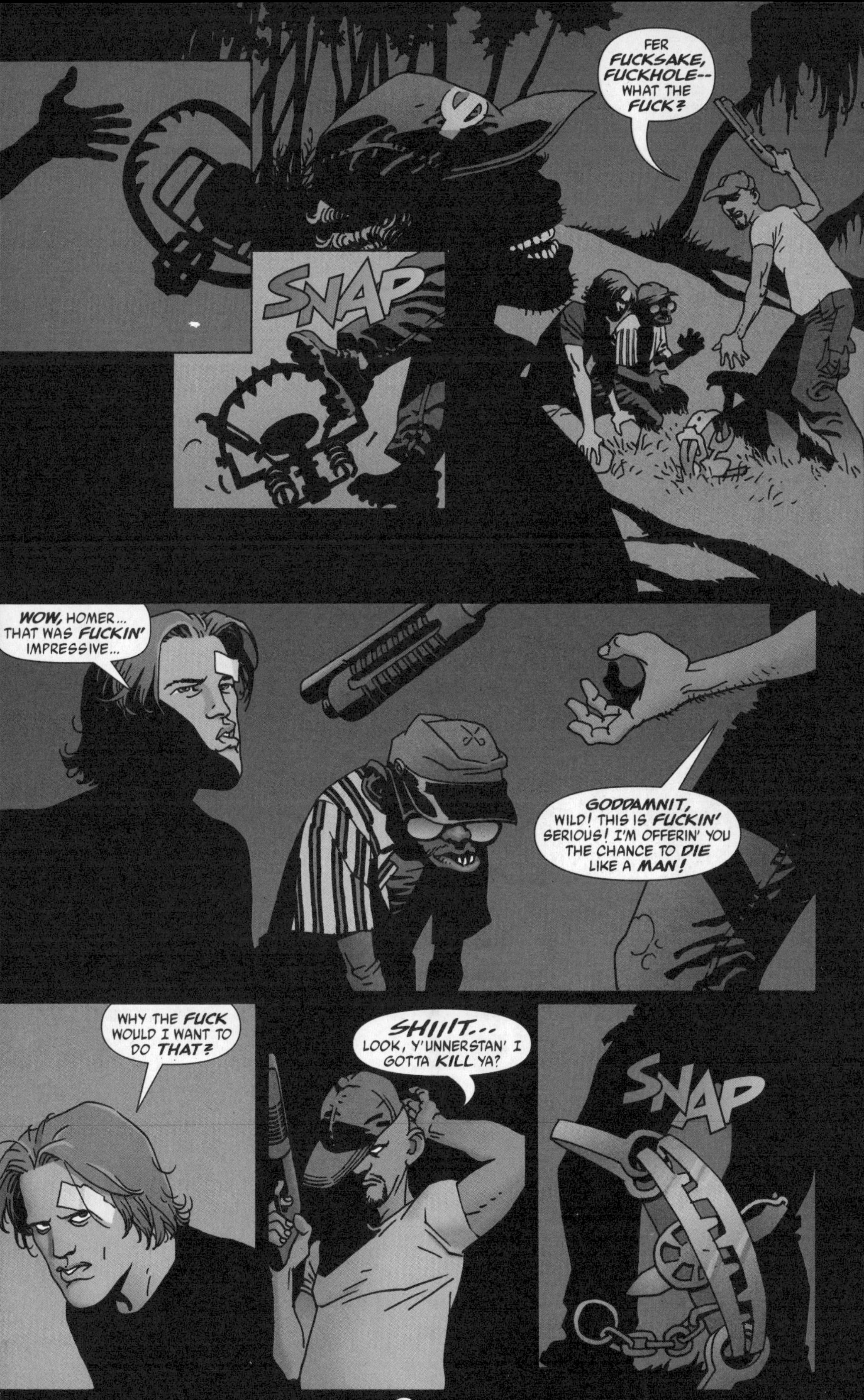
FER FUCKSAKE, FUCKHOLE-- WHAT THE FUCK?
SNAP
WOW, HOMER... THAT WAS FUCKIN' IMPRESSIVE...
GODDAMNIT, WILD! THIS IS FUCKIN' SERIOUS! I'M OFFERIN' YOU THE CHANCE TO DIE LIKE A MAN!
WHY THE FUCK WOULD I WANT TO DO THAT?
SHIIIT... LOOK, Y'UNNERSTAN' I GOTTA KILL YA?
SNAP

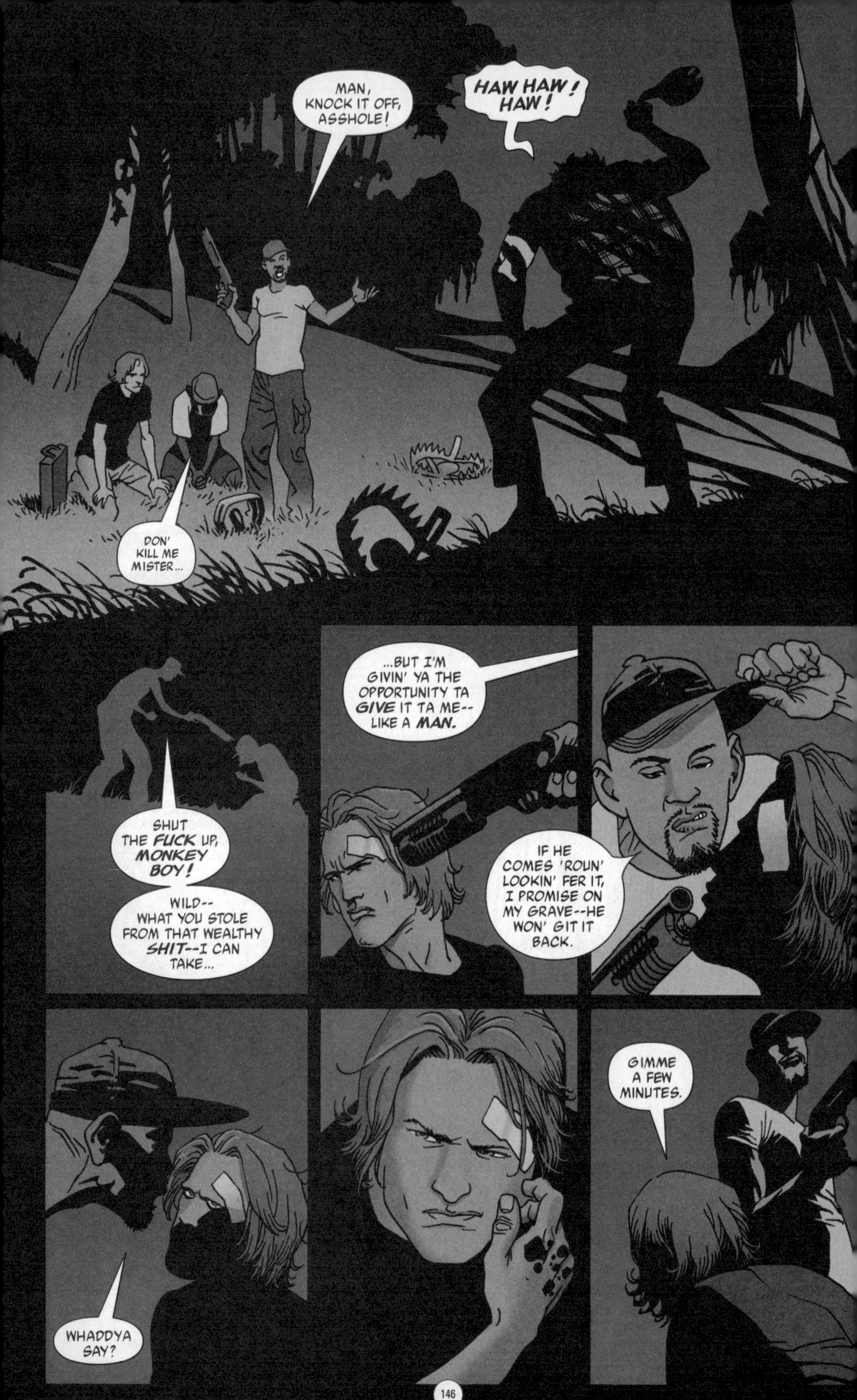
MAN, KNOCK IT OFF, ASSHOLE!
HAW HAW! HAW!
DON' KILL ME MISTER...
SHUT THE FUCK UP, MONKEY BOY!
WILD-- WHAT YOU STOLE FROM THAT WEALTHY SHIT--I CAN TAKE...
...BUT I'M GIVIN' YA THE OPPORTUNITY TA GIVE IT TA ME-- LIKE A MAN.
IF HE COMES 'ROUN' LOOKIN' FER IT, I PROMISE ON MY GRAVE--HE WON' GIT IT BACK.
WHADDYA SAY?
GIMME A FEW MINUTES.

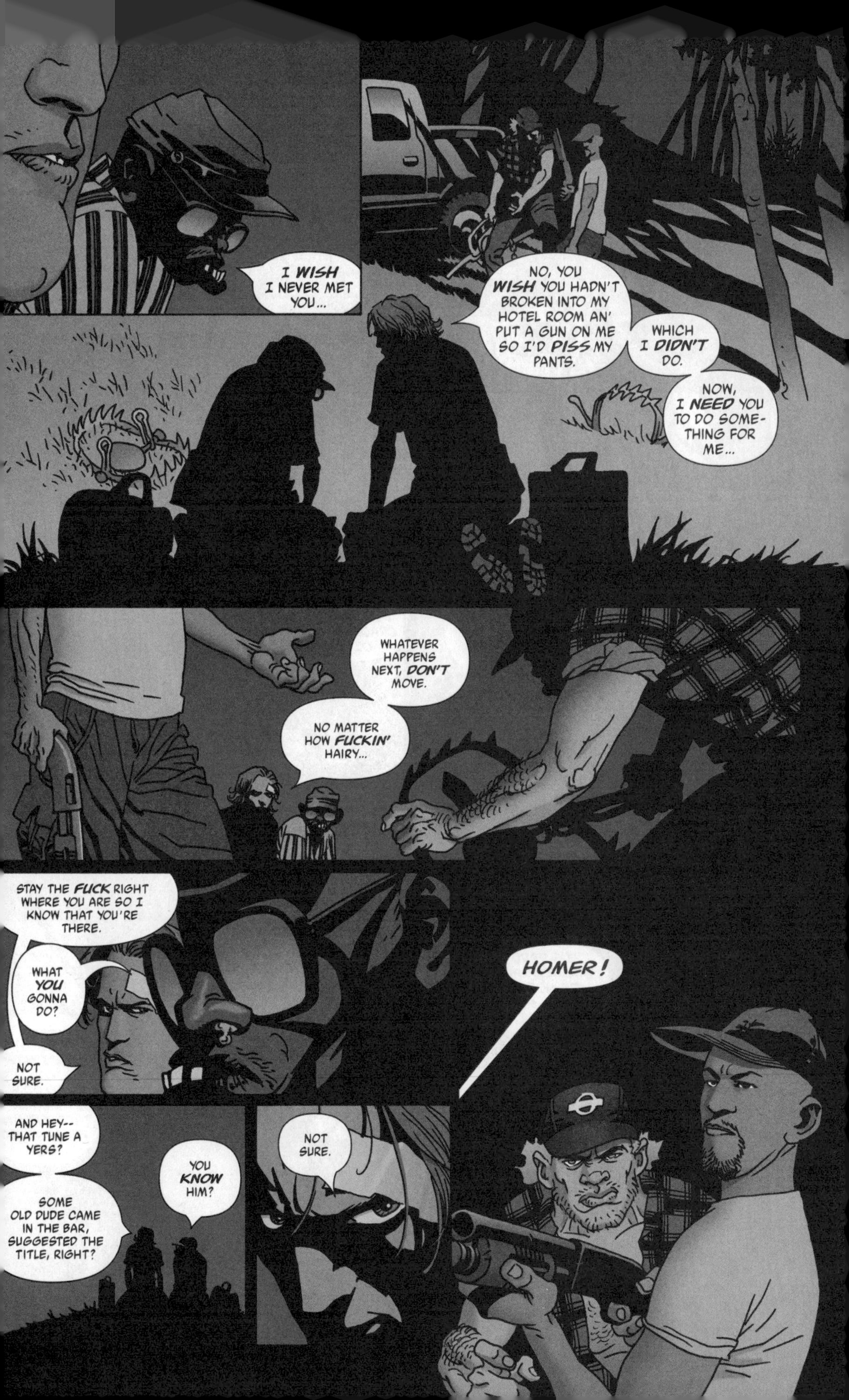

I WISH I NEVER MET YOU...
NO, YOU WISH YOU HADN'T BROKEN INTO MY HOTEL ROOM AN' PUT A GUN ON ME SO I'D PISS MY PANTS.
WHICH I DIDN'T DO.
NOW, I NEED YOU TO DO SOME-THING FOR ME...
WHATEVER HAPPENS NEXT, DON'T MOVE.
NO MATTER HOW FUCKIN' HAIRY...
STAY THE FUCK RIGHT WHERE YOU ARE SO I KNOW THAT YOU'RE THERE.
WHAT YOU GONNA DO?
NOT SURE.
AND HEY-- THAT TUNE A YERS?
SOME OLD DUDE CAME IN THE BAR, SUGGESTED THE TITLE, RIGHT?
YOU KNOW HIM?
NOT SURE.
HOMER!

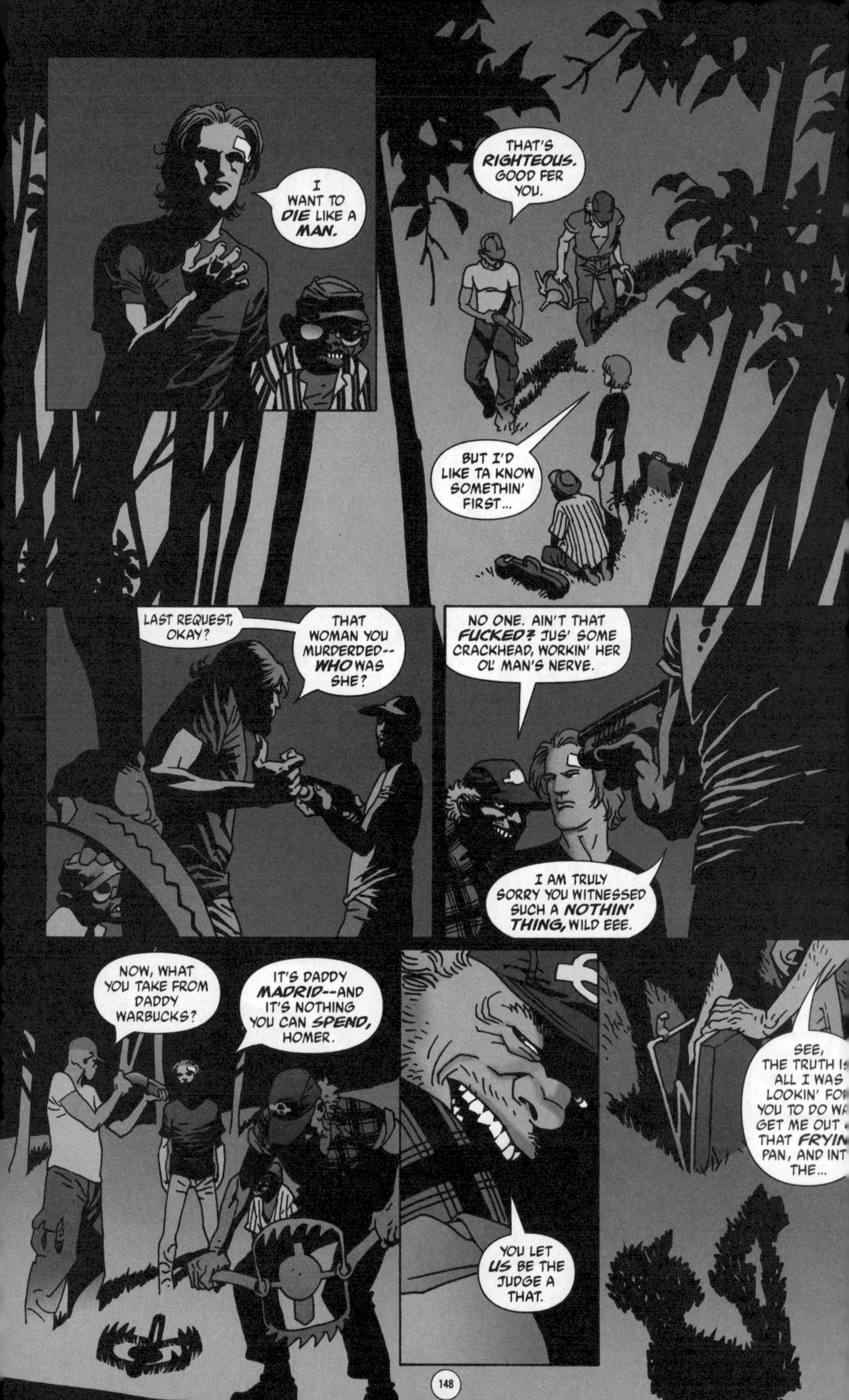

I WANT TO DIE LIKE A MAN.
THAT'S RIGHTEOUS. GOOD FER YOU.
BUT I'D LIKE TA KNOW SOMETHIN' FIRST...
LAST REQUEST, OKAY?
THAT WOMAN YOU MURDERDED-- WHO WAS SHE?
NO ONE. AIN'T THAT FUCKED? JUS' SOME CRACKHEAD, WORKIN' HER OL' MAN'S NERVE.
I AM TRULY SORRY YOU WITNESSED SUCH A NOTHIN' THING, WILD EEE.
NOW, WHAT YOU TAKE FROM DADDY WARBUCKS?
IT'S DADDY MADRID--AND IT'S NOTHING YOU CAN SPEND, HOMER.
YOU LET US BE THE JUDGE A THAT.
SEE, THE TRUTH I ALL I WAS LOOKIN' FO YOU TO DO W GET ME OUT THAT FRYIN PAN, AND INT THE...

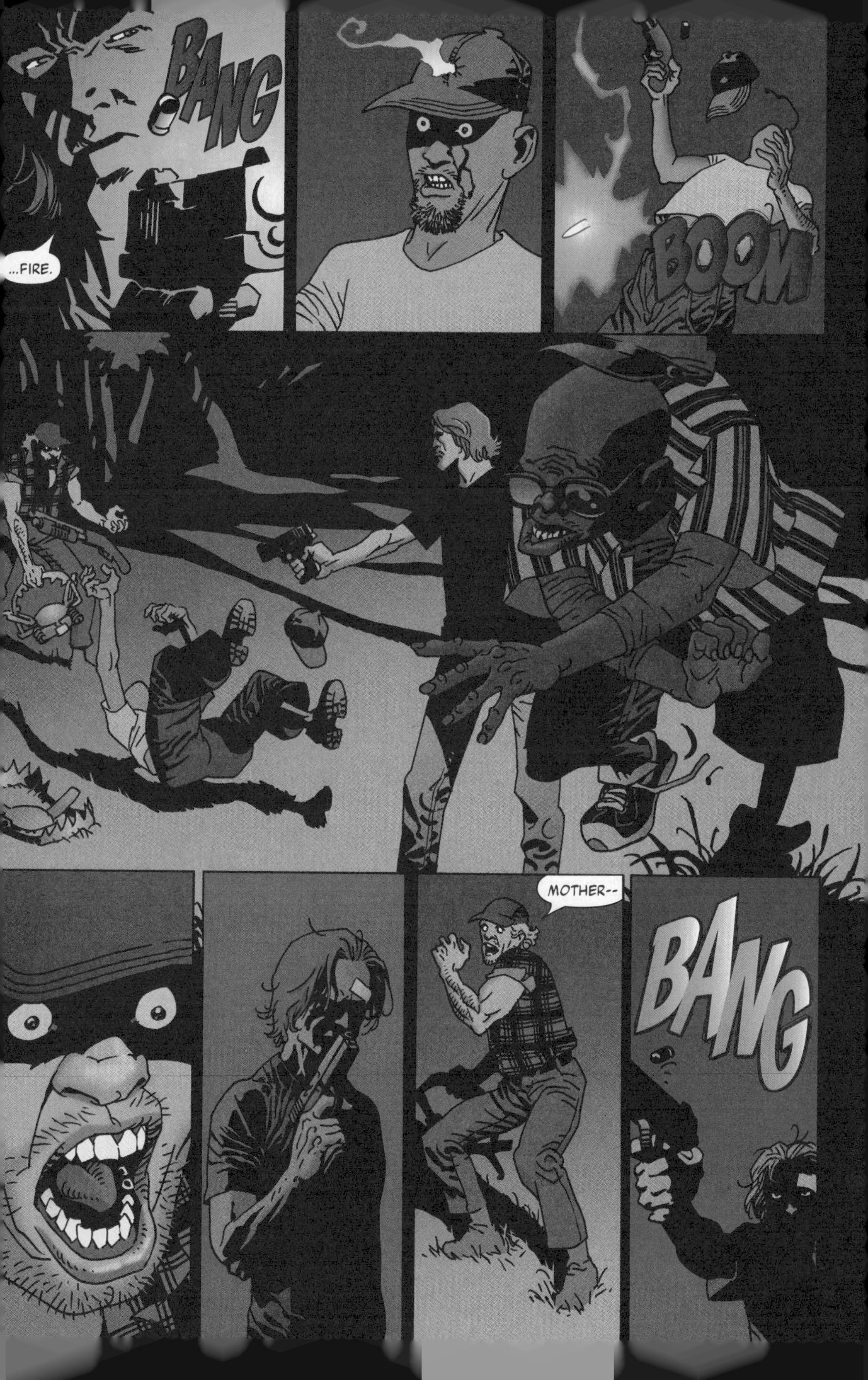
BANG
...FIRE.
BOOM
MOTHER--
BANG

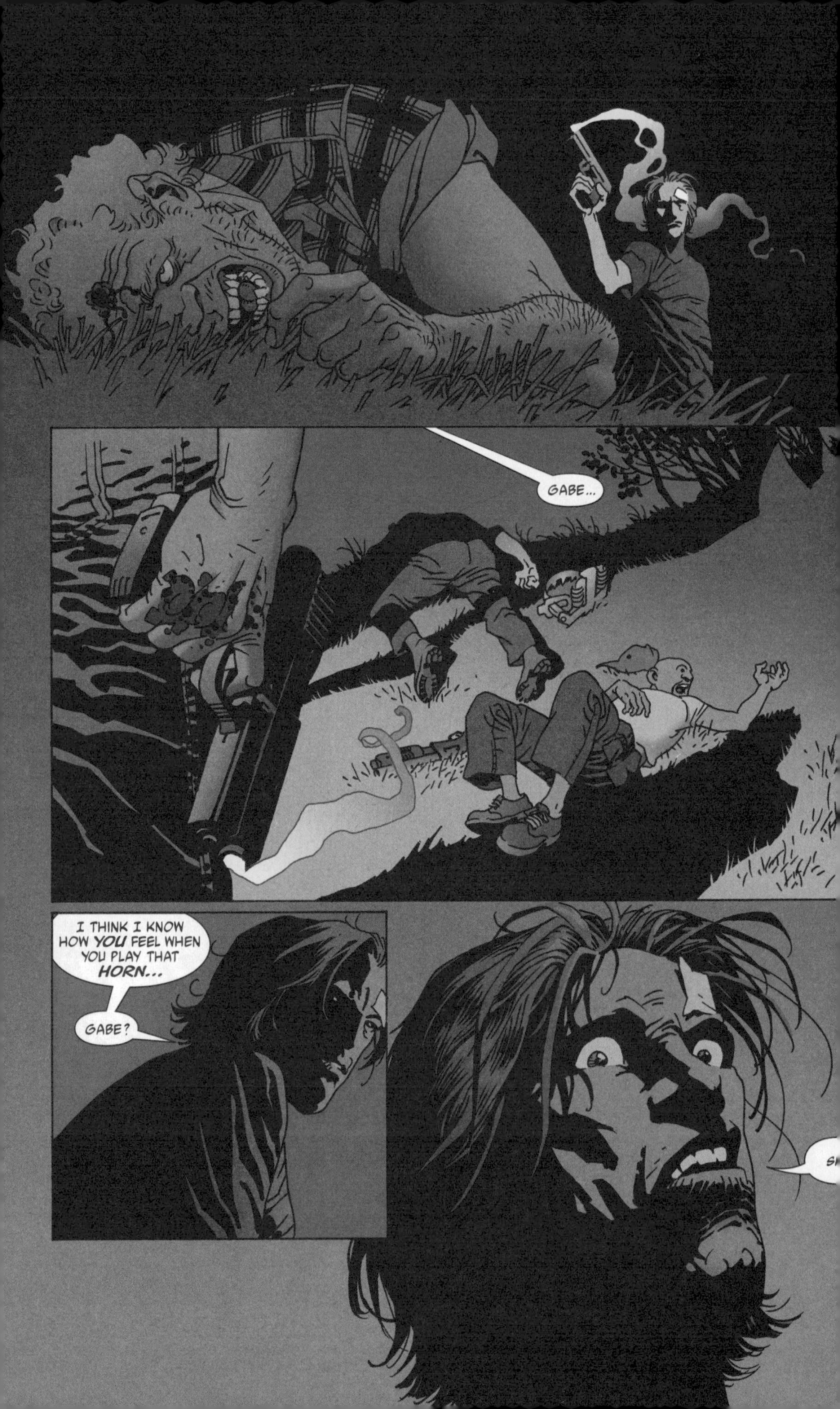
GABE...
I THINK I KNOW HOW YOU FEEL WHEN YOU PLAY THAT HORN...
GABE?

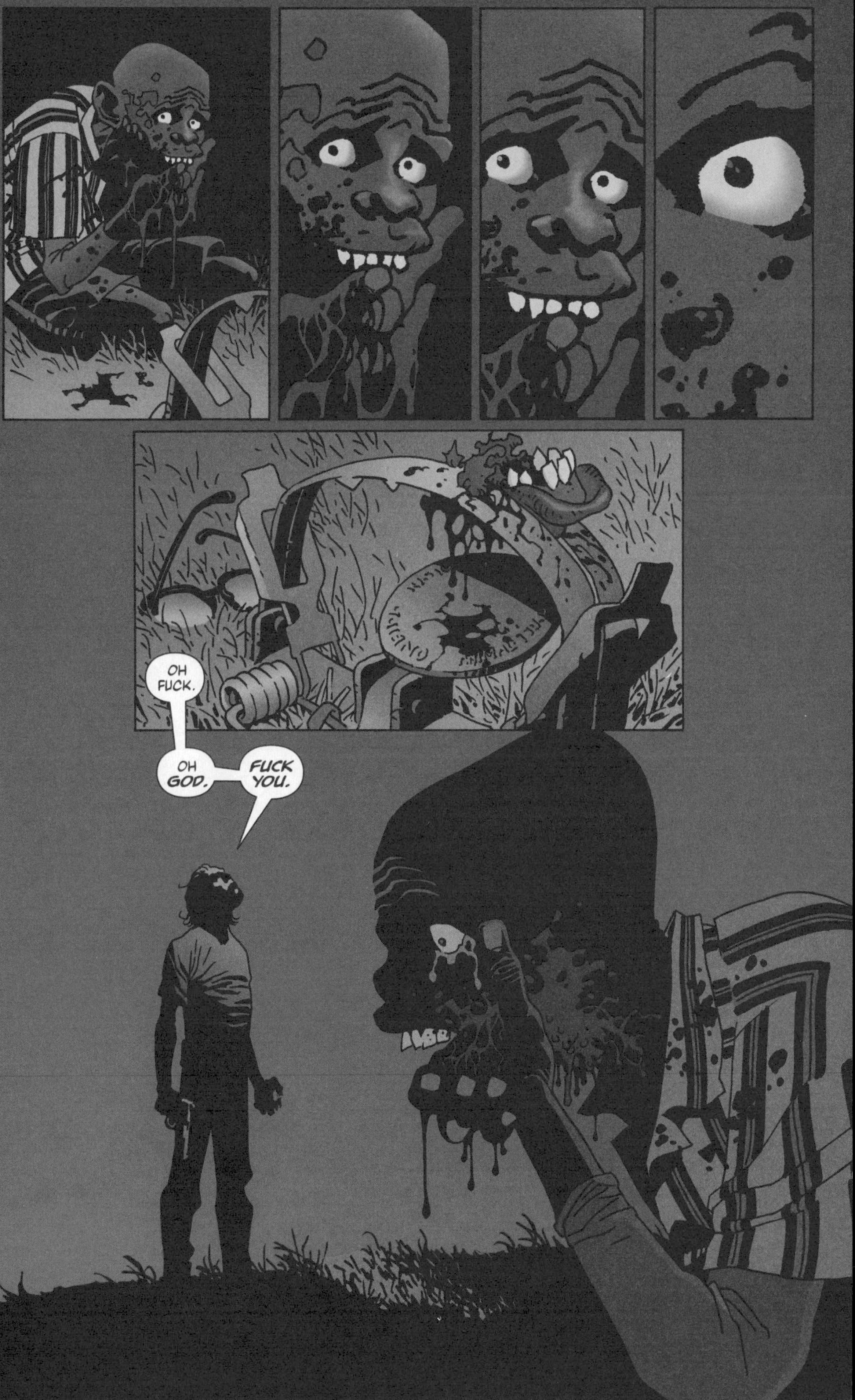
OH FUCK.
OH GOD.
FUCK YOU.

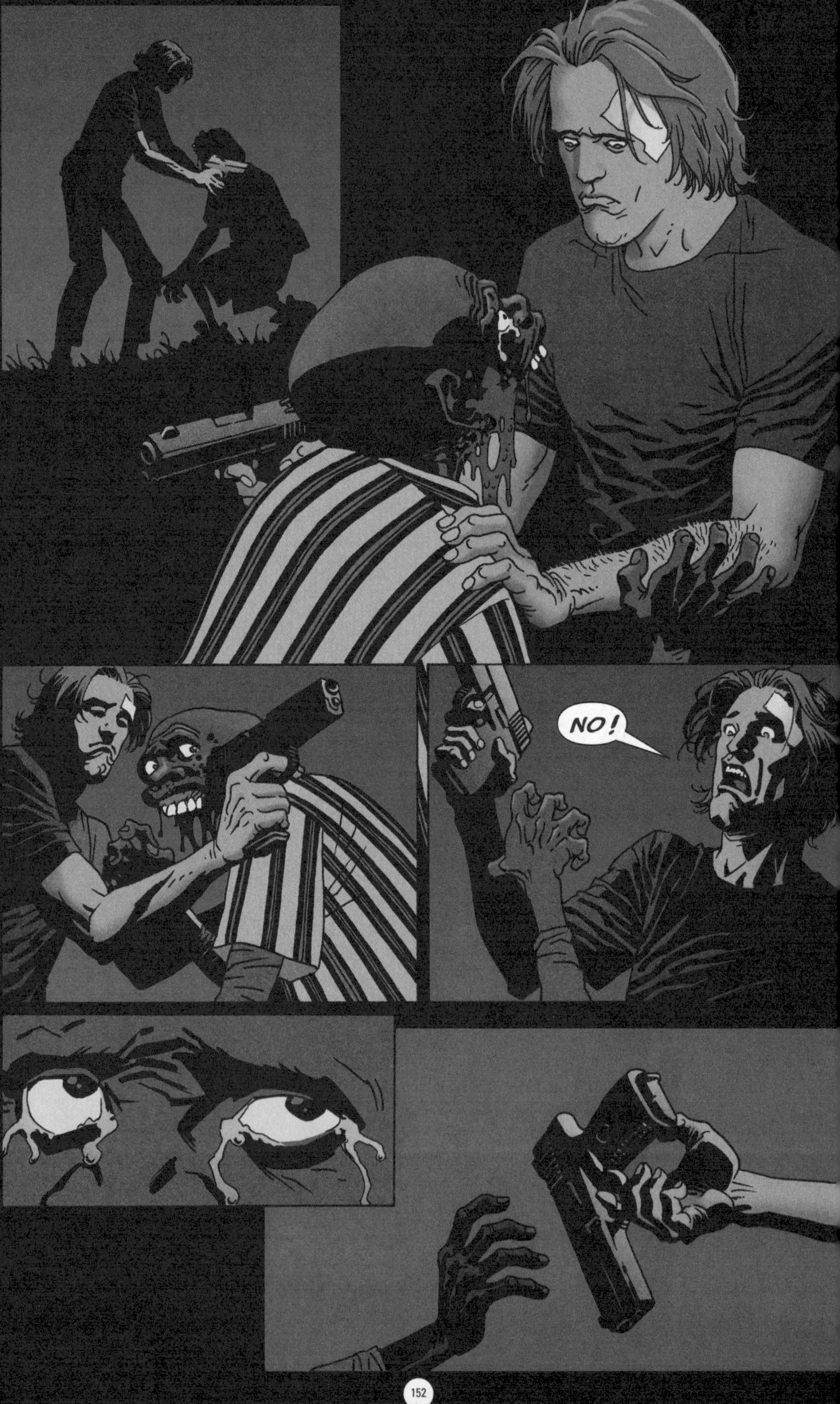

NO!

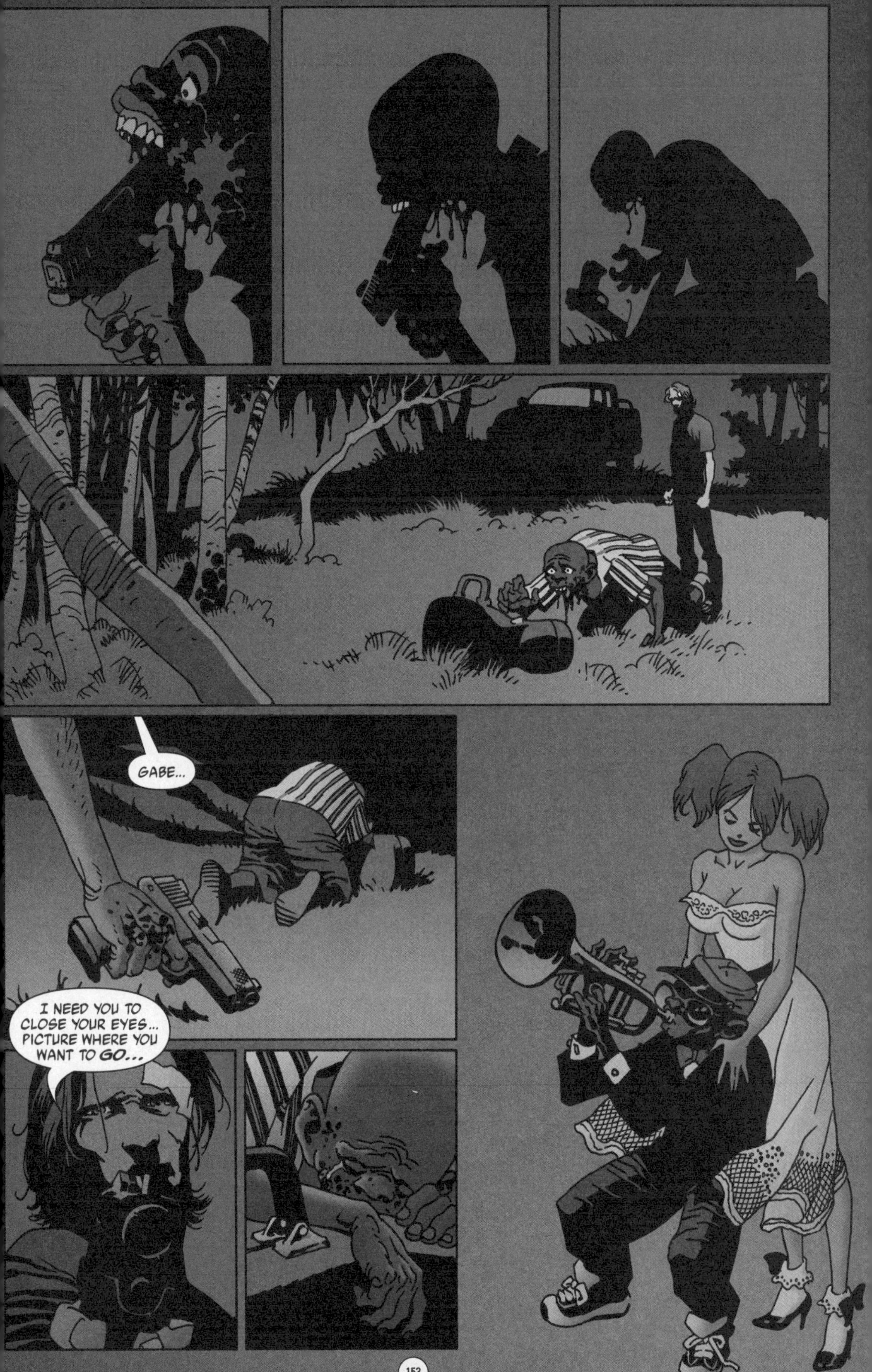
GABE...
I NEED YOU TO CLOSE YOUR EYES... PICTURE WHERE YOU WANT TO GO...

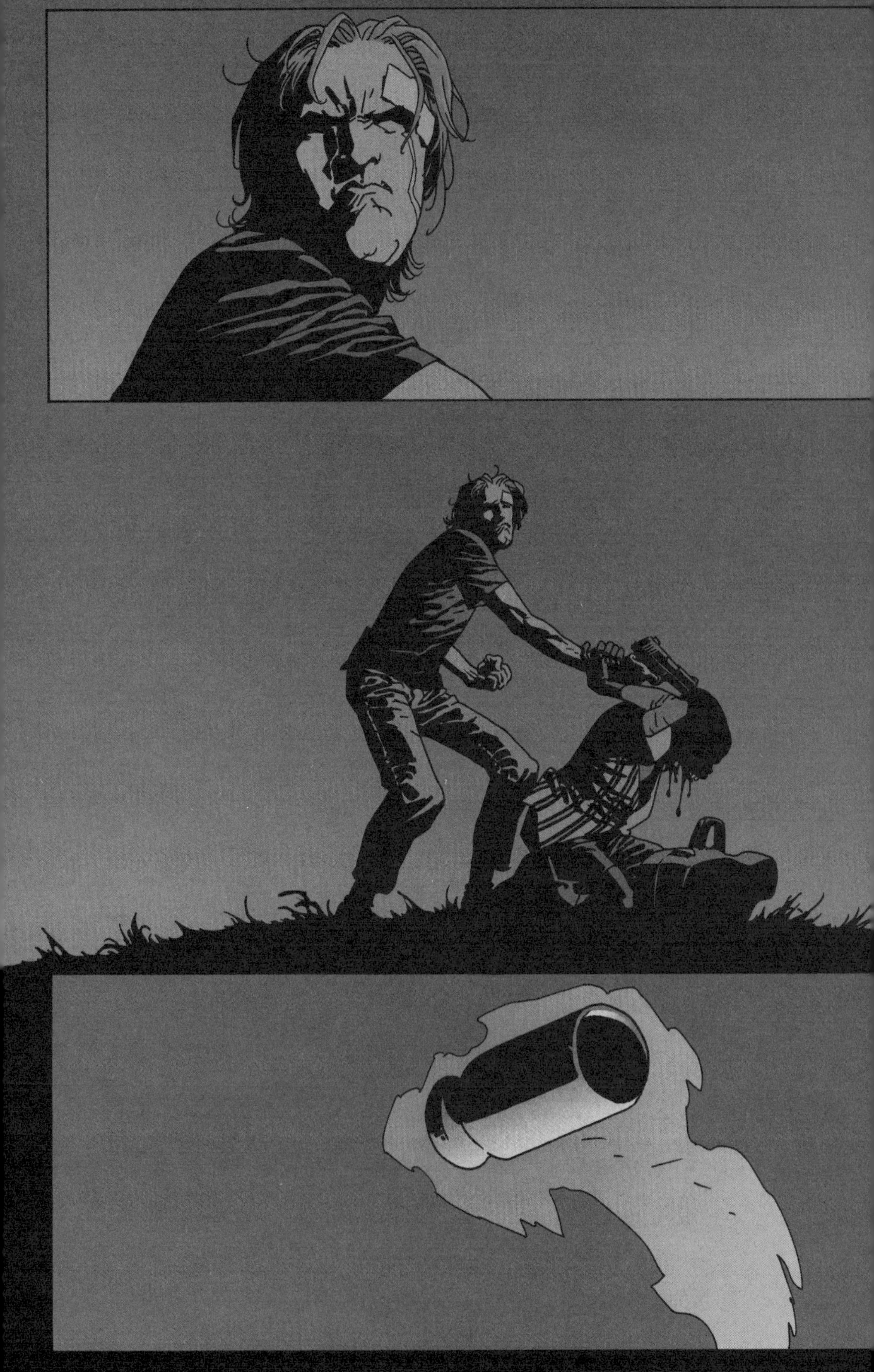

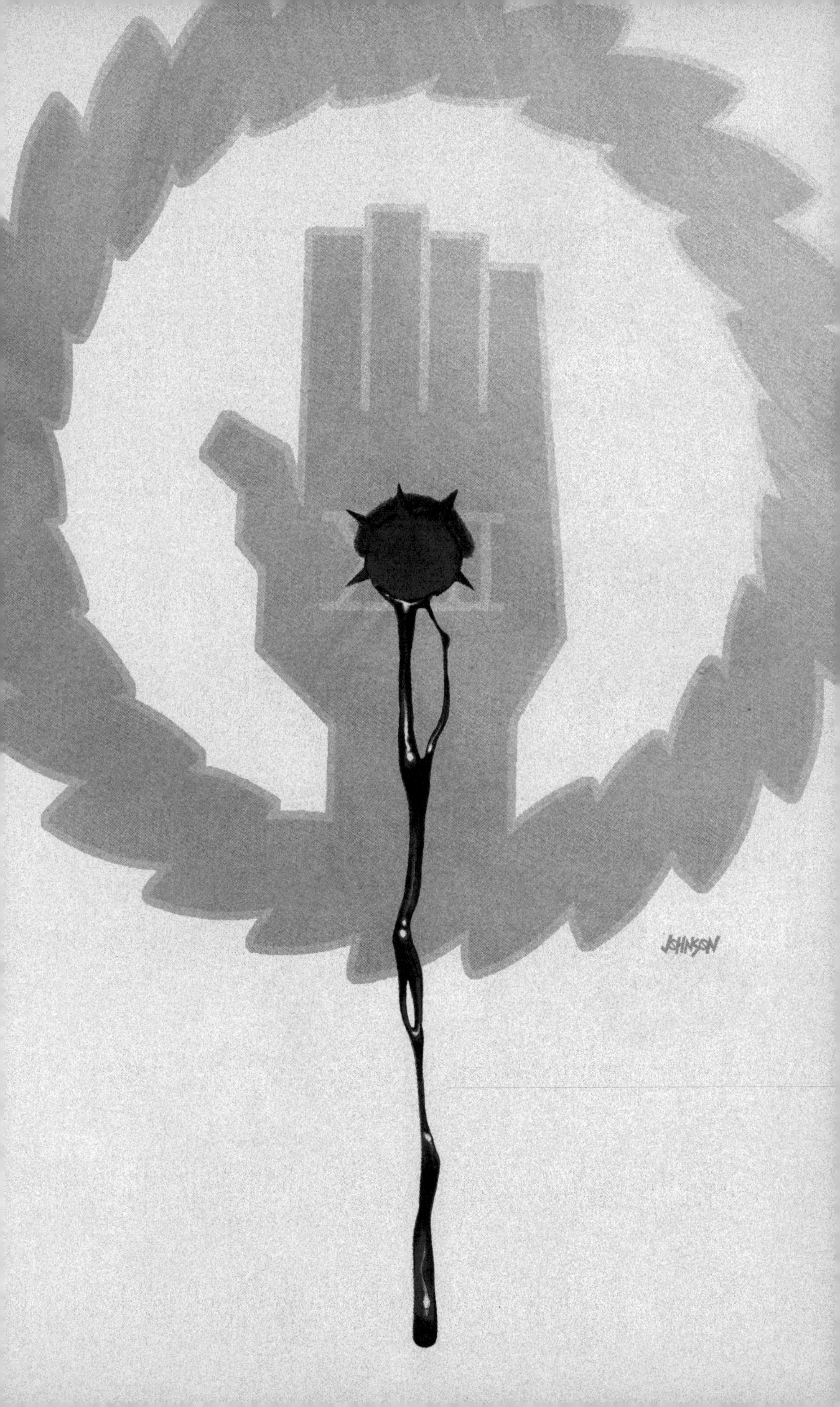
JOHNSON

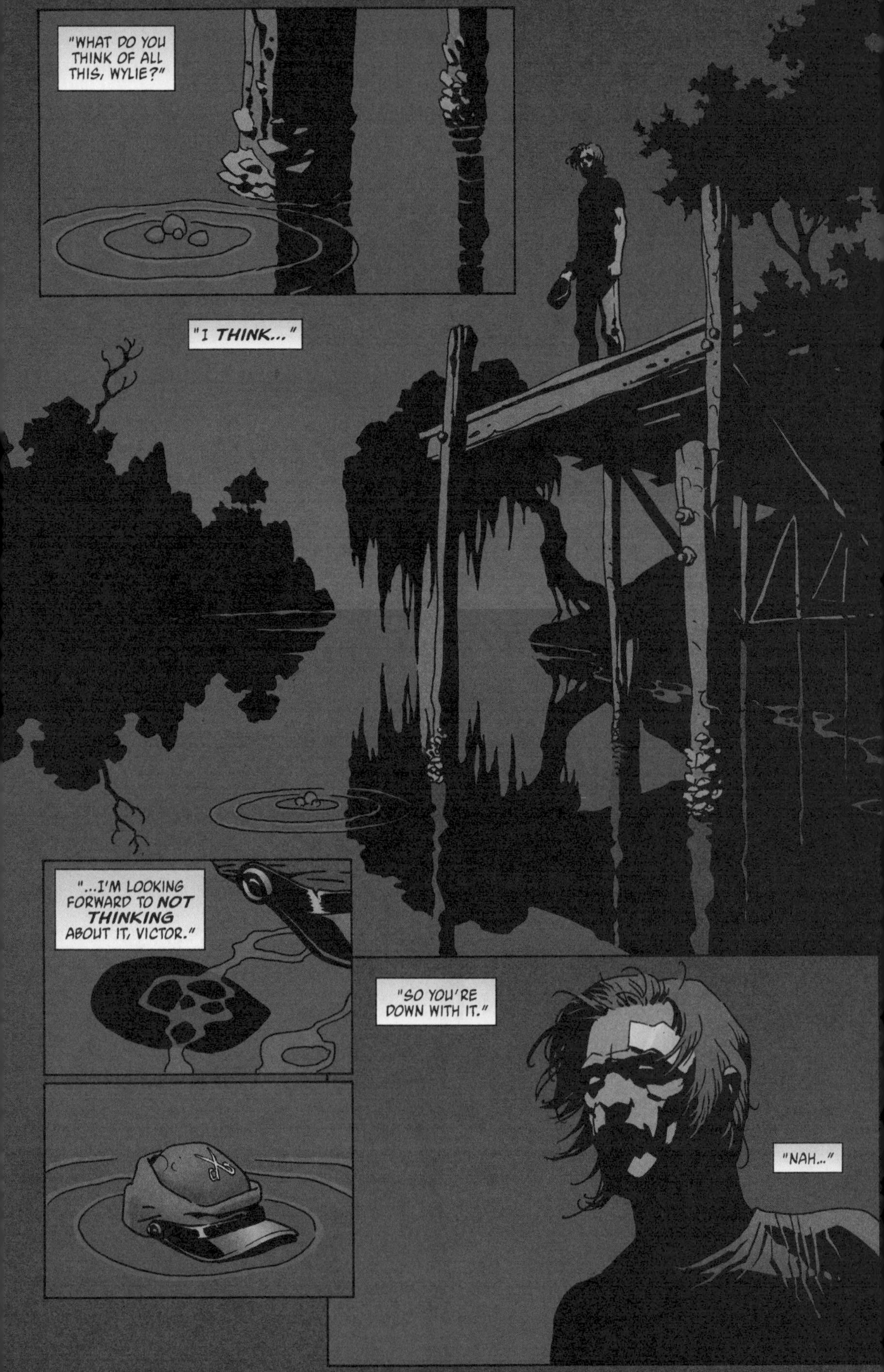
"WHAT DO YOU THINK OF ALL THIS, WYLIE?"
"I *THINK...*"
"...I'M LOOKING FORWARD TO **NOT THINKING** ABOUT IT, VICTOR."
"SO YOU'RE DOWN WITH IT."
"NAH..."

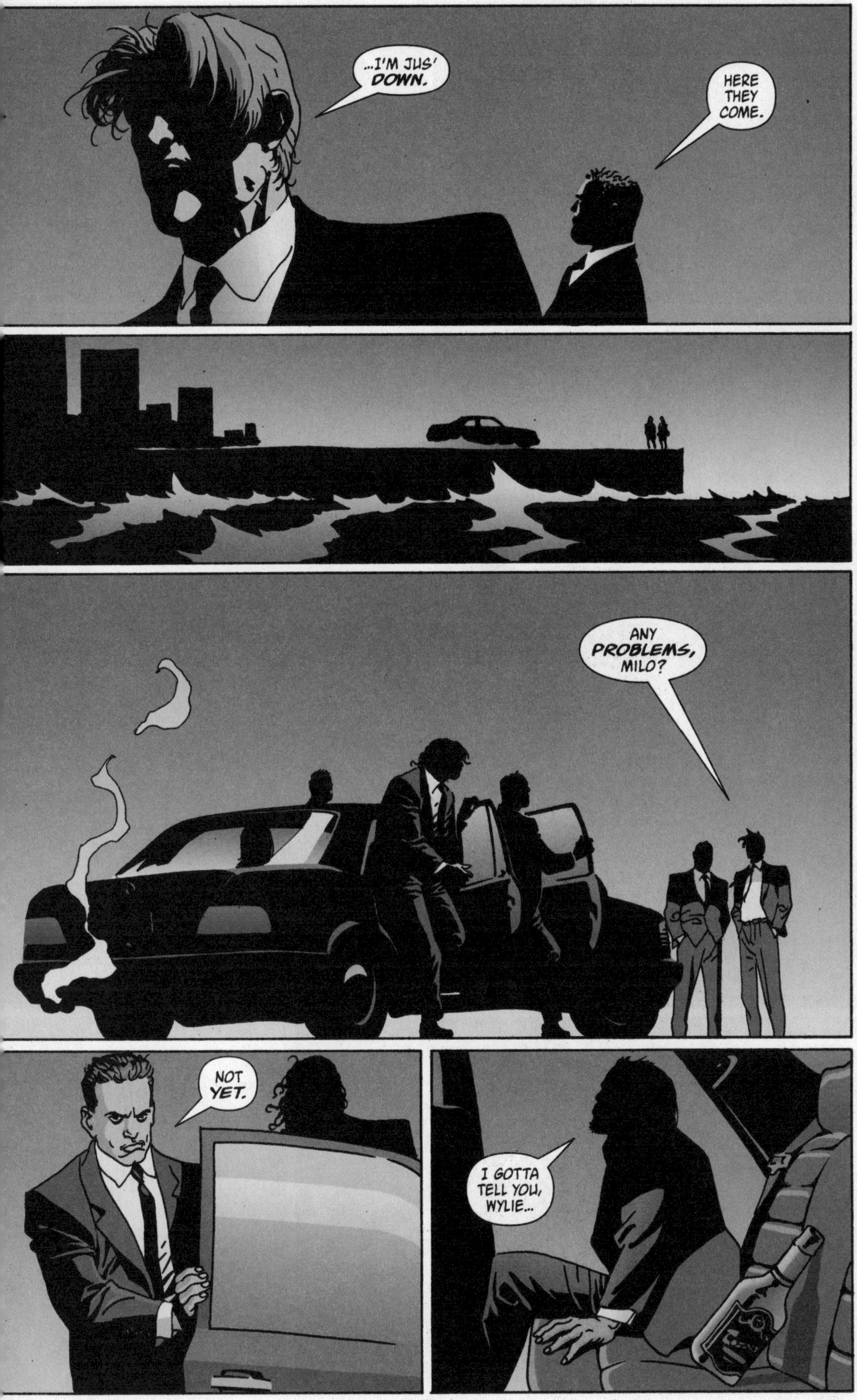
...I'M JUS' DOWN.
HERE THEY COME.
ANY PROBLEMS, MILO?
NOT YET.
I GOTTA TELL YOU, WYLIE...

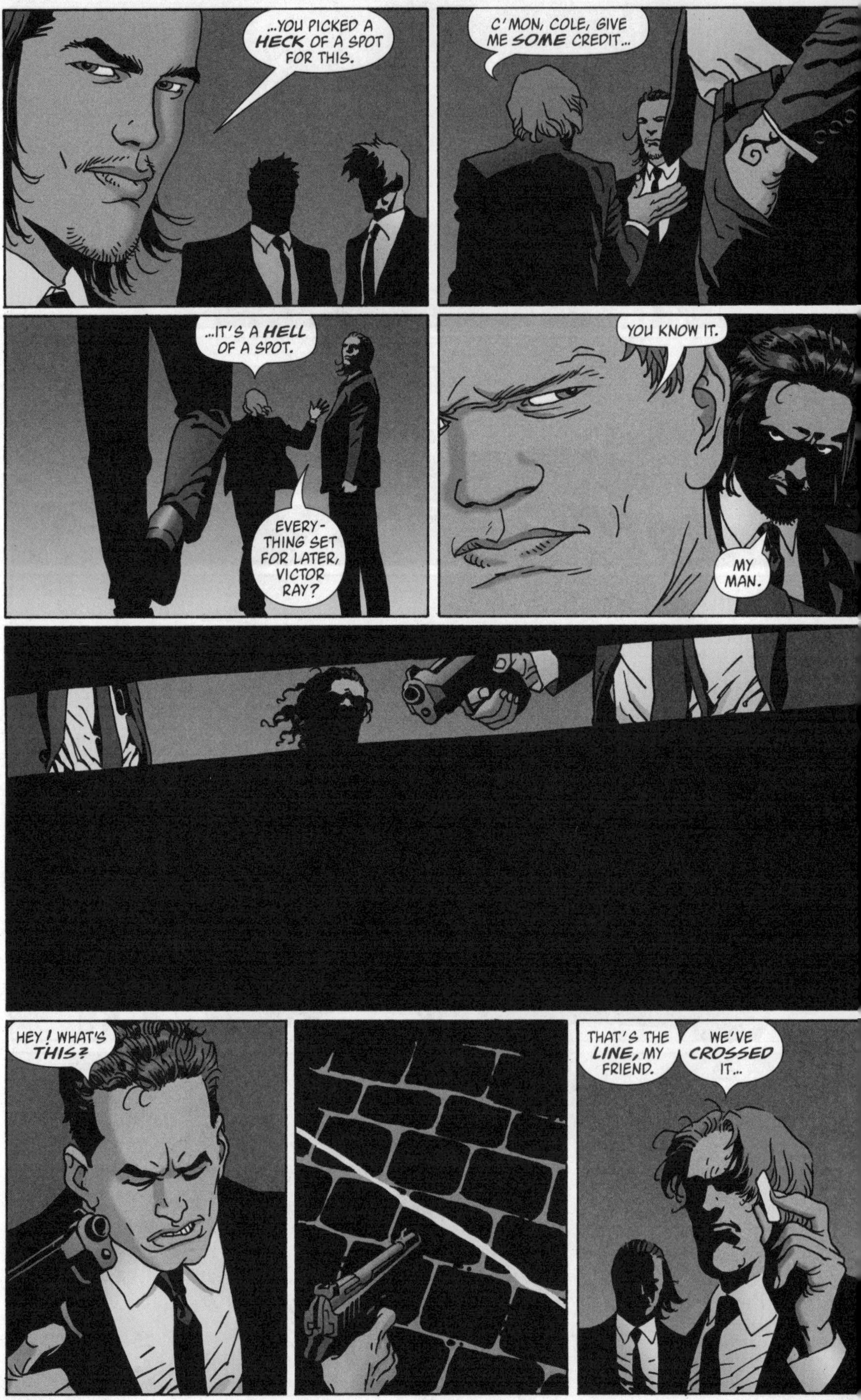
...YOU PICKED A HECK OF A SPOT FOR THIS.
C'MON, COLE, GIVE ME SOME CREDIT...
...IT'S A HELL OF A SPOT.
EVERY-THING SET FOR LATER, VICTOR RAY?
YOU KNOW IT.
MY MAN.
HEY! WHAT'S THIS?
THAT'S THE LINE, MY FRIEND.
WE'VE CROSSED IT...

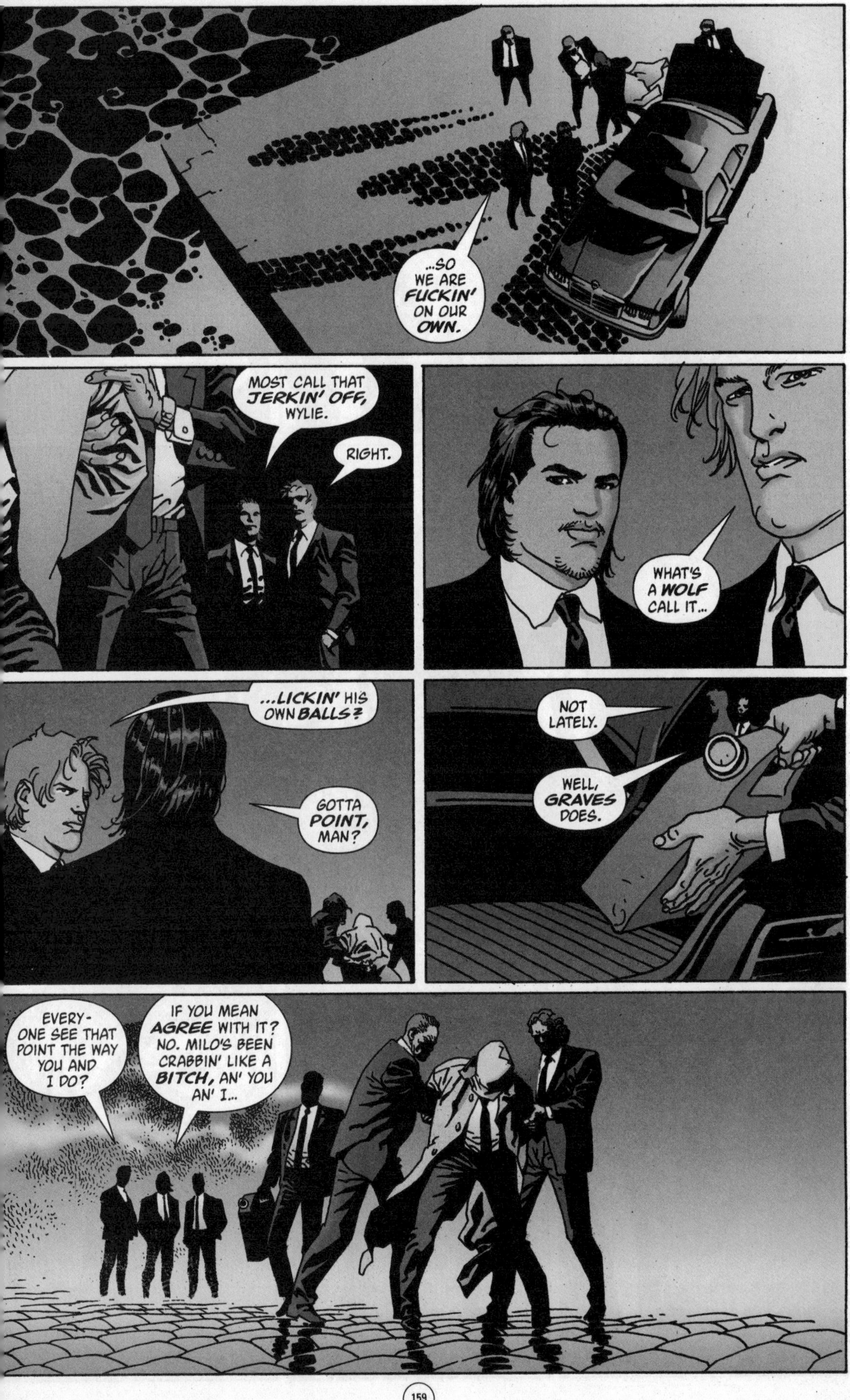
...SO WE ARE FUCKIN' ON OUR OWN.
MOST CALL THAT JERKIN' OFF, WYLIE.
RIGHT.
WHAT'S A WOLF CALL IT...
...LICKIN' HIS OWN BALLS?
GOTTA POINT, MAN?
NOT LATELY.
WELL, GRAVES DOES.
EVERY-ONE SEE THAT POINT THE WAY YOU AND I DO?
IF YOU MEAN AGREE WITH IT? NO. MILO'S BEEN CRABBIN' LIKE A BITCH, AN' YOU AN' I...

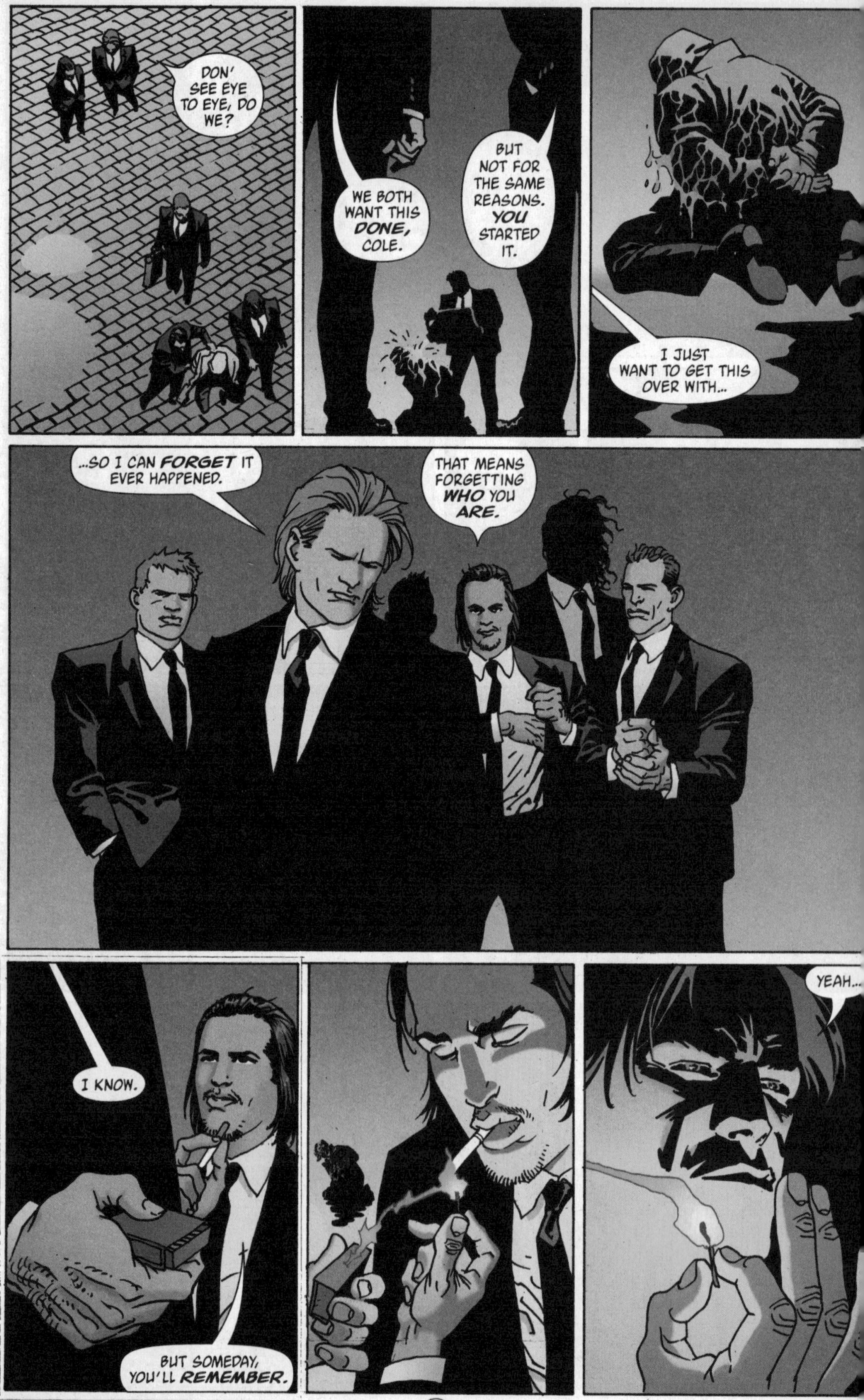

DON' SEE EYE TO EYE, DO WE?
WE BOTH WANT THIS DONE, COLE.
BUT NOT FOR THE SAME REASONS. YOU STARTED IT.
I JUST WANT TO GET THIS OVER WITH...
...SO I CAN FORGET IT EVER HAPPENED.
THAT MEANS FORGETTING WHO YOU ARE.
I KNOW.
BUT SOMEDAY, YOU'LL REMEMBER.
YEAH...

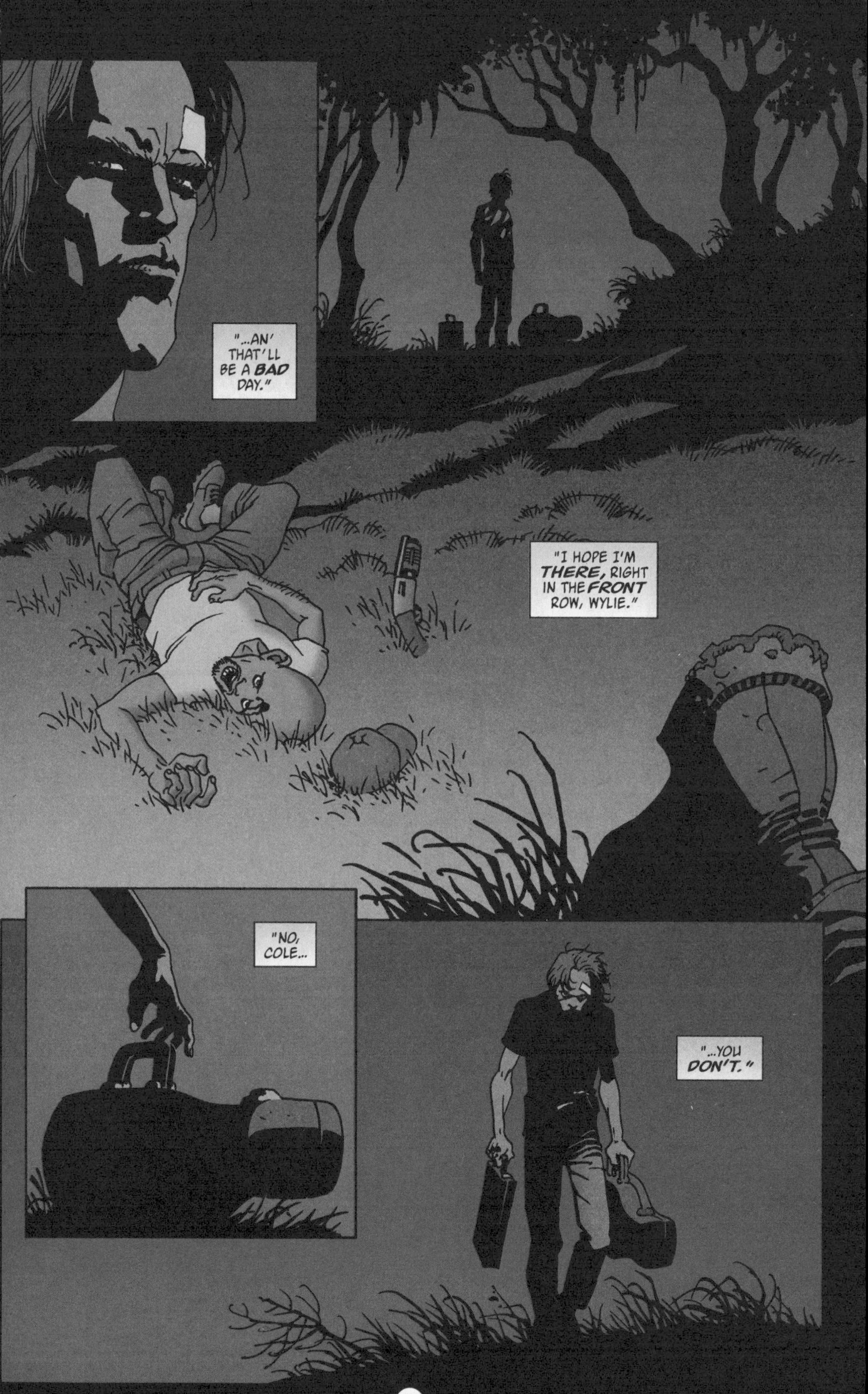
"...AN' THAT'LL BE A **BAD** DAY."
"I HOPE I'M **THERE,** RIGHT IN THE **FRONT** ROW, WYLIE."
"NO, COLE...
"...YOU **DON'T.**"

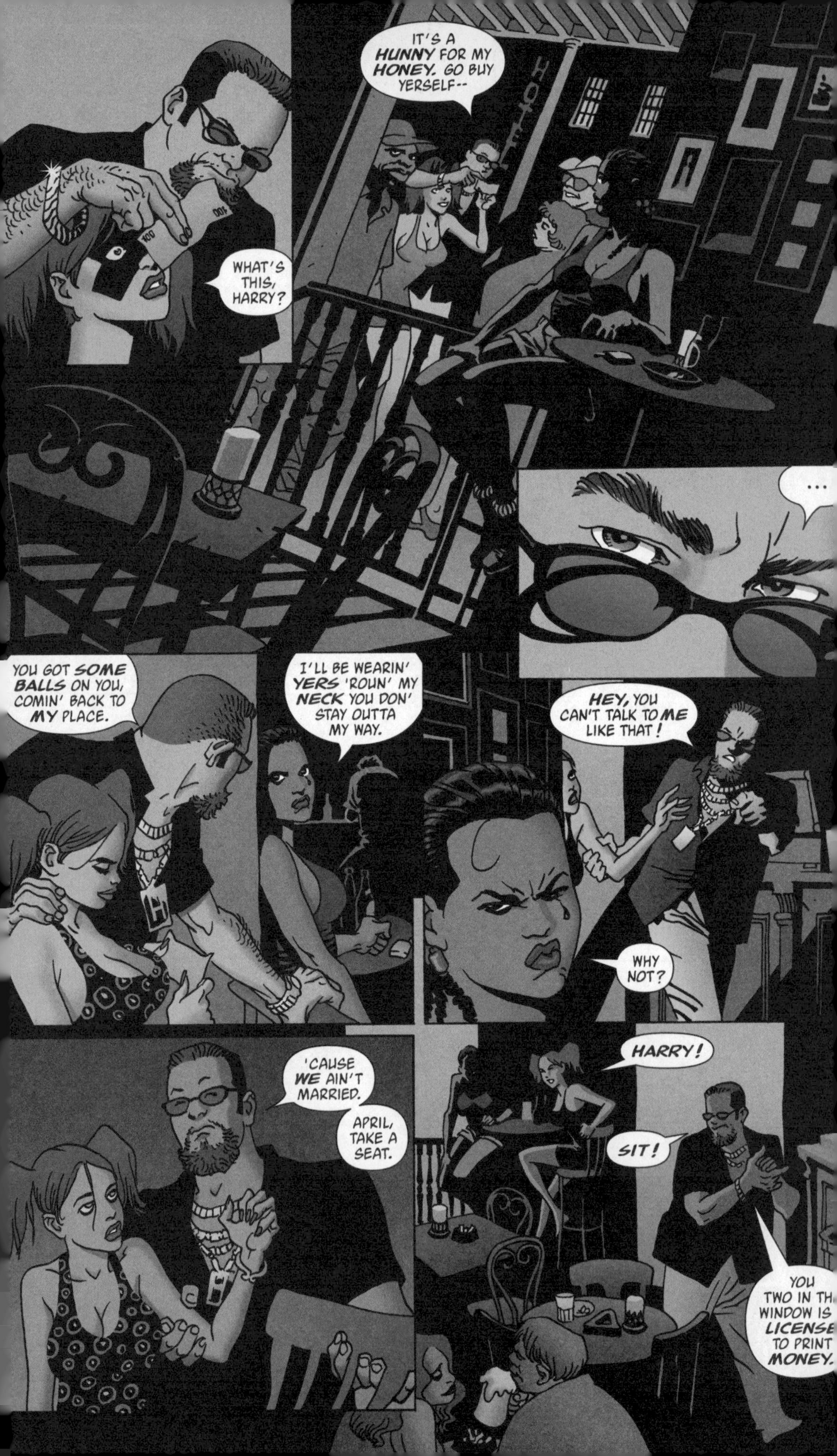
WHAT'S THIS, HARRY?
IT'S A HUNNY FOR MY HONEY. GO BUY YERSELF--
...
YOU GOT SOME BALLS ON YOU, COMIN' BACK TO MY PLACE.
I'LL BE WEARIN' YERS 'ROUN' MY NECK YOU DON' STAY OUTTA MY WAY.
HEY, YOU CAN'T TALK TO ME LIKE THAT!
WHY NOT?
'CAUSE WE AIN'T MARRIED.
APRIL, TAKE A SEAT.
HARRY!
SIT!
YOU TWO IN TH WINDOW IS LICENSE TO PRINT MONEY.

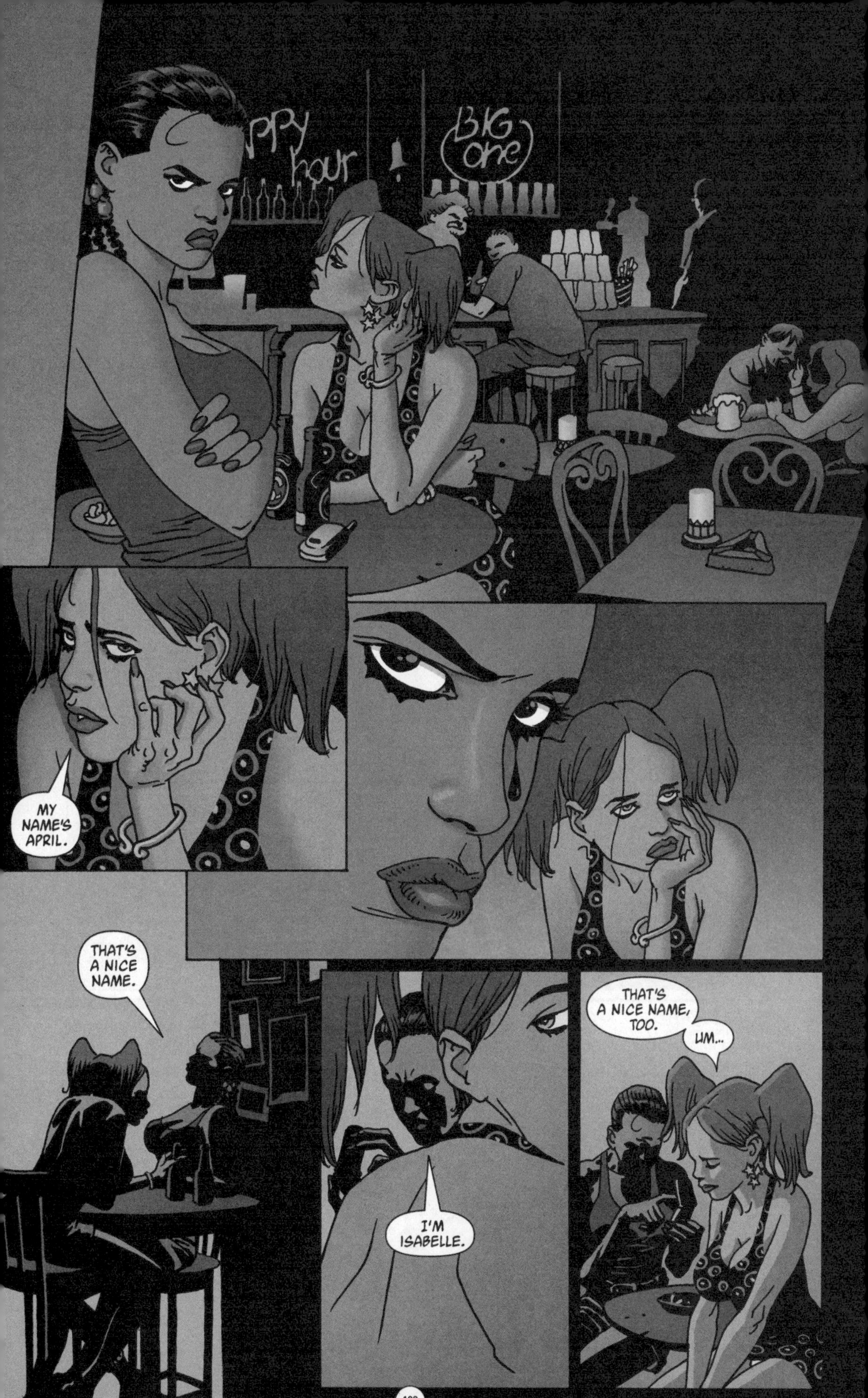

PPY
hour
BIG
one
MY NAME'S APRIL.
THAT'S A NICE NAME.
I'M ISABELLE.
THAT'S A NICE NAME, TOO.
UM...

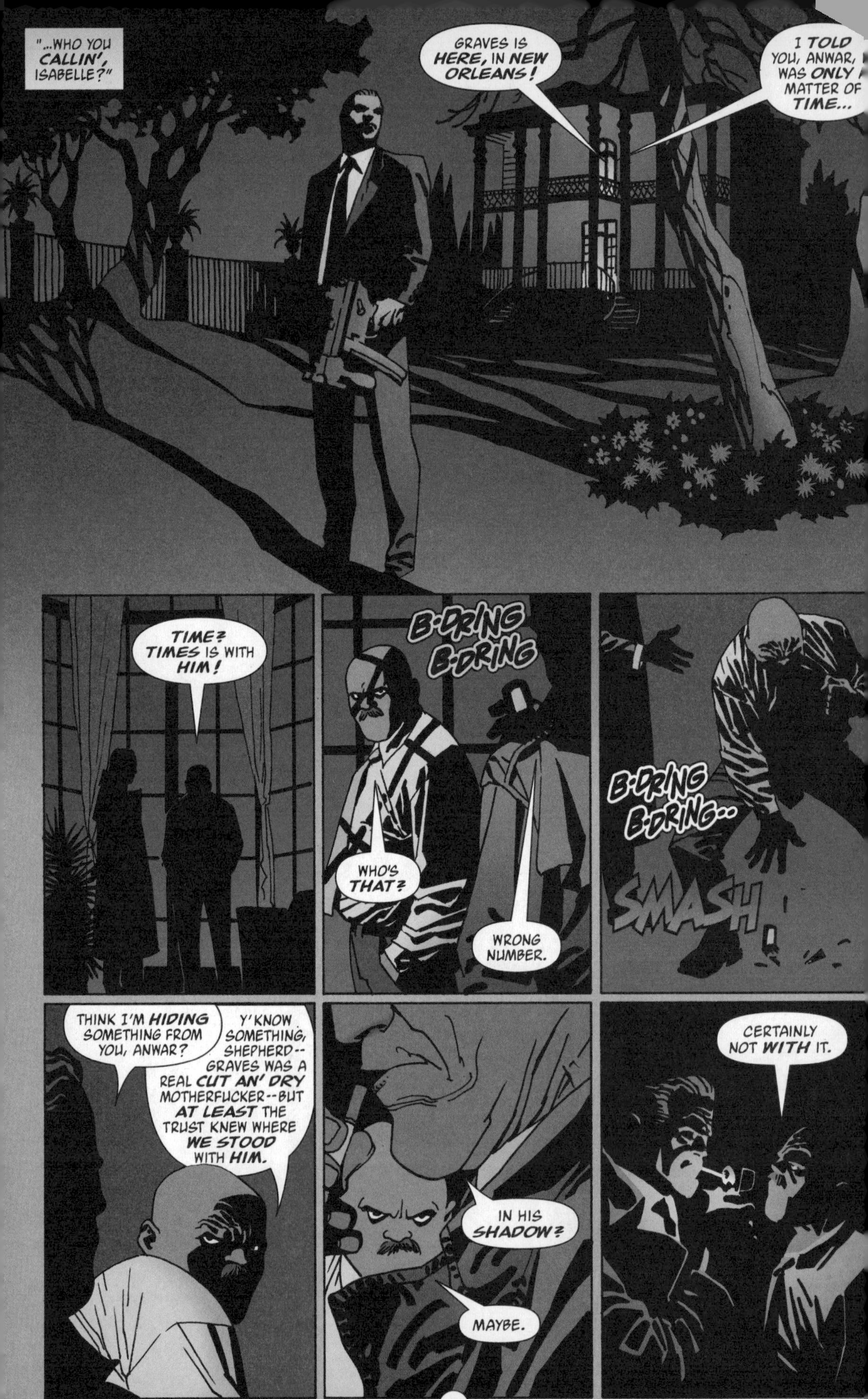
"...WHO YOU CALLIN', ISABELLE?"
GRAVES IS HERE, IN NEW ORLEANS!
I TOLD YOU, ANWAR, WAS ONLY A MATTER OF TIME...
TIME? TIMES IS WITH HIM!
B-DRING B-DRING
WHO'S THAT?
WRONG NUMBER.
B-DRING B-DRING..
SMASH
THINK I'M HIDING SOMETHING FROM YOU, ANWAR?
Y'KNOW SOMETHING, SHEPHERD-- GRAVES WAS A REAL CUT AN' DRY MOTHERFUCKER--BUT AT LEAST THE TRUST KNEW WHERE WE STOOD WITH HIM.
IN HIS SHADOW?
MAYBE.
CERTAINLY NOT WITH IT.

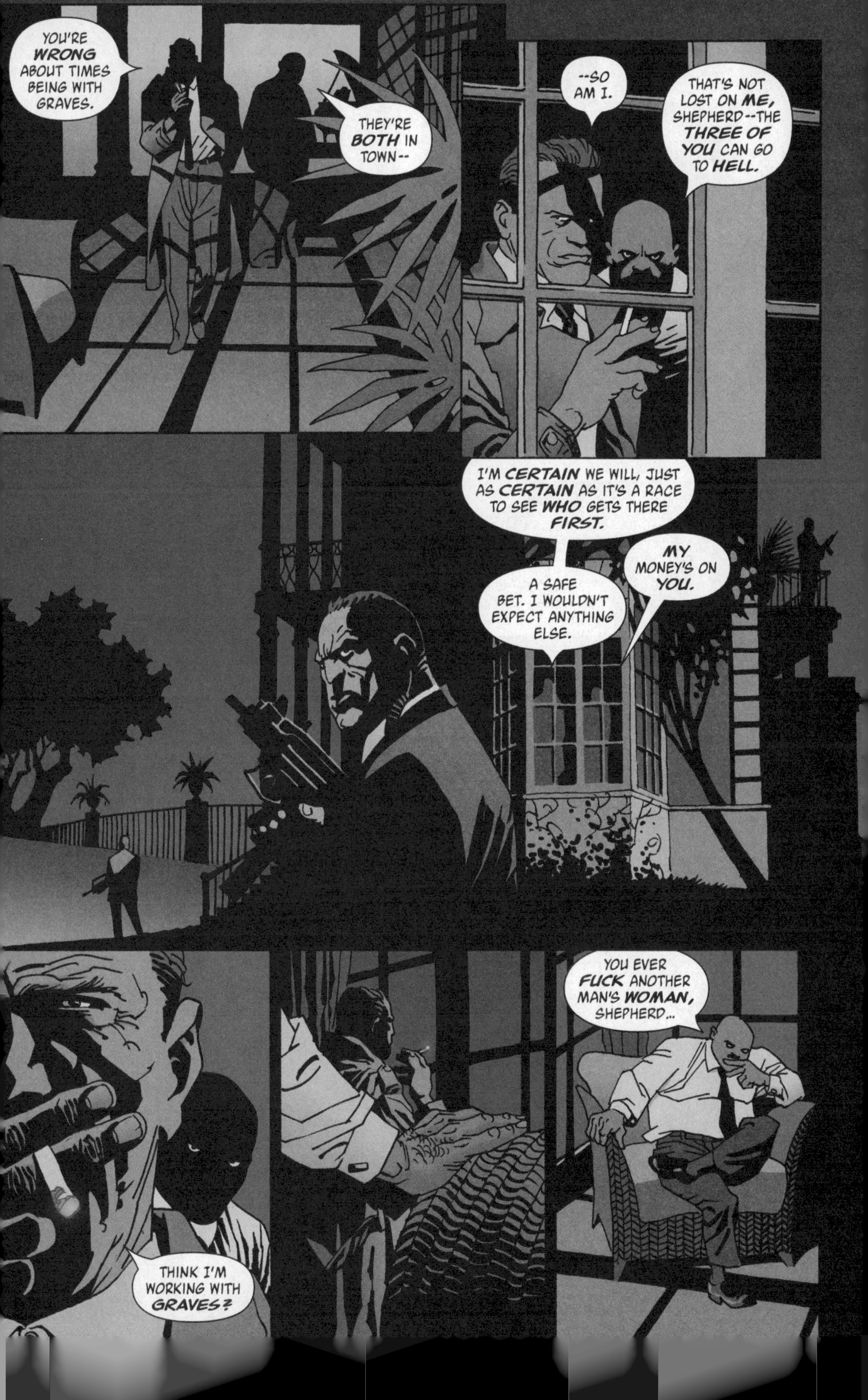
YOU'RE WRONG ABOUT TIMES BEING WITH GRAVES.
THEY'RE BOTH IN TOWN--
--SO AM I.
THAT'S NOT LOST ON ME, SHEPHERD--THE THREE OF YOU CAN GO TO HELL.
I'M CERTAIN WE WILL, JUST AS CERTAIN AS IT'S A RACE TO SEE WHO GETS THERE FIRST.
A SAFE BET. I WOULDN'T EXPECT ANYTHING ELSE.
MY MONEY'S ON YOU.
THINK I'M WORKING WITH GRAVES?
YOU EVER FUCK ANOTHER MAN'S WOMAN, SHEPHERD...

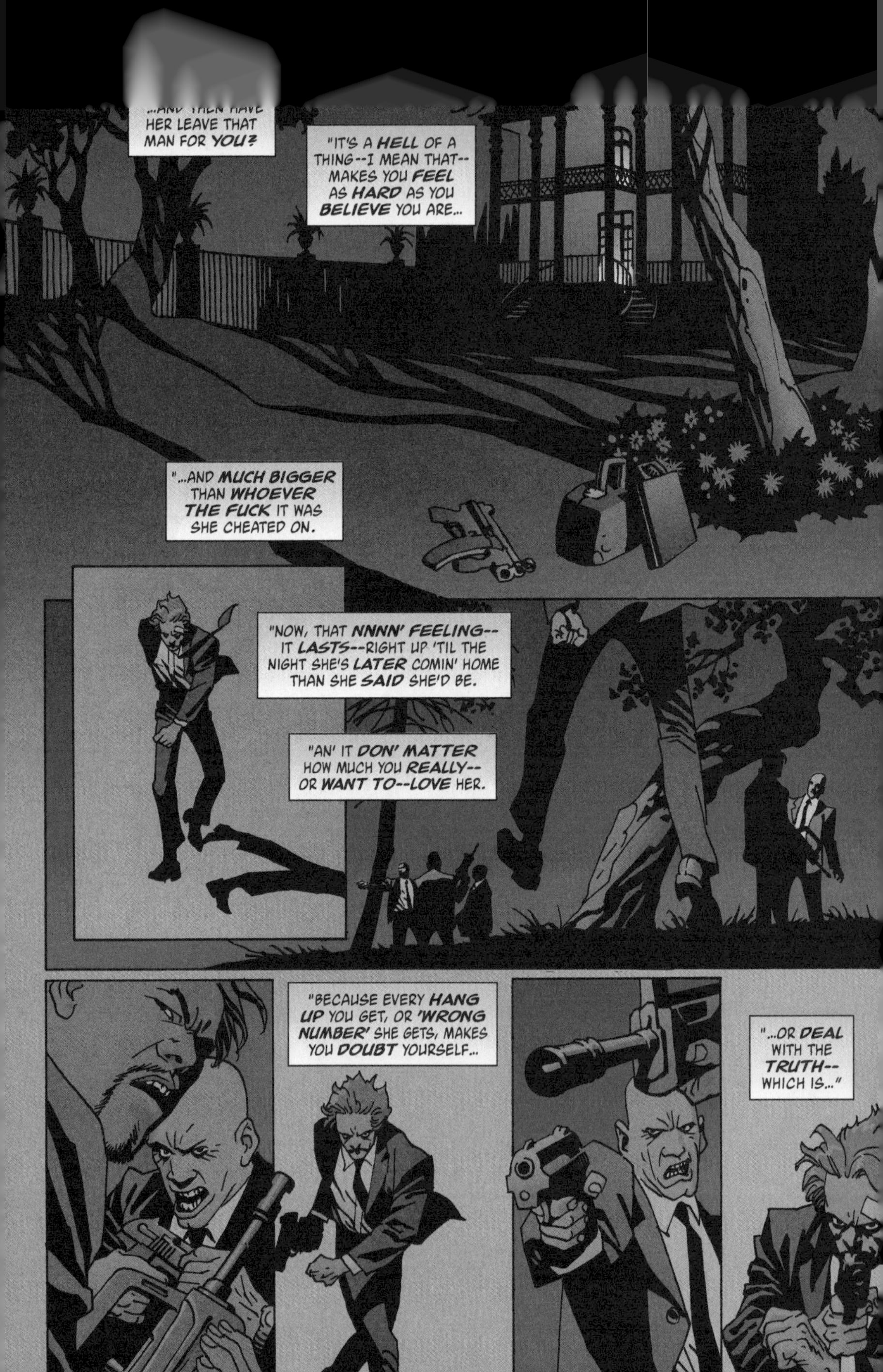
HER LEAVE THAT MAN FOR YOU?
"IT'S A HELL OF A THING--I MEAN THAT--MAKES YOU FEEL AS HARD AS YOU BELIEVE YOU ARE...
"...AND MUCH BIGGER THAN WHOEVER THE FUCK IT WAS SHE CHEATED ON.
"NOW, THAT NNNN' FEELING--IT LASTS--RIGHT UP 'TIL THE NIGHT SHE'S LATER COMIN' HOME THAN SHE SAID SHE'D BE.
"AN' IT DON' MATTER HOW MUCH YOU REALLY--OR WANT TO--LOVE HER.
"BECAUSE EVERY HANG UP YOU GET, OR 'WRONG NUMBER' SHE GETS, MAKES YOU DOUBT YOURSELF...
"...OR DEAL WITH THE TRUTH--WHICH IS..."

IF SHE DID IT **ONCE**, SHE CAN DO IT **AGAIN**.

AN' YOU MIGHT BE THE "WHOEVER THE **FUCK** IT WAS" THIS TIME.

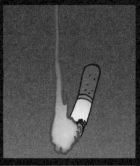

BANG

GET DOWN.

BAMBAMBAM

BANG

JESUS...

WHAT?

BAM BAMBAM BANG

NOT A WASTED ROUND...

...EVERY **SHOT** HAS A **POINT**.

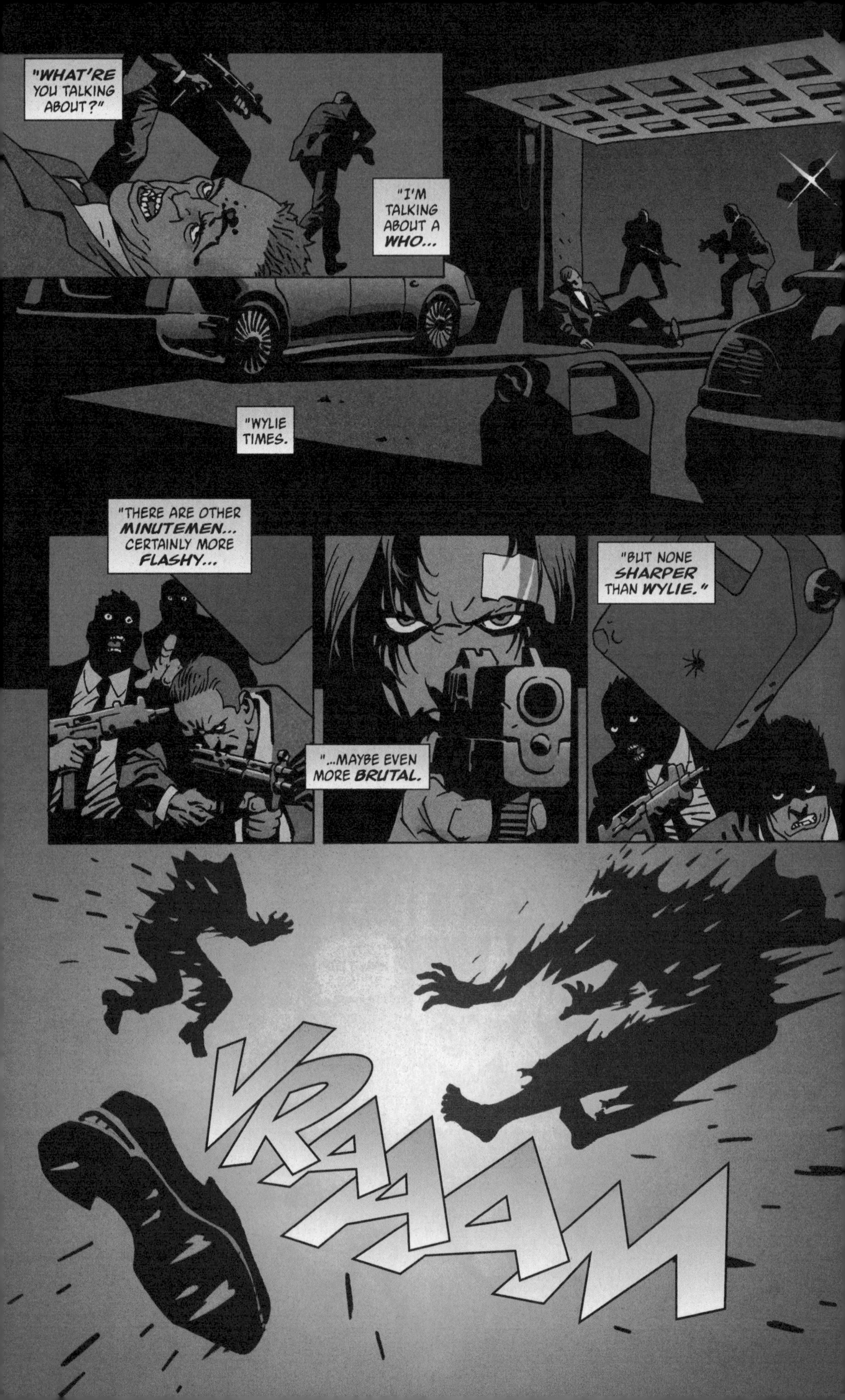
"WHAT'RE YOU TALKING ABOUT?"
"I'M TALKING ABOUT A WHO...
"WYLIE TIMES.
"THERE ARE OTHER MINUTEMEN... CERTAINLY MORE FLASHY...
"...MAYBE EVEN MORE BRUTAL.
"BUT NONE SHARPER THAN WYLIE."
VRAAAM

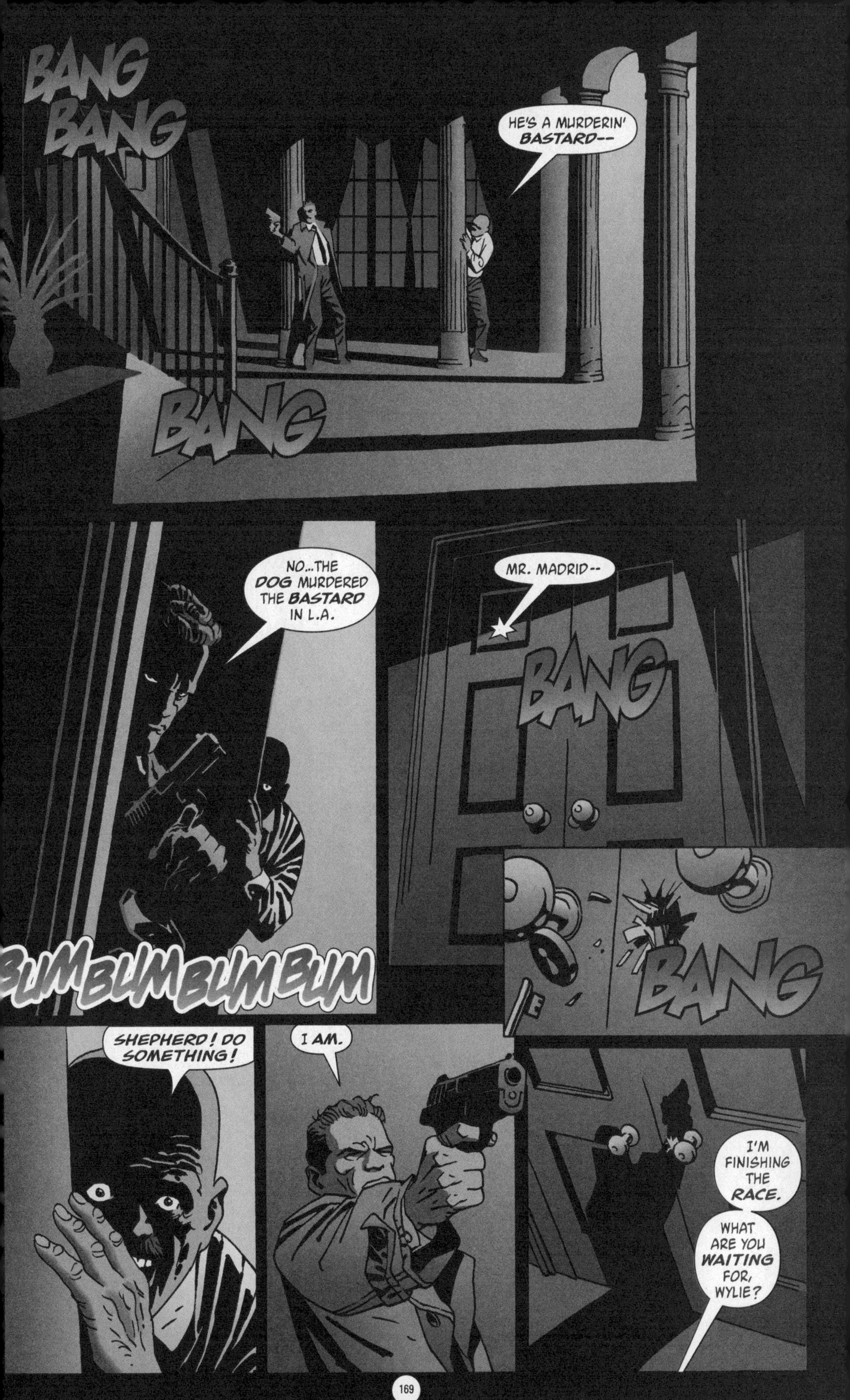
BANG
BANG
HE'S A MURDERIN' BASTARD--
BANG
NO...THE DOG MURDERED THE BASTARD IN L.A.
BLIM BLIM BLIM BLIM
MR. MADRID--
BANG
BANG
SHEPHERD! DO SOMETHING!
I AM.
I'M FINISHING THE RACE.
WHAT ARE YOU WAITING FOR, WYLIE?

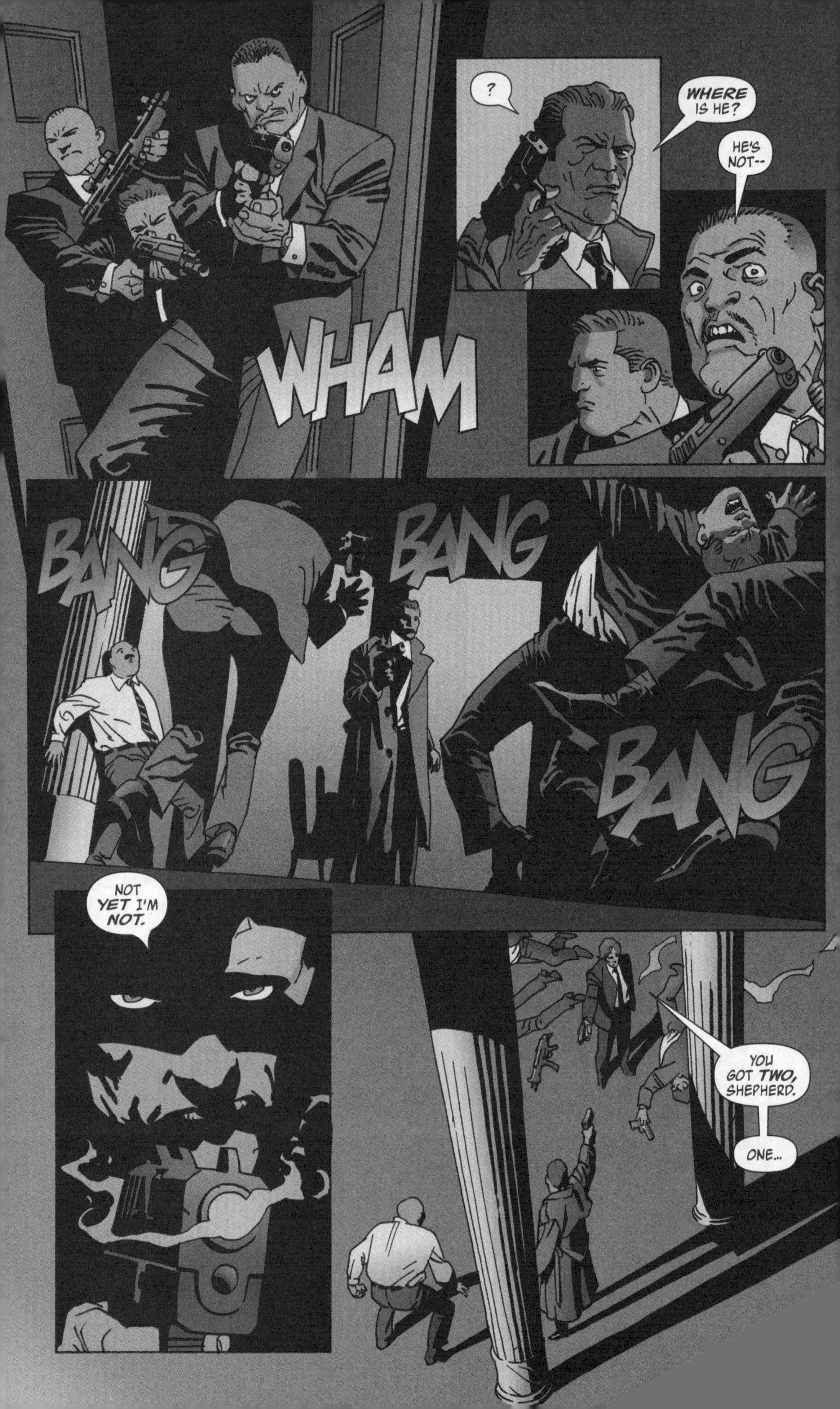
WHAM
?
WHERE IS HE?
HE'S NOT--
BANG
BANG
BANG
NOT YET I'M NOT.
YOU GOT TWO, SHEPHERD.
ONE...

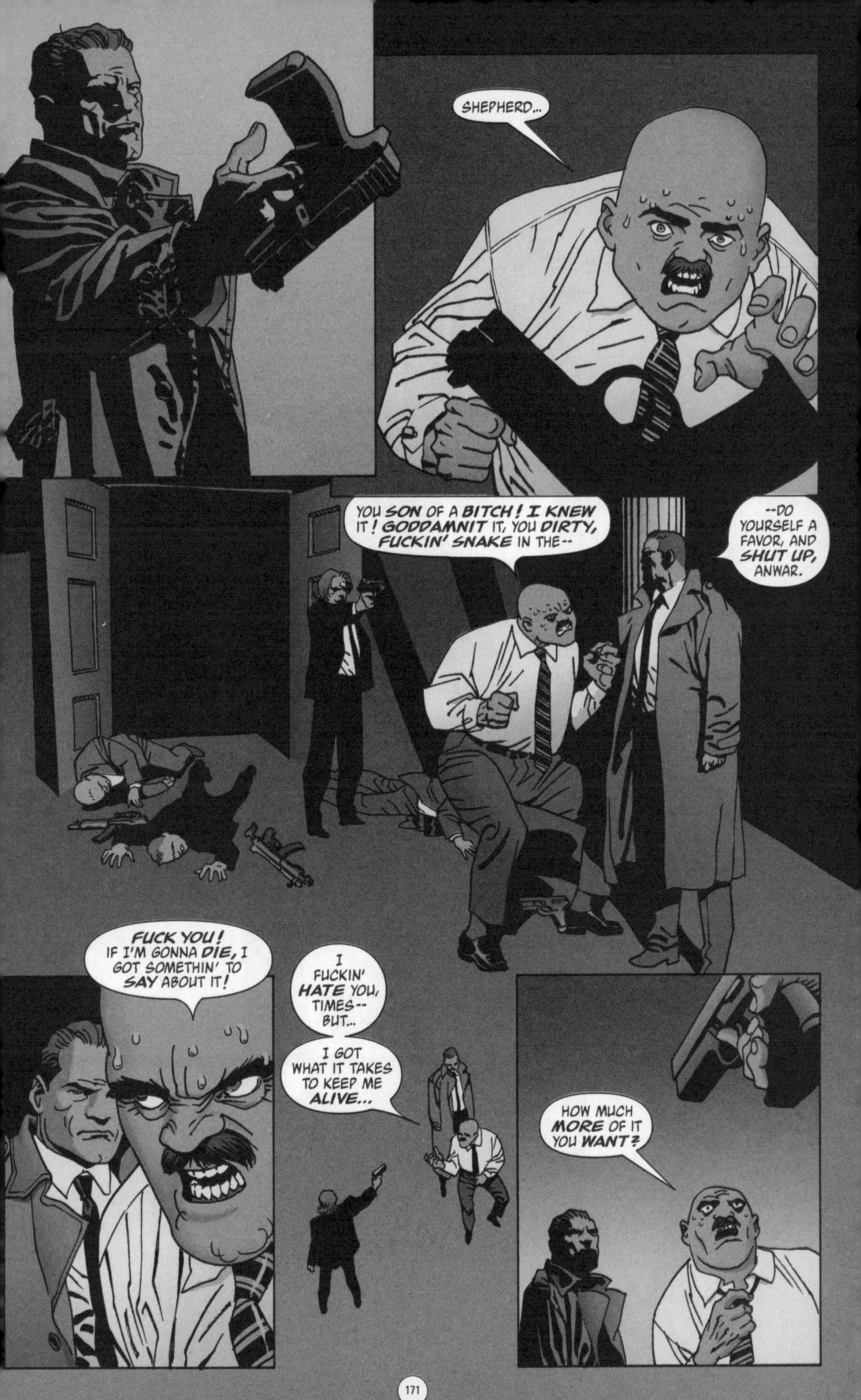

SHEPHERD...
YOU SON OF A BITCH! I KNEW IT! GODDAMNIT IT, YOU DIRTY, FUCKIN' SNAKE IN THE--
--DO YOURSELF A FAVOR, AND SHUT UP, ANWAR.
FUCK YOU! IF I'M GONNA DIE, I GOT SOMETHIN' TO SAY ABOUT IT!
I FUCKIN' HATE YOU, TIMES-- BUT...
I GOT WHAT IT TAKES TO KEEP ME ALIVE...
HOW MUCH MORE OF IT YOU WANT?

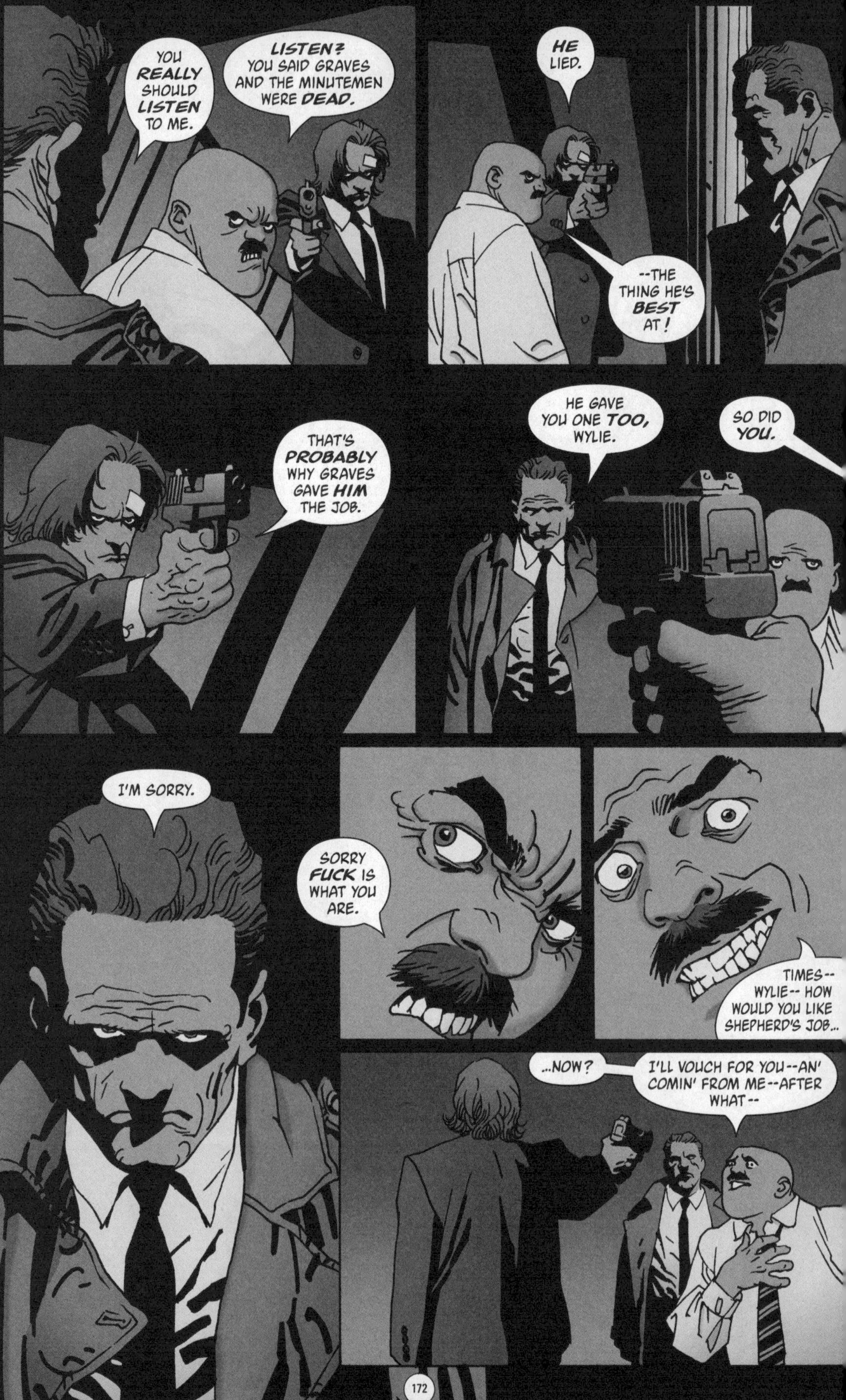
YOU REALLY SHOULD LISTEN TO ME.
LISTEN? YOU SAID GRAVES AND THE MINUTEMEN WERE DEAD.
HE LIED.
--THE THING HE'S BEST AT!
THAT'S PROBABLY WHY GRAVES GAVE HIM THE JOB.
HE GAVE YOU ONE TOO, WYLIE.
SO DID YOU.
I'M SORRY.
SORRY FUCK IS WHAT YOU ARE.
TIMES-- WYLIE-- HOW WOULD YOU LIKE SHEPHERD'S JOB...
...NOW?
I'LL VOUCH FOR YOU--AN' COMIN' FROM ME--AFTER WHAT--

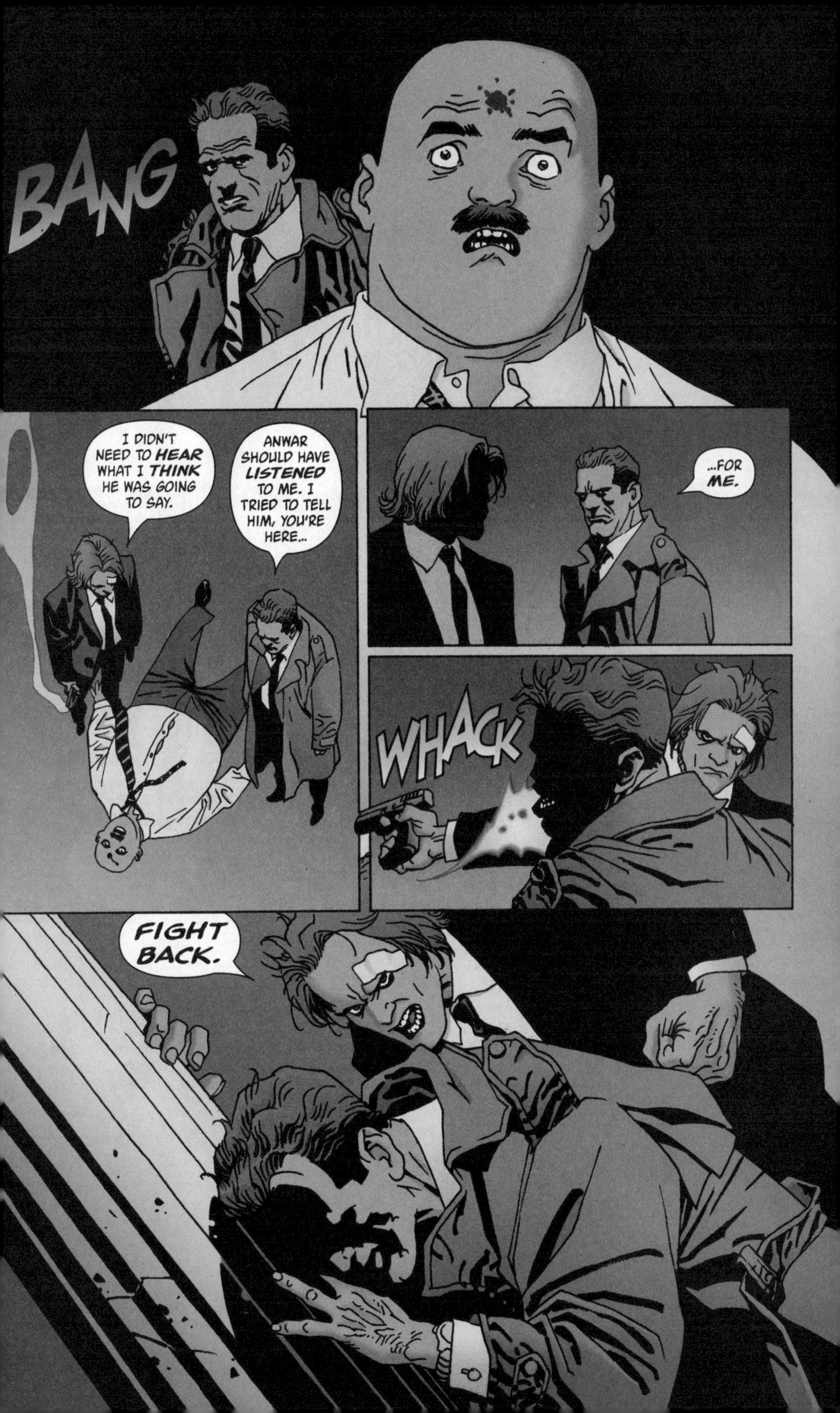
BANG
I DIDN'T NEED TO HEAR WHAT I THINK HE WAS GOING TO SAY.
ANWAR SHOULD HAVE LISTENED TO ME. I TRIED TO TELL HIM, YOU'RE HERE...
...FOR ME.
WHACK
FIGHT BACK.

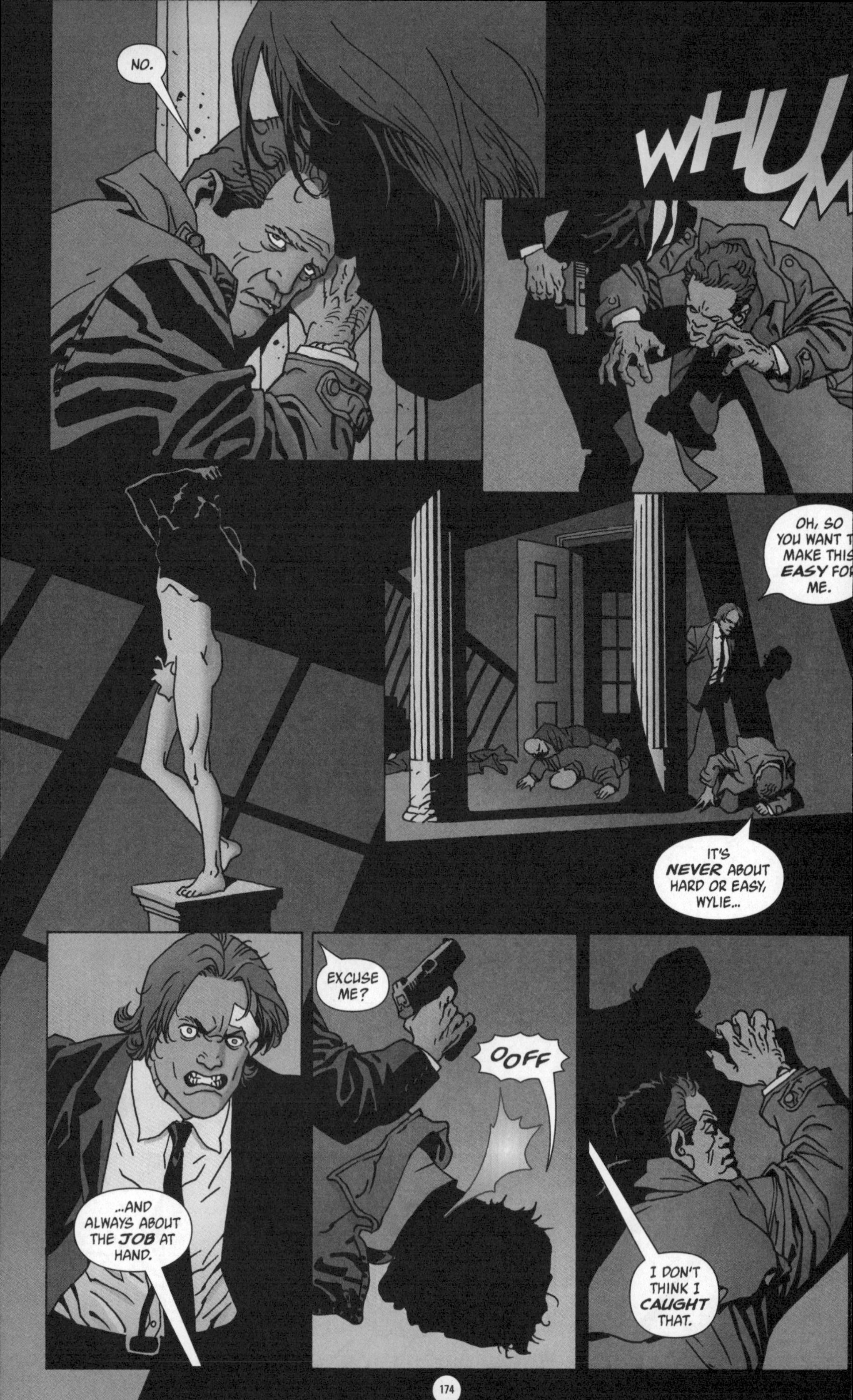
NO.
WHUM
OH, SO YOU WANT T MAKE THIS EASY FO ME.
IT'S NEVER ABOUT HARD OR EASY, WYLIE...
...AND ALWAYS ABOUT THE JOB AT HAND.
EXCUSE ME?
OOFF
I DON'T THINK I CAUGHT THAT.

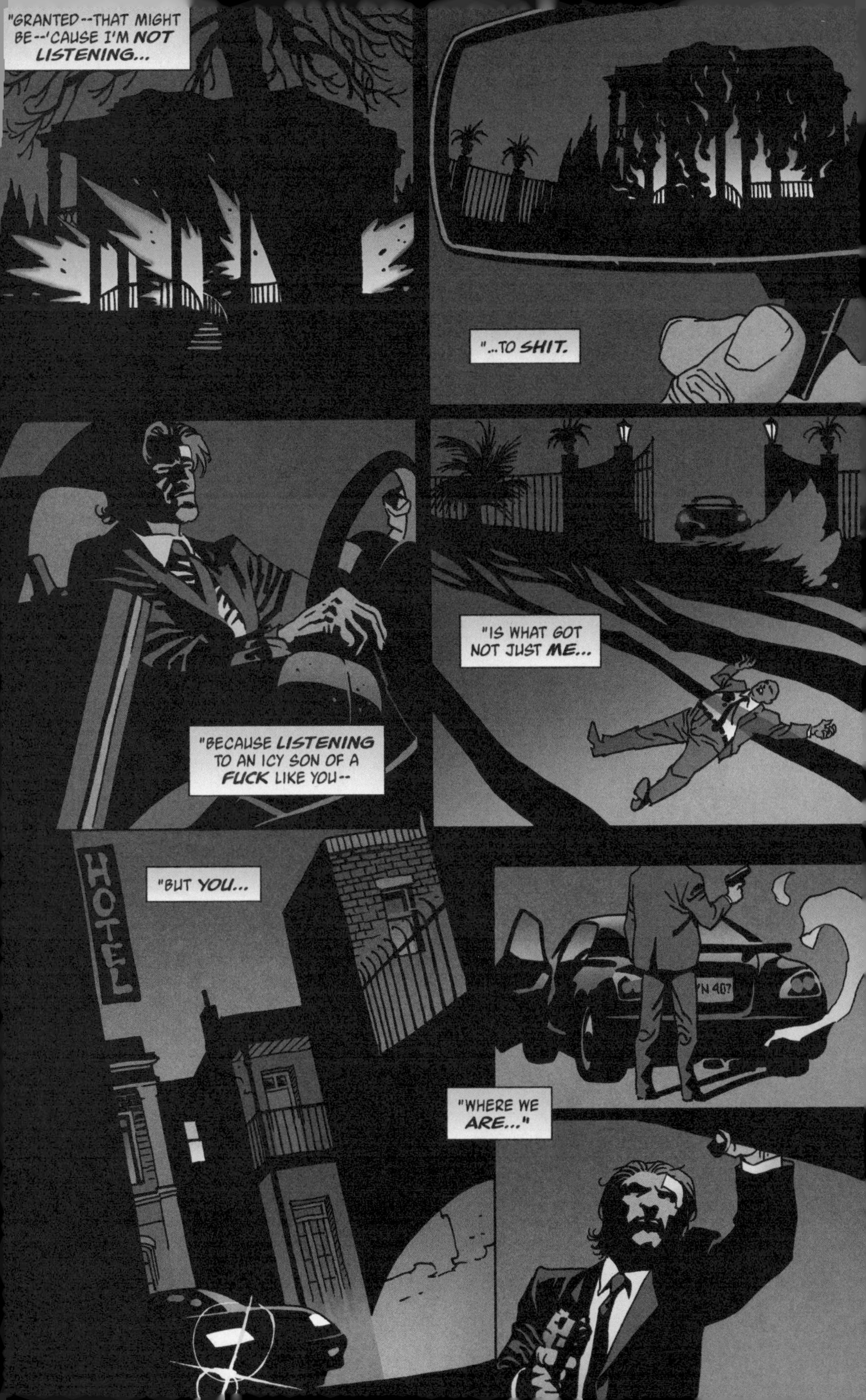
"GRANTED--THAT MIGHT BE--'CAUSE I'M NOT LISTENING...
"...TO SHIT.
"BECAUSE LISTENING TO AN ICY SON OF A FUCK LIKE YOU--
"IS WHAT GOT NOT JUST ME...
HOTEL
"BUT YOU...
"WHERE WE ARE..."

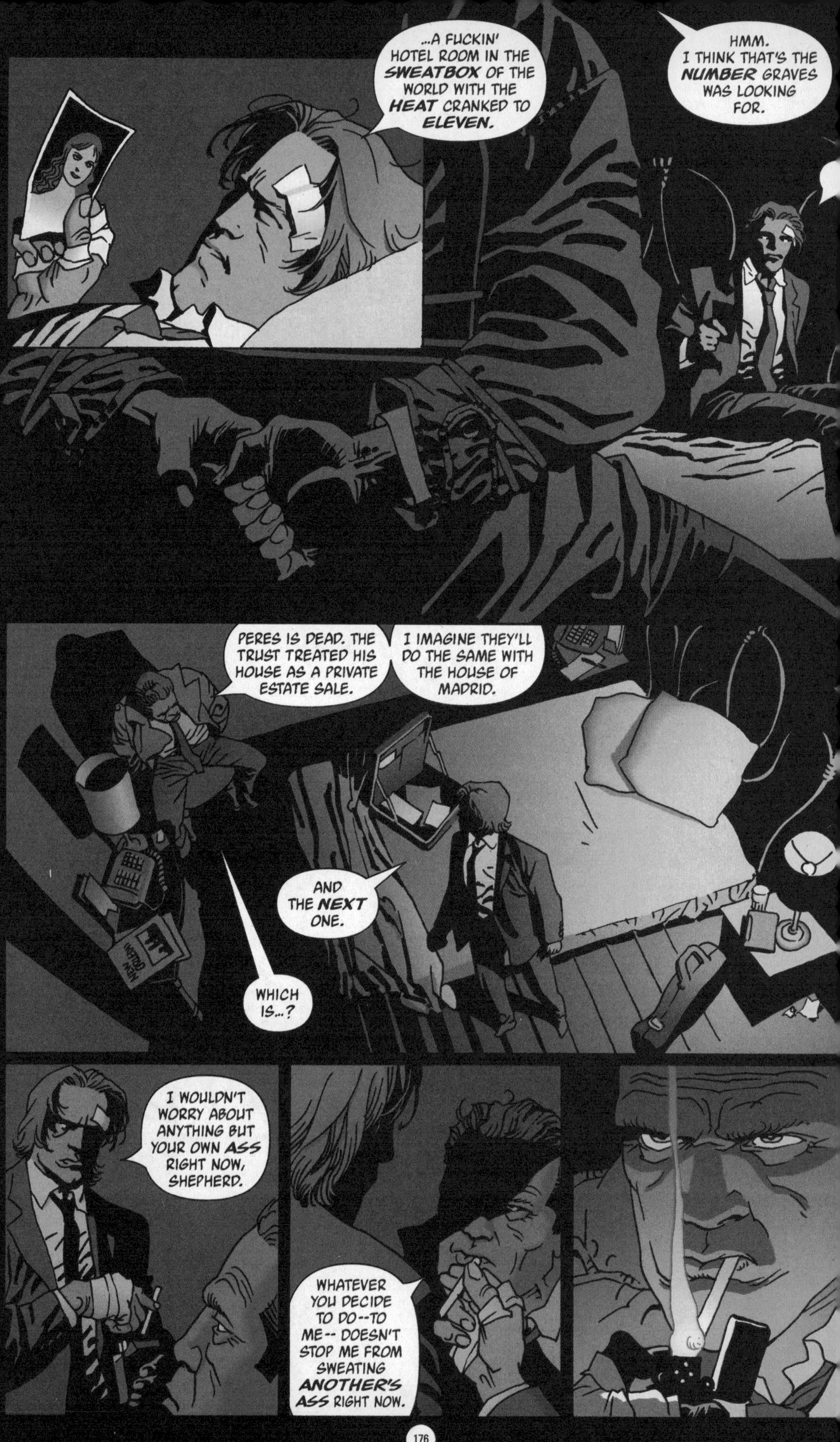
...A FUCKIN' HOTEL ROOM IN THE SWEATBOX OF THE WORLD WITH THE HEAT CRANKED TO ELEVEN.
HMM. I THINK THAT'S THE NUMBER GRAVES WAS LOOKING FOR.
PERES IS DEAD. THE TRUST TREATED HIS HOUSE AS A PRIVATE ESTATE SALE.
I IMAGINE THEY'LL DO THE SAME WITH THE HOUSE OF MADRID.
AND THE NEXT ONE.
WHICH IS...?
I WOULDN'T WORRY ABOUT ANYTHING BUT YOUR OWN ASS RIGHT NOW, SHEPHERD.
WHATEVER YOU DECIDE TO DO--TO ME-- DOESN'T STOP ME FROM SWEATING ANOTHER'S ASS RIGHT NOW.

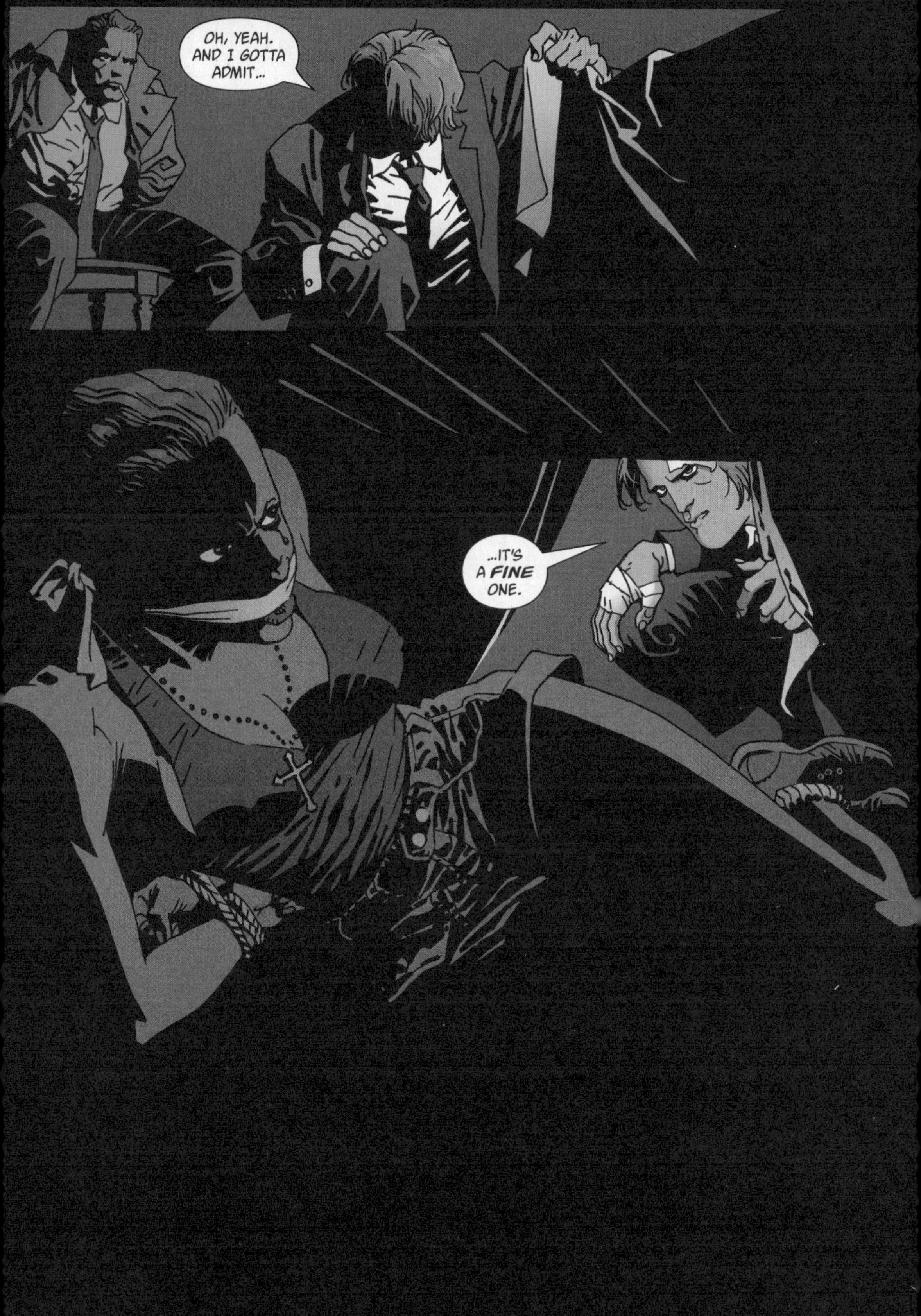
OH, YEAH. AND I GOTTA ADMIT...
...IT'S A FINE ONE.

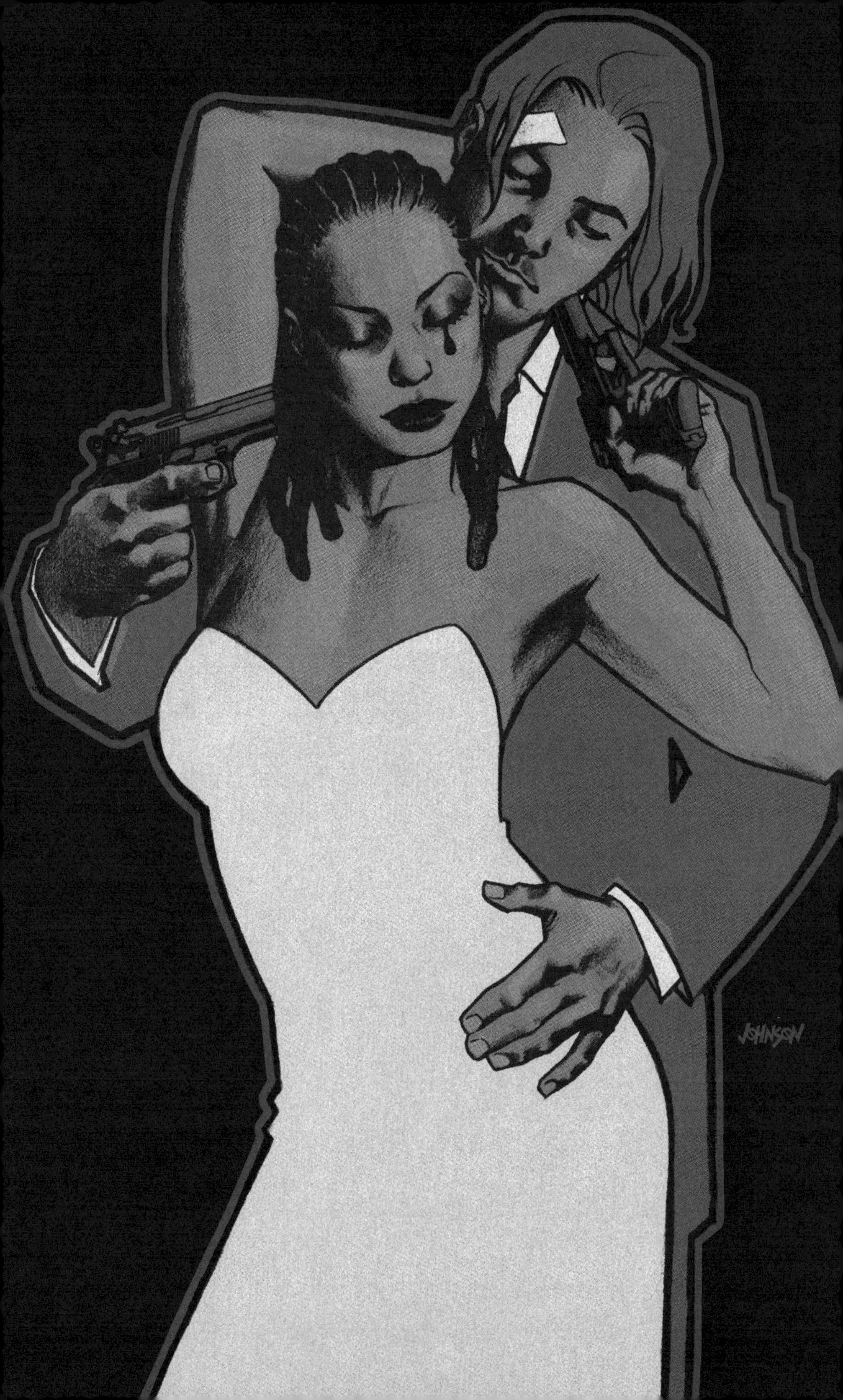
JOHNSON

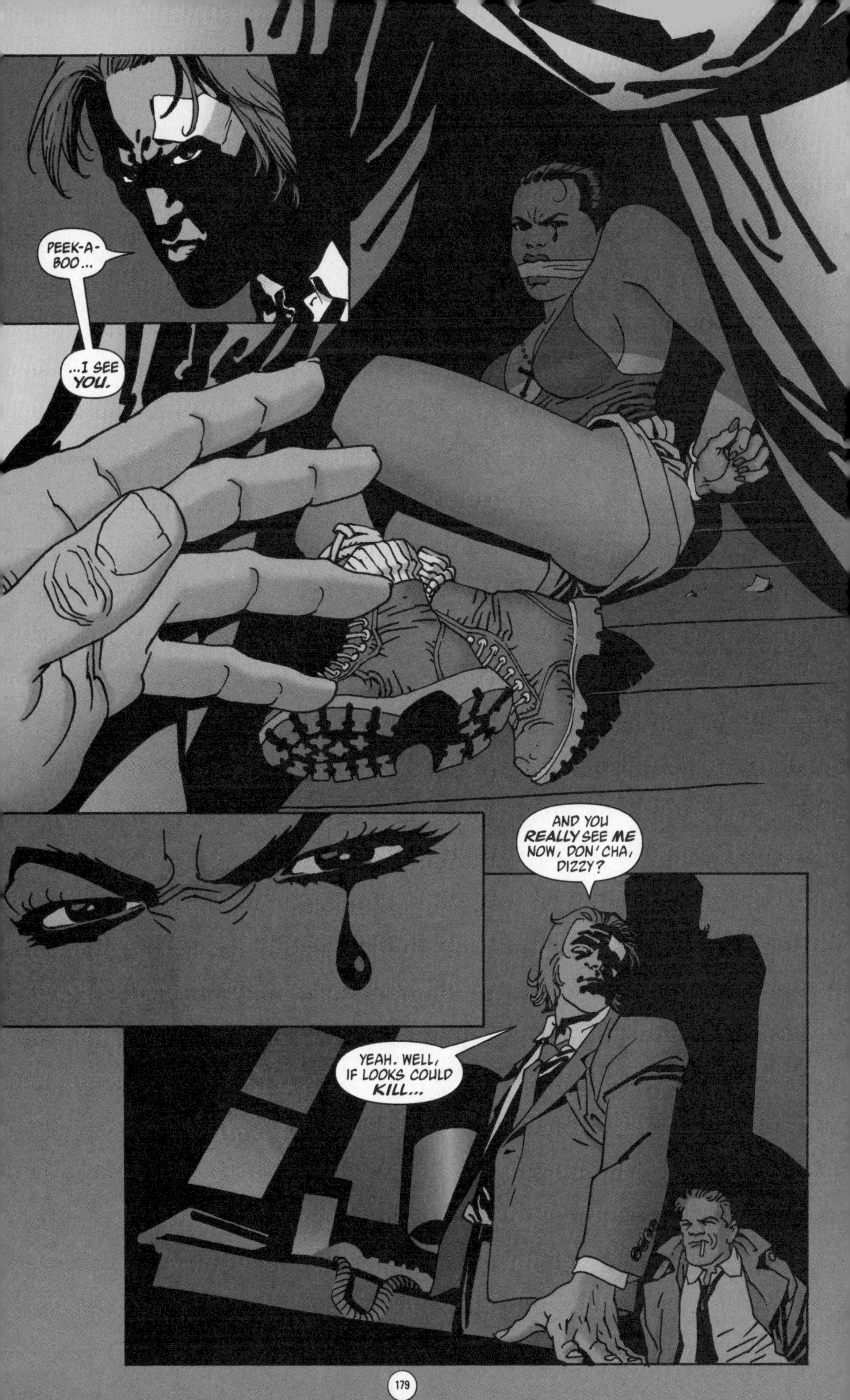
PEEK-A-BOO...
...I SEE YOU.
AND YOU REALLY SEE ME NOW, DON'CHA, DIZZY?
YEAH. WELL, IF LOOKS COULD KILL...

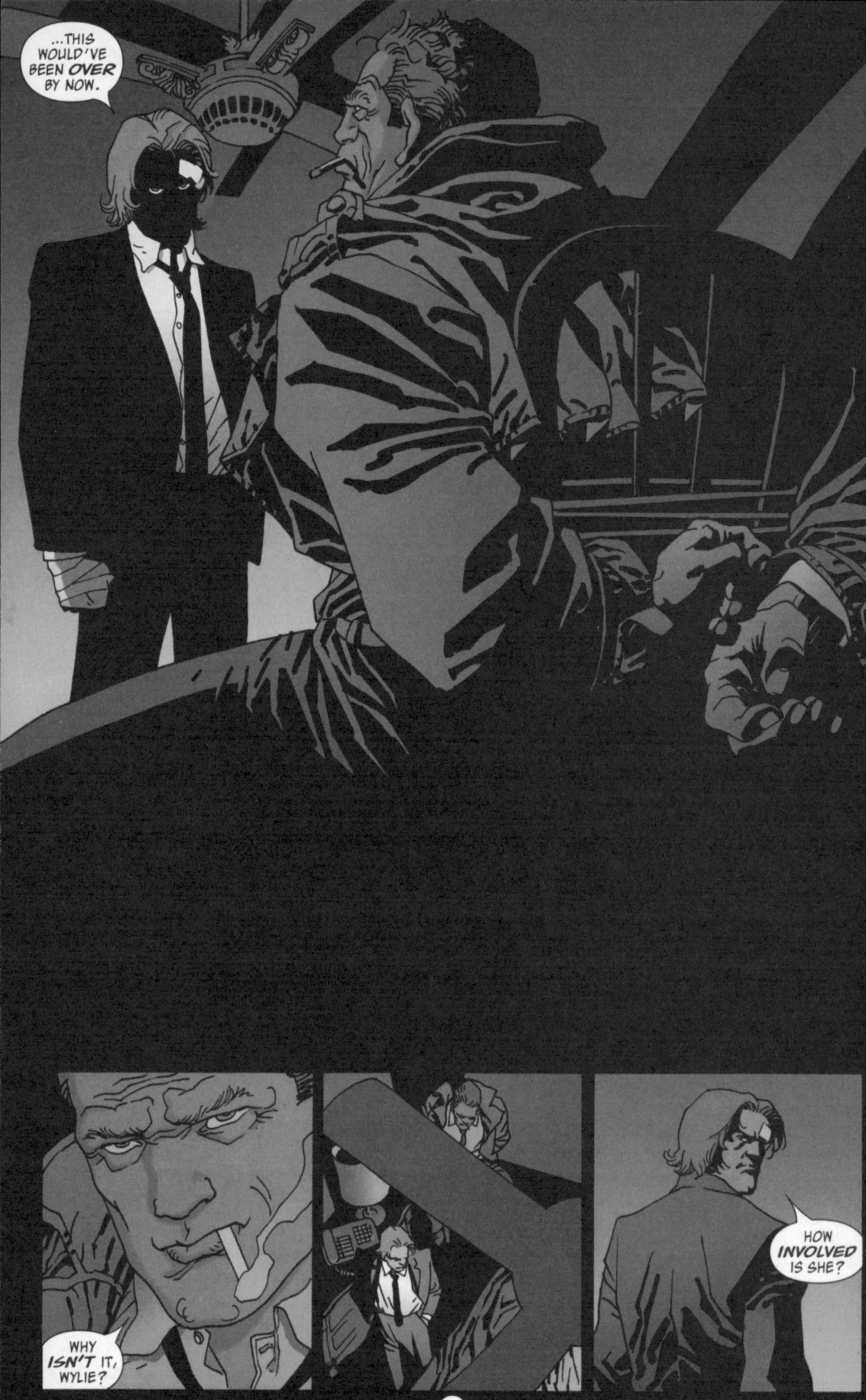

...THIS WOULD'VE BEEN *OVER* BY NOW.
WHY *ISN'T* IT, WYLIE?
HOW *INVOLVED* IS SHE?

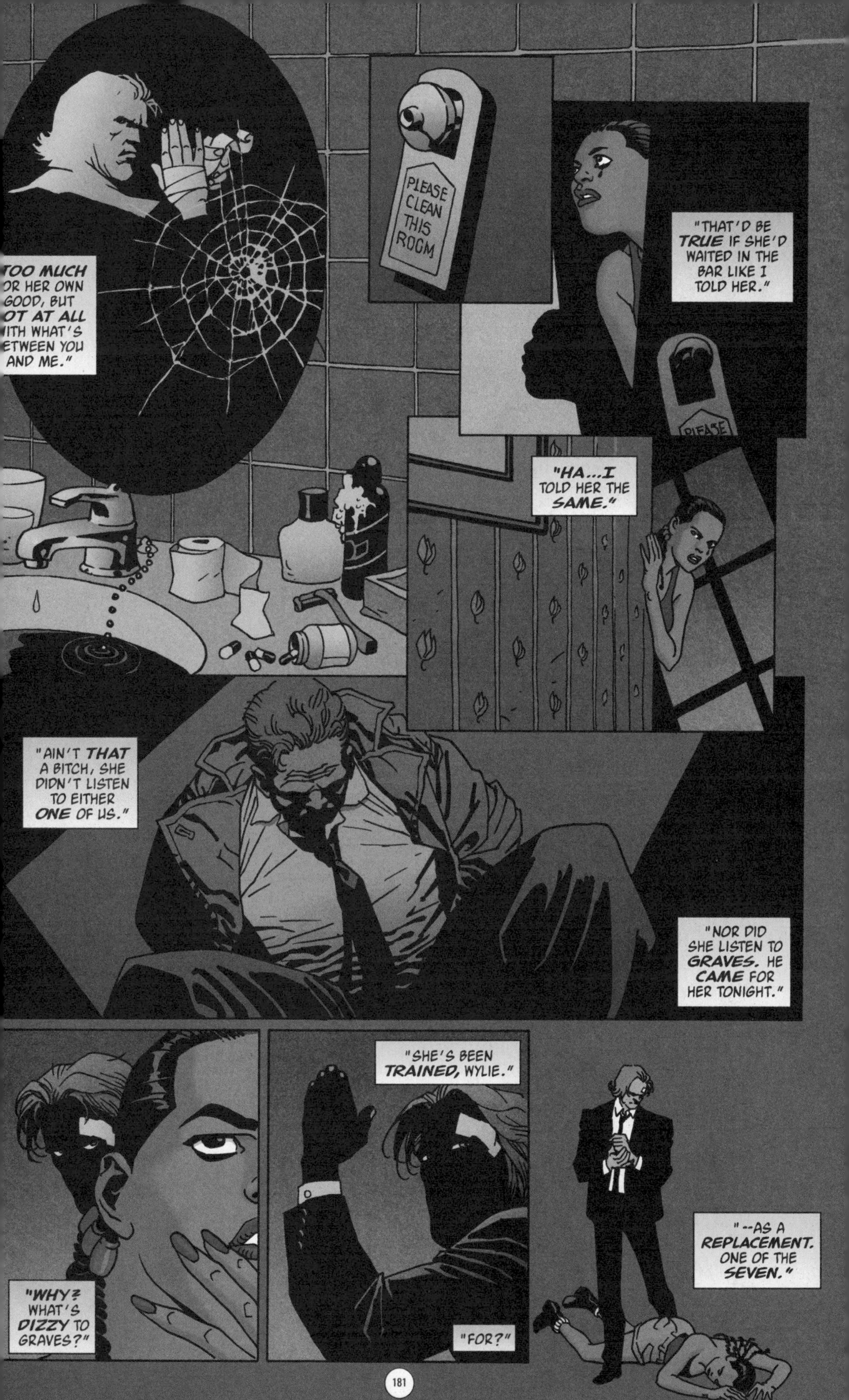
TOO MUCH
OR HER OWN
GOOD, BUT
OT AT ALL
ITH WHAT'S
ETWEEN YOU
AND ME."
PLEASE CLEAN THIS ROOM
"THAT'D BE TRUE IF SHE'D WAITED IN THE BAR LIKE I TOLD HER."
"HA...I TOLD HER THE SAME."
"AIN'T THAT A BITCH, SHE DIDN'T LISTEN TO EITHER ONE OF US."
"NOR DID SHE LISTEN TO GRAVES. HE CAME FOR HER TONIGHT."
"WHY? WHAT'S DIZZY TO GRAVES?"
"SHE'S BEEN TRAINED, WYLIE."
"FOR?"
"--AS A REPLACEMENT. ONE OF THE SEVEN."

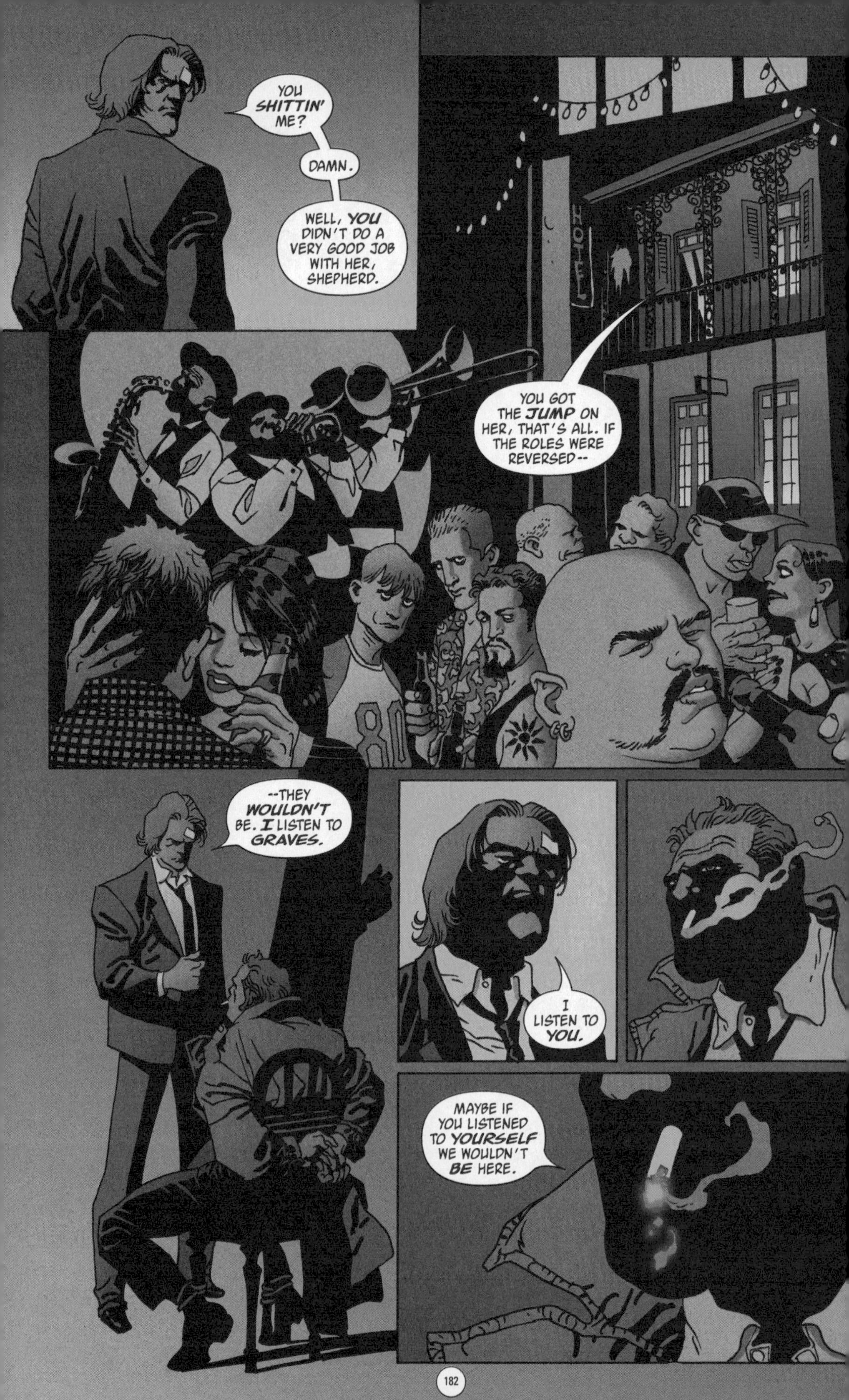

YOU SHITTIN' ME?
DAMN.
WELL, YOU DIDN'T DO A VERY GOOD JOB WITH HER, SHEPHERD.
HOTEL
YOU GOT THE JUMP ON HER, THAT'S ALL. IF THE ROLES WERE REVERSED--
--THEY WOULDN'T BE. I LISTEN TO GRAVES.
I LISTEN TO YOU.
MAYBE IF YOU LISTENED TO YOURSELF WE WOULDN'T BE HERE.

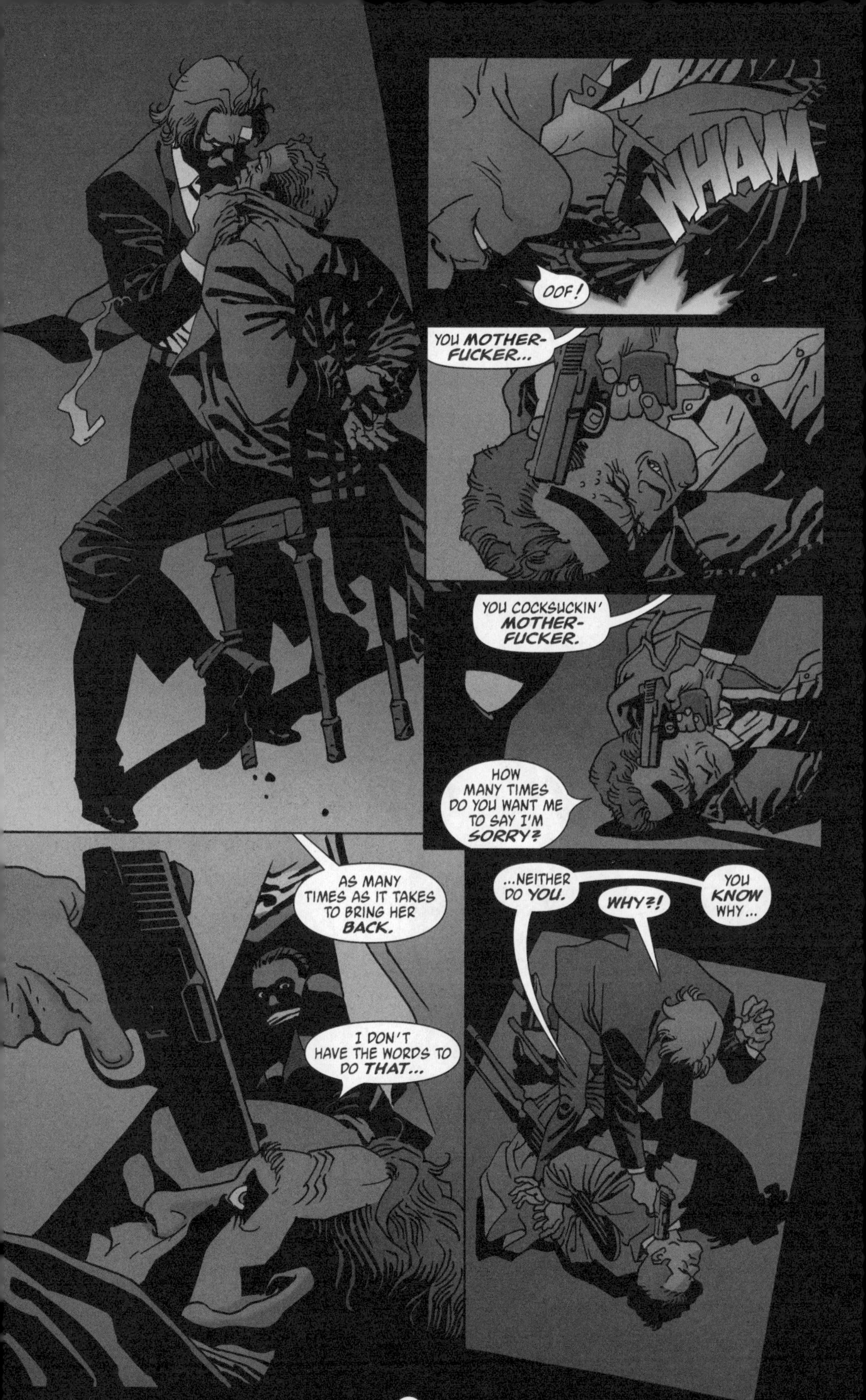
WHAM
OOF!
YOU MOTHER-FUCKER...
YOU COCKSUCKIN' MOTHER-FUCKER.
HOW MANY TIMES DO YOU WANT ME TO SAY I'M SORRY?
AS MANY TIMES AS IT TAKES TO BRING HER BACK.
I DON'T HAVE THE WORDS TO DO THAT...
...NEITHER DO YOU.
WHY?!
YOU KNOW WHY...

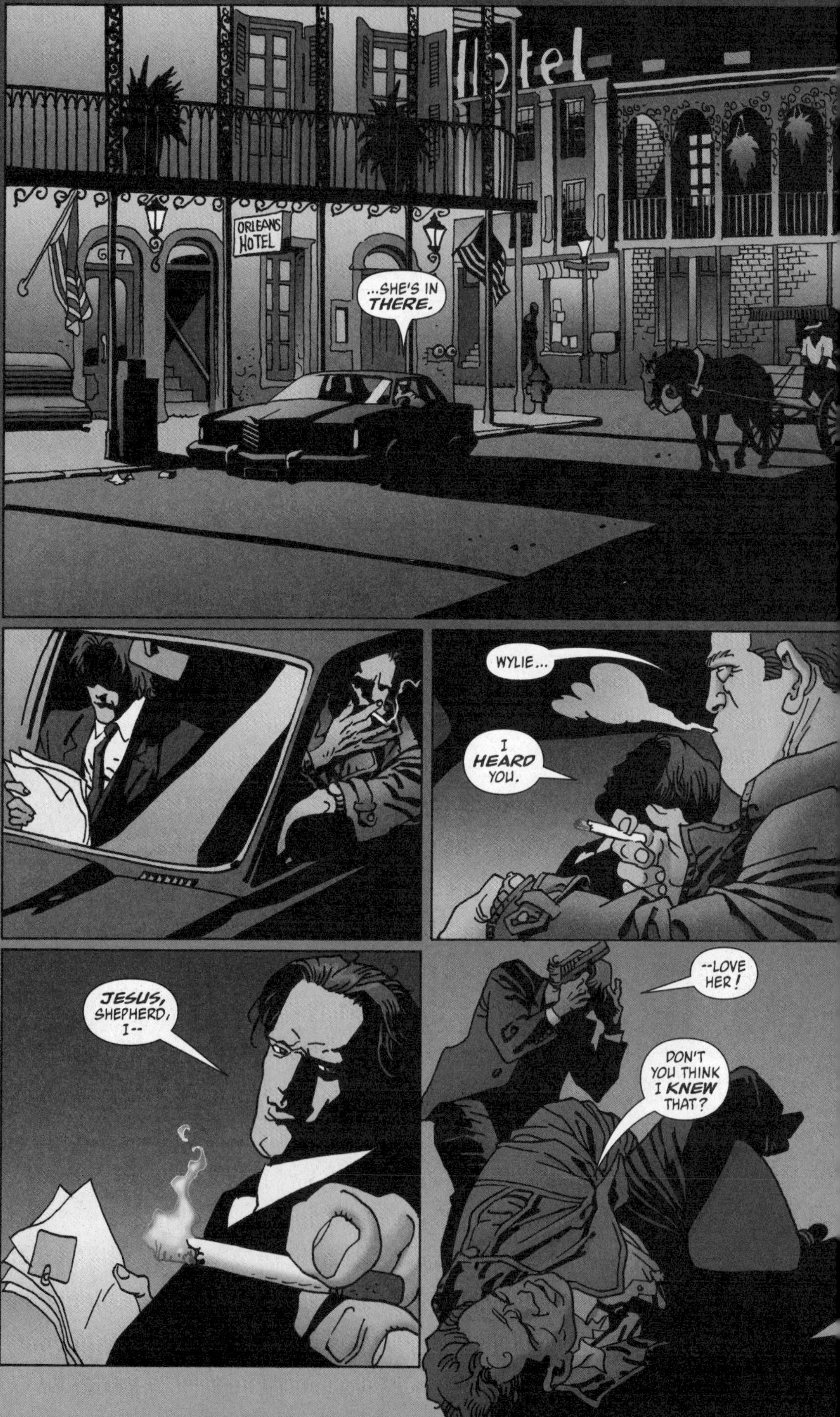
ORLEANS HOTEL
Hotel
...SHE'S IN THERE.
WYLIE...
I HEARD YOU.
JESUS, SHEPHERD, I--
--LOVE HER!
DON'T YOU THINK I KNEW THAT?

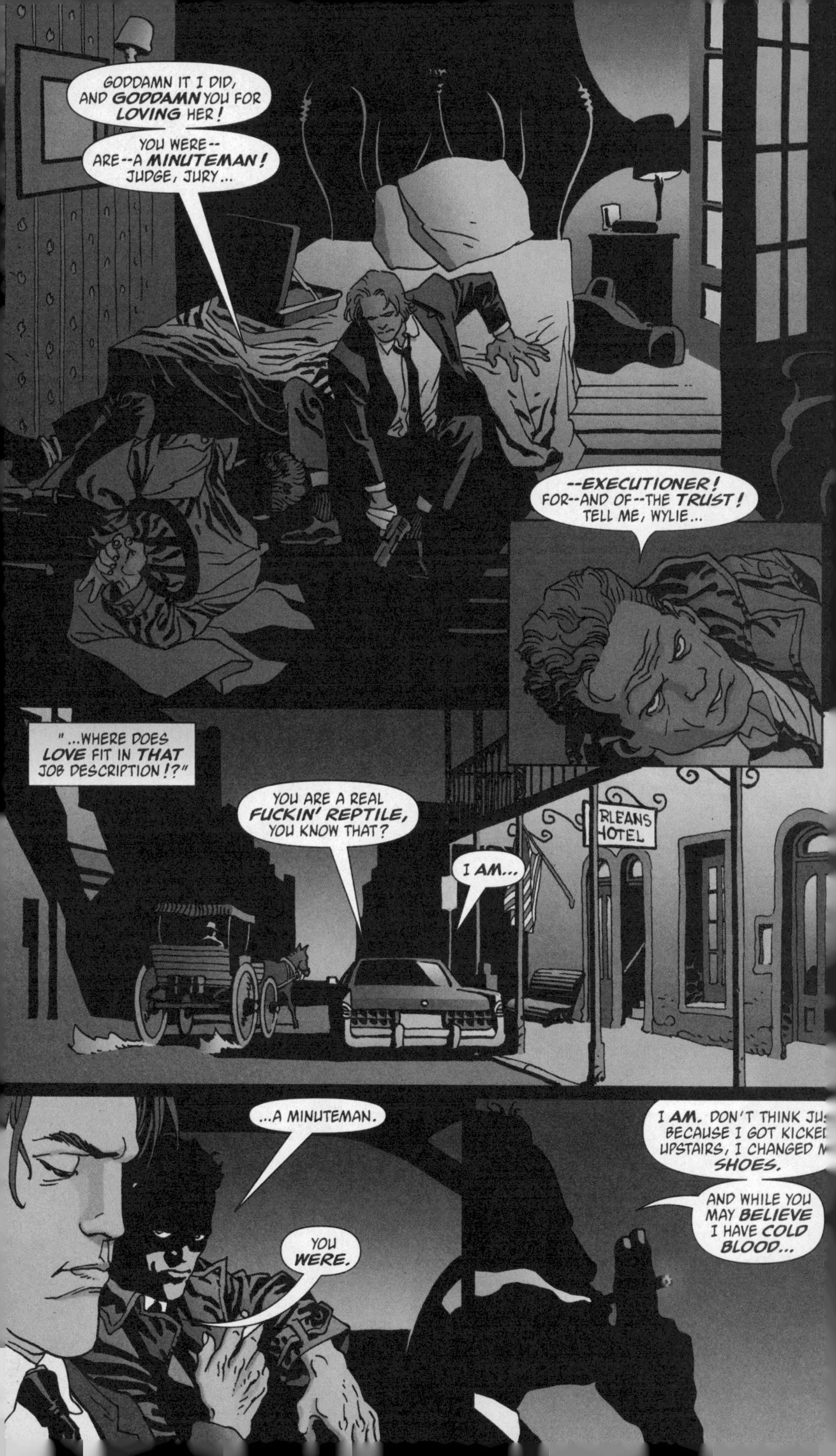
GODDAMN IT I DID, AND GODDAMN YOU FOR LOVING HER!
YOU WERE-- ARE--A MINUTEMAN! JUDGE, JURY...
--EXECUTIONER! FOR--AND OF--THE TRUST! TELL ME, WYLIE...
"...WHERE DOES LOVE FIT IN THAT JOB DESCRIPTION!?"
YOU ARE A REAL FUCKIN' REPTILE, YOU KNOW THAT?
I AM...
RLEANS HOTEL
...A MINUTEMAN.
YOU WERE.
I AM. DON'T THINK JUS BECAUSE I GOT KICKED UPSTAIRS, I CHANGED M SHOES.
AND WHILE YOU MAY BELIEVE I HAVE COLD BLOOD...

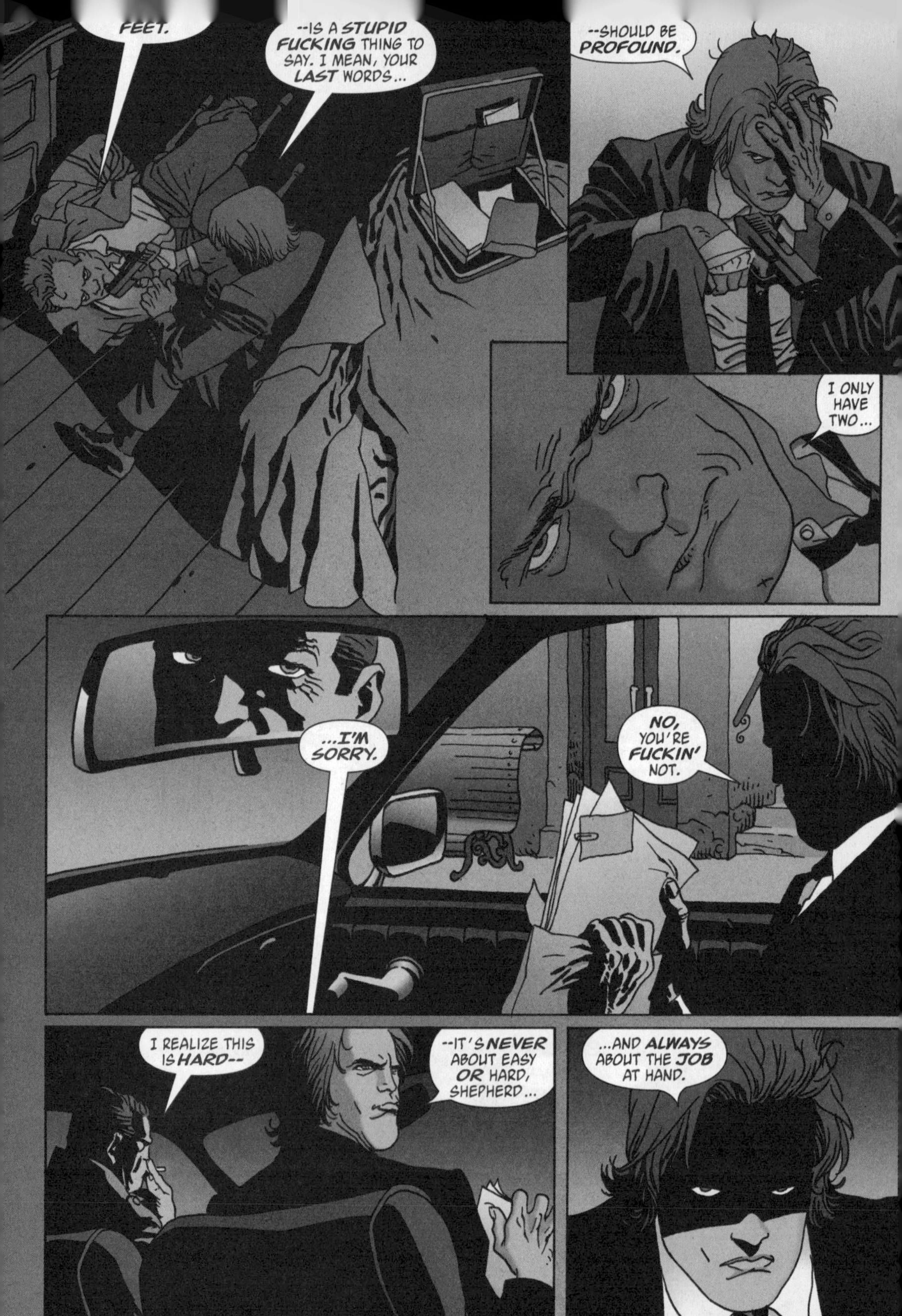
FEET.
--IS A STUPID FUCKING THING TO SAY. I MEAN, YOUR LAST WORDS...
--SHOULD BE PROFOUND.
I ONLY HAVE TWO...
...I'M SORRY.
NO, YOU'RE FUCKIN' NOT.
I REALIZE THIS IS HARD--
--IT'S NEVER ABOUT EASY OR HARD, SHEPHERD...
...AND ALWAYS ABOUT THE JOB AT HAND.

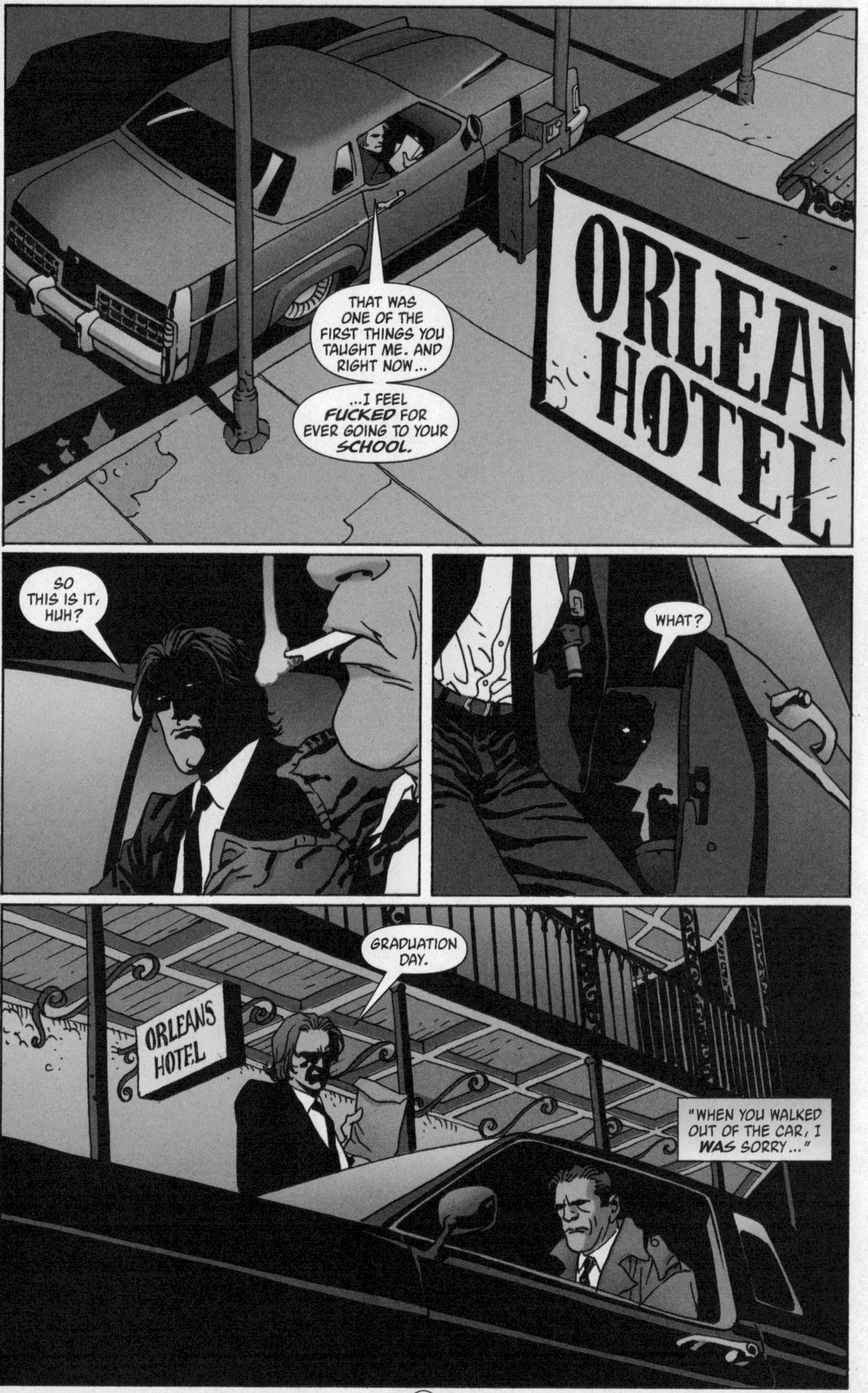
ORLEAN
HOTEL
THAT WAS ONE OF THE FIRST THINGS YOU TAUGHT ME. AND RIGHT NOW...
...I FEEL FUCKED FOR EVER GOING TO YOUR SCHOOL.
SO THIS IS IT, HUH?
WHAT?
GRADUATION DAY.
ORLEANS HOTEL
"WHEN YOU WALKED OUT OF THE CAR, I WAS SORRY..."

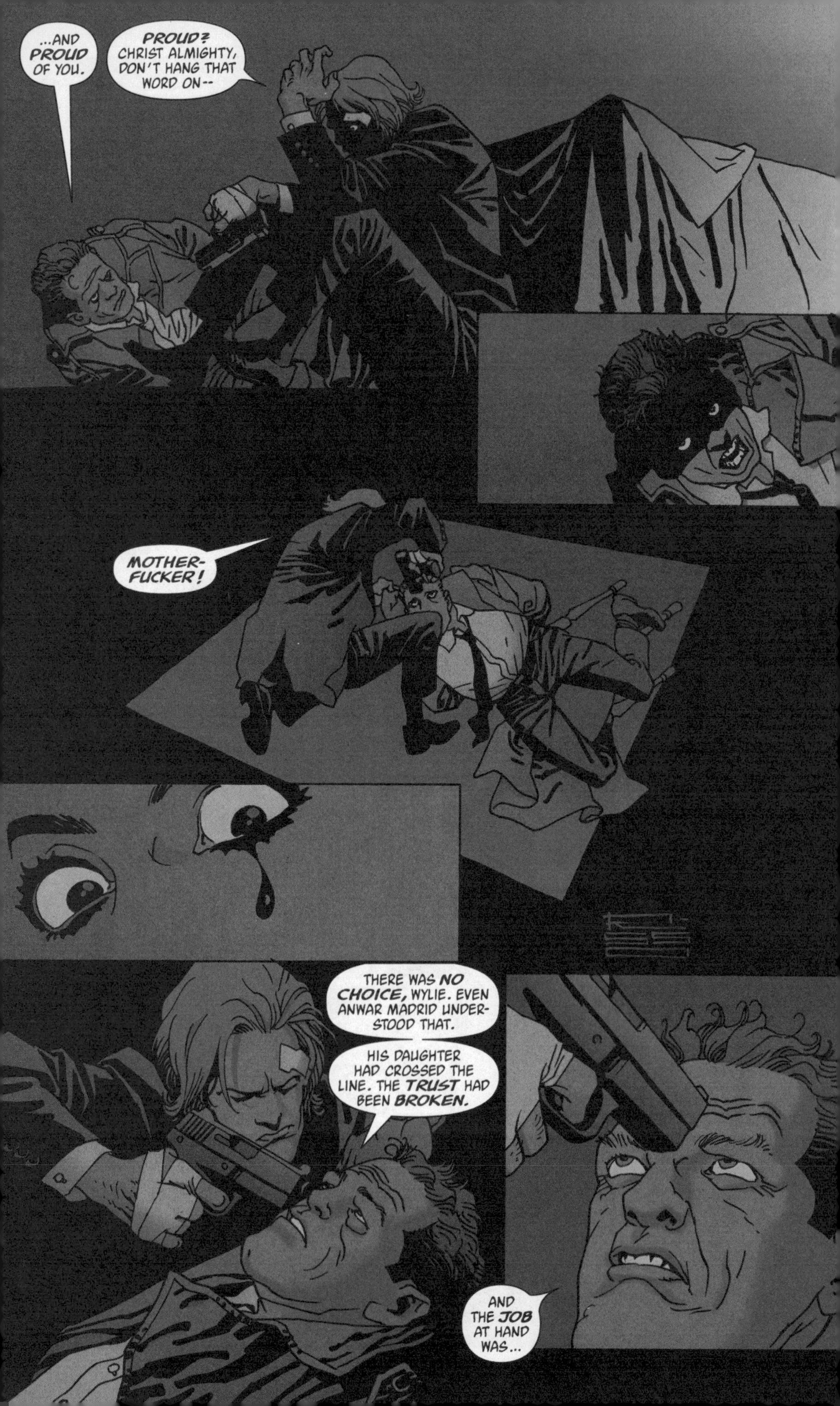
...AND PROUD OF YOU.
PROUD? CHRIST ALMIGHTY, DON'T HANG THAT WORD ON--
MOTHER-FUCKER!
THERE WAS NO CHOICE, WYLIE. EVEN ANWAR MADRID UNDER-STOOD THAT.
HIS DAUGHTER HAD CROSSED THE LINE. THE TRUST HAD BEEN BROKEN.
AND THE JOB AT HAND WAS...

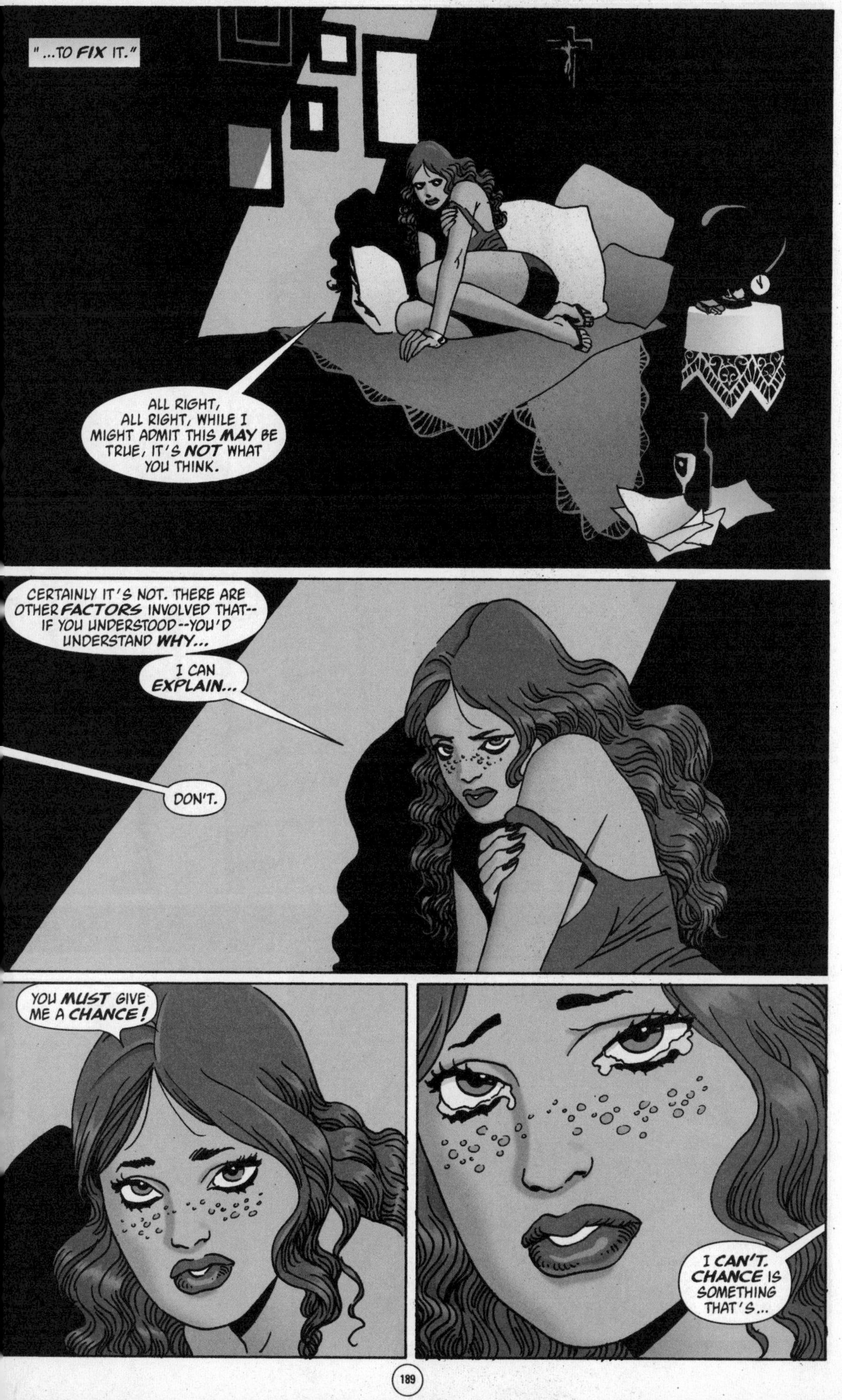
"...TO FIX IT."
ALL RIGHT, ALL RIGHT, WHILE I MIGHT ADMIT THIS MAY BE TRUE, IT'S NOT WHAT YOU THINK.
CERTAINLY IT'S NOT. THERE ARE OTHER FACTORS INVOLVED THAT-- IF YOU UNDERSTOOD--YOU'D UNDERSTAND WHY...
I CAN EXPLAIN...
DON'T.
YOU MUST GIVE ME A CHANCE!
I CAN'T. CHANCE IS SOMETHING THAT'S...

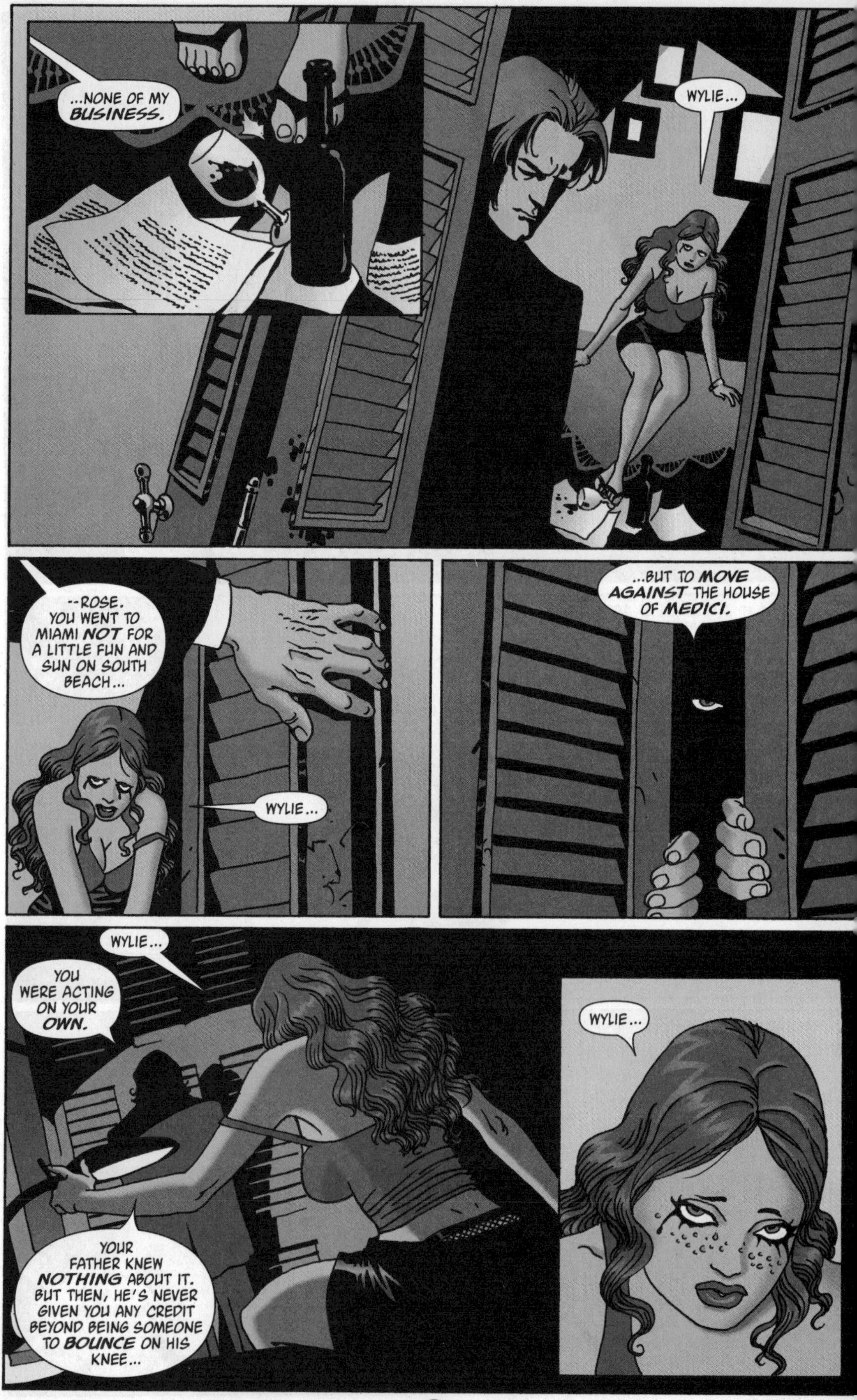

...NONE OF MY BUSINESS.
WYLIE...
--ROSE. YOU WENT TO MIAMI NOT FOR A LITTLE FUN AND SUN ON SOUTH BEACH...
WYLIE...
...BUT TO MOVE AGAINST THE HOUSE OF MEDICI.
WYLIE...
YOU WERE ACTING ON YOUR OWN.
YOUR FATHER KNEW NOTHING ABOUT IT. BUT THEN, HE'S NEVER GIVEN YOU ANY CREDIT BEYOND BEING SOMEONE TO BOUNCE ON HIS KNEE...
WYLIE...

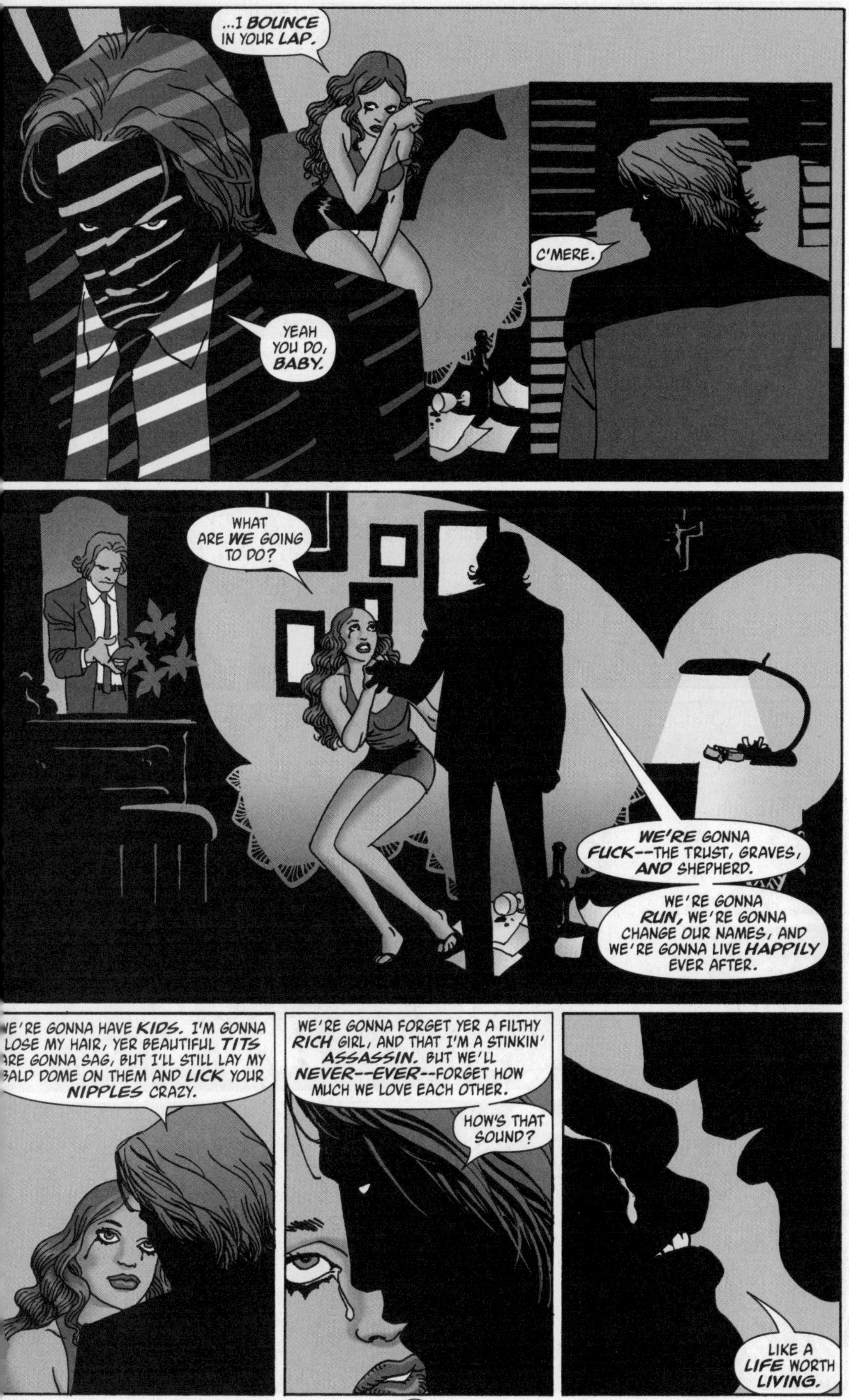
...I BOUNCE IN YOUR LAP.
YEAH YOU DO, BABY.
C'MERE.
WHAT ARE WE GOING TO DO?
WE'RE GONNA FUCK--THE TRUST, GRAVES, AND SHEPHERD.
WE'RE GONNA RUN, WE'RE GONNA CHANGE OUR NAMES, AND WE'RE GONNA LIVE HAPPILY EVER AFTER.
WE'RE GONNA HAVE KIDS. I'M GONNA LOSE MY HAIR, YER BEAUTIFUL TITS ARE GONNA SAG, BUT I'LL STILL LAY MY BALD DOME ON THEM AND LICK YOUR NIPPLES CRAZY.
WE'RE GONNA FORGET YER A FILTHY RICH GIRL, AND THAT I'M A STINKIN' ASSASSIN. BUT WE'LL NEVER--EVER--FORGET HOW MUCH WE LOVE EACH OTHER.
HOW'S THAT SOUND?
LIKE A LIFE WORTH LIVING.

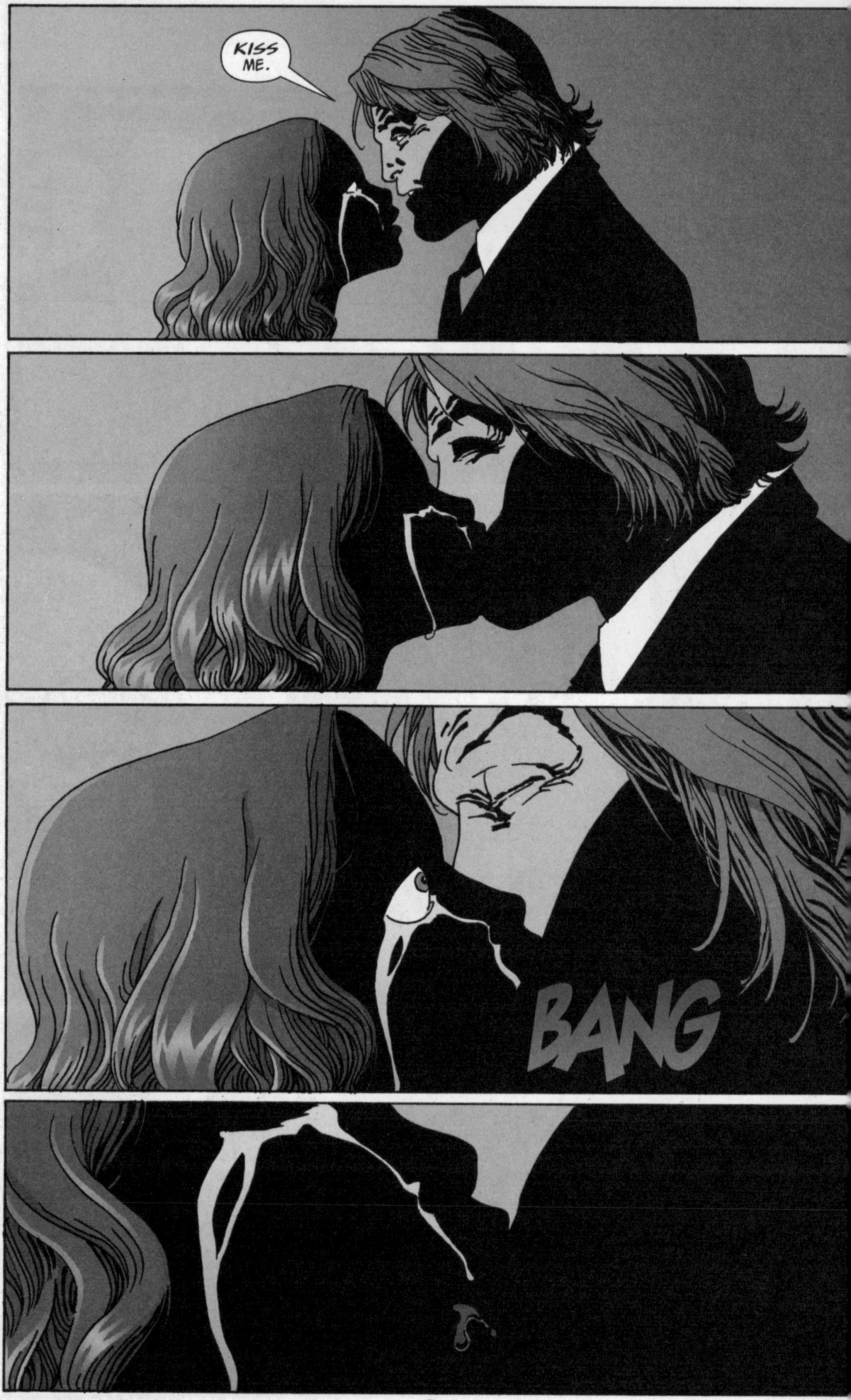
KISS ME.
BANG

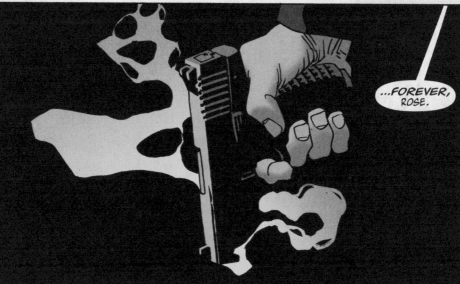

...FOREVER, ROSE.

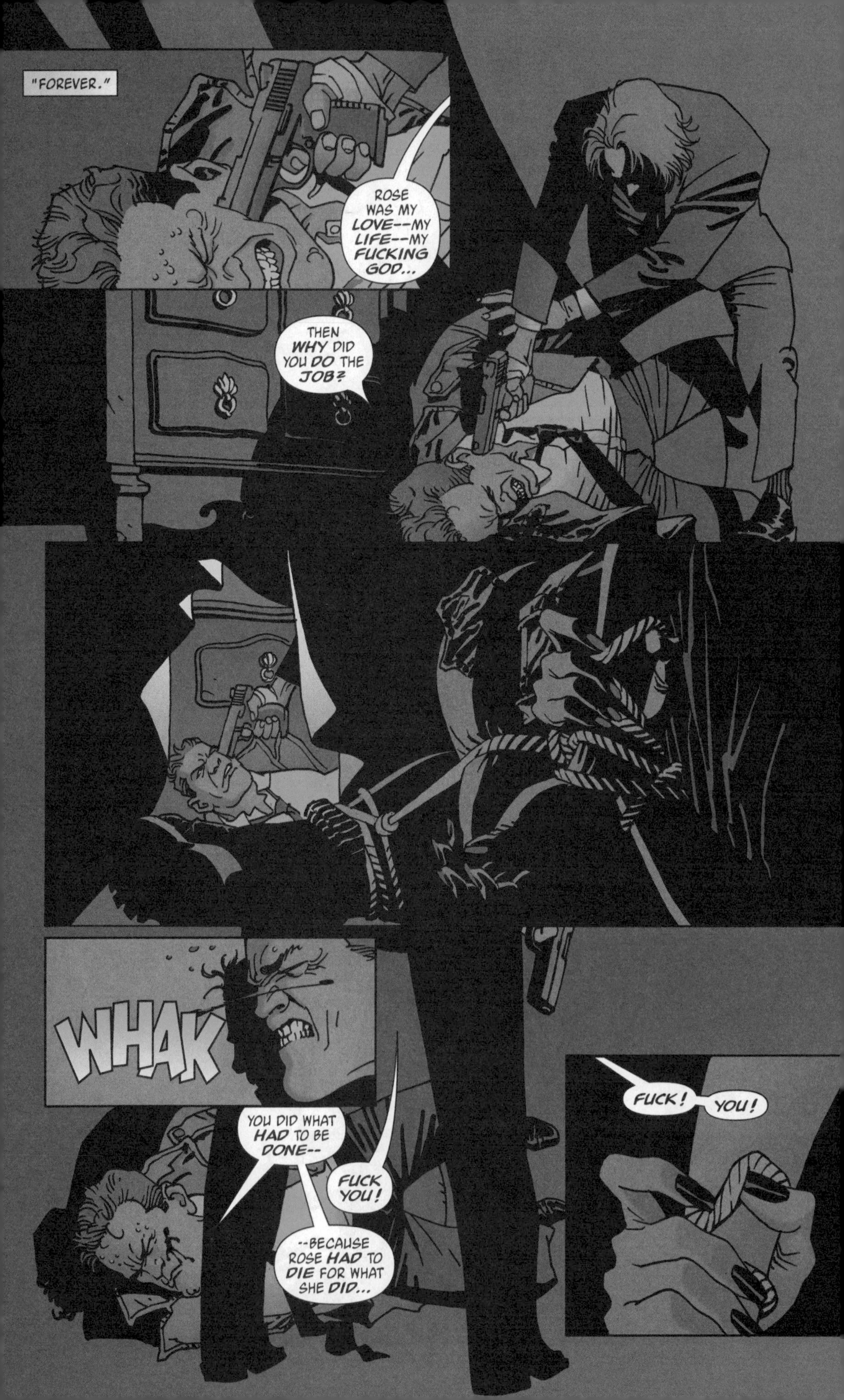
"FOREVER."
ROSE WAS MY LOVE--MY LIFE--MY FUCKING GOD...
THEN WHY DID YOU DO THE JOB?
WHAK
YOU DID WHAT HAD TO BE DONE--
FUCK YOU!
--BECAUSE ROSE HAD TO DIE FOR WHAT SHE DID...
FUCK!
YOU!

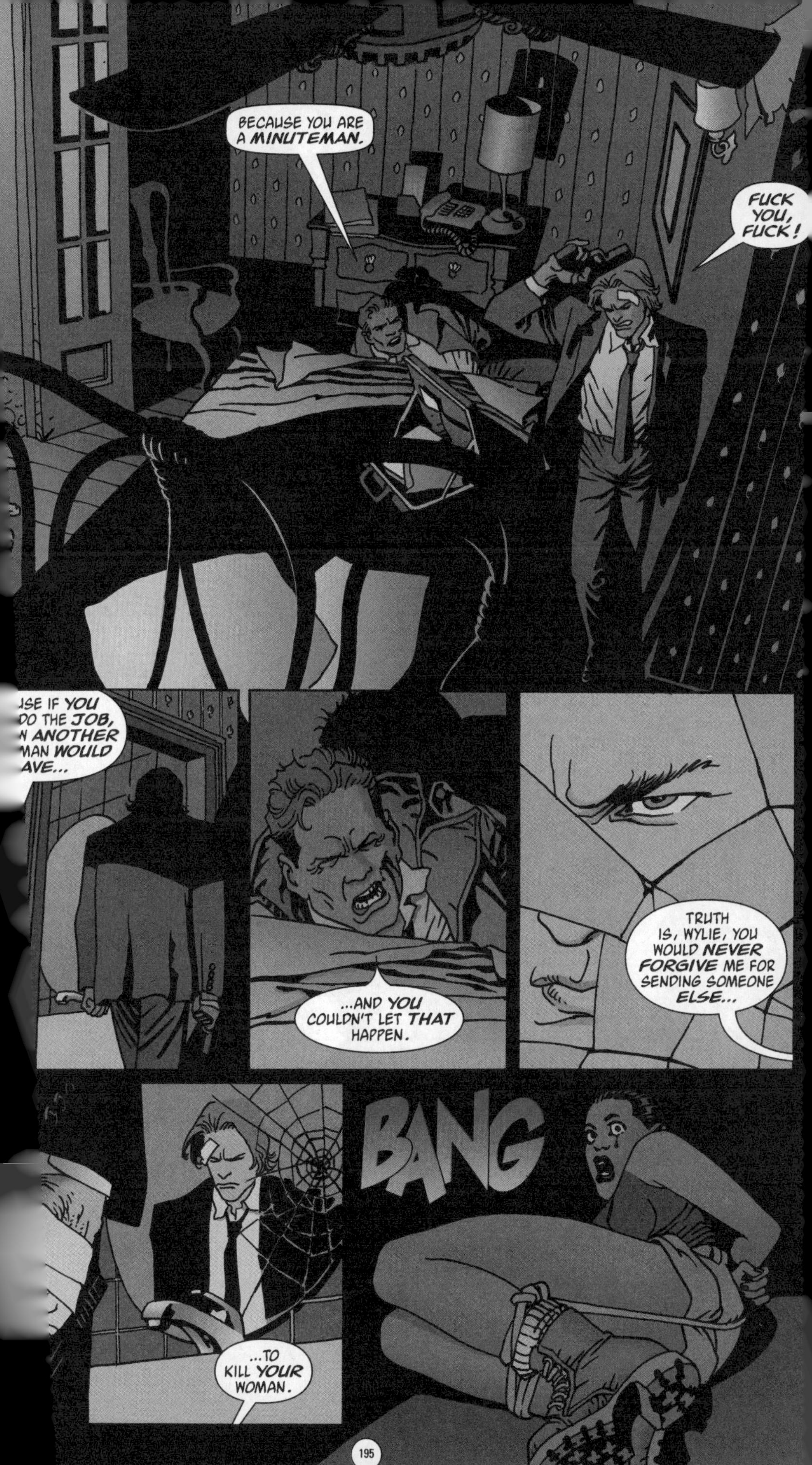

BECAUSE YOU ARE A MINUTEMAN.
FUCK YOU, FUCK!
...AND YOU COULDN'T LET THAT HAPPEN.
TRUTH IS, WYLIE, YOU WOULD NEVER FORGIVE ME FOR SENDING SOMEONE ELSE...
...TO KILL YOUR WOMAN.
BANG

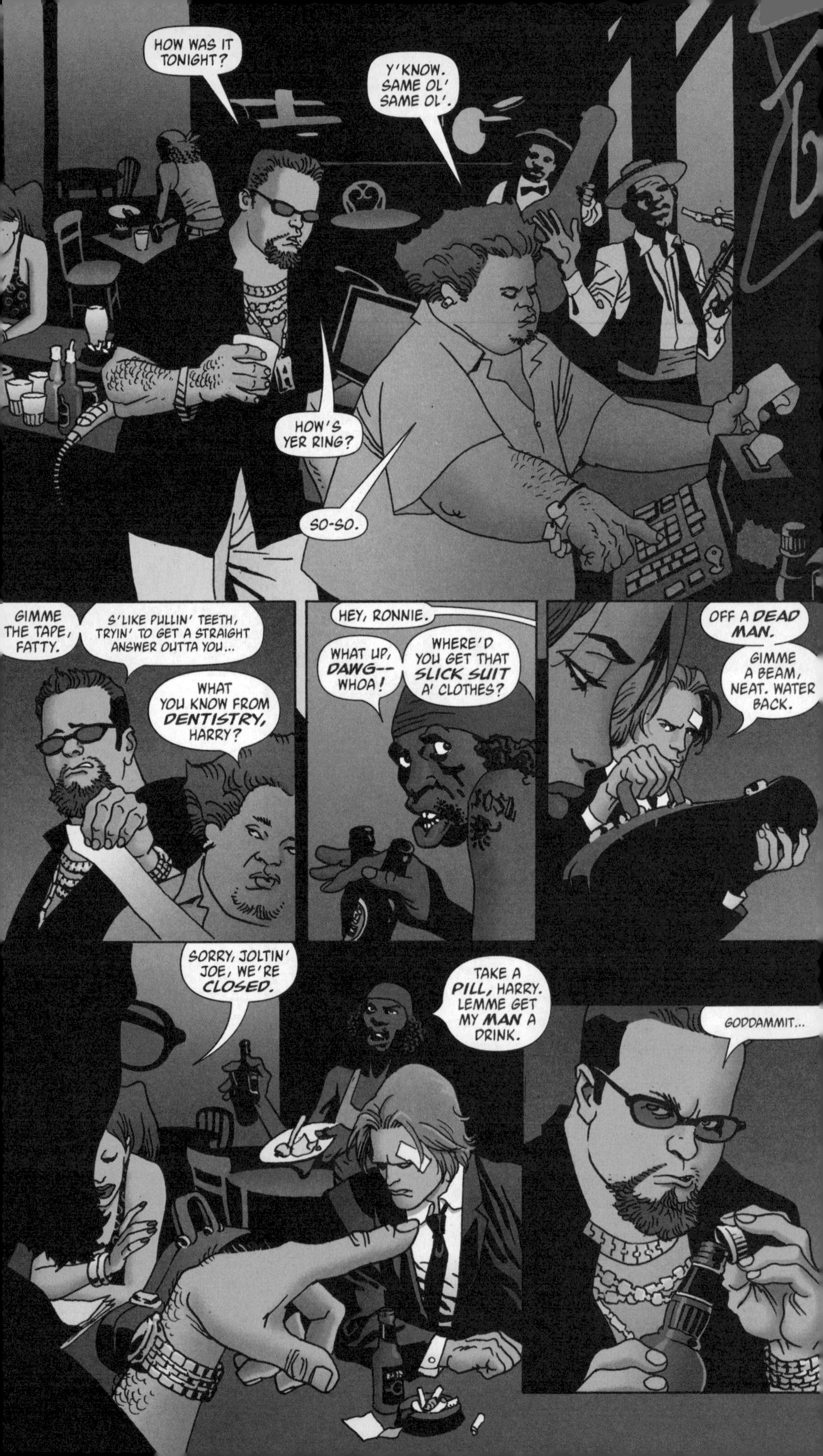

HOW WAS IT TONIGHT?
Y'KNOW. SAME OL' SAME OL'.
HOW'S YER RING?
SO-SO.
GIMME THE TAPE, FATTY.
S'LIKE PULLIN' TEETH, TRYIN' TO GET A STRAIGHT ANSWER OUTTA YOU...
WHAT YOU KNOW FROM DENTISTRY, HARRY?
HEY, RONNIE.
WHAT UP, DAWG-- WHOA!
WHERE'D YOU GET THAT SLICK SUIT A' CLOTHES?
OFF A DEAD MAN.
GIMME A BEAM, NEAT. WATER BACK.
SORRY, JOLTIN' JOE, WE'RE CLOSED.
TAKE A PILL, HARRY. LEMME GET MY MAN A DRINK.
GODDAMMIT...

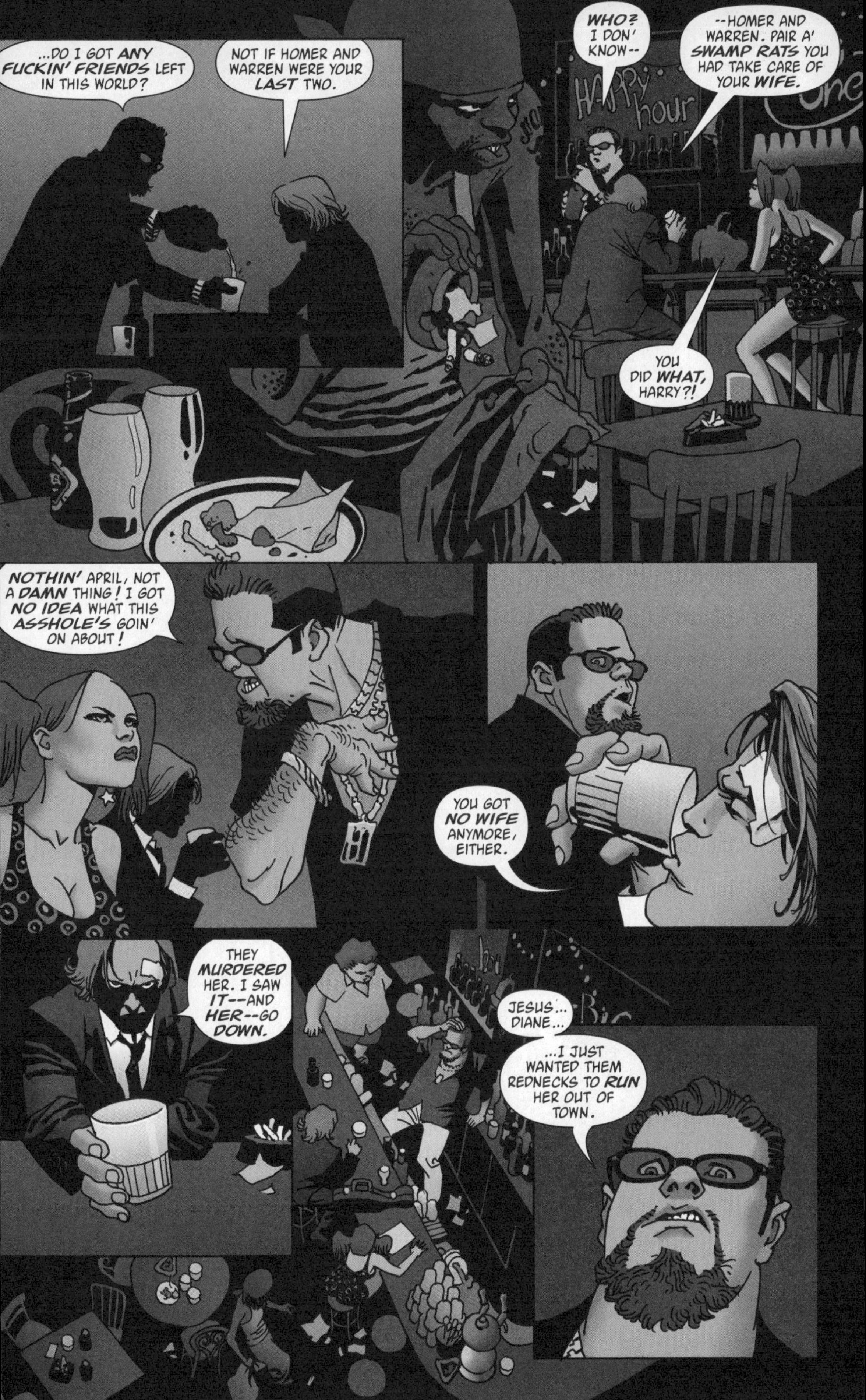
...DO I GOT ANY FUCKIN' FRIENDS LEFT IN THIS WORLD?
NOT IF HOMER AND WARREN WERE YOUR LAST TWO.
WHO? I DON' KNOW--
--HOMER AND WARREN. PAIR A' SWAMP RATS YOU HAD TAKE CARE OF YOUR WIFE.
YOU DID WHAT, HARRY?!
NOTHIN' APRIL, NOT A DAMN THING! I GOT NO IDEA WHAT THIS ASSHOLE'S GOIN' ON ABOUT!
YOU GOT NO WIFE ANYMORE, EITHER.
THEY MURDERED HER. I SAW IT--AND HER--GO DOWN.
JESUS... DIANE...
...I JUST WANTED THEM REDNECKS TO RUN HER OUT OF TOWN.

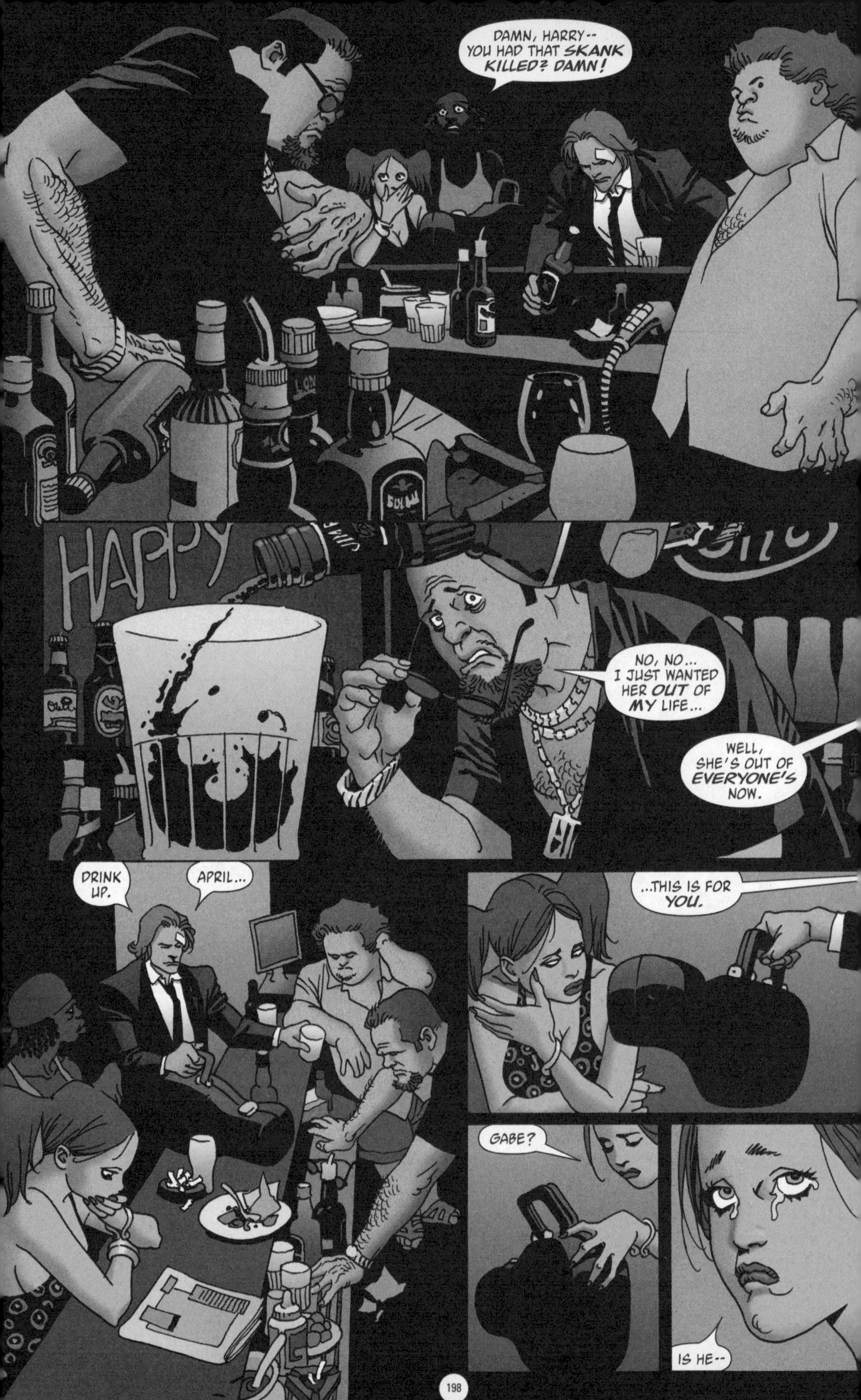
DAMN, HARRY-- YOU HAD THAT SKANK KILLED? DAMN!
NO, NO... I JUST WANTED HER OUT OF MY LIFE...
WELL, SHE'S OUT OF EVERYONE'S NOW.
DRINK UP.
APRIL...
...THIS IS FOR YOU.
GABE?
IS HE--

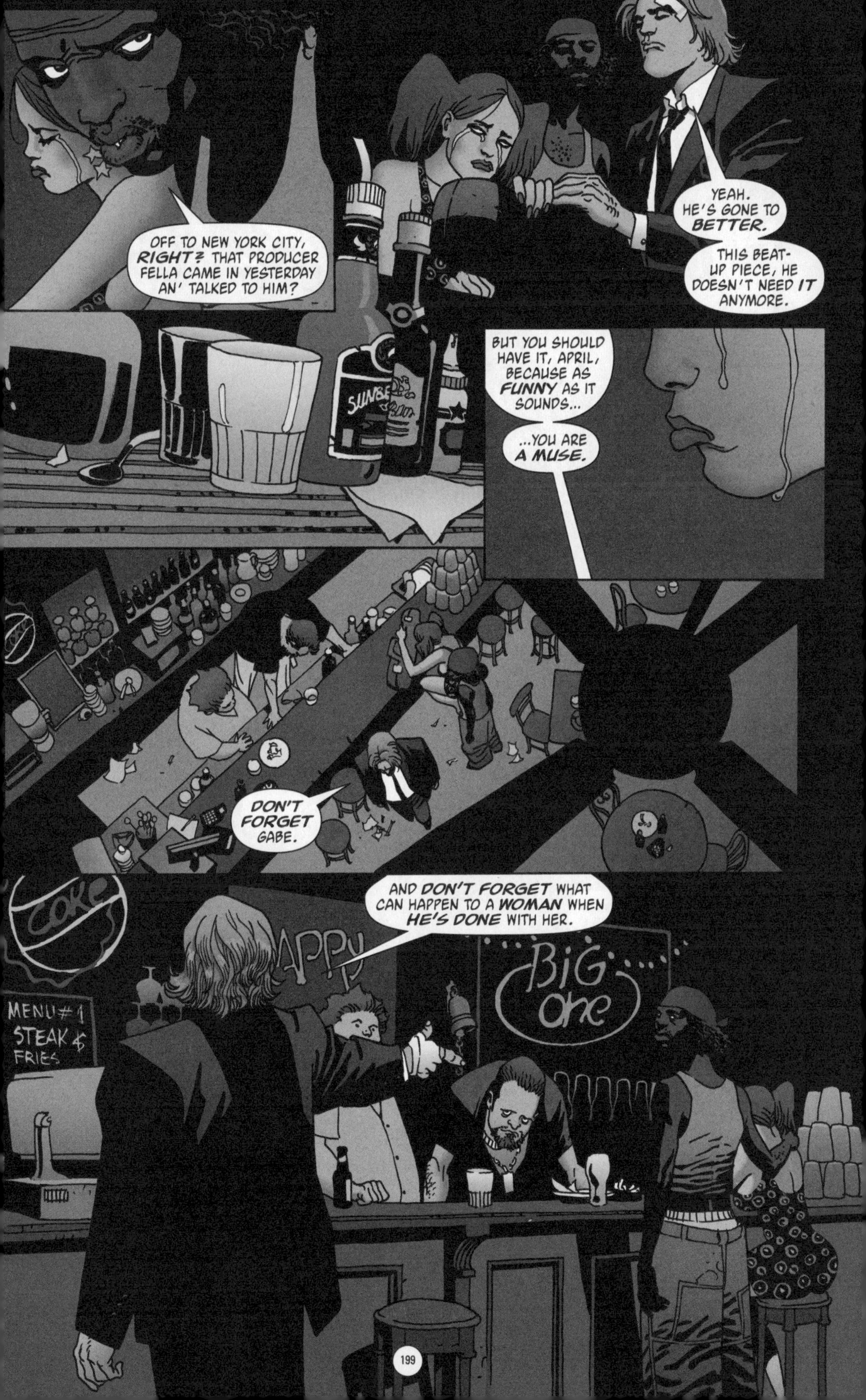

OFF TO NEW YORK CITY, RIGHT? THAT PRODUCER FELLA CAME IN YESTERDAY AN' TALKED TO HIM?
YEAH. HE'S GONE TO BETTER.
THIS BEAT-UP PIECE, HE DOESN'T NEED IT ANYMORE.
BUT YOU SHOULD HAVE IT, APRIL, BECAUSE AS FUNNY AS IT SOUNDS...
...YOU ARE A MUSE.
DON'T FORGET GABE.
AND DON'T FORGET WHAT CAN HAPPEN TO A WOMAN WHEN HE'S DONE WITH HER.
COKE
APPY
BIG ONE
MENU #1 STEAK & FRIES

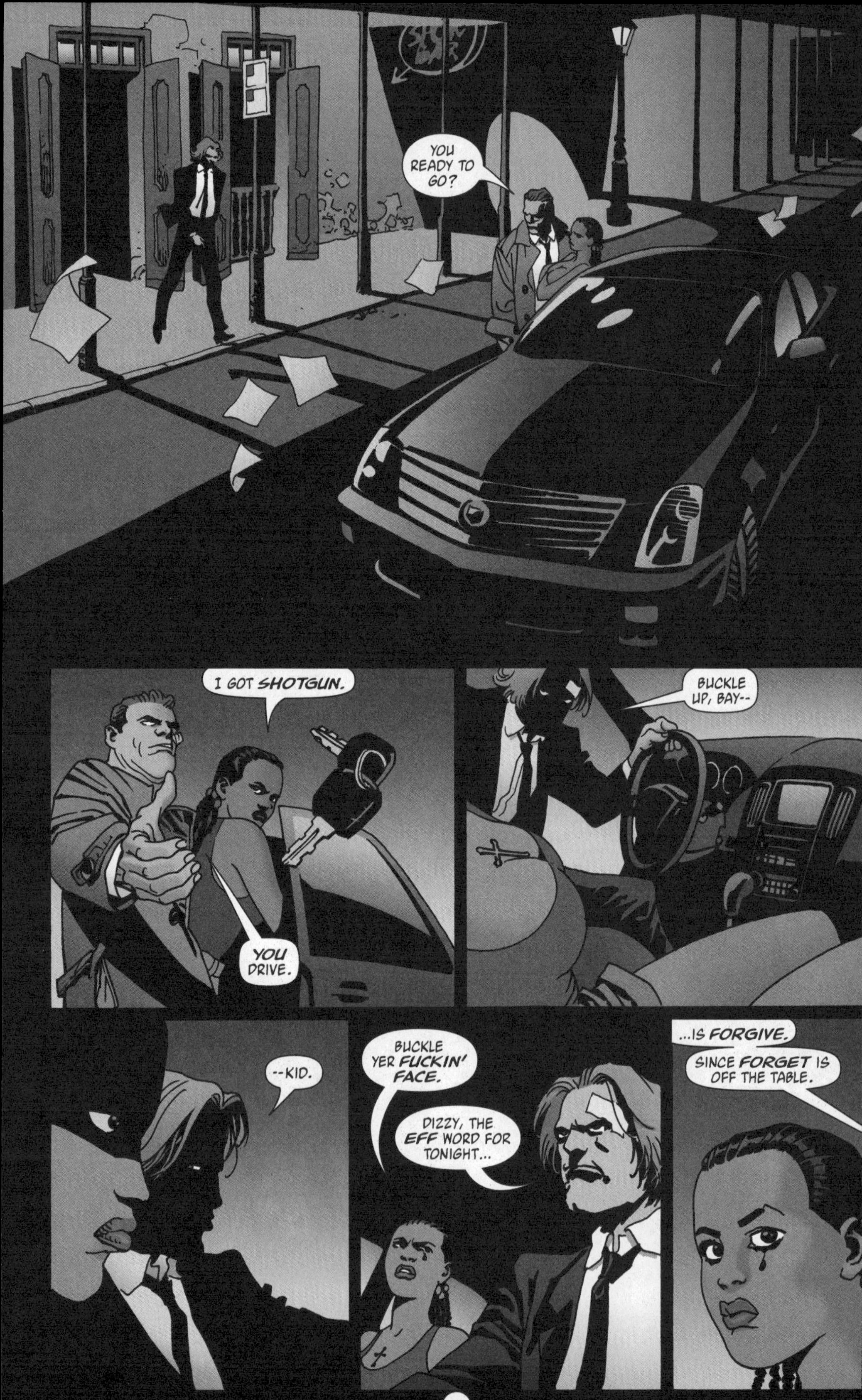
YOU READY TO GO?
I GOT SHOTGUN.
YOU DRIVE.
BUCKLE UP, BAY--
--KID.
BUCKLE YER FUCKIN' FACE.
DIZZY, THE EFF WORD FOR TONIGHT...
...IS FORGIVE.
SINCE FORGET IS OFF THE TABLE.

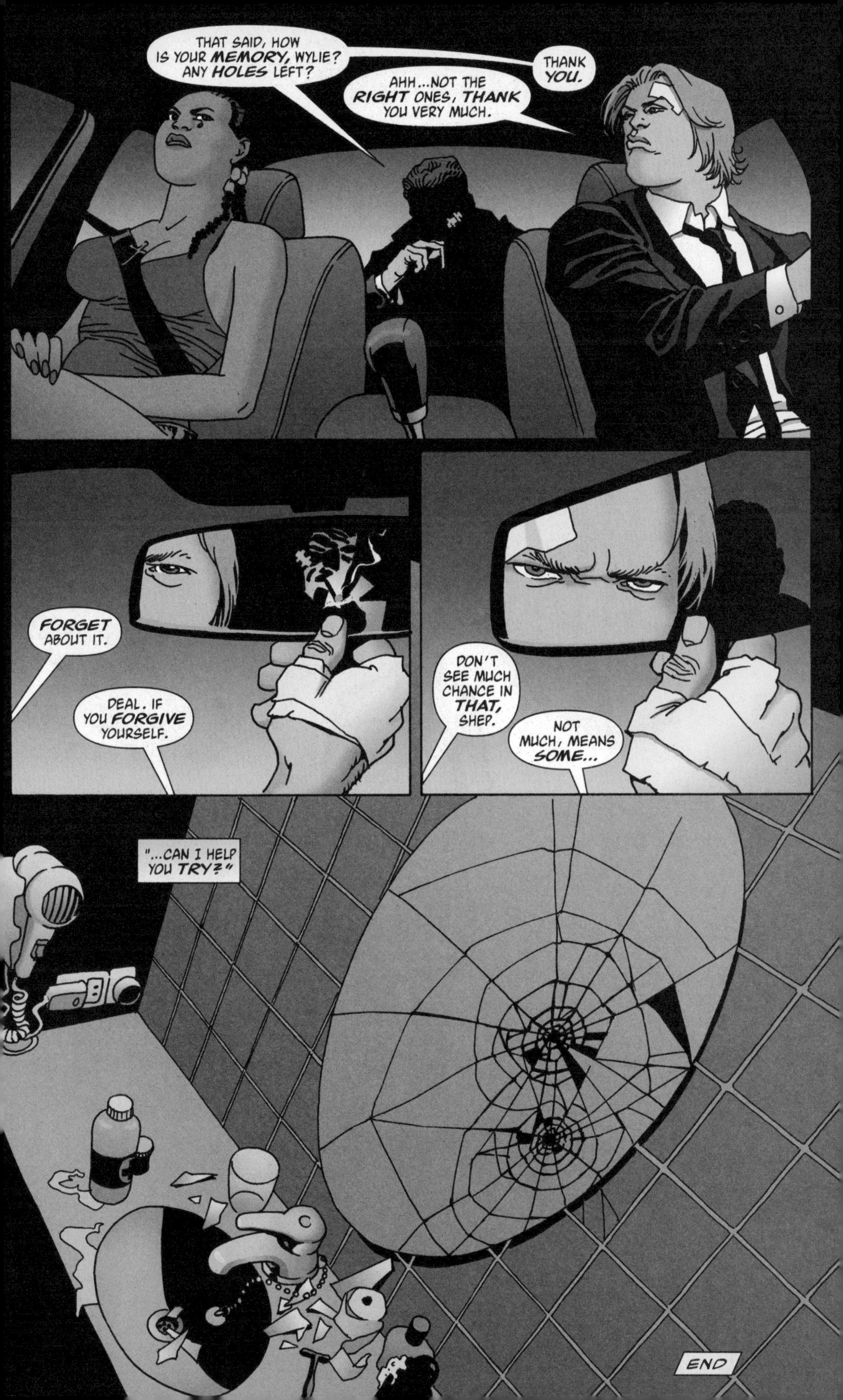
THAT SAID, HOW IS YOUR MEMORY, WYLIE? ANY HOLES LEFT?
AHH...NOT THE RIGHT ONES, THANK YOU VERY MUCH.
THANK YOU.
FORGET ABOUT IT.
DEAL. IF YOU FORGIVE YOURSELF.
DON'T SEE MUCH CHANCE IN THAT, SHEP.
NOT MUCH, MEANS SOME...
"...CAN I HELP YOU TRY?"
END

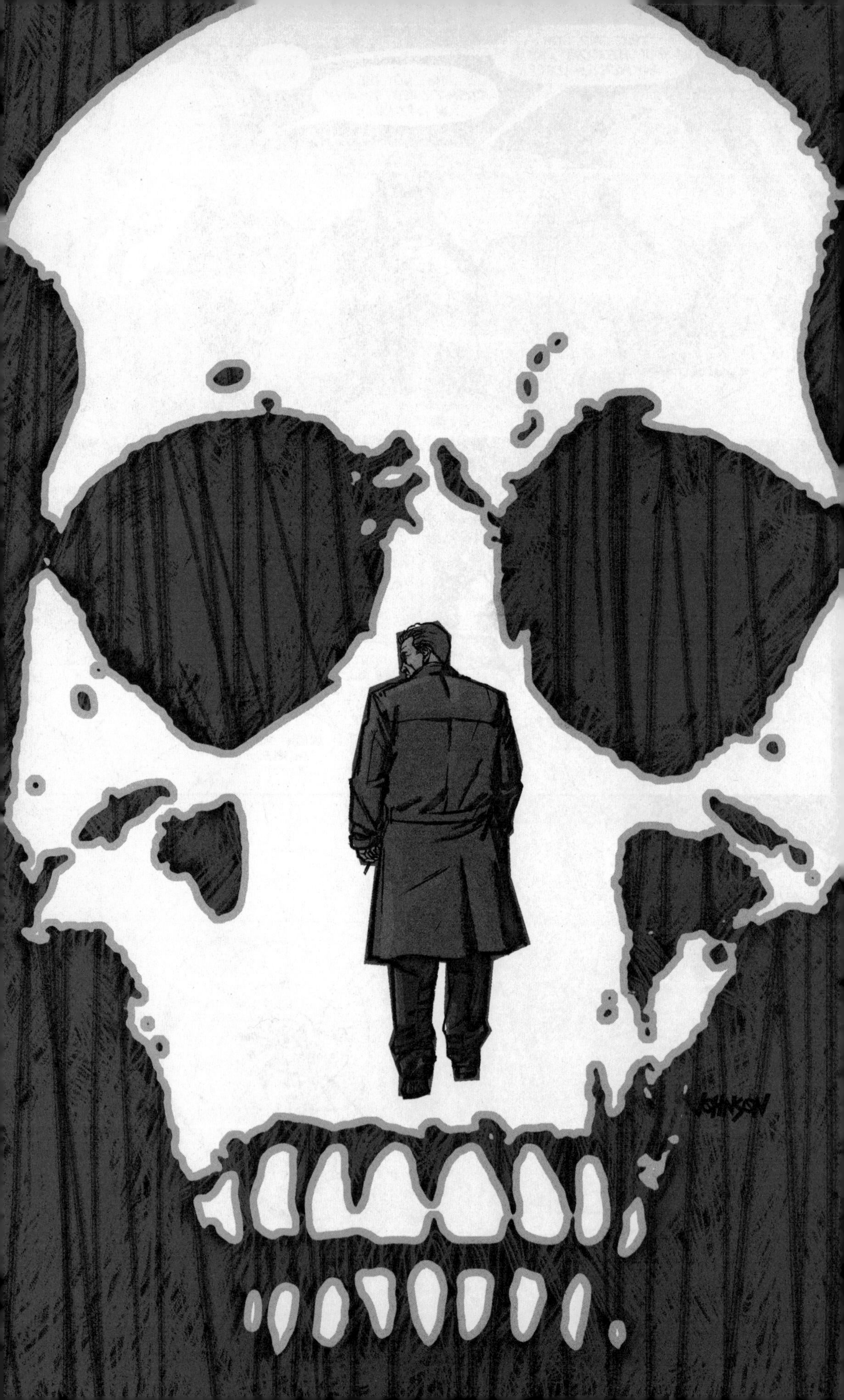
JOHNSON

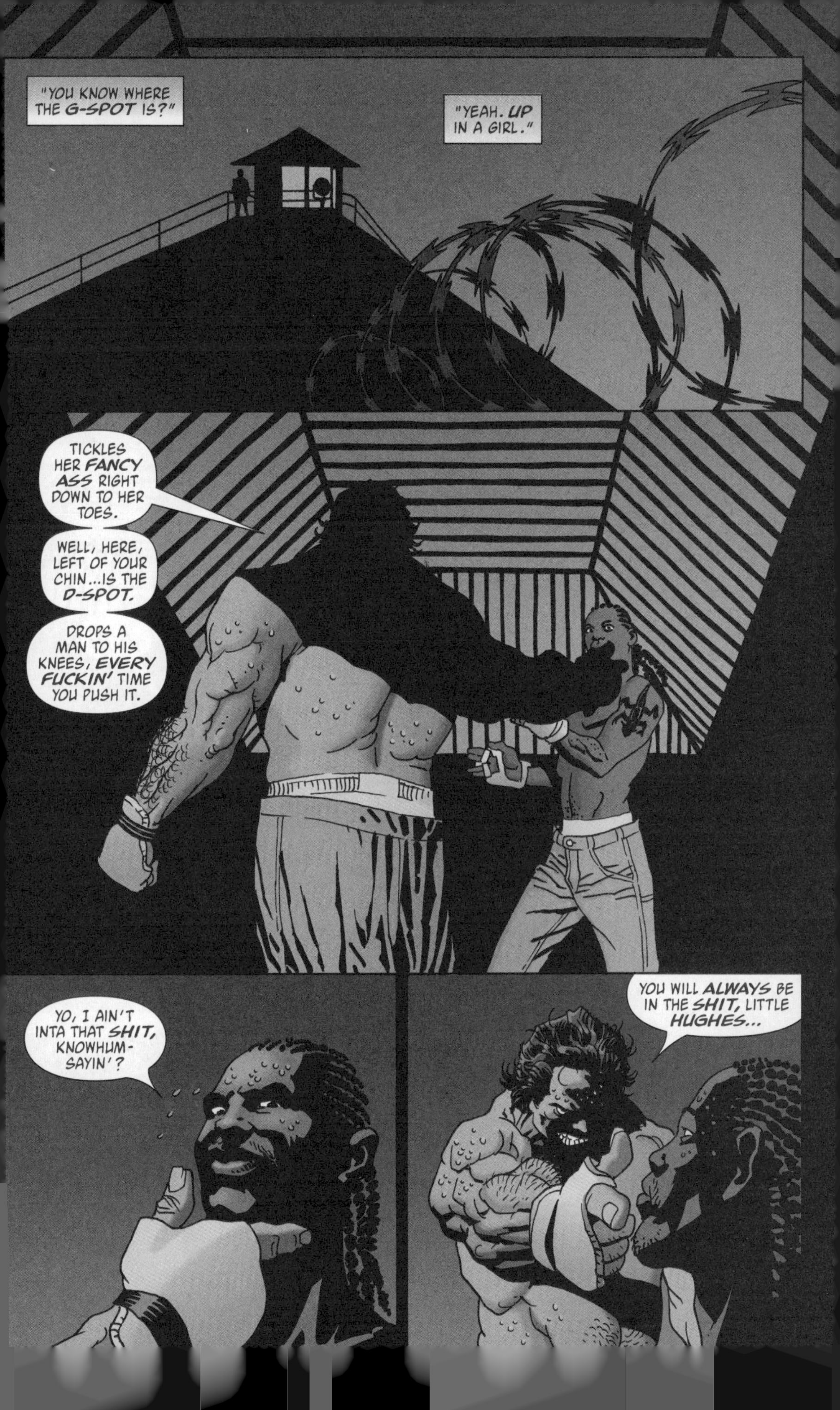
"YOU KNOW WHERE THE G-SPOT IS?"
"YEAH. UP IN A GIRL."
TICKLES HER FANCY ASS RIGHT DOWN TO HER TOES.
WELL, HERE, LEFT OF YOUR CHIN...IS THE D-SPOT.
DROPS A MAN TO HIS KNEES, EVERY FUCKIN' TIME YOU PUSH IT.
YO, I AIN'T INTA THAT SHIT, KNOWHUM-SAYIN'?
YOU WILL ALWAYS BE IN THE SHIT, LITTLE HUGHES...

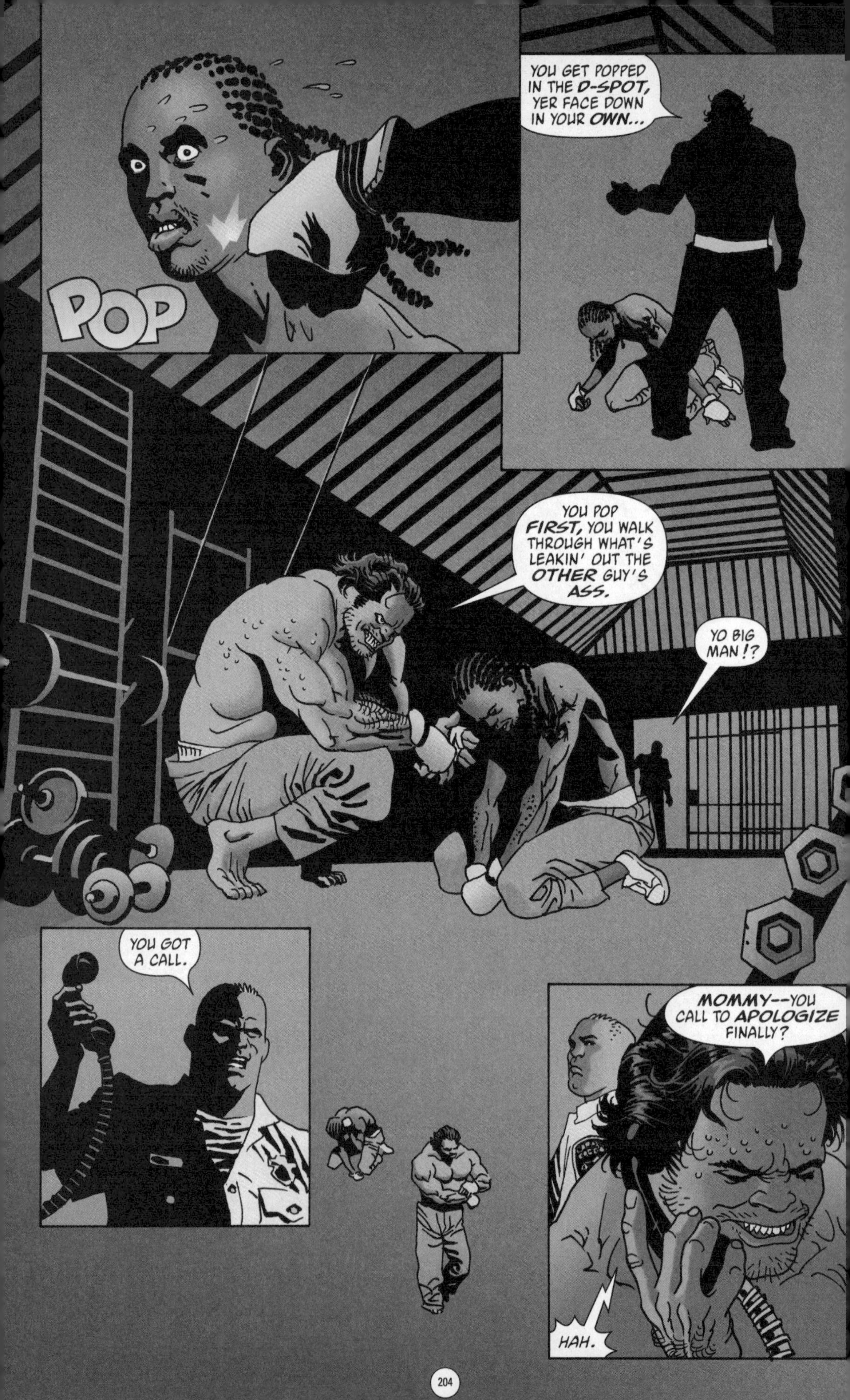
POP
YOU GET POPPED IN THE D-SPOT, YER FACE DOWN IN YOUR OWN...
YOU POP FIRST, YOU WALK THROUGH WHAT'S LEAKIN' OUT THE OTHER GUY'S ASS.
YO BIG MAN!?
YOU GOT A CALL.
MOMMY--YOU CALL TO APOLOGIZE FINALLY?
HAH.

HAHAHAHA...
LONO...LEAVE IT TO YOU TO MAKE ME LAUGH AT A TIME LIKE THIS.
SHEPHERD? YOU SOUND OUTTA BREATH...WHAT'RE YOU DOIN'?
KEEP IT SHOR
I'M...
...DYING.
Coda Smoke

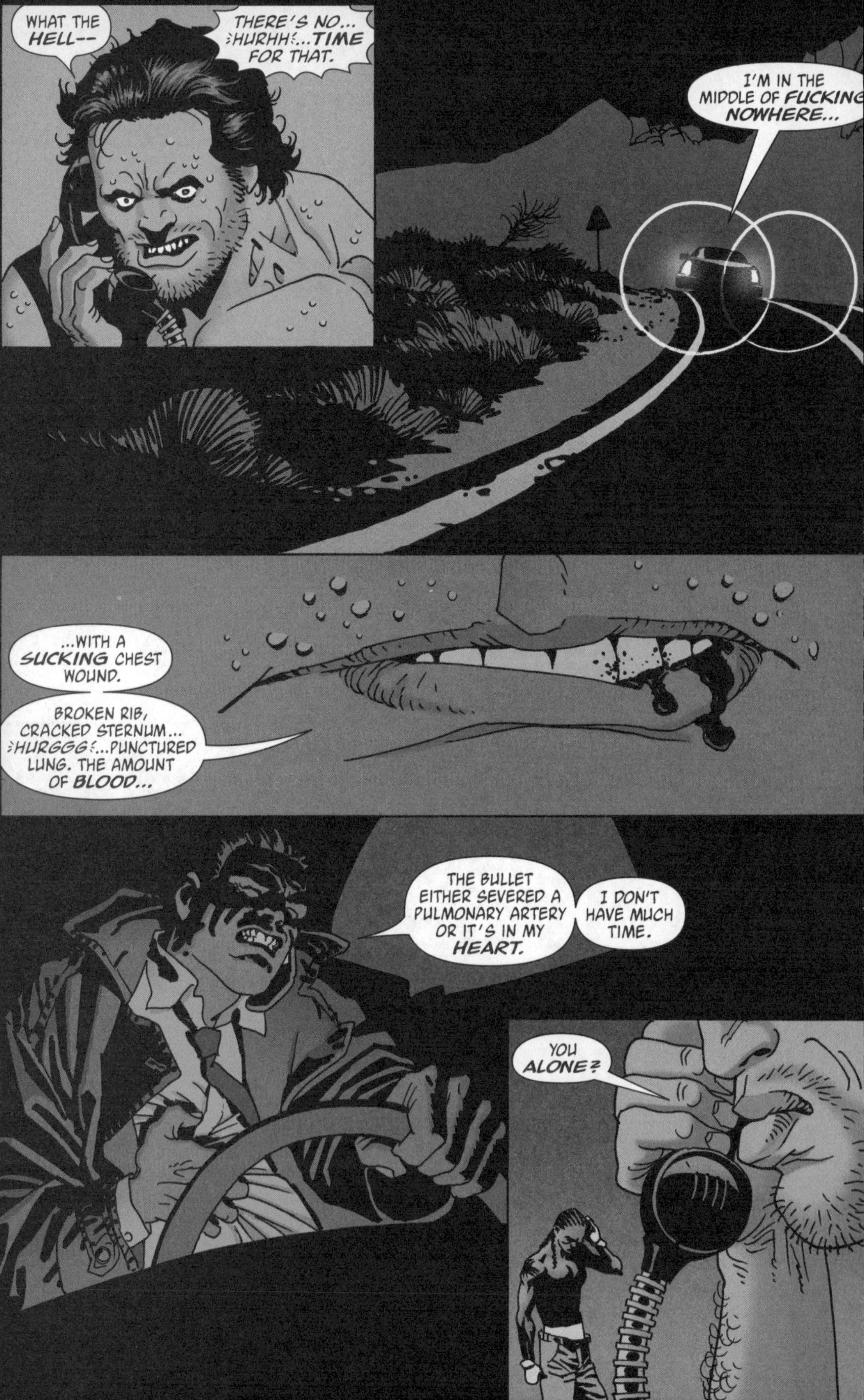
WHAT THE HELL--
THERE'S NO... ≷HURHH≷...TIME FOR THAT.
I'M IN THE MIDDLE OF FUCKING NOWHERE...
...WITH A SUCKING CHEST WOUND.
BROKEN RIB, CRACKED STERNUM... ≷HURGGG≷...PUNCTURED LUNG. THE AMOUNT OF BLOOD...
THE BULLET EITHER SEVERED A PULMONARY ARTERY OR IT'S IN MY HEART.
I DON'T HAVE MUCH TIME.
YOU ALONE?

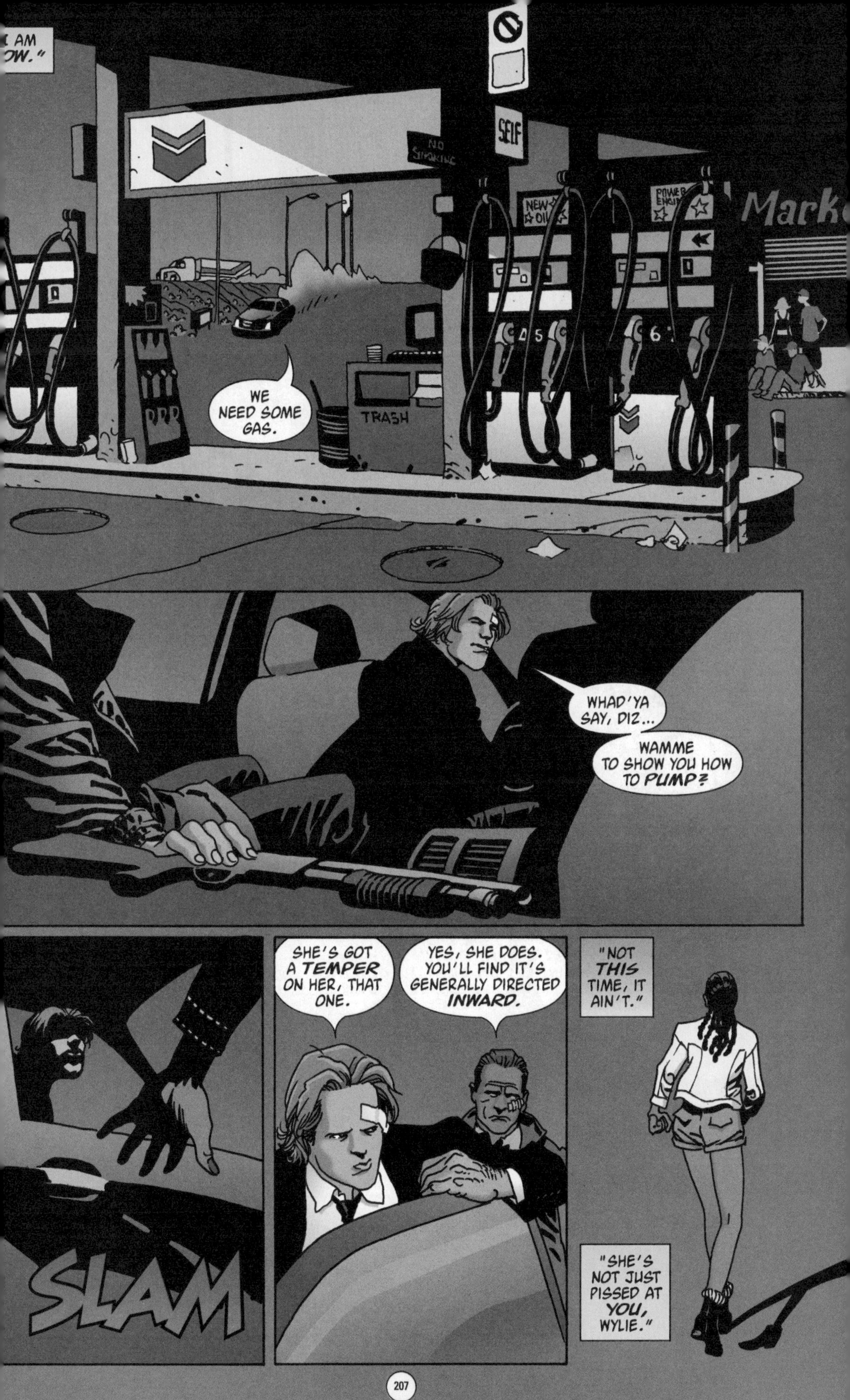
SELF
NO SMOKING
TRASH
WE NEED SOME GAS.
WHAD'YA SAY, DIZ...
WAMME TO SHOW YOU HOW TO *PUMP?*
SLAM
SHE'S GOT A *TEMPER* ON HER, THAT ONE.
YES, SHE DOES. YOU'LL FIND IT'S GENERALLY DIRECTED *INWARD.*
"NOT *THIS* TIME, IT AIN'T."
"SHE'S NOT JUST PISSED AT *YOU,* WYLIE."

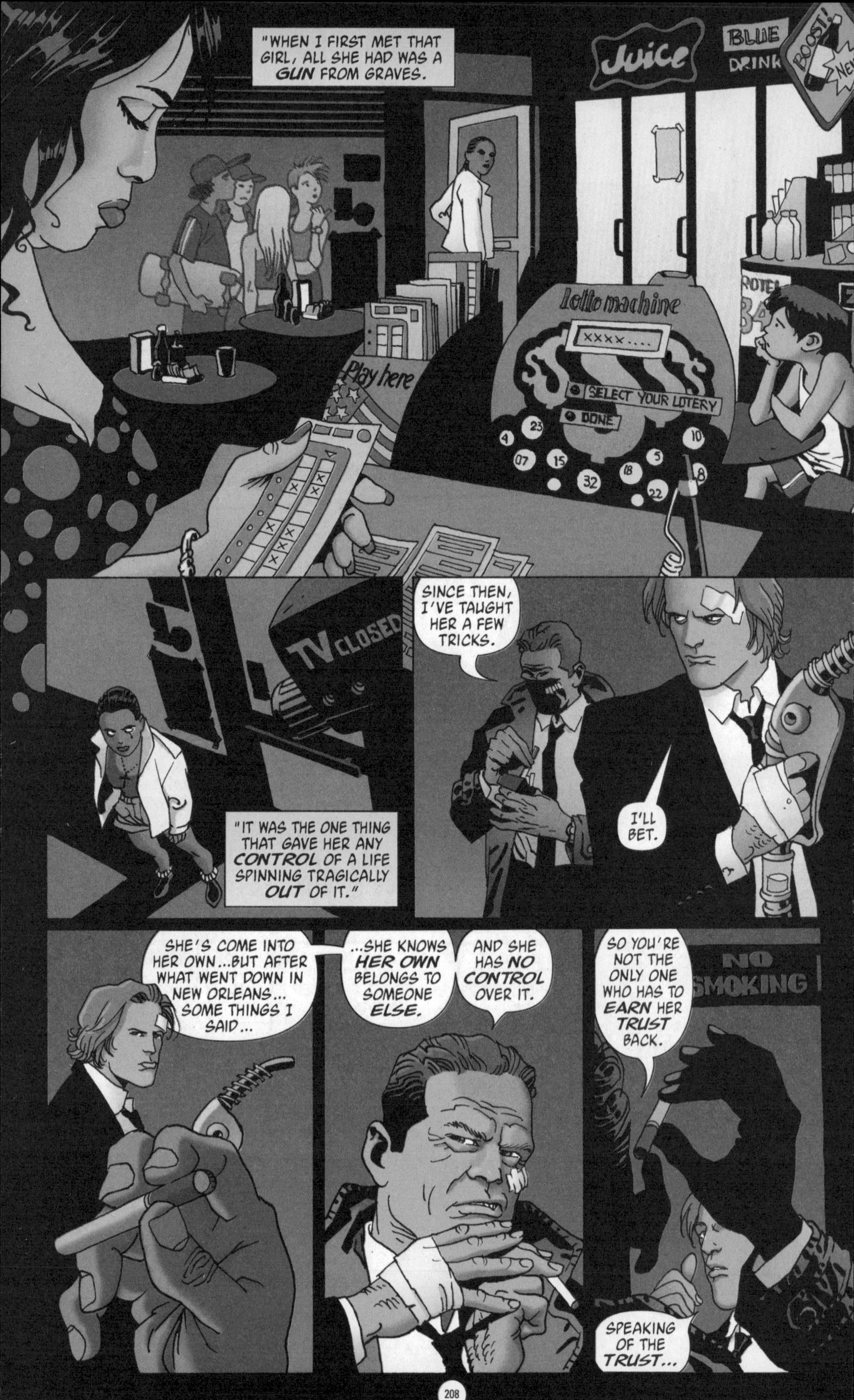
"WHEN I FIRST MET THAT GIRL, ALL SHE HAD WAS A GUN FROM GRAVES.
Juice
BLUE DRINK
BOOST! New
Lotto machine
XXXX....
SELECT YOUR LOTERY
DONE
Play here
TV CLOSED
"IT WAS THE ONE THING THAT GAVE HER ANY CONTROL OF A LIFE SPINNING TRAGICALLY OUT OF IT."
SINCE THEN, I'VE TAUGHT HER A FEW TRICKS.
I'LL BET.
SHE'S COME INTO HER OWN...BUT AFTER WHAT WENT DOWN IN NEW ORLEANS... SOME THINGS I SAID...
...SHE KNOWS HER OWN BELONGS TO SOMEONE ELSE.
AND SHE HAS NO CONTROL OVER IT.
NO SMOKING
SO YOU'RE NOT THE ONLY ONE WHO HAS TO EARN HER TRUST BACK.
SPEAKING OF THE TRUST...

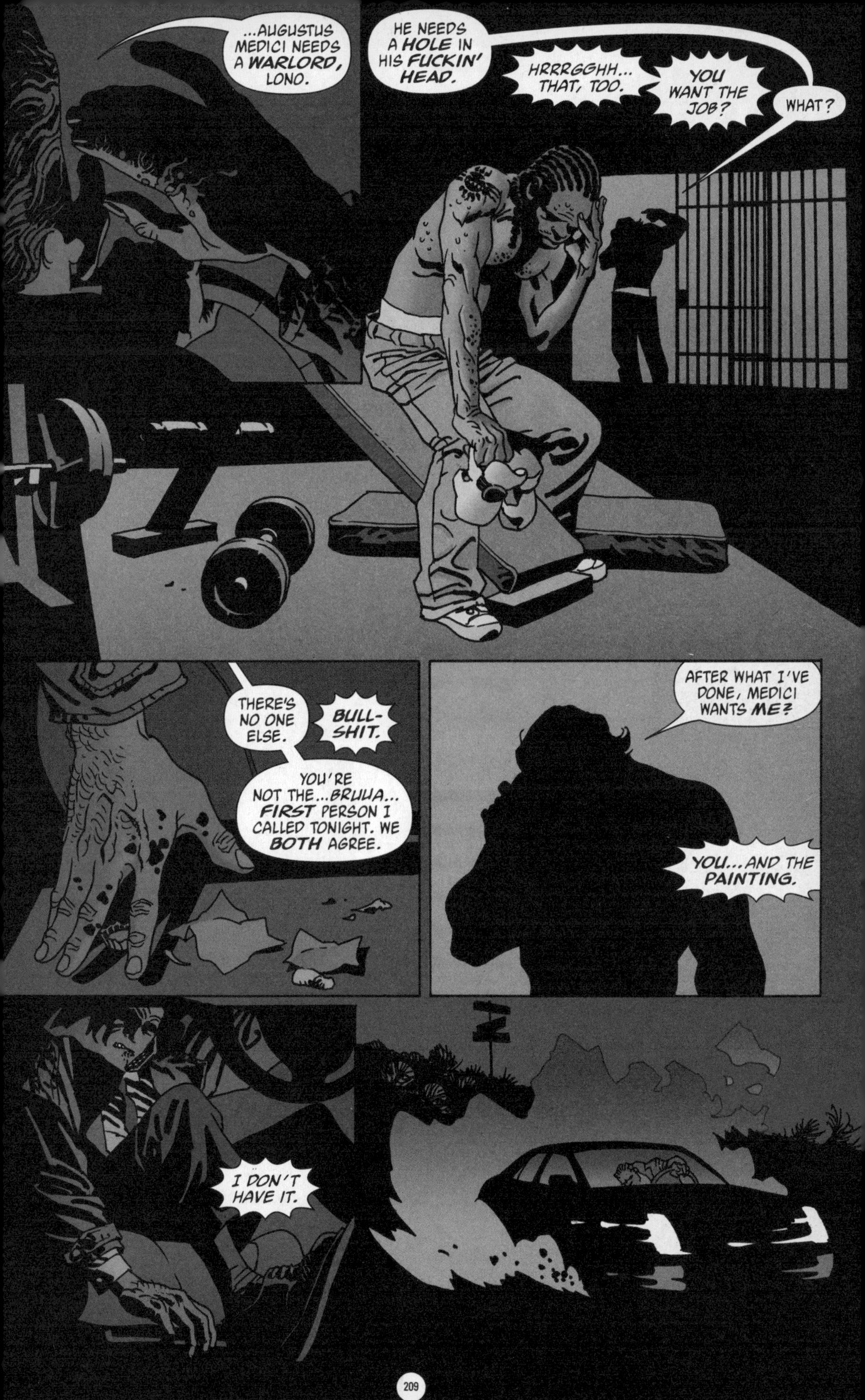
...AUGUSTUS MEDICI NEEDS A WARLORD, LONO.
HE NEEDS A HOLE IN HIS FUCKIN' HEAD.
HRRRGGHH... THAT, TOO.
YOU WANT THE JOB?
WHAT?
THERE'S NO ONE ELSE.
BULL-SHIT.
YOU'RE NOT THE...BRUJA... FIRST PERSON I CALLED TONIGHT. WE BOTH AGREE.
AFTER WHAT I'VE DONE, MEDICI WANTS ME?
YOU...AND THE PAINTING.
I DON'T HAVE IT.

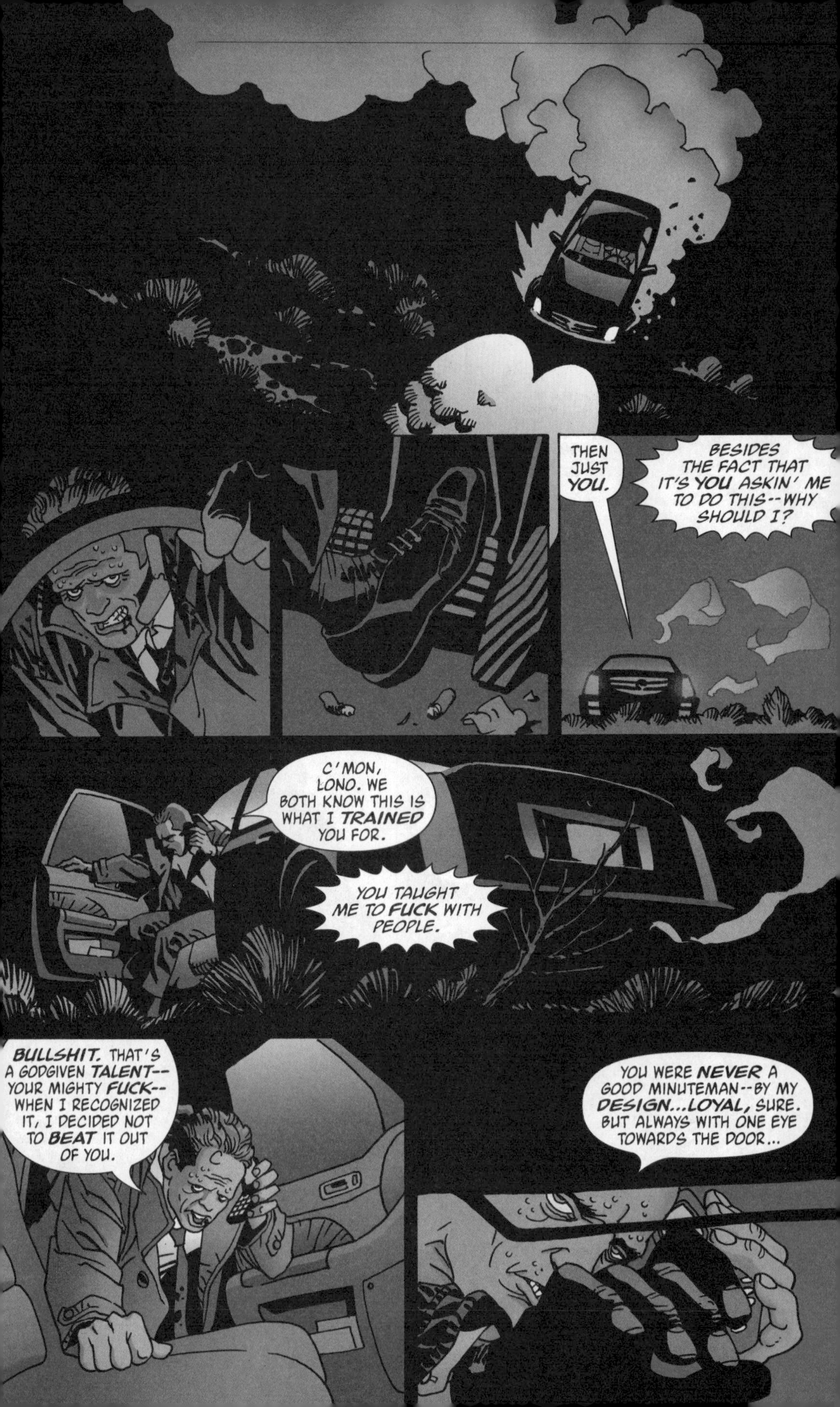
THEN JUST YOU.
BESIDES THE FACT THAT IT'S YOU ASKIN' ME TO DO THIS--WHY SHOULD I?
C'MON, LONO. WE BOTH KNOW THIS IS WHAT I TRAINED YOU FOR.
YOU TAUGHT ME TO FUCK WITH PEOPLE.
BULLSHIT. THAT'S A GODGIVEN TALENT--YOUR MIGHTY FUCK--WHEN I RECOGNIZED IT, I DECIDED NOT TO BEAT IT OUT OF YOU.
YOU WERE NEVER A GOOD MINUTEMAN--BY MY DESIGN...LOYAL, SURE. BUT ALWAYS WITH ONE EYE TOWARDS THE DOOR...

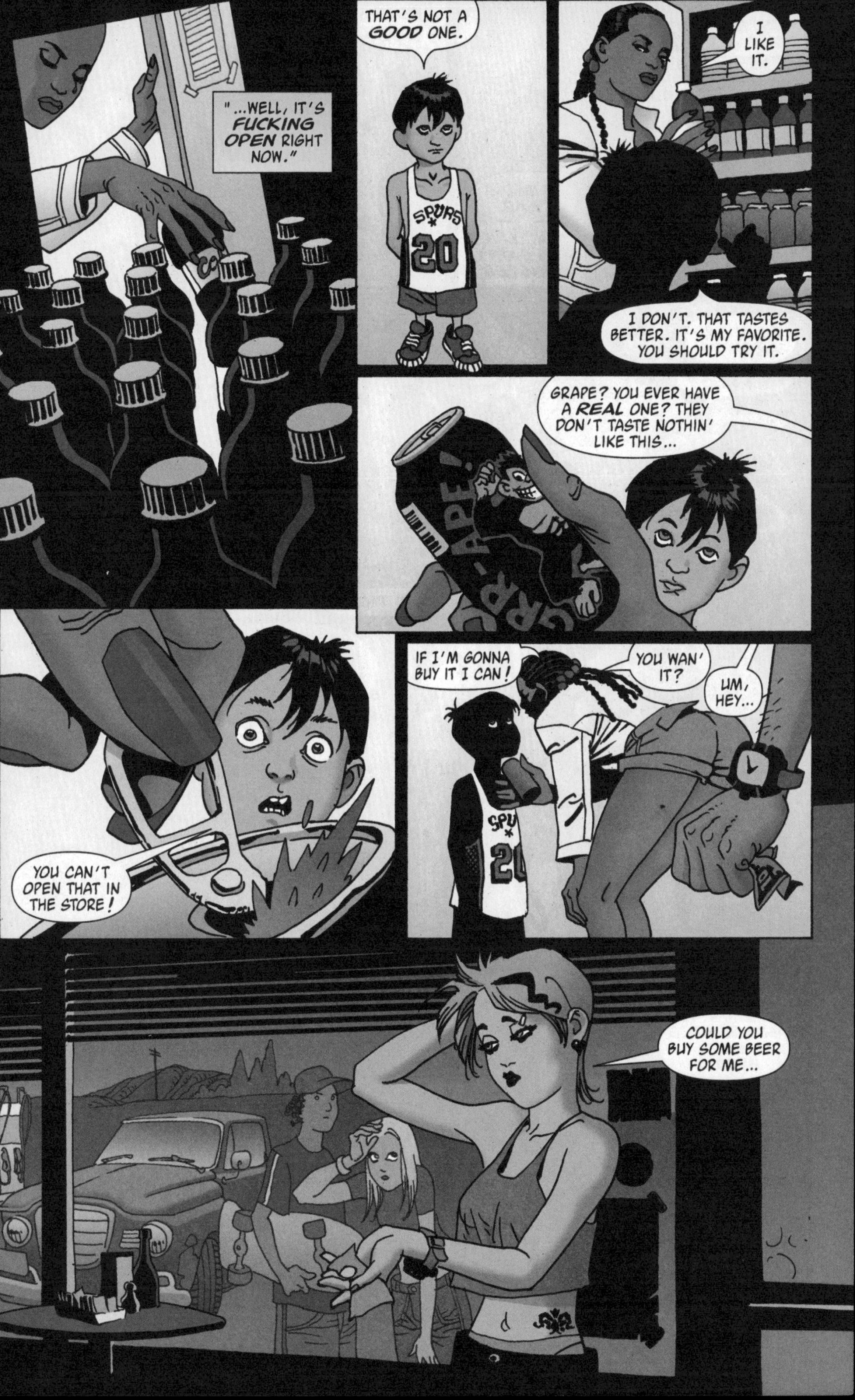
"...WELL, IT'S FUCKING OPEN RIGHT NOW."
THAT'S NOT A GOOD ONE.
I LIKE IT.
I DON'T. THAT TASTES BETTER. IT'S MY FAVORITE. YOU SHOULD TRY IT.
GRAPE? YOU EVER HAVE A REAL ONE? THEY DON'T TASTE NOTHIN' LIKE THIS...
GRR-APE!
YOU CAN'T OPEN THAT IN THE STORE!
IF I'M GONNA BUY IT I CAN!
YOU WAN' IT?
UM, HEY...
COULD YOU BUY SOME BEER FOR ME...

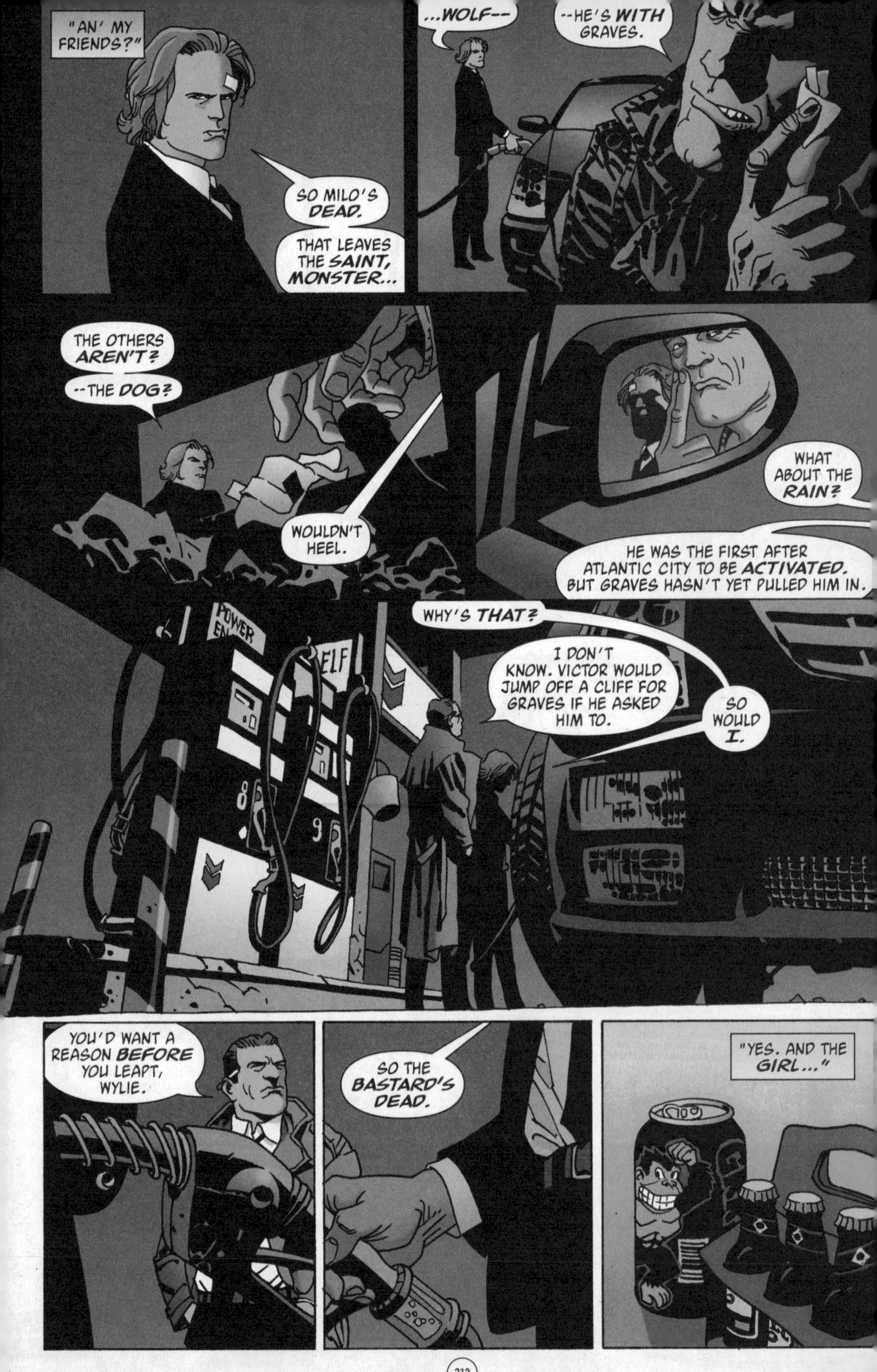
"AN' MY FRIENDS?"
SO MILO'S DEAD.
THAT LEAVES THE SAINT, MONSTER...
...WOLF--
--HE'S WITH GRAVES.
THE OTHERS AREN'T?
--THE DOG?
WOULDN'T HEEL.
WHAT ABOUT THE RAIN?
HE WAS THE FIRST AFTER ATLANTIC CITY TO BE ACTIVATED. BUT GRAVES HASN'T YET PULLED HIM IN.
WHY'S THAT?
I DON'T KNOW. VICTOR WOULD JUMP OFF A CLIFF FOR GRAVES IF HE ASKED HIM TO.
SO WOULD I.
YOU'D WANT A REASON BEFORE YOU LEAPT, WYLIE.
SO THE BASTARD'S DEAD.
"YES. AND THE GIRL..."

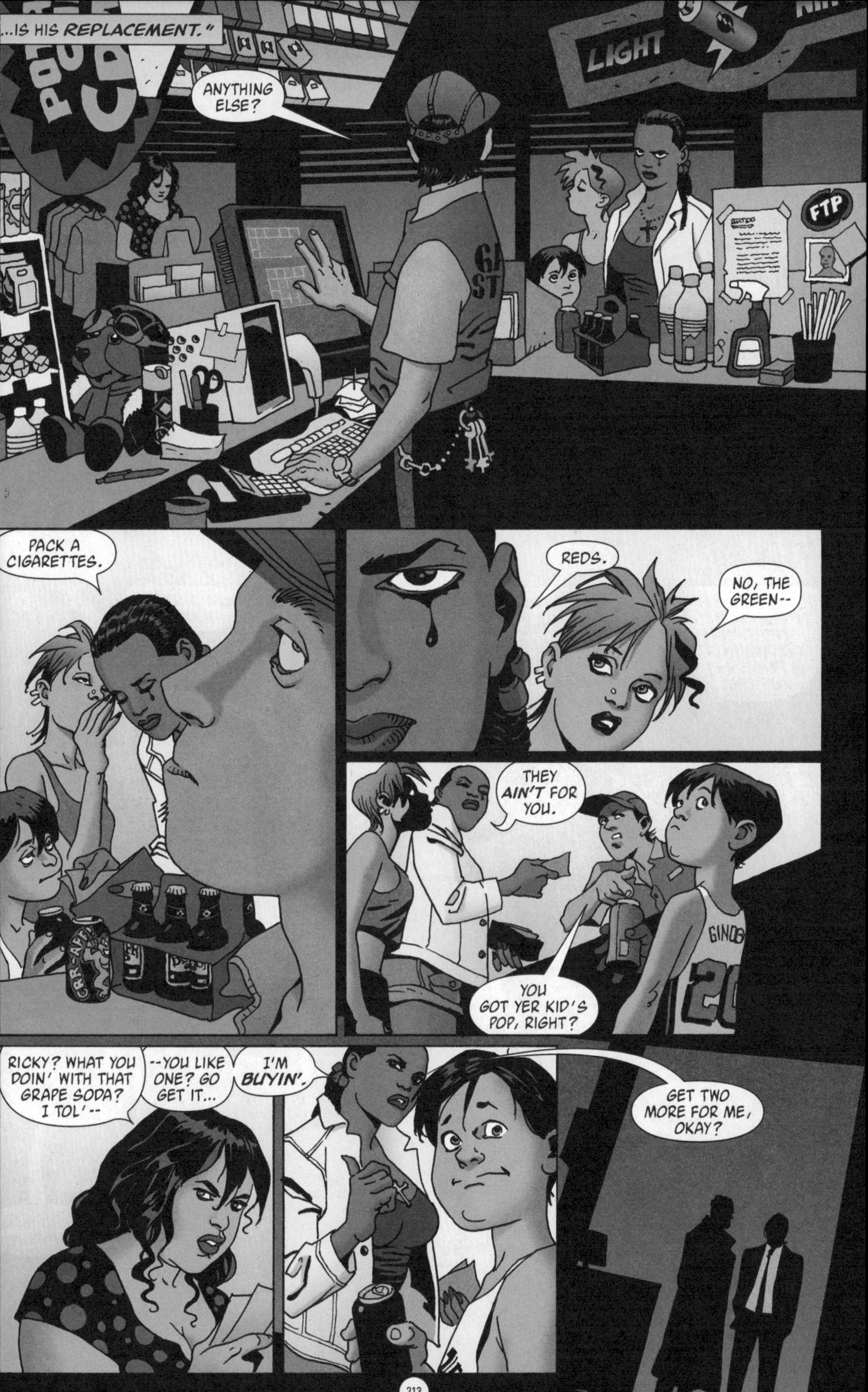

...IS HIS REPLACEMENT."
LIGHT
ANYTHING ELSE?
FTP
PACK A CIGARETTES.
REDS.
NO, THE GREEN--
THEY AIN'T FOR YOU.
YOU GOT YER KID'S POP, RIGHT?
RICKY? WHAT YOU DOIN' WITH THAT GRAPE SODA? I TOL'--
--YOU LIKE ONE? GO GET IT...
I'M BUYIN'.
GET TWO MORE FOR ME, OKAY?

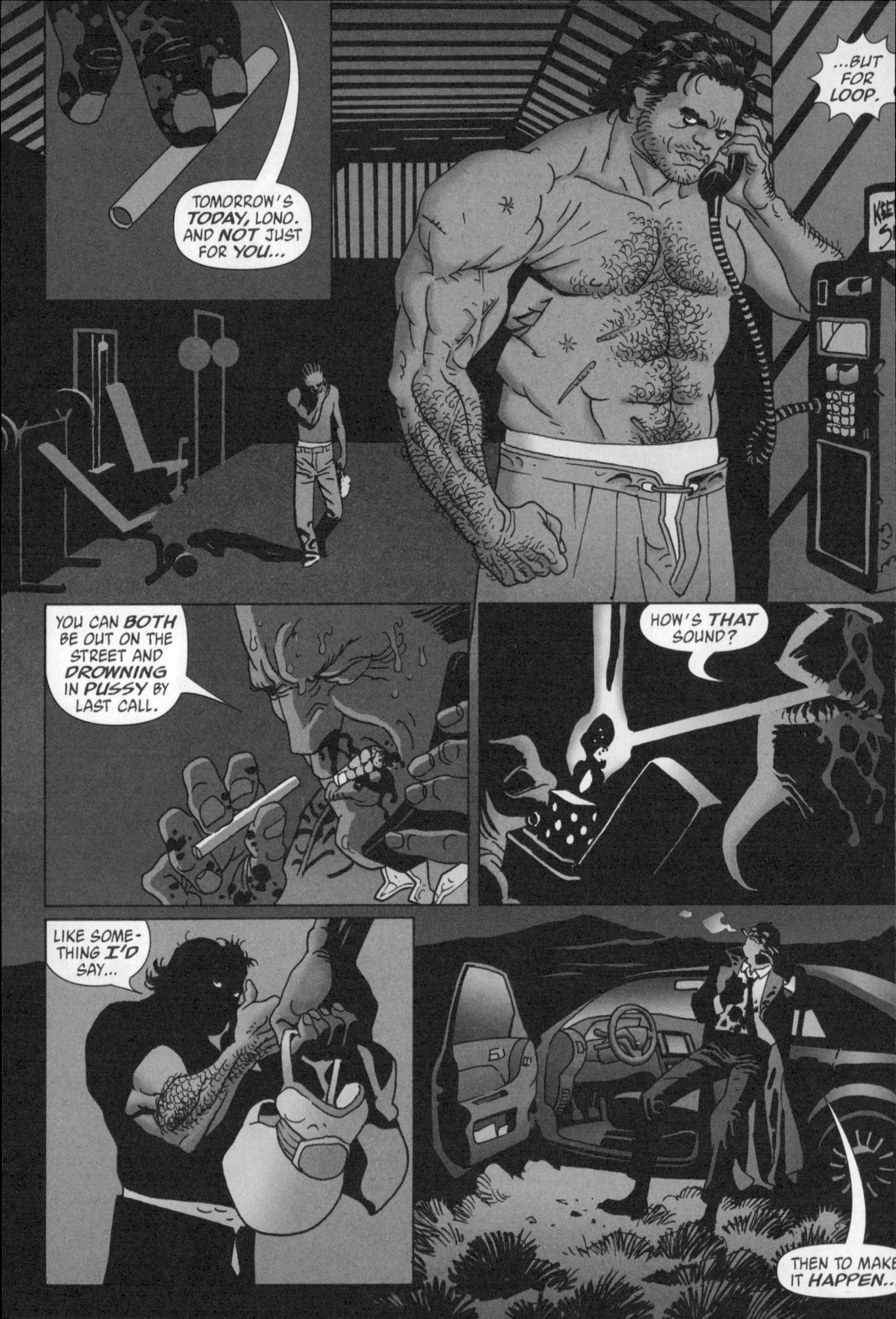
TOMORROW'S TODAY, LONO. AND NOT JUST FOR YOU...
...BUT FOR LOOP.
YOU CAN BOTH BE OUT ON THE STREET AND DROWNING IN PUSSY BY LAST CALL.
HOW'S THAT SOUND?
LIKE SOME-THING I'D SAY...
THEN TO MAKE IT HAPPEN...

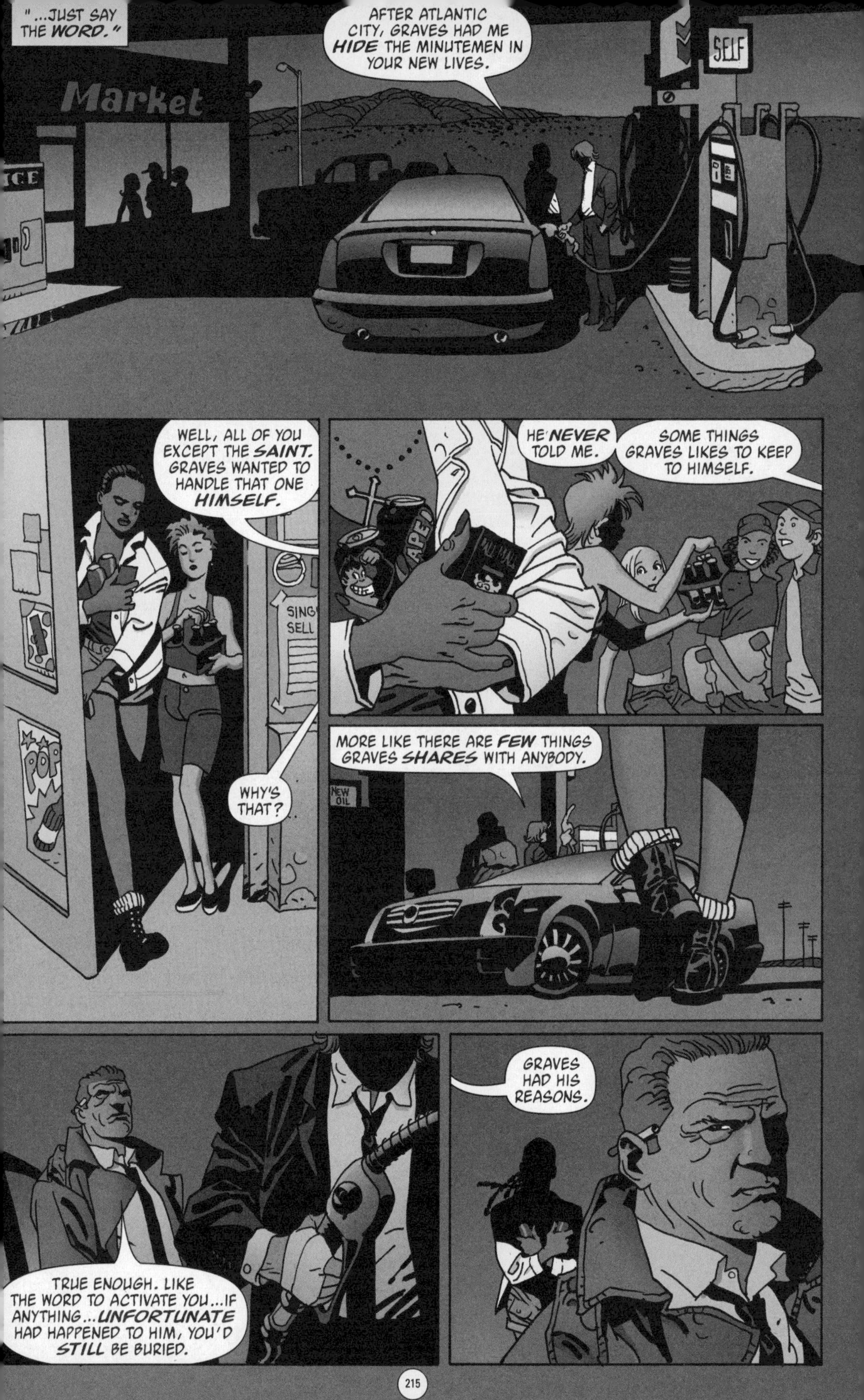
"...JUST SAY THE WORD."
AFTER ATLANTIC CITY, GRAVES HAD ME HIDE THE MINUTEMEN IN YOUR NEW LIVES.
Market
SELF
WELL, ALL OF YOU EXCEPT THE SAINT. GRAVES WANTED TO HANDLE THAT ONE HIMSELF.
WHY'S THAT?
HE NEVER TOLD ME.
SOME THINGS GRAVES LIKES TO KEEP TO HIMSELF.
MORE LIKE THERE ARE FEW THINGS GRAVES SHARES WITH ANYBODY.
NEW OIL
TRUE ENOUGH. LIKE THE WORD TO ACTIVATE YOU...IF ANYTHING...UNFORTUNATE HAD HAPPENED TO HIM, YOU'D STILL BE BURIED.
GRAVES HAD HIS REASONS.

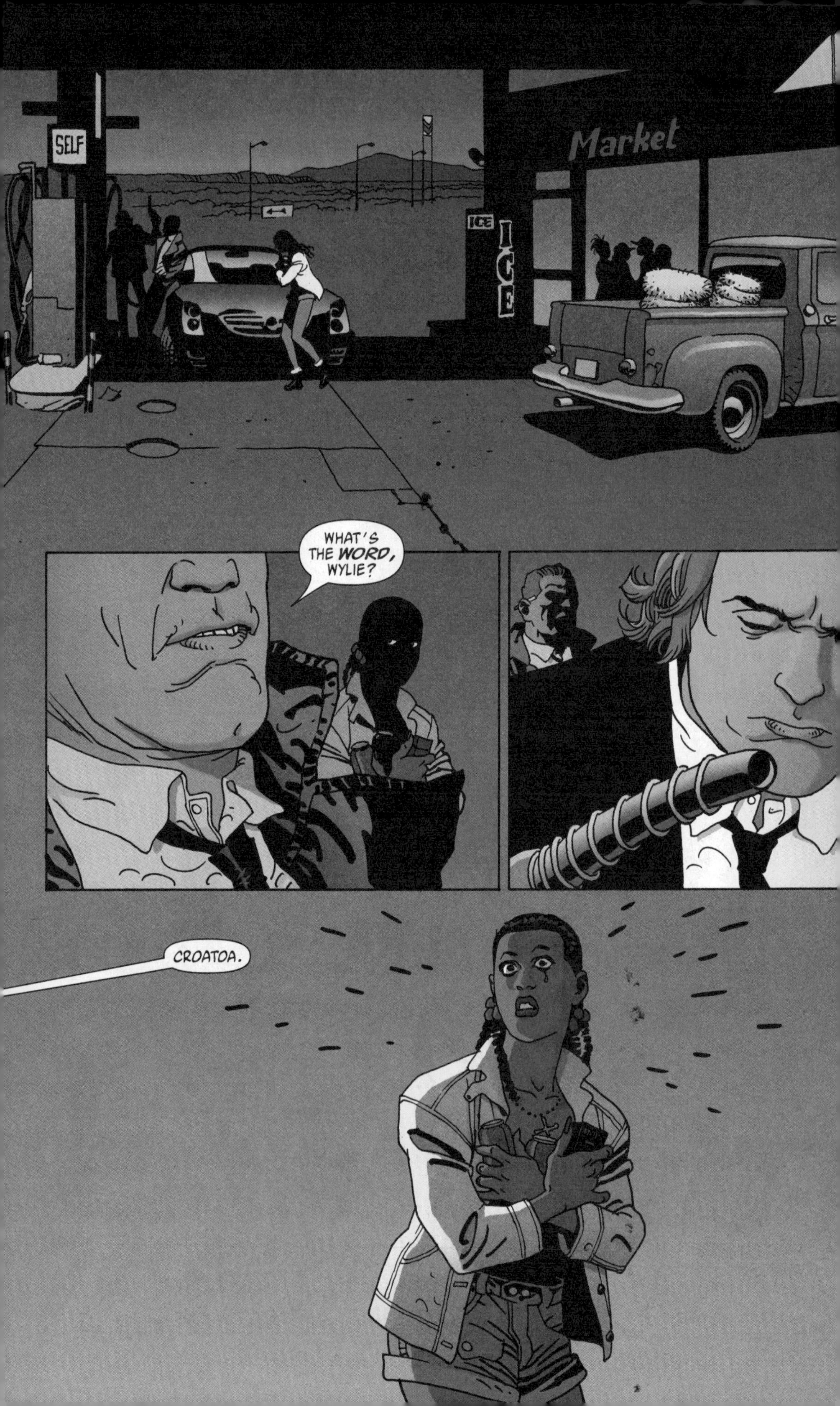
SELF
Market
ICE
ICE
WHAT'S THE WORD, WYLIE?
CROATOA.

SO WHAT'S THE **PLAN?**

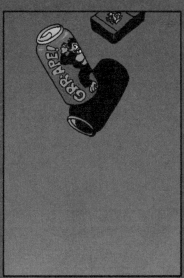

IN MY OPINION? FLAWED.

MAYBE EVEN BY **DESIGN.**

YOU BETTER THINK ABOUT WHAT YER SAYING, SHEPHERD.

GRAVES' PLAN IS TO PREVENT AUGUSTUS MEDICI FROM GRABBING **SOLE** CONTROL OF THE TRUST.

WHY THEN DOES EVERY MOVE WE MAKE HAND MEDICI **MORE** CONTROL?

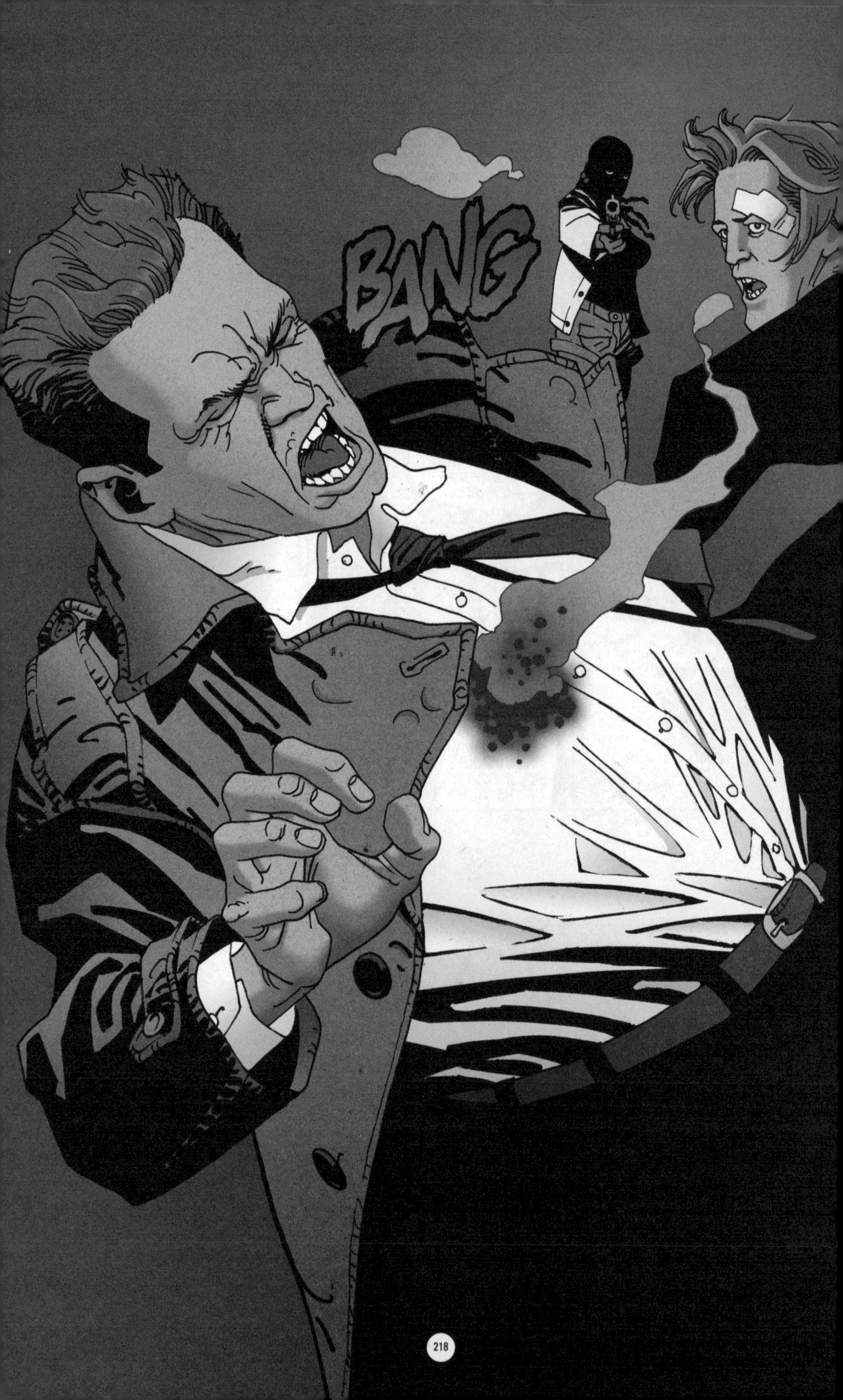
BANG

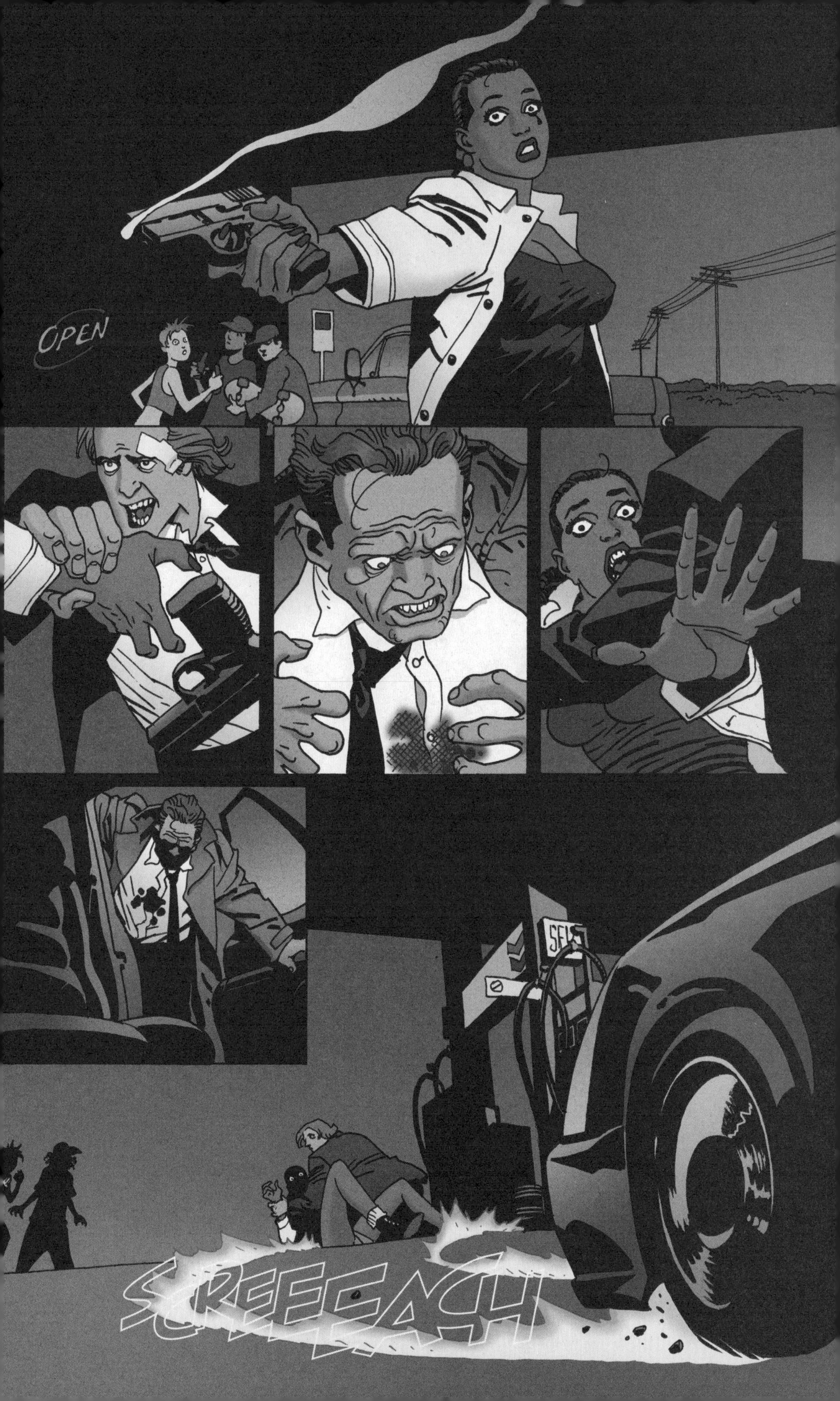
OPEN
SCREEEACH

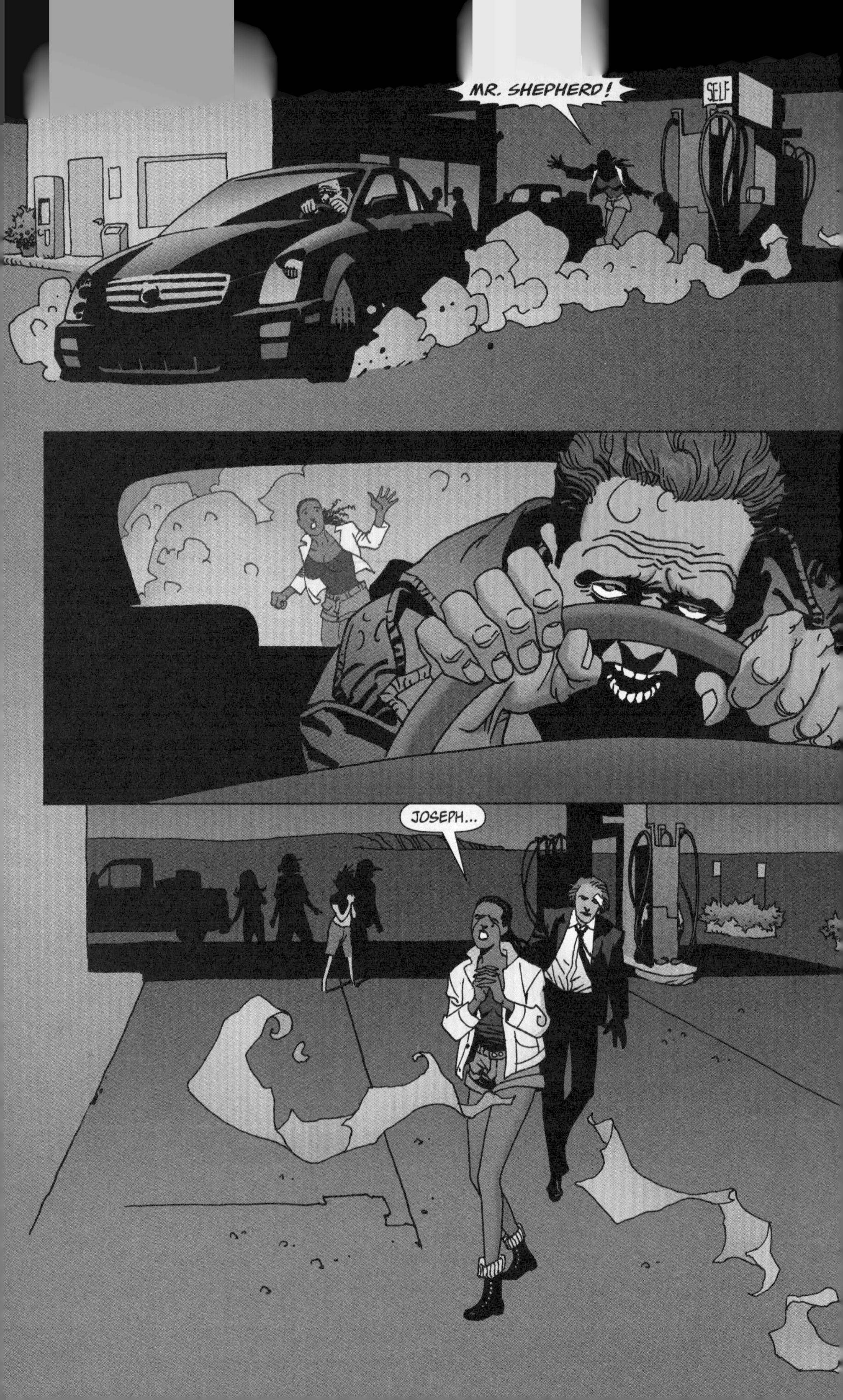
MR. SHEPHERD!
SELF
JOSEPH...

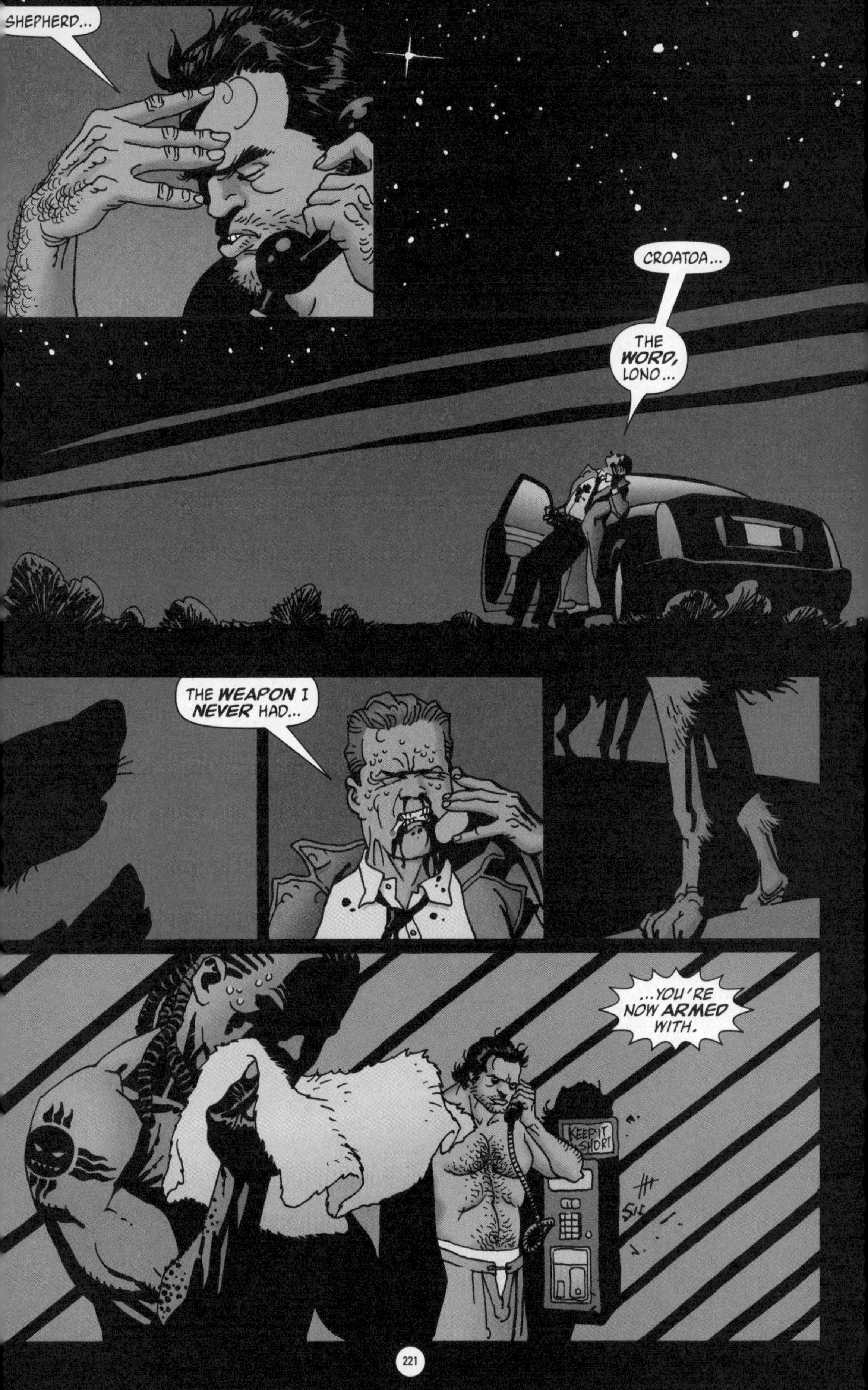
SHEPHERD...
CROATOA...
THE WORD, LONO...
THE WEAPON I NEVER HAD...
...YOU'RE NOW ARMED WITH.
KEEP IT SHORT

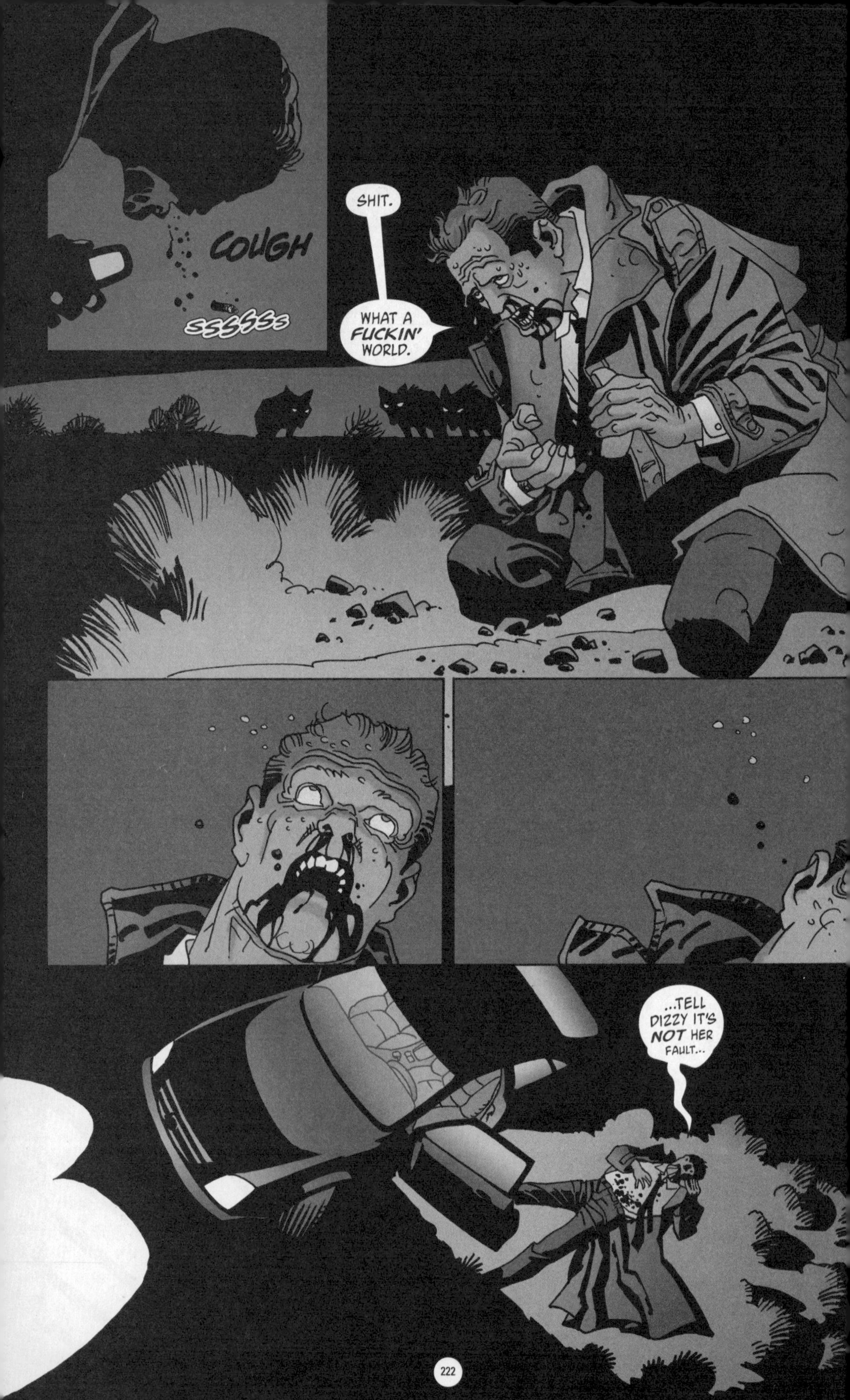
COUGH
SSSSSS
SHIT.
WHAT A FUCKIN' WORLD.
...TELL DIZZY IT'S NOT HER FAULT...

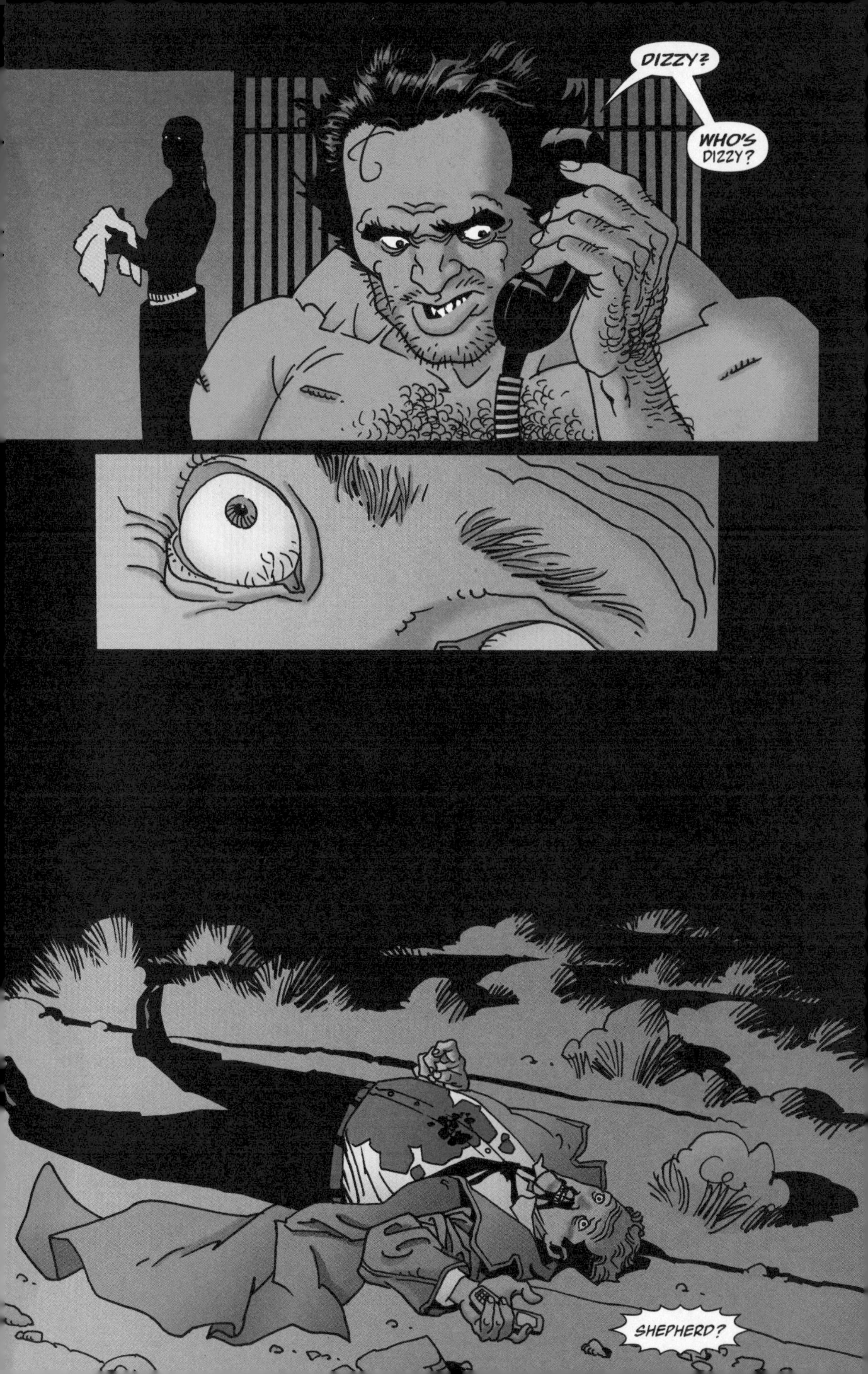
DIZZY?
WHO'S DIZZY?
SHEPHERD?

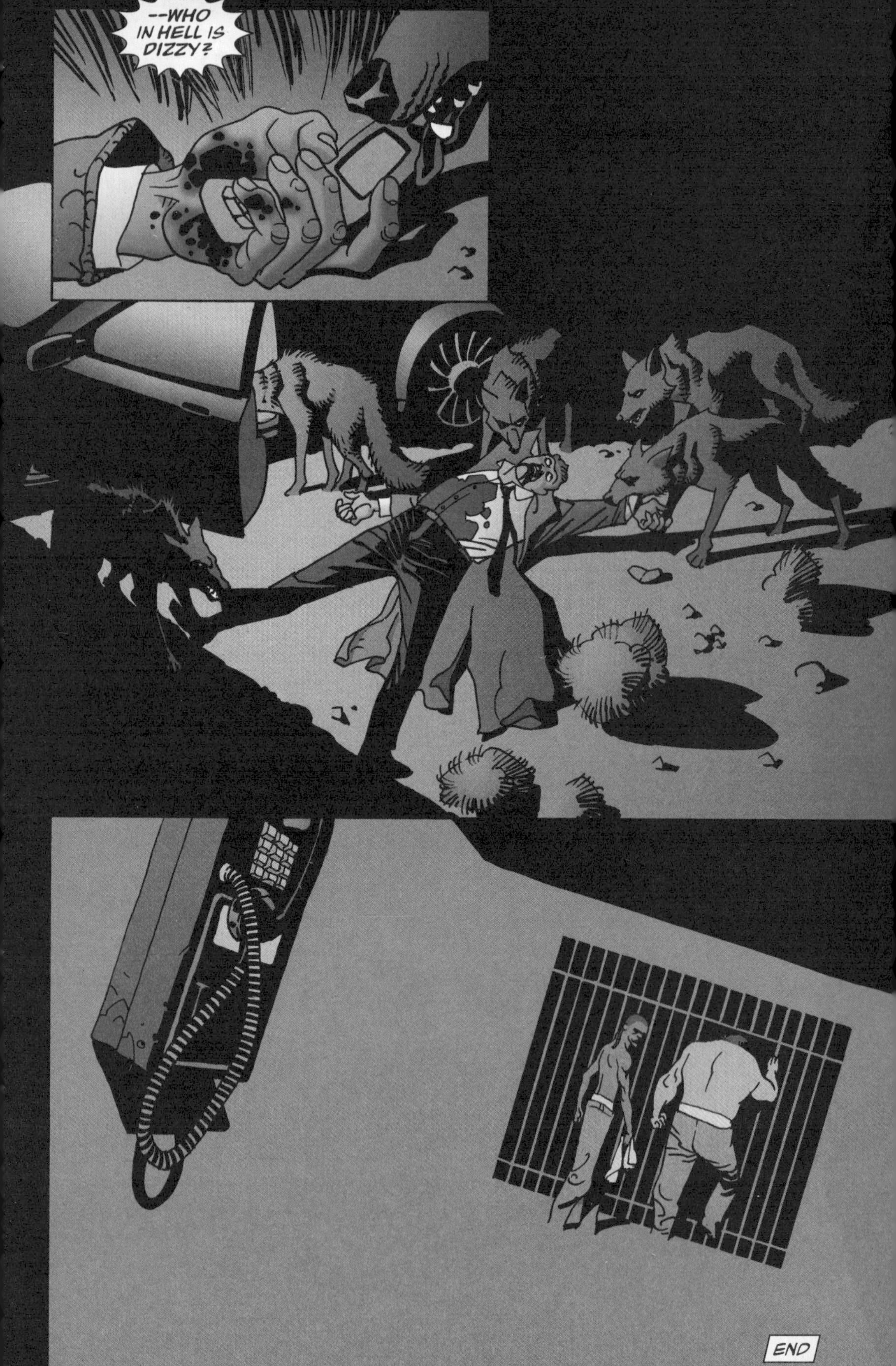
--WHO IN HELL IS DIZZY?
END